CONCISE COLLEGE TEXTS

4009094

CRIMINAL LAW

By

Peter Seago, J.P., LL.M.

Dean of Faculty of Law,
Senior Lecturer in Law at the
University of Leeds

Third Edition

LONDON
SWEET & MAXWELL
1989

First Edition 1981
Second Edition 1985
Third Edition 1989
Reprinted 1991
Reprinted 1992

Published by
Sweet & Maxwell Limited of
South Quay Plaza, 183 Marsh Wall, London E14 9FT
Laserset by P.B. Computer Typesetting, Pickering, N. Yorks.
Printed in Great Britain by
Richard Clay (The Chaucer Press) Ltd., Bungay, Suffolk

British Library Cataloguing in Publication Data

Seago, Peter
    Criminal law.—3rd ed. (Concise college
    texts)
    1. England. Criminal law
    I. Title   II. Series
    344.205

    ISBN 0-421-39280-0

PREFACE

This book is intended as an introduction for those who are beginning their studies of Criminal Law. As in previous editions I have followed a fairly traditional path, looking first at those principles which are common to crimes in general before dealing with the specific crimes which are included in most A Level and undergraduate courses. However, I remain convinced that total adherence to this format can be confusing. Students, not unreasonably, expect Criminal Law to be about crimes and so in the previous editions I have begun with a look at one well known crime, namely murder. The following chapters on the general principles can then be discussed against the background of this offence. Although recent developments may have rendered murder less suitable as an introductory offence, having weighed all the arguments in favour of using another, I have decided to start, yet again, with murder; it has the distinct advantage of being a readily understandable concept even if its finer points may be somewhat impenetrable.

Once again the Appellate Courts have ensured that changes were necessary to almost every part of the book. This is particularly true in the areas of intoxication, duress, homicide and indecent assault, while the problems relating to the definition of intention and recklessness continue to tease the judiciary. However, the most important development since the last edition is undoubtedly the publication of the Law Commission's Draft Criminal Code (Law Commission No. 177; 1989). The Draft Code is based upon the Report of a working party of academic lawyers under the chairmanship of Professor J. C. Smith C.B.E., Q.C. It is an attempt to produce in a single statute the present law relating to the general principles of Criminal Law and the central specific offences, although the opportunity has been taken to incorporate certain proposals for reform. The ultimate aim, which is dependent upon the Government's willingness to find Parliamentary time, is the creation of a complete Criminal Code to replace the present rag bag of statutory and common Law provisions. Whatever its eventual fate, the Draft Code is essential reading for all students of Criminal Law.

I am grateful to all those who have taken the trouble to send comments and suggestions on the previous edition; these have been most useful in the preparation of this new edition. I am particulary grateful to the Commandant and staff ot the West Yorkshire Police Officers Training School at Wakefield for the preparation of the cover photograph and to Sergeant John Jones for resisting all suggestions by the photographer to make it even more realistic.

I have attempted to state the law as I understood it to be on January 1, 1989, though I have been able to incorporate a few later cases.

Peter Seago

Leeds
June 1989

CONTENTS

TABLE OF CASES

TABLE OF STATUTES

CHAPTER 1

INTRODUCTION

MOST people have heard of the saying that "ignorance of the law is no defence" which is the result of another well-known phrase or saying that "everyone is presumed to know the law." Unlike many maxims which have no basis in reality, these do represent the very harsh rule in criminal law that it is no defence to a criminal charge that the person charged was unaware that the act he was performing was a criminal offence. Nor would it make any difference to his guilt or innocence that he had consulted a lawyer who had told him that there was no such offence.

This gives rise to several questions. For instance what is a crime and how do you know whether given conduct is or is not a crime? What such questions are not unreasonably looking for is a definition of crime which will at the same time act as an infallible test by which to determine whether given conduct is a crime. Unfortunately no such definition has ever, or is ever, likely to be found. The best that can be offered is to say that a criminal offence is conduct which may be followed by criminal proceedings and sentence. This is very little help to the man in the street who wants to know whether it is a criminal offence to drive a car without properly working windscreen wipers, but given that you can find out whether or not certain conduct can or cannot be followed by criminal proceedings, it is a watertight definition of a crime. Thus in this country adultery cannot be followed by criminal proceedings so therefore it is not a crime. Intercourse with a woman without her consent can be followed by criminal proceedings and is therefore a crime.

Before we go any further we should stop for a moment to say something about the term criminal proceedings. In this country we tend to divide lawsuits into criminal and civil proceedings. The basic difference is that criminal proceedings are normally handled by the Crown Prosecution Service acting on behalf of the state with the ultimate aim that a court shall, if it finds him guilty, impose a criminal sentence on the offender. (Until recently the police were responsible for not only the investigation of suspected criminal offences, but also for the decision of whether or

1

not there should be a prosecution. Since the Prosecution of Offences Act 1985 the final decision on whether to prosecute lies with the newly-created Crown Prosecution Service whose head is the Director of Public Prosecutions.) This sentence may take many forms including imprisonment, fine, probation, and absolute discharge. Where the person is ordered to pay a fine he pays it to the state and not to the victim, though the criminal courts have the power to order that a guilty party pays compensation to the victim. Civil proceedings on the other hand take many forms, but the general pattern is of an action brought by one individual against another often seeking some form of monetary compensation (damages) from that other; the basic notion is the redress of the grievance between the two parties and not primarily one of punishing a wrongdoer.

A given act may lead to both criminal and civil proceedings in which case it is both a crime and a civil wrong. Thus if X punches Y on the nose, the Crown Prosecution Service (or Y, since private prosecutions are possible) may prosecute X in criminal proceedings for an assault, and Y may bring an action in the civil courts to get damages from X for his injuries. There is generally nothing to stop both forms of action from being taken, though it is likely that the criminal proceedings will get off the ground first. It may seem rather silly to have to bring separate proceedings, one to punish X and the other to compensate Y. The answer is that in many cases it is a waste of public resources and it is precisely for this reason that the courts have been given powers in criminal cases to order an accused person to pay compensation to his victim.

Is there, therefore, no way in which the man in the street can tell whether something he is about to do will be a crime or not? Criminal law tends to represent society's attitude towards conduct. It is a decision that certain conduct should not be permitted and that it should not be left to the "victims" of this conduct to bring the matter to court. A good example of this is the law relating to brothels. If you find that a brothel has been opened up in the house next door, you can clearly sue its owners for a civil action in nuisance, but the law takes the view that this is a situation in which the private citizen should not be forced to make the running. It is therefore made a criminal offence and the state, through the Crown Prosecution Service, can take action in the criminal courts to stop the activity.

The question, however, of what acts can be followed by criminal proceedings can only be answered by reference to the law as laid down by Parliament in statutes and regulations, and in the decisions of the courts over the last few centuries. Of course most people know that it is a crime to kill, rape, steal, injure and equally that it is not an offence to wear bow ties. In the middle however is a great band of conduct over which various societies take differing views. Thus it is possible to take widely differing views on such matters as homosexual activity, incest, drug possession and adultery. But in relation to what we can, for the moment, call real crimes such as murder, rape, assault, theft, and damage to property, most people have a reasonable idea of what activity is or is not criminal.

However the picture has been complicated over the last 50 years by the increasing use of regulations (which have the force of statutes, but are passed without full Parliamentary debate) to control all aspects of everyday life. Thus, in relation to road traffic, most citizens are aware of the major offences relating to bad, or drunken driving, which are contained in statutes passed by full Parliamentary discussion, but very few would know of the detailed regulations (not contained in the statute) concerning depth of tread on the tyres. Breach of such regulations is often sanctioned by fines and this makes the activity a criminal offence. There are literally hundreds of such regulations passed each year in all spheres of everyday life, and they make a mockery of the notion that all people are presumed to know the law. In fact some countries have taken the view that breach of such regulations should not be classified as criminal offences, with all the stigma that involves; instead breaches are termed violations or contraventions to distinguish them from true crimes (see Justice Report, "Breaking The Rules," 1980). It is indeed highly questionable that any conduct should be made sanctionable with any form of penalty unless there has been the opportunity for full Parliamentary discussion.

In the remainder of this chapter we shall look briefly at the criminal courts and the way in which a case may proceed through these courts, before proceeding to a discussion of the general principles of criminal liability.

1. Classification of Offences and Mode of Trial

(1) Treasons, felonies and misdemeanours; arrestable offences

Until 1967 offences in this country were classified as treasons, felonies or misdemeanours. Thus with the exception of the various forms of treason all offences were either felonies or misdemeanours; felonies being the more serious. Certain consequences flowed from the distinction, but it was generally felt that the classification was somewhat arbitrary and unsatisfactory. Since the major use of the distinction was to identify those crimes where a police officer might arrest a suspect without a warrant it was decided to replace the classification of felonies and misdemeanours with a new one based on the right to arrest without warrant. So by the Criminal Law Act 1967 the old categories of felonies and misdemeanours were replaced with the new ones of arrestable and non-arrestable offences.

The law in this area is now to be found in Part III of the Police and Criminal Evidence Act 1984. Under section 24 an arrestable offence is defined as one in which the sentence is fixed by law (e.g. murder; see below, p. 15); an offence for which a person of 21 years of age or over (not previously convicted) may be sentenced to imprisonment for a term of five years (or might be so sentenced but for the restrictions imposed by section 33 of the Magistrates' Courts Act 1980); or the offence is one of a number listed in section 24(2) of the Act. Section 24 outlines the powers of arrest without warrant for arrestable offences available to both police and private individuals. Section 25 provides police constables with new general powers of arrest in the case of non-arrestable offences subject to certain criteria (see Zander, *Police and Criminal Evidence Act 1984*).

The terms felonies and misdemeanours are still widely used in other common law jurisdictions and, of course, feature largely in pre-1967 cases (See also accessories; below, p. 112).

(2) Summary and indictable offences; summary trial and trial on indictment

There are two methods of trial for criminal cases; summary trial and trial on indictment. Summary trial is the term used to describe trial before lay magistrates, or a stipendiary magistrate, in the magistrates courts where there will be no jury. Trial on indictment is the name given to trial in the Crown Court before a legally qualified judge where, following a plea of guilty, there will be trial by jury. (The indictment is the formal document which contains a statement of the charge or charges against the accused and to which the accused is asked to plead at the beginning of the trial. Each charge is listed in a separate count in the indictment; any count which reveals in substance more than one offence will be held to be bad for duplicity).

It is probably common knowledge that the more serious cases are tried in the Crown Court and the less serious before the magistrates' court. It must be remembered that although in an ideal world every accused should be entitled to a trial before a legally qualified judge sitting with a jury, there are simply not sufficient resources to achieve this, so that somewhat more than 95 per cent. of all criminal cases are disposed of by magistrates without a jury. On the other hand it is recognised that certainly for offences which carry heavy penalties no accused ought to be deprived of his right to jury trial. It would be a wonderfully simple solution if we could then simply designate offences as either summary or indictable offences, thereby indicating from the outset the mode of trial applicable to each offence. There are of course some offences where this is possible. For example murder, manslaughter and rape are offences which should always be dealt with by a legally qualified judge and so these offences are categorised as indictable offences, indicating that in no circumstances can they be tried summarily by the magistrates. On the other hand we can say that certain offences should not be the concern of the Crown Court and should only be triable by magistrates. Examples of these would include parking offences and very minor assaults. In 1977 it was decided that all offences involving drinking and driving should be heard solely by magistrates' courts, unless of course they form part of a more serious charge such as causing death by reckless driving. Under the Criminal Justice Act 1988 yet more offences were made summary only offences including the serious offences of driving while disqualified, and taking a motor vehicle without the owners consent.

However in the middle there are a great band of offences where no easy classification is possible. Take, for example, theft. Quite clearly since it is an offence requiring dishonesty and in which large sums of money may be involved, it would be totally inappropriate to reserve it solely for the magistrates' jurisdiction. On the other hand many instances of theft, although morally serious, involve trivial amounts of money or property and are cases where the penalty imposed by the court is not likely to include imprisonment. Since theft accounts for a very high proportion of prosecuted offences it would be totally impractical to send all such cases to the Crown Court; the criminal process would soon grind to a halt. A halfway house had to be found which met the requirement of justice in the individual case whilst ensuring, as far as possible, that the Crown Court was not overloaded. Following, to a large extent, the recommendations of the James Committee (Distribution of Business between the Magistrates' Courts and the Crown Court, Cmnd. 6323 (1975)) a new classification of offences for the purpose of determining the mode of trial was provided by the Criminal Law Act 1977. The present statutory provisions are to be found in the Magistrates' Courts Act, 1980, Part I. The halfway house was achieved by designating this middle band of criminal offence as offences triable either way, meaning that offences so classified may be tried either summarily or on indictment but that the accused's consent was necessary before he could be tried summarily. It was hoped that in this way many accused persons would accept the offer of summary trial which would mean that the case may well be disposed of immediately, but that he was not deprived of a jury trial if that was what he wanted. Basically all offences which were either summary only or indictable only, before 1977 remain so unless specifically altered by the Act and all other offences which previously fell into one of three intermediate categories are now classified as offences triable either way unless specifically placed into the summary only or indictable only categories.

A person charged with an offence which is classified as summary only will be brought before the magistrates' court on an information containing the charge against him and tried in that court. Following the trial various appeals are open as shown on the diagram (see p. 10, below). Where he is charged with an offence which is triable only on indictment he will be brought before the magistrates who will sit as examining justices to decide whether the prosecution's case is strong enough to warrant committing the accused for trial in the Crown Court. It is difficult to describe exactly what suffices at this stage, but theoretically the justices should not commit for trial unless they feel that a reasonable jury could possibly find the accused guilty. These proceedings are known as the committal proceedings and the evidence may be presented solely in the form of written documents under section 6(2) of the Magistrates' Courts Act 1980, in which case the proceedings are purely formal and the magistrates simply commit the accused on the papers without considering them. This procedure can only be used where the accused so wishes and is represented; it has the effect of saving considerable time. On the other hand the accused may elect to have an old style committal under section 6(1) of the Magistrates' Courts Act 1980 in which case the evidence is presented, both orally and in writing, and the magistrates must make a decision as to whether there is a case to be answered in the Crown Court. (For further details, see, *e.g.* Smith and Bailey, *The Modern English Legal System*, pp. 500 *et seq.*).

Where the accused is charged with an offence which is triable either way he is brought before the magistrates as if to committal proceedings. The procedure which is then followed is possibly best illustrated as a series of steps. Let us suppose for the purpose of explanation that the accused has been charged with stealing a bottle of rum from the local supermarket. He has been charged with theft contrary to section 1 of the Theft Act 1968. Theft is an offence which carries a maximum of 10 years, though in this case it is unlikely, unless there is a criminal record, that the accused, if convicted, would receive any sentence of imprisonment. The maximum sentence that can be imposed by magistrates is six months' imprisonment and/or a £2,000 fine. It would seem that this type of case ought therefore to be disposable by summary trial. At the outset the magistrates would hear details of the offence together with representations from both sides as to which type of trial was desired. If the magistrates take the view that the case is unsuitable for summary trial, they will proceed, as examining justices, to see whether there is sufficient evidence to commit the accused for trial in the Crown Court, though up till the time when they commit him for trial they may still decide to offer him the chance of summary trial. If, on the other hand, they feel that they would be prepared to try the case, they will invite the defendant to choose where he wishes to be tried. Before he makes this decision he must be warned that even if he elects summary trial he may still be sent to the Crown Court for sentence where he may receive the maximum sentence for the offence. The magistrates have, in effect, decided that their sentencing powers are adequate to deal with the offence. Once the defendant has pleaded guilty or been found guilty the magistrates will pass sentence and if there are no previous convictions recorded against the defendant the magistrates will be unable to commit the defendant for sentence to the Crown Court; they will be restricted to their own sentencing powers. If, however, the defendant is shown to have previous convictions, the magistrates may take the view that their sentencing powers are inadequate and commit him to the Crown Court for sentence. If the defendant elects to be tried summarily by the magistrates, the magistrates retain the power to change their mind and commit him for trial to the Crown Court right up until the close of the case for the prosecution.

Although the threefold classification of offences would in
itself greatly simplify the previous law relating to the distribution of business between the magistrates' and Crown Court, the
James Committee took the view that it was necessary to direct
more work towards the magistrates. The Committee reported
that a great deal of time was taken up in the Crown Court by
cases of theft where the sums involved were small and criminal
damage where the damage inflicted could be cheaply repaired.
They thus recommended that where the accused was charged
with theft involving less than £20 or criminal damage where the
damage caused was less than £100 the accused should not be
entitled to trial by jury. Parliament refused to accept the
recommendations relating to theft, largely because theft is a
crime which always requires dishonesty and where a conviction
is always a serious one to place on a person's record; but it is
quite conceivable that further attempts will be made to restrict
some cases of theft to the magistrates' court. However,
Parliament, in the Criminal Law Act 1977 followed the advice
of the James Committee on criminal damage and in fact
increased the sums involved to £200. This figure is now £2,000
(Criminal Justice Act 1988 s. 38). The effect of this recent
increase will mean that virtually all criminal damage offences,
save those where arson or explosives are involved, will be tried
in magistrates' courts. As a result, where the accused is charged
with criminally damaging property of another, there are now, in
effect, two separate offences depending upon the value of the
damage caused. Where the accused is charged with an offence
contrary to section 1 of the Criminal Damage Act 1971 (except
where the damage or destruction is caused by fire), or where the
accused is a secondary party to such an offence, or where he has
attempted or incited its commission, there is an extra step for
the magistrates to follow. They must first ascertain the financial
amount of the damage or destruction caused. (See the
Magistrates' Courts Act 1980, s.22, Sched. 2). They will hear
representations from both sides in an attempt to discover the
cost of replacement where the property has been destroyed or
irreparably damaged, or repair or replacement (whichever is
less) where the goods have been damaged. The relevant cost is
the cost it would take to repair or replace the property at the
time of the commission of the alleged offence. It is provided
that the decisions of the magistrates on the estimate of the
damage shall not be subject to appeal.

If the magistrates find that the damage exceeds £2,000 then
the offence is one triable either way and the procedure outlined

above will be followed. If the magistrates find that the damage is below £2,000 then the offence is triable summarily only. In this case the maximum that can be imposed is three months imprisonment or a fine of £500. As with other purely summary offences there is no power to commit for sentence since the maximum sentence is within the magistrates' jurisdiction.

If the magistrates are unable to decide whether the damage does or does not exceed £2,000, then the accused will be told that the choice is up to him. If he wishes the offence will be treated as purely summary, in which case the maximum sentence he may receive is three months or a fine of £500. He will be told that since it is purely summary there is no question of a later decision to commit for trial or of committal for sentence. If the accused chooses not to accept this offer to treat the offence as a purely summary one then the offence is regarded as one triable either way and technically the procedure outlined above (p. 7) will be followed. The reason for saying "technically" is that his refusal to allow the offence to be treated as a purely summary offence can only be on the grounds that he wants to be tried by a jury. There therefore seems little point in following through the procedure outlined above for offences triable either way. [It is possibly worth mentioning that the procedure to determine whether the cost of the damage exceeds a certain amount is rarely called into play—the sides having generally agreed the amount. With the increase in the figure to £2,000 it will be even rarer.]

2. Appeals

It would be beyond the scope of this book to cover in any detail the system of appeals operating in criminal cases. The following diagrams illustrate the routes the cases may follow through the courts. (See further Smith and Bailey, Chap. 19).

SUMMARY TRIALS: APPEALS

HOUSE OF LORDS

Either side may appeal on points of law.

Divisional Court must certify point of law of general public importance.

AND either the House of Lords or the Divisional Court must grant leave to appeal.

DIVISIONAL COURT OF THE QUEEN'S BENCH DIVISION OF THE HIGH COURT

Appeal by either prosecutor or defendant by way of case stated. The appeal must be based either on a point of law or excess of jurisdiction by the magistrates.

CROWN COURT

Appeal by defendant only

(1) Appeal against conviction on points of law or fact (but only if defendant pleaded not guilty at his trial)

(2) Appeal against sentence.

MAGISTRATES' COURTS

Summary Trial

— No jury.

TRIAL ON INDICTMENT: APPEALS

HOUSE OF LORDS

Appeal on points of law only.

Court of Appeal must certify point of law of general public importance; *AND* Court of Appeal or House of Lords must grant leave to appeal.

Either side may appeal.

(Attorney General's references may reach H. of L.).

(Attorney General's references on sentence may also reach H. of L.).

COURT OF APPEAL (CRIMINAL DIVISION)

Appeal by accused only.

(1) against conviction — on a point of law — no leave required.

(2) against conviction — on a point of fact or mixed law and fact — leave required.

(3) against sentence — leave required.

Following an acquittal in the Crown Court the Attorney General may refer a point of law for clarification to Court of Appeal — but this does not affect the acquittal.

Where the Attorney General believes that the trial judge has imposed a sentence which is unduly lenient (in certain serious offences) he may refer the case to the Court of Appeal where the sentence can be replaced by one the Court of Appeal considers to be more appropriate (Criminal Justice Act, ss. 35, 36).

CROWN COURT

Trial on indictment before judge and a jury.

MAGISTRATES' COURTS

Preliminary Investigation (committal proceedings).

CHAPTER 2

MURDER

1. INTRODUCTION

In the study of criminal law it is always useful to bear in mind that however theoretical the subject may appear, its *raison d'être* is extremely practical. In each criminal prosecution which is brought before the courts it will be up to the prosecutor to prove that the accused has committed the offence with which he has been charged. We shall see that each crime has what may be described as a list of ingredients, all of which must be established to the court's satisfaction before a conviction can be returned. It is analogous to a doctor who is trying to diagnose a patient's ailment from the list of symptoms he has been given. On the surface it may seem that the patient is suffering from a particular disease, but one important symptom is missing and so the doctor will have to consider other possibilities. In criminal law the particular ingredients obviously vary from one crime to another and can only be discovered from a study of the statute books and previous decisions of the courts. However, there are principles which are common to crimes in general. Questions such as, can more than one person be liable for a single offence and what defences are open to the accused, are questions which can be asked about all crimes and in many cases the answer will be the same whether the crime is murder, stealing or assault. It is thus normal to study these so-called general principles before moving to a study of particular crimes, but this can lead to an air of unreality. We shall therefore begin with an analysis of the basic requirements of murder so that the general principles can be examined against the background of an actual offence.

2. UNLAWFUL HOMICIDE

Murder is one of a group of offences which are generally

referred to as unlawful homicides. The word homicide simply means the killing of a human being which in itself is not necessarily a criminal offence. Some killings are purely accidental, others may be justified or authorised; for instance a killing of another in self-defence may be held to be justified. Such killings will not be classified as unlawful and will not, therefore, attract criminal liability, though it may take a trial to establish this. Other homicides which do not possess these qualities are said to be unlawful homicides and do attract criminal liability. Even within the category of unlawful homicides it is possible to detect varying degrees of culpability. Thus it has become common to subdivide unlawful homicides into more specific offences according to our perception of their gravity. In this country we have attempted to identify those killings which we regard as the most serious and to these we have attached the name, "murder." Those we regard as less serious we classify as manslaughter, infanticide and causing death by reckless driving. Once it has been decided that unlawful homicides must be subdivided, it is necessary to specify the criteria upon which a given killing will be assigned to one category or to another, and this will form the basis of this and later chapters.

Before we look at the way in which we assign unlawful homicides to one category or another it may be useful to have a look at the Criminal Statistics in order to get some idea of the size of the problem. For the moment we use the term homicide to cover murder, manslaughter and infanticide, we can say that in 1987, 687 deaths were initially recorded as homicides. This represents a record high, the previous highest figure being 660 in 1986. However, it must be remembered that since there are relatively few homicides, it is to be expected that the numerical variations from year to year will be more noticeable than in those crimes, such as theft, where the numbers are far greater. It is also worth noting that the 1987 figure includes 16 deaths resulting from one incident in Hungerford. As in the past, about 12 per cent. of these deaths were eventually recorded as non homicides. In 64 per cent. of the cases the victim was acquainted with the suspect (between 1977 and 1986 the average was 73 per cent.) and in 37 per cent. of the cases the victim was a member of the suspect's family or was the suspect's cohabitee or lover. This means that only about three in 10 victims are unknown to the suspect. Because of the high proportion of victims who are known to the suspects, it is hardly surprising that 50 per cent. of the deaths arise out of quarrels or bouts of temper and that the most frequently-used implement is a sharp instrument (about one third of the cases). About 1 in 10 deaths arose out of robberies or similar incidents and only 7 deaths were attributable to terrorism. After sharp instruments, hitting and kicking was the next most frequent cause of death (approximately 1 in 6), strangulation and asphyxiation accounted for about 1 in 7 and a blunt instrument 1 in 8. Shooting was responsible for 1 in 8 of the deaths, which represents an increase on the average 1 in 13; without Hungerford, however, this number falls to 1 in 10. By the middle of 1988 the convictions for these homicides recorded in 1987 stood at: murder—124; manslaughter—174; infanticide—0. Causing death by reckless driving is not included in these statistics. In 1987, 292 cases of causing death by reckless driving were recorded. By way of contrast, it is worth noting that in 1987 two million cases of theft were recorded. Of these the most common types were 660,000 thefts from motor vehicles, 247,000 thefts from shops, 119,000 thefts of pedal cycles and 290,000 thefts or unlawful takings of motor vehicles. Obviously murder attracts more attention than nearly any other crime because of its extremely serious and potentially sensational nature. On the other hand it makes less appearances in the courts than media coverage might tend to lead one to expect. (Figures extracted from Criminal Statistics; England and Wales Cm 498 (1987).)

3. MURDER

As we have said previously, once you have taken the view that there is a need to categorise unlawful homicides, you must then decide upon the criteria to be used. We have traditionally taken the view that the most heinous killings should be labelled as murder and that the less serious killings be called manslaughter (or possibly infanticide or causing death by reckless driving). It would, of course, be quite feasible for Parliament to provide that in future there should be only one category known as unlawful homicide and that the sentence should vary according to the severity of the offence. This would have the effect of rendering the law a great deal more simple, though it would be open to the criticism that it would leave too much discretion in the hands of the sentencer. In any case there is no serious possibility that Parliament would ever be attracted to such a drastic change which would remove from our law the opportunity to label our worst killers as murderers. How, therefore, do we decide which killings merit the label "murder"? In this country we have normally, though not invariably, distinguished murder from manslaughter by reference to the state of the accused's mind at the time of the killing. Thus we have normally held it to be murder where the accused has intentionally brought about the death of the victim. This, however, is not the only workable method for classifying killings. It would be possible to hold that murder—the most serious of the homicides—should include all killings committed in the furtherance of thefts, terrorism and rapes or any killings where the victim was a police officer or killings which involved the use of guns or explosives. We have come to reject this type of approach on the basis that we find it to be unacceptable that a chance killing can be held to be murder simply because it happened during the commission of another offence or because the victim happened to be a police officer. Other jurisdictions have taken the view that to treat as murder any killing which results from the furtherance of, for example robbery, serves as a deterrent to would-be robbers; they will be convicted of murder if any death results from the robbery even if the victim is shot by a policeman who is chasing the robbers (but see below, p. 46).

Whatever criteria are selected to distinguish murder from manslaughter the problem remains the same; you must identify factually those killings which you consider to be the most heinous and then find a form of statutory provision which will cover those and no others. The complexity of the problem can be seen by a consideration of two types of killing. If we assume for the moment that only a killing in which the accused has deliberately taken the life of his victim shall be murder, then in the absence of any mercy killing defence, a father who deliberately kills his child, who is terminally and painfully ill, will be a murderer. The bank robber, however, who sprays bullets round the bank will not necessarily be covered because he may not intend to kill anyone. (For further discussion and proposals for future reform see the 14th Report of the Criminal Law Revision Committee, Offences Against the Person.)

The penalty for murder

Although the classification of homicides as murder and manslaughter serves to allow the society to stigmatise those

killings which it regards as most heinous as murder, this in itself
might not seem to warrant the complexities which arise from
having such a distinction unless the more serious offence is seen
to attract a heavier penalty. Clearly in those jurisdictions where
murder still attracts the death penalty the distinction is crucial.
In this country, however, Parliament has, at least for the
foreseeable future, abolished the death penalty for murder and
so the distinction has become less important (Murder (Abolition
of Death Penalty) Act 1965).

Murder in our jurisdiction carries a mandatory sentence of life
imprisonment; the trial judge has no discretion to vary the
sentence. The Home Secretary may release such a person on
licence at any time during the term, but the trial judge has the
power to make a recommendation that such a step should not
be taken for a certain number of years. Thus he may, in
sentencing the convicted murderer to life imprisonment,
recommend that he should serve at least 20 years before being
released. This type of recommendation will be made when the
judge feels that he is dealing with, for example, a particularly
brutal murder. The Home Secretary is clearly not bound to
follow such a recommendation, though failure to do so would
almost certainly increase the pressure for a return of the death
penalty. Where the accused is convicted of manslaughter then
the judge has a discretion to award any sentence up to and
including life imprisonment. Here, however, he is able to take
account of aggravating an mitigating factors in arriving at what
he considers to be the correct sentence. If the judge believed
that, in the circumstances, no punishment was merited, he could
award an absolute discharge. The Criminal Law Revision
Committee (Report on Offences Against the Person, Cmnd.
7844 (1980) para. 42) was divided in its opinion as to whether or
not the mandatory life sentence for murder should be preserved.
If it were to be removed, then the need for a distinction
between murder and manslaughter would become arguably very
much weaker.

The basic elements of murder

We said earlier that in every crime the prosecution must
establish certain ingredients in order to gain a conviction. In the
next chapter we shall see that these ingredients fall into two
categories. In one category are all those elements of the crime
which have noting to do with the accused's state of mind; for

the moment we can call these the external elements of the crime. In the other category, are those elements relating to the accused's state of mind at the time of the commission of the offence; these we can call the internal elements. Adopting this classification we can say that the external elements for both murder and manslaughter are the same. The distinction between the two crimes lies in the internal elements.

(a) *The external elements*

The external elements of murder and manslaughter are the unlawful killing of a human being who was within the Queen's Peace where the death occurred within a year and a day of the last act done by the accused to the victim. Murder and manslaughter are exceptional crimes in that any citizen of the United Kingdom and Colonies who is alleged to have committed murder or manslaughter may be tried in this country wherever the killing was alleged to have occurred. Our courts also have jurisdiction over any such crimes alleged to have been committed by non-British subjects in the United Kingdom or on a British ship or aircraft. We can now examine each of the external elements in turn.

(i) *Unlawful.* The killing must be an unlawful killing. This indicates that the law recognises that in certain circumstances a killing may be either justified or authorised. For example, the execution in the prescribed manner of a man sentenced to death would clearly be a lawful killing. Though if the executioner secretly entered the condemned man's cell on the eve of his execution and poisoned him, this would clearly be an unlawful homicide. Equally the law recognises that it may be justifiable for X to kill Y in order to prevent Y killing either X or someone else (see Chap. 6, p. 173). It is for the prosecution to prove that the killing was unlawful, though the accused may have the burden of introducing some evidence that he was acting, for example, in self-defence in order to make a live issue of self defence. (See further below, p. 91).

(ii) *Killing of a human being.* The prosecution must prove that the accused caused the death of a human being. In most cases it will be obvious that if the facts are as the prosecution alleged the accused has killed a human being. However, difficulties can arise over whether the accused's act was really the cause of the victim's death and whether or not the victim was a human being protected by the law of homicide. The problem of causation will be examined later (see p. 42). A few words are required here as to the definition of human being. Difficulties can arise at each end of life's spectrum as to when a person becomes or ceases to be a human being.

At what precise moment does a child come under the protection of the law of homicide? It is normally said that the child must be expelled entirely from the mother's body and that it must have an independent existence of its own. What exactly constitutes independent existence is difficult to state. It is generally accepted that it is not necessary that the after-birth must have been expelled or severed. Equally it is clear that independent existence would be established by proof that the child had begun to breathe, though whether this is a requirement is disputed since this may not occur for quite some time after the baby has been completely expelled from the mother. Other judges seem to favour the test that the baby shall have established an independent circulation. This test, however, is no longer really tenable since medical evidence would suggest that the foetus is maintaining an independent blood circulation within a month of conception. There is no authoritative answer to such a question, though it is possibly safe to say that it acquires an independent existence at the latest when it starts breathing. There are, of course, separate offences of child destruction and abortion to deal with the "killing" of a child which has not yet achieved an independent existence. Further the injuring of a foetus in the womb, which is then born alive, but later dies of the injuries, may constitute murder or manslaughter (*West* (1848)).

At the other end of life's span it is not difficult to think of problems which might occur as to the precise moment at which a human being died and thus ceased to be capable of being killed. With the advancement of medical science it is now quite possible to maintain heart beats and breathing by artificial means even though the patient has no chance of making a recovery or of even regaining consciousness. The issue has been further complicated by the fact that organs for the use in transplants need realistically to be taken from a body in which the heart is still beating. The problem could therefore arise where the accused has seriously wounded the victim who is then artificially maintained on a respirator. If another person then turns off the respirator, who has killed the victim? The initial assailant or the person (possibly a doctor) who has turned off the respirator? Although there is no definitive statement on the law relating to this issue, it seems likely that in future the courts will accept the test as being that of "brain death" rather than cessation of heart beat. Brain death occurs where medical evidence shows that the brain has been irreparably damaged and that none of its major centres is functioning (see *Malcherek* (1981)).

(iii) *Queen's Peace.* If the accused has killed an enemy during the heat of war and in the exercise thereof the killing will not be an unlawful homicide.

(iv) *Death within a year and a day.* The old definitions of murder and manslaughter provide that the prosecution must prove that the victim died within a year and a day of the wounds inflicted by the accused and, if this was a series of wounds, within a year and a day of the last. This rule still persists today (see *Dyson* (1908)). Its original function was to act as a sort of a test of whether or not the actions of the accused actually caused the death of the victim. If the victim survived more than a year and a day after the attack then it was assumed that the real cause of death was something other than the accused's action. As medical science has advanced it is now obviously much easier to state with relative conviction what, in the opinion of medically qualified persons, the accused actually died from, yet in its 1980 Report on Offences Against the Person, the Criminal Law Revision Committee recommended that the rule be retained though they suggested the reduction of the term to a year. We shall see later that more refined rules have been developed over the years to determine whether, at law, the accused could be said to have caused the death of the victim and there really seems little point in retaining the old rule. What would be the position today of a would-be assassin who managed to infect his victim with a slow growing cancer? (For further discussion of causation see below, p. 42).

It would seem that the year and a day rule applies to other offences where the defendant is alleged to have brought about death.

In *The Coroner for Inner West London, ex p. De Luca* (1988) the Divisional Court held that the year and a day rule had applied to suicide when suicide was a crime and that it still applied to offences under Homicide Act 1957, section 4(1) (killings in the furtherance of a suicide pact; see below p. 235) and offences under Suicide Act 1961, section 2(1) (aiding,

abetting, counselling or procuring suicide). It seems fairly clear
that the rule also applies to the crime of infanticide (section 1
Infanticide Act 1938). There may be some doubt as to whether
it applies to causing death by reckless driving (Road Traffic Act,
section 1 1988) but since this crime is now defined in a way
which makes it scarcely distinguishable from manslaughter it
would seem highly illogical if it were not to apply here (see
below p. 223 *et seq.*). In *ex p. De Luca* the applicant had sought
to quash a coroner's verdict that his son had committed suicide.
The Divisional Court ruled that although suicide was no longer
a crime, the fact that the son's death had occurred more than a
year and a day after he had shot himself prevented the coroner
from returning a verdict that the son had killed himself.

(b) *The internal elements*

Unless the prosecution can prove all of the external elements
discussed in the preceding section, there can be no conviction
for murder (or manslaughter). However, proof of these
elements alone will not suffice. The prosecution must prove also
that at the time the accused brought about the death of another
human being he possessed a certain state of mind. In essence,
the prosecution must establish the existence of some mental
element on each of the external elements. This can best be
illustrated by an example. If, for the moment, we assume that
murder is a crime requiring intention on each element of the
external elements then the prosecution would have to prove:

(i)   that the accused *intended* to kill a human being;
(ii) that the accused *intended* that the victim should die
      within a year and a day;
(iii) that the accused *intended* that the victim be within the
      Queen's Peace. This sounds a little odd and this is
      because this element of the crime is neither an act nor a
      result; it is a circumstance (see further below, p. 31).
      You cannot really intend circumstances, you can only
      know whether or not they exist. Thus in relation to
      circumstances, knowledge is the equivalent of intention.
      The requirement should thus be rephrased—that the
      accused *knew* that the victim was within the Queen's
      Peace.
(iv) That the accused *knew* that no circumstances of
      justification existed. Because the burden of proving the
      killing was unlawful rests upon the prosecution, it is

difficult to phrase the mental element in relation to the requirement of unlawfulness in the way we have expressed the other three. What we are concerned with here is the existence of circumstances which the law recognises as justifying the killing; possibly the best example is self-defence. Where the accused relies upon such a defence it is incumbent upon him to introduce some evidence that at the time he killed the victim he believed that it was necessary to do so in order to protect his own life (he does not have to know that the law regards this as a circumstance in which the killing of another would be lawful). Once he has introduced such evidence the prosecution would have to prove, beyond reasonable doubt that the accused knew that no such circumstances existed.

Thus suppose that we can establish that X intentionally killed Y, that there were no circumstances of justification, that the death occurred within a year and a day, can we now say that X murdered Y. Clearly not. We still have not said that, for example, X knew that there were no circumstances of justification existing at the time of the killing. Until we have established this and the necessary intent on all the other external elements there can be no conviction for murder.

If the law really was that *intention* and nothing less had to be established on each of the external elements of the offence, we should end up with a very narrow crime of murder. In reality we shall find that the requirements are much less stringent. We can now look at each of the external elements and examine what mental state is required in relation to each.

(i) *Killing of a human being.* This is clearly the central feature of the crime of murder and the state of mind required on this element, which has traditionally been described as the malice aforethought of murder, has been differently defined at various times in our history. In harsher times it was very widely defined. Writing in the sixteenth century Coke said that if a man shot an arrow at a deer intending to steal that deer "and the arrow killeth a boy that is hidden in the bush" he was guilty of murder! This may seem very draconian, but until the Homicide Act 1957 it was still murder for a man intending to commit certain violent crimes, such as rape or robbery, to cause death during the commission of the crime. This was known as the felony murder rule; the only mental state required was that of the crime he was committing when the death occurred.

It was also murder for a man intending to resist arrest to cause the death of an officer of justice. In both of these cases, sometimes referred to as constructive murder, the death itself could have been entirely accidental and quite unintended or unforeseen, but the accused could be convicted of murder and hanged. Although this harsh extension of malice aforethought is still prevalent in some states of the United States of America it was abolished in this country by section 1 of the Homicide Act 1957. There still, however, remains uncertainty as to the precise definition of malice aforethought for murder. Obviously it includes an intention to kill, but it goes further than this.

The killing of a human being. Let us start by considering the facts of a recent case; *Hancock and Shankland* (1986). In that case two striking Welsh miners had information that a non-striking miner was being driven to work in a taxi. At the time when the taxi was due to pass along a stretch of dual carriageway, they positioned themselves on a footbridge over the road and as the taxi approached they dropped heavy slabs of concrete into the road in its path. As a result the taxi crashed and the driver was killed. Hancock and Shankland were charged with murder. The case is instructive, because unlike the situation where the defendant has simply shot his victim or stuck a knife into his back, it is less easy to determine the state of mind of the two miners in relation to the dead driver. It might be relatively easy for a jury to reach the conclusion that the defendants intended to stop the non-striking miner reaching his work. It might even be easy to hold that they intended to damage the taxi in order to achieve their main purpose. But can you say that they intended to kill or even injure the driver or anyone in the taxi? (We shall see later that if it was found that they intended to kill the non-striking miner, the law would permit a conviction of murdering the taxi driver; see below p. 77). Possibly they foresaw a risk that the occupants of the car would be killed or injured, but do you consider that this should be enough to convict them of murder?

Following the decision of the House of Lords in *Moloney* (1985) the trial judge directed the jury that they could only convict the two miners if they were satisfied that they intended either to kill another human being or to cause that other human being really serious bodily harm. It is thus sufficient in relation to this element of the crime that the prosecution establish that the defendant:

EITHER intended to kill another human being
OR intended to cause him really serious bodily harm.

Leaving aside, for the moment, the question why we should convict a man of murder when he only intended to cause harm and not death, we are faced with the question of what is meant by the word "intend." (In the actual case of *Hancock and Shankland*, although the trial judge had rightly told the jury that they could only convict the defendants of murder if they found that they either intended to kill or cause really serious bodily harm, their convictions for murder were quashed by the Court of Appeal and replaced by convictions for manslaughter. This decision was upheld by the House of Lords on the basis that the trial judge in trying to explain what was meant by intention might have misled the jury). In a case where the defendant has shot or stabbed his victim the jury will probably have no difficulty in deciding, without any help from the judge, whether or not the defendant intended to kill or seriously injure him. However, in cases like *Hancock and Shankland* the jury may not unreasonably ask for some guidance. It is quite likely that they will reach a position where they can say 'We have no difficulty in reaching the conclusion that the two defendants foresaw that it was quite likely that someone would be seriously injured by the concrete slabs; but is that enough? The answer quite simply is "No!" Foreseeing that something might happen is not the same thing as intending to cause it to happen. In the next chapter we shall look at the meaning of the word "intend" in more detail (below, page 53). For the moment we can say that a person intends to produce a result when he desires that result and deliberately sets about to cause it. This is an over narrow view; but will suffice for the purpose of this introductory chapter.

Consider the following examples. Do any of the following intend to cause death or serious bodily harm? Should they be guilty of murder?

(i) During a bank robbery A sprays bullets indiscriminately around the bank. One bullet strikes a metal part of the till, ricochets and kills a customer.

(ii) B has sent a cargo of worthless material to New York on a passenger airliner. In the cargo he has secreted a bomb which will explode while the aircraft is over the sea. He has no desire to injure any of the passengers. He simply wishes to claim insurance on his cargo.

(iii) C, a terrorist, throws a bomb into a crowded pub and gives a warning which he hopes will suffice to clear the pub, but which he realises might be insufficient. Several customers are killed.

(iv) C's bomb, in example (iii), fails to explode. An hour later a bomb disposal expert is killed wile trying to defuse it.

Intention to cause serious harm. Throughout the decision of the House of Lords in *Moloney* (1985), Lord Bridge talks of an intention to cause serious harm. This is the modern equivalent of saying that the jury must find that the accused intended to cause grievous bodily harm. In *D.P.P.* v. *Smith* (1961) the House of Lords examined the meaning of the phrase "grievous bodily harm." Viscount Kilmuir L.C. said the phrase should be given its ordinary natural meaning. "Bodily harm needs no explanation and 'grievous' means no more and no less than 'really serious'." What constitutes really serious bodily harm is a question of fact for the jury. In *Saunders* (1985) the Court of Appeal held that there was no need to use the prefix "really" in connection with the phrase "serious harm" since it does nothing more than to emphasise that the harm must be—actually or really—serious.

It may strike you as odd that an accused person can be convicted of murder even though his only intention is to cause serious harm and he does not even contemplate death as a remote possibility. Some explanation, therefore, of the history of this category of malice aforethought might be useful.

We mentioned before that in earlier days an accused could be convicted of murder on the basis that the killing had occurred while he was furthering some other crime. The only intention required was the intention to commit that other crime. Thus if X accidentally killed Y while raping her, this was murder. This type of murder, referred to as felony murder or constructive murder, was abolished by section 1 of the Homicide Act 1957. Now before 1957 it was never doubted that if X intentionally caused Y grievous bodily harm and Y died as a result, X was guilty of murder. Was this by virtue of the felony murder rule? An intention to cause grievous bodily harm was the necessary mental state for the separate crime of causing grievous bodily harm with intent. Thus it could be argued that for this state of mind to afford the necessary malice aforethought of murder was, in effect, to utilise the felony murder rule. On the other hand others might argue that before 1957 there were, in reality, three categories of malice aforethought; express malice was the correct term where the accused intended to kill the victim; constructive malice covered the felony murder situation; implied malice was the term used to describe the situation where the accused intended to cause his victim grievous bodily harm. After 1957 it became important to know whether an intention to cause grievous bodily harm sufficed as malice aforethought by virtue of the felony murder rule, in which case it would no longer do so after 1957, or whether it was a separate head of malice which was not affected by section 1 of the Homicide Act 1957. In *Vickers* (1957) the Court of Criminal Appeal held that it was a separate head of malice aforethought and therefore survived the Act. This was not challenged until 1975 when Lords Diplock and Kilbrandon in *Hyam* argued that *Vickers* had been wrongly decided. Lord Diplock in a detailed review of the history of this head of malice aforethought came to the conclusion that it was part of the doctrine of constructive malice and was therefore abolished by section 1 of the Homicide Act 1957. He said that the prosecution should have to prove either that the accused intended to kill or that he intended to cause any bodily harm which he knew was likely to kill. Since Viscount Dilhorne and Lord Hailsham supported the correctness of the decision in *Vickers*, it fell to the fifth member of the House, Lord Cross, to cast the deciding vote. He declared that in the absence of more detailed discussion he was forced to assume that *Vickers* had been rightly decided; an intention to cause grievous bodily harm sufficed as malice aforethought for murder. This was scarcely a satisfactory state of affairs on such an important issue and in *Cunningham* (1982) the House of Lords returned to the question again. This time a unanimous House rejected Lord Diplock's argument and affirmed the decision in *Vickers*.

In *Moloney* the House of Lords expressly approves the decision in *Cunningham*. Indeed it held that "the restricted definition" of the mental element, favoured in *Hyam* by Lord Diplock and Lord Kilbrandon, could now only be adopted by legislative, not by judicial, intervention.

Thus we can safely say that if X intentionally causes Y serious bodily harm and Y dies as a result, X will have the necessary malice aforethought of murder. Whether the malice aforethought of murder *should* be established by a state of mind which does not even contemplate death as a remote possibility is a matter which must now be left to Parliament.

(ii) *The other external elements.* The major difference between the mental state required on the other external elements and the element just discussed is that whereas the prosecution will always have to lead evidence that the accused intended to kill or seriously harm a human being, once this is established it will be assumed that the necessary mental element on the other external factors exist unless the accused actually introduces some evidence to the contrary. However once the accused has introduced evidence that he did not possess the necessary mental state on one of the other elements it will be up to the prosecution to prove beyond reasonable doubt that he did. We can take the other three elements in turn.

That the victim should die within a year and a day. Although there is no authority on this point it seems likely that no mental element is required here at all. It is unlikely that a court would be sympathetic to a defendant who said that he was not guilty of murder since he did not intend his victim to die within a year and a day; the poison he had introduced was meant to take 18 months to kill him. Since we have already said that an accused can be convicted of murder when he intends to cause serious harm it would be highly illogical to introduce a requirement that the accused must intend or even foresee that death would occur within a year and a day. This external element is one upon which the accused simply takes his chance. The death must actually occur within a year and a day, but no mental element is required on this eventuality.

That the victim should be within the Queen's Peace. It is suggested that the prosecution would succeed if they can prove either that the accused knew that the victim was within the Queen's Peace or that he realised that the victim was probably within the Queen's Peace. In other words intention or foresight suffices on this element.

That the killing should be unlawful. Clearly where the accused raises a defence of justification it will suffice if the prosecution can prove that the accused did not know of the existence of any circumstances which would, in law, justify the killing. Equally if the accused thought it probable that no circumstances of justification existed the prosecution would also succeed on this issue. Again something less than intention suffices on this element.

Thus it is suggested that only on the central element of the offence is liability restricted to intentional conduct. On the other elements something less suffices. We have described this as foresight; in the next section we will see that it is often described as recklessness (see below, p. 59).

4. Conclusion

As we said at the beginning of this chapter once you subscribe to the view that there needs to be more than one category of unlawful homicide, you must select your criteria upon which such classification will be made. We have now seen that in this country we distinguish between murder and manslaughter by reference to what was in the accused's thoughts at the time he caused the death of the victim. The result is that we have produced an offence of murder which can be proved against an accused even though he had given no thought to the possibility that a human being might be killed. When the opportunity is taken by Parliament to reform the law relating to unlawful homicide it is unlikely that the present definition of malice aforethought will appeal to the legislators. An amusing and instructive exercise you can undertake is to try to identify factually those killings you consider ought to be classified as murder, and then attempt to draft criteria which will cover those killings and none other.

CHAPTER 3

ACTUS REUS AND MENS REA; THE INGREDIENTS OF A CRIME

FROM a consideration of the particular crime of murder we may proceed to a consideration of the general principles of criminal liability. It will have become apparent that on a charge of murder the prosecution must establish at least two things. First it must establish that the accused brought about the (external) elements required to satisfy the definition of murder, namely the death within a year and a day of a human being within the Queen's Peace. These elements comprise, what is known as the *actus reus* of the offence of murder. Secondly, it must be proved that the accused brought about those elements with a certain state of mind. The requisite state of mind is called the *mens rea*.

Whatever the crime (whether it is murder at one extreme or dropping litter at the other) there is no exception to the requirement that the prosecution must establish every part of the *actus reus. Dyson* (1908) is a good illustration of this. That case shows that if the death occurred by so much as one hour or even one second over one year and a day from the infliction of the harm causing the death, the accused cannot be convicted of murder or manslaughter. Of course it may be a matter of chance whether the victim dies just inside or just outside the stated period and it can make no difference to the accused's culpability whether the victim dies on one day or the next. But for legal purposes it is crucial; the elements constituting the crime must always be strictly proved. So on a charge of obtaining property by deception the prosecution will fail if it cannot establish that the accused made a false statement—it is not enough that the accused believed that he was making a false statement and intended to act dishonestly (*Deller* (1952)). So on a charge of receiving stolen goods it has to be proved that the goods were, in fact, stolen at the time they were received—it is not enough that the accused and everyone else thought that the goods were stolen (*Haughton* v. *Smith* (1975), but see below, p. 202). The reason for this strict

28

requirement is that the law has set its face against imposing criminal liability simply on the basis of the accused's intentions; the law requires, in addition, strict proof of all the elements which the law says constitutes the crime.

The reason for the second requirement—of a certain state of mind—is even more obvious. A broad distinction needs to be drawn between persons who deliberately cause harm and those who cause harm unavoidably and accidentally; the former, it may be supposed are rightly brought within the purview of the criminal law, while the latter are not. In relation to "serious" crimes (sometimes referred to as crimes *mala in se*) this is normally the position; but in relation to "minor" crimes (crimes *mala prohibita*) criminal liability is frequently imposed even though the accused has not deliberately brought about the harm (the *actus reus*). Where liability is imposed though the accused is not at fault, the crime is known as an offence of strict (or absolute) liability. These crimes, and the policies which are claimed to justify their existence, are dealt with later in Chap. 4, though some incidental mention will be made of them in this chapter.

Even if the prosecution establish these two requirements (*viz.* the forbidden act deliberately brought about by the accused) it does not necessarily follow that a crime has been committed. Take a case where the accused is charged with murdering another and pleads that he was acting in self defence. The prosecution may have no difficulty in establishing that the accused has caused the forbidden act and that he did so deliberately; but the accused claims that he killed the victim because, had he not done so, the victim would have killed him. Killing, even deliberate killing, is not always a crime. This is true of other crimes also; the law admits of certain circumstances in which even the deliberate causing of a forbidden act is held to be justified.

Obviously not every case raises an issue of justification but where the issue is raised it is not for the accused to prove the justification, but for the prosecution to negative it. The prosecution will have to prove beyond reasonable doubt that the accused acted without grounds which in law would justify his act (see below, p. 146). This is because lack of justification is regarded as one of the ingredients of the crime—the definition of many offences contains the phrase "without lawful authority or excuse"; for murder the killing must be "unlawful."

As to whether circumstances of justification should be classified as part of the *actus reus* or part of the *mens rea* no general agreement exists. If the accused kills in lawful self-defence is he to be excused because there is no *actus reus* of murder, or because he lacks *mens rea?* It will be appreciated that the accused will not care very much how lawyers analyse his situation so long as self-defence is recognised in exculpating him, and rightly so. The really important issue is not whether lawyers ascribe certain elements to *actus reus* and others to *mens rea*, but whether there is a crime.

But cases can arise—they are very rare cases—where it might make a difference whether circumstances of justification relate to the *mens rea* or *actus reus*. Suppose that Anne sees Ben running out of a bank. She does not know why he is running but she vividly recalls that on the previous evening he insulted her at a disco. To take her revenge she trips him up and beats him half to death with her umbrella. Imagine Anne's surprise when she is surrounded by staff from the bank who congratulate her on capturing the man who had just robbed the bank. Is Anne a criminal? She thought that she was assaulting Ben and could hardly offer her desire to take revenge as justification for the assault. Or is she a heroine? She has brought a villain to justice. *Ought* she to be regarded as a villain or heroine? If lack of justification is part of the *actus reus* of assault then a prosecution of Anne must fail because the prosecution would have to meet the requirement not only of proving an assault but also that it was an assault in circumstances which provided no justification. On our facts the prosecution would clearly be unable to prove that Anne's assault was unjustified. If, however, justification is regarded as part of the mental element, it would be material to consider whether Anne knew of the circumstances of justification. Since she did not know of the circumstances, on this view she ought to be convicted.

In *Dadson* (1850) the accused was a police constable charged with shooting at another with intent to cause him grievous bodily harm. Dadson had been posted to guard a copse from which there had been several thefts of wood. When he saw P emerge from the copse carrying wood which he had, in fact stolen, Dadson called to him to stop but P ran off. In order to stop him Dadson shot him in the leg. At the time it was assumed that it was permissible for a police constable to shoot an escaping felon. Unfortunately stealing wood was not in itself a felony unless the accused had two previous convictions for the same offence. As it turned out P had two previous convictions for the offence, but Dadson did not know of this at the time. Dadson was convicted of the offence despite the existence of circumstances of justification, and on a case reserved the conviction was upheld. The case would seem to be authority for the proposition that where the accused raises justification as a defence to a criminal charge he will fail if the prosecution establishes that at the time of the commission of the offence the accused was not aware of the facts which would justify his action. What should be the position if in similar circumstances the defendant had said "I don't know if he is a felon; but there is at least a fifty-fifty chance that he is? [But see Police and Criminal Evidence Act 1984, s. 24(4).]

In *Miller* (1983) Lord Diplock said that it would be conducive to clarity in analysing the ingredients of a crime that was created by statute, as the great majority of criminal offences now were, if one were to avoid bad Latin and instead to think of and speak about the conduct of the accused and his state of mind at the time of that conduct, instead of speaking of *actus reus* and *mens rea*. Clearly to translate *actus reus* and *mens rea* as "guilty act and guilty mind" would be misleading. However, most lawyers regard the terms as useful symbols for the various elements of a criminal offence, and their disappearance from common usage seems rather unlikely.

1. ACTUS REUS

Actus literally means "act" but while most crimes require that the accused commits a certain act this is not always the case. Criminal liability may also arise through failure to act and so *actus* can cover an omission as well as an act. Perhaps it would be better to speak of conduct since conduct can be taken to include commission and omission. Even this enlarged meaning of *actus* may not cover all cases since on occasion, as we shall see (below, p. 36) criminal liability may be imposed for a state of affairs without any requirement for conduct on the part of the accused.

A crime, however, requires more than conduct: the *actus* must be *reus*. If X fires a rifle he is engaged in conduct; but to fire a rifle, without more, is not a crime. Suppose then that X aims his rifle at Y and deliberately kills him. X has now brought about a consequence which consequence is normally proscribed by the law of murder—*normally* but not always. Whether or not X will be guilty of murder depends upon the circumstances surrounding the killing. X will not be guilty of murder if Y is an enemy in time of war or if X is acting in circumstances of self-defence. Thus we can say that crimes generally are comprised of (a) some conduct, (b) a prohibited consequence, and (c) certain surrounding circumstances and that each individual crime will consist of one, two or all of such elements. Murder is a crime involving all three elements, whereas the crime of rape involves only (a) and (c).

(1) Voluntary nature of the act

Ordinarily the prosecution must prove that the accused voluntarily brought about the *actus reus* of the crime. To put it another way the act or omission must have occurred because of a conscious exercise of will on the part of the accused. Thus there would be no voluntary act where the act alleged to constitute the crime was performed by the accused while he was asleep, or suffering from concussion caused by a blow on the head. In these types of case it is usually said that the accused is acting in a state of automatism (or more accurately non-insane automatism; see below, p. 34). But these are not the only situations in which the action of the accused may be said to be involuntary. For example if X were to hold Y's hand and force him to stick a knife in Z, Y's action could not be said to have been a voluntary one. It is also necessary to distinguish the requirement for a voluntary act from the requirement in many, but not all crimes, that the accused intentionally, caused the *actus reus*. Whereas the prosecution will always fail if it cannot prove that the accused acted voluntarily, in certain crimes (crimes of strict liability) it will be excused from the need to show that the accused acted intentionally. Suppose that A is charged with failing to stop at a red traffic light, it will be no defence for him to say that he had not seen any traffic lights let alone that they were showing red; this is an offence of strict liability which does not require that the police prove that he knew the lights were red. However a plea that he suffered a blackout just before his car reached the lights would, if accepted, mean that there was no voluntary act of driving and this would be fatal to the prosecution's case. It is pointless to worry about whether voluntariness is rightly described as part of the *actus reus* or as part of the *mens rea* of a given crime; the point to remember is that it is an essential part of every crime.

Let us consider the following hypothetical situations:

(i) A pushes B so that B loses his balance and falls against C;

(ii) While driving his car D is attacked by a swarm of bees; in instinctively brushing them away from his face he loses control of his car which mounts the pavement and injures E;

(iii) While driving his car F is subject to an attack of angina pectoris, which causes him to lose control of the car which then mounts the pavement;

(iv) While asleep H stabs and kills J, his wife;

(v) K suffers from arteriosclerosis which causes a blackout. During the blackout K hits his son L, with a hammer;

(vi) M is under the influence of alcohol to such an extent that he is no longer aware of what he is doing. In this state he strikes his friend, N, with a beer mug.

In each of these situations a criminal charge may be laid and in all of them the accused might raise the same defence, namely that there was no voluntary conduct of his which caused the *actus reus*. But it does not necessarily follow that the same result would be reached in all six examples.

In example (i) A may well be liable for assaulting both B and C, but B has not assaulted C since there is absolutely no voluntary conduct at all on B's part. This should clearly result in an absolute acquittal for B.

Example (ii) differs in that D is the only human agent involved, but his action is purely reflexive and the view would no doubt be taken (*cf. Hill* v. *Baxter* (1958)) that it was not a voluntary act—or a sufficiently voluntary act—for D to incur criminal liability either for injuring E or for driving the car without due care and attention.

In example (iii) F is prima facie not guilty for the same reasons. There is no truly conscious control of movements by F during the angina attack and thus he cannot be said to be driving the car. But here it becomes necessary to consider F's knowledge of the nature and frequency of his attacks. If this was the first attack suffered by F then he would incur no liability, but if F was aware that he was frequently subject to attacks there would be no difficulty in saying that, by virtue of taking the risk of an attack whilst driving, he was guilty of careless driving—from the moment he started to drive. So in *Kay* v. *Butterworth* (1945) the accused was found guilty of driving even though he had fallen asleep at the time when the accident occurred; his culpability consisted of continuing to drive when he knew he was feeling drowsy. A more refined example is provided by *Jarmain* (1946) where in the course of a robbery J pointed a loaded pistol at a cashier knowing that it had no safety catch and required only a light touch on the trigger to fire. The cashier, a brave woman, told him to go away and this so disconcerted J that, according to his version of the facts, while he was trying to work out what he should do he involuntarily pressed the trigger and the cashier was killed. The court declined to regard J's last action separately from the rest of the transaction. The death was caused by pointing a loaded pistol at the cashier at point blank range, and there was no doubt that this had been done voluntarily.

Example (iv) is straightforward. Acts done in a state of somnambulism are evidently not voluntary. Cases of killings done by persons in such a state are rare but they have occurred and resulted in acquittals. In *Cogdon* (1951), Mrs. Cogdon a woman with a record of bizarre dreams and of excessive worry over her 19-year-old daughter Pat, on the night in question dreamt that the Korean War was taking place all round her house and that a Korean soldier was attacking Pat who was in bed. In a state of somnambulism she took an axe and attacked the "Korean" thereby killing her daughter. At her trial for murder she pleaded that her act was an involuntary one and she was acquitted.

In these first four examples the defendant may be said to have raised the defence of *automatism*, or more accurately, *non-insane automatism* (see below, p. 36). The defendant, in each case, is saying that the conduct which is alleged to constitute the criminal offence was not brought about by an exercise of his free will; it was involuntary conduct. Unless the prosecution can prove that the conduct was voluntary, the defendant will be entitled to be found "not guilty." On the face of it, this seems a potent defence. It is surely very easy for a defendant to swear that he blacked out, and extremely difficult, if not impossible, for the prosecution to prove that he did not. However, in practice, automatism is a defence of very limited application. Thus Lord Denning was able to say that it was confined to "acts done while unconscious and to spasms, convulsions and reflex actions" (*Bratty* (1963)). The case of *Broome* v. *Perkins* (1987) reveals just how limited the defence is. In that case the defendant was charged with driving without due care and attention. He had clearly driven erratically during the course of a five mile journey from his place of work to his home, but he could recall nothing. The damaged state of his car caused him to realise what must have happened and he immediately reported to the police. Evidence from witnesses showed that at certain times during the journey he had effected course corrections, and medical evidence suggested that it was perfectly possible for a person in his condition to react to gross stimuli—but to react imperfectly. In other words he would have enough awareness and control to miss a ten tonne truck. The Divisional Court held that this did not amount to automatism since he had acted consciously during the driving and not totally automatically; a logical if rather harsh decision. The court is, in effect, saying that there is a gradual progression from a state of total control of one's actions to complete automatism where no control at all exists. It is only when one reaches the state of complete lack of control that the defence of automatism exists. Thus sleepwalking would constitute automatism, but nothing short of this. *Broome* v. *Perkins* must cast doubt on the case of *Charlson* (1955) where a father who was suffering from a brain tumour struck his small son with a mallet and threw him out of a window. The court treated this as a case of non-insane automatism and we shall see later it is now generally accepted that he should have been acquitted on the basis of insanity (see below, p. 152). However, even accepting for the moment that it did not fall within the definition of insanity, it is difficult to reconcile the case with *Broome* v. *Perkins*. It is inconceivable that Charlson exercised absolutely no control over his movements. Charlson's action was surely not within Denning's definition of "acts done while unconscious and . . . spasms, convulsions and reflex actions."

The defence is further limited by the imposition upon the defendant of a strong evidential burden which he must discharge before the issue can be left to the jury (for the explanation of evidential burden, see below p. 90). Although it is up to the prosecution to prove, beyond reasonable doubt, that the accused was not acting as an automaton, he is not obliged to do this unless the accused has first laid a satisfactory foundation that he was acting as an automaton. Mere testimony from the accused will not generally suffice. He will be expected to produce some evidence, possibly medical, to support his claim that he blacked out and acted as an automaton. If he fails to produce such evidence the court will assume that he was acting voluntarily and will not then expect the prosecution to deal specifically with the issue of voluntariness.

The case posed in example (v) is more complicated. There is no doubt that K is entitled to an acquittal but the real question is whether he is entitled to a verdict of not guilty or to a verdict of not guilty by reason of insanity which would result in a commitment during Her Majesty's pleasure. It will be appreciated that K's case, unlike those of B and D, raises the possibility of repetition. Of course, it is just possible that on some future occasion B may again be pushed by A or that D might again be attacked in his car by a swarm of bees, but these are contingencies against which no precautions can be taken. With K it is different. The prognostication may be that he will have further blackouts leading to further impulsive and motiveless violence.

What the courts have done is to draw a line, as best they can, between sane and insane automatism. Both forms of automatism result in an acquittal but only the former enables the defendant to leave the court a free man. Example (v) would no doubt result in a verdict of not guilty by reason of insanity because K would be held to be suffering from a disease of the mind within the M'Naghten rules. These rules are amplified below (p. 150); for now it is important to note that there is an important practical distinction between automatism which is based on a disease of the mind (insane automatism) and other forms of automatism (non-insane automatism). It may seem odd that the somnambulist who has killed in his sleep will be acquitted and subject to no further restraints, especially since there may be reason to believe that if he can kill once in his sleep he can do it again. The explanation is simply that somnambulism, as such, is not a disease of the mind. It is perhaps worth drawing attention to the fact that if in example (iii) F had suffered a heart attack this would almost certainly result in a finding of non-insane automatism, though the effect of disrupting the blood supply to the brain is exactly what happens in arteriosclerosis. It can't be imagined, however, that we would classify the heart attack victim as insane.

Example (vi) is given to draw attention to the fact that automatism arising from the non-medical and voluntary consumption of alcohol or drugs is not generally a defence. There are said to be special policy reasons for treating such cases in an exceptional way (see below, p. 161).

(2) Criminal liability in the "state of affairs" cases

While there is notionally no criminal liability unless the *actus reus* is brought about by some voluntary act or omission on the part of the accused, there is no rule of law which says that criminal liability cannot be imposed without some such voluntary act by the accused. Parliament could, for example, make it a criminal offence to be over six feet tall. In such an unlikely event it would be no defence for the accused to claim that he had no control over the mechanisms of his body which had caused him to be over six feet in height. While it is inconceivable that Parliament would create such an offence it has to be acknowledged that it is theoretically open to Parliament to do so and there are, as it happens, some crimes which might be taken to impose criminal liability without proof of any voluntary act on the part of the accused.

Under Road Traffic Regulation Act 1984, section 107, and for the purposes of ensuring that certain fixed penalties such as parking fines, are paid, "it shall be conclusively presumed ... that [the owner] was the driver at that time ... that acts or omissions of the driver of the vehicle at that time were his acts or omissions." Thus if the accused's son has parked the accused's car illegally, the accused will be liable even though he is sleeping in his bed in New York at the time. It is, however, a defence for the accused to show that the car was in the possession of the other person without the consent of the accused, thus liability is incurred only if the accused consented to the possession of the car. Nevertheless, given an actual consent to possession, the accused is liable for certain crimes committed thereafter without any proof of any voluntary act on his part. It is easy to appreciate what led Parliament to take this unusual step. Many parking tickets were left unpaid and when the police served a summons on the owner they would be met by the impossibility of proving whether it was the owner, his wife or some other member of the family who had been responsible for the illegal parking.

A much more extreme case is provided by *Larsonneur* (1933). A French woman, L, went from England to Ireland where she was arrested by the Irish police and sent back to England where she was taken into police custody. She was charged with being an alien who was "found" in the United Kingdom without permission. Strictly speaking, of course, she was "found" in this country the moment she set foot off the boat from Ireland. However she did not want to come back to England but she was forced back by the Irish police. Once the boat docked here she had no alternative but to get off on to British soil—straight into the arms of the English police—at which stage she was "found" here without permission. There was no voluntary action on her part and nothing she could do to prevent herself stepping on to British soil. Nevertheless she was convicted of the offence. Her conviction was upheld because she literally came within the prohibition. She was "an alien" to whom permission to land was refused and she was "found" here. As a matter of fact her conduct was not involuntary (conduct is not involuntary merely because it is done under duress) but the implication in the judgment is that she would have been convicted even if she had been physically carried into England by the police.

The decision in *Larsonneur* has been justly and universally condemned. Nonetheless a similar decision was reached in *Winzar* v. *Chief Constable of Kent* (1983) where the police had been called to remove the accused from a hospital corridor. They found that he was drunk and removed him to a police car which was parked in the highway. He was later charged with being found drunk in the highway, though in reality he was "found" by the police in the hospital corridor. Cases such as these can be defended by a very literal approach to statutory interpretation. Statutory offences rarely specify that such issues as insanity and duress should be a defence but these are implied as a matter of course; it would be no more difficult to read in the fundamental requirement that the *actus reus* must be caused by some voluntary act of the accused. Of course, if, as is the case with section 107 of the Road Traffic Regulation Act 1984 (referred to above), Parliament has patently dispensed with the need to prove that the *actus reus* was caused by some conduct of the accused, then that has to be accepted. Obviously Miss Larsonneur would be liable to be convicted of the offence under Road Traffic Regulation Act, section 107 if, while on holiday or even imprisoned in Liverpool, her brother, using her car with her permission, had parked it illegally in London. But *Larsonneur* and *Winzar* were not cases where they were made liable (justifiably in view of the difficulties of otherwise enforcing the law) for the acts of others. They were made liable for *their own conduct* in circumstances where that conduct was controlled by others. Are we to say that if, having legally parked her car in a two hour zone and being about to remove it before the time on the meter expires, she is unable to do so because she is kidnapped by terrorists or arrested for theft, she is liable for a parking offence? Should it make a difference whether she has been unlawfully abducted or lawfully arrested?

(3) Liability for failing to act

In most criminal prosecutions the prosecutor will be seeking to prove that a prohibited situation or result has been brought about by the acts of the accused. However in certain situations it will be the fact that the accused failed to act that led to the prohibited event occurring. For example, if A pushes B under the water in a swimming pool and holds him there until B is dead then it is clear that A's actions have caused B's death. On the other hand if A sees B drowning in the swimming pool in a situation where it would be easy to rescue B, but A does nothing, the result will be the same—B will die. However this time B would have died whether or not A had been there. Should the law therefore hold A responsible for B's death? It would be easy to say yes, for most of us would find the picture of A simply watching B drown morally abhorent. Yet if we hold, in principle, that A should be liable for failing to act, we would probably cause more problems than the law could handle. It would be easy to hold that A should be liable for the death of B where B is a small child drowning in about two or three feet of water, but such straightforward cases are unlikely to occur. The water may be much deeper, and there may be strong currents, or A may be only a modest swimmer. How much of a risk can the law expect A to take with his own life in order to save another from death or lesser injury? The answer that he should take such risks as the court deems reasonable in all the circumstances would merely involve the courts in a minute examination of all the surrounding factors and possibly A's appreciation of them.

For these sorts of reasons most jurisdictions, including our own, have not adopted a general principle of liability for failing to act. Instead the law has enumerated certain factual situations in which persons shall be under a duty to act, and if they fail to act in these situations thereby causing a prohibited criminal result, they shall be liable for that result. Where the law imposes such a duty to act, this duty forms part of the *actus reus* for that particular charge and the prosecution will have to prove not only the existence of the duty to act, but also that the accused unreasonably failed to act.

The situations in which such duties are imposed can be found in both statute law and in the decisions of the courts. Examples of statutory crimes which will be committed by a failure to act include certain failures by drivers to report a road traffic accident caused by the presence of their vehicles on the road (see, *e.g.* the Road Traffic Act 1988, s.170; failure by a motorist to provide a police constable with a specimen of breath for a breath test (the Road Traffic Act 1988, s.7(6)). Where statute has made it an offence to perform a certain act without first obtaining the necessary authority (for example operating a television without a licence) there is both an act and an omission, but the crux of the offence is the act and so these are not true examples of omissions.

Certain persons are liable to act because of their status. For example sea captains are under a duty to take reasonable steps to protect the lives of their passengers and crew. Parents are under an obligation to look after the welfare of their children and guardians their wards, though the guardian's duty probably arises as much out of the specific undertaking by the guardian. (See *Sheppard* (1981).)

It is possible to bring oneself under a duty to act through contractual obligations. For example if A is employed by a Seaside Council to act as lifeguard and to use all reasonable endeavours to protect the life of swimmers on the beach, although his contract is with the council there arises a duty to look after swimmers on the beach who are not privy to the contract. The leading case in this area is *Pittwood* (1902) where the accused, who was under a contractual obligation to look after a railway level crossing, negligently left his post with the gates in such a position to suggest to road users that no trains were coming. As a result a man was killed when his cart, which was crossing the railway lines, was struck by a train. Clearly the action of the accused could be regarded as grossly negligent and clearly his negligent conduct had lead to the death. He argued that he owed no duty to the users of the level crossing; his contractual obligations lay solely with the railway company. The court, however, held that this contractual undertaking was sufficient to place him under a duty to the road users and thus the prosecution were able to establish the remaining part of the *actus reus* and the accused was convicted of manslaughter (for manslaughter by gross negligence see below, p. 226).

The courts have also found a duty to exist where the accused has voluntarily assumed responsibility for another's care and then simply failed to fulfil that undertaking. One example of this is the case of *Instan* (1893) where the accused undertook to look after her aged and helpless aunt, but then caused her death by failing to give her food. Although there may be a contractual situation here in relation to the food, the court held that there was also a duty arising out of the voluntary undertaking to look after the aunt.

In some jurisdictions the courts have held that where a person has created a dangerous situation, he is under a duty to take reasonable steps to avert danger. Thus, whereas A, who comes upon a burning house, is under no obligation to take any action to extinguish the fire, if it was he who caused the fire, he would be under an obligation to do his best to get the fire extinguished. In *Miller* (1983) the accused had fallen asleep while smoking a cigarette in a house where he was squatting. He awoke to find that his mattress was on fire, but instead of taking steps to put the fire out, he simply moved to another room leaving the fire to spread. The House of Lords decided that common sense dictated that he should bear responsibility for the result of his failure to avert the danger and it was necessary to formulate an approach to such cases which Crown Court judges could explain clearly to lay jurors. Thus it was held that where an accused had unwittingly created a risk that the property of another would be damaged or destroyed, he should bear the responsibility for the resulting damage if he subsequently became aware of the risk and failed to take steps to avert it. The prosecution would, of course, have to show that the failure to take action was accompanied by the necessary *mens rea* (see below, p. 61 and *Fagan* v. *M.P.C.* (1969), below, p. 75).

Once the prosecution have proved that the accused failed to act in a situation where the law imposes a duty to act then the general principles of criminal liability operate as in any other case. The prosecution will have to establish any remaining elements of the *actus reus* together with any requirements relating to the state of mind of the accused. It is very tempting in situations where the accused has failed to look after someone properly as a result of which the person has died, to say that this will at most amount to manslaughter. However if the prosecution can establish that the accused deliberately withheld food so that the victim would suffer serious bodily harm or death, then this is a proper case for a conviction for murder (see *Gibbins and Proctor* (1918)).

This is not intended to be an exhaustive list of duty situations; the courts may well add further categories. The law in this area is, possibly of necessity, vague. There is little authority on just how much of a risk people under a duty to act must take in order to perform their duty, but the majority of cases are concerned with situations where no risk at all is involved and the accused has simply abandoned his responsibility. In some American states where there has been codification it has been common to include in the provisions dealing with liability for omissions some such phrase as "or the omission to perform a duty which the law imposes upon him and which he is physically capable of performing," and this is probably implicit in the English decisions.

(4) Causation

It has been seen in Chap. 2 (Murder) that the *actus reus* of that offence required that the death occur within a year and a day of the final act or omission of the accused. The purpose of that rule was quite clear; it was an early, somewhat rough and ready, type of test to ensure that the death was in fact caused by the accused. Today medical science has advanced and we can have sounder evidence on which to decide whether it was, in fact, the accused's actions which brought about the death of the victim. However, we shall also see that the courts are reluctant simply to hand over such decisions to medical experts. In this section we shall examine the basic problems surrounding the question of whether the accused's actions "caused" the prohibited consequence. The principles discussed are applicable in general to criminal offences the *actus reus* of which involves a prohibited consequence, but most of the reported decisions concern the responsibility of an accused for the death of another.

In cases of murder and manslaughter the jury will have to be satisfied that the action of the accused was a factual cause of the victim's death and the judge may have to direct them as to whether it is also capable of amounting in law to the cause of the victim's death. What then do we mean by factual and legal causes? Take for example a simple situation in which A invites B to his house for dinner and on the way to A's house B is run over by a car driven by C who is drunk, and as a result B dies. To be a factual cause of the death the action of the accused must be an event without which the death would not have occurred. So in a sense the invitation by A was a factual cause of B's death since without this invitation B would not have left his house, though it would seem odd to say that A caused B's death. Clearly we shall be looking at the actions of C and again we can say that if C had not hit him with his car B would not have died. Thus we can say that C's driving was a factual cause of B's death. There may be other factors the absence of which may have spared B's life; for example the fact that C was drunk and possibly the way B was behaving as a pedestrian. All of these can be said to be factual causes of B's death. The action of the accused must at least amount to a factual cause. In the case of *White* (1910) the accused tried to poison his mother and gave her a drink containing poison. She was later found dead having drunk a little of the mixture. It was found, however, that she had died of a heart attack and there was no evidence to show that this was brought about by the poison. White, therefore, had to be acquitted of murder since the prosecution failed to show that without the actions of White the woman would not have died (he was convicted of attempted murder).

Even if it were possible for a jury to find the accused's actions a factual cause of the *actus reus* of the crime it is still possible for the judge to direct the jury that they cannot be held in law to be the cause of the *actus reus*. Take for example a situation in which the accused has injured X in a minor public house brawl and as a result X is taken to the local hospital where, while being treated for minor cuts, he is savagely attacked by a masked intruder and killed. Of course, it is possible to say that if the accused had not injured X in the first place X would not have been in hospital at the time of the attack. However the judge would rule that in law the assault by the accused could not be regarded as the cause of X's death. What then can amount to the legal cause of an *actus reus*?

In the first place it must be the unlawful actions of the accused which bring about the prohibited result. In *Dalloway* (1847) the accused was driving a horse and cart in a negligent fashion when a young child ran out into the road ahead of him. Dalloway was unable to stop and the young child was killed. It was held that the jury should have been directed that if they found that even if Dalloway had been driving properly he would still have run over the child then they must acquit him since the negligent way in which he was driving could not be said to be the legal cause of the child's death. To gain a conviction the prosecution would have to prove that it was the negligent element of the driving that was the cause of the child's death not just simply the fact that Dalloway was driving and that a child was killed in his cart. In other words if the jury acquitted they would in effect be saying that the real cause of death was the way in which the child ran out in front of the cart.

It is often said that the action of the accused must be a substantial cause of the *actus reus*. So in the crimes of unlawful homicide since everyone is in a sense dying from the moment of birth, killing is defined as an acceleration of death. It is just as much an unlawful killing to kill someone who is on the point of dying from an incurable disease as it is to kill someone who, under normal circumstances, can expect to go on living for years. This of course poses problems in the realms of medical treatment where painkilling drugs given to terminal patients may have the effect of accelerating the death of the patient (see the trial of *Bodkin Adams* (1957)). At present mercy killing is still murder, however well motivated, and the debate on whether some properly controlled form of mercy killing should be permitted is likely to continue for many years.

Thus in unlawful homicide offences the accused must have accelerated the death of the victim in a substantial manner (see *Armstrong* (1989)). The example is often posed of a man dying from a slit throat when another assailant sticks a pin in him causing him to lose another drop of blood. It might be argued that that drop of blood caused the victim to die a fraction of a second earlier, but the judge would be bound to direct the jury that the pin prick cannot be regarded as a legal cause of the death. This might be explained on the ground that the pin prick did not substantially accelerate the death, and so was not a substantial cause. In reality, however, the use of the expression gives no more help in predicting what the courts will accept as being a legal cause of the *actus reus*, than to say that in some cases the judge will have to decide which of several factual causes can be regarded as the legal cause and that his decision will be based on feelings of common sense. For example in the illustration of the invitation to dinner it would be so obviously absurd to hold the invitation to dinner as being the legal cause of the death. A more difficult case would be the assault victim who is killed by a completely unforeseeable attack while receiving medical attention in hospital. Again the judge is surely going to find that the legal cause of the death was the attack by the masked man in the hospital, though this time it would be less absurd to hold that the initial assault which caused him to be in hospital at the time of the attack could be regarded as a legal cause of the death. If we alter the situation again and imagine a situation in which the accused assaulted the victim causing him to require minor surgery and as a result of a mistake by the surgeon during the operation the victim died, clearly we now have two factual causes; the initial assault and the surgeon's negligence. Without either of these two events the victim would have survived. In this case, however, a holding that the initial assault could be regarded as a legal cause of the death would not be at all absurd since it is a very reasonable argument to say that if you cause another to require hospital treatment you must accept the risk that the hospital may be a long way away, that the surgeons at the hospital may not be as good as others at another hospital and that even brilliant surgeons make mistakes. On the other hand it would be just as reasonable to argue that though the initial assailant should remain liable for the minor injuries caused by the assault, he should not be blamed for the mistakes of the hospital. One thing is quite clear, it is the duty of the judge to rule on what can or cannot be regarded as a legal cause of the *actus reus*. We shall return to the hospital type of case later.

It must also be realised that an *actus reus* can have more than one legal cause. For example if A and B both assault X at the same time, neither inflicting mortal wounds, but as a result of the combined attack X dies, then both sets of wounds will be regarded as the legal cause of X's death and thus both men could be charged with an unlawful homicide offence. Similarly if A attacks X and leaves him dying from the wounds inflicted, and later B inflicts further wounds as a result of which X dies considerably more quickly, then both A and B can be held to have caused the death of X. If A's wounds were not mortal and B's attack was totally unforeseeable then only B would be liable for the death. If A administered poison to X but before it had a chance to have any effect B shoots and kills X instantaneously, then only B will be held to be the cause of X's death. As we said earlier it is largely a question of common sense, and it should always be remembered that although a decision on causation may exempt a party from the ultimate and more serious consequence—most of the cases revolve round killing situations where there is an intervening act between the initial assault and the death—the party so relieved from liability will still remain liable to the extent of his initial attack.

We can now look at those cases in which the initial action of the accused and the final consequence are separated by an intervening event which may or may not be foreseeable. Since nearly all the cases in this area are concerned with the question of whether the accused caused the death of another our examples will be based on unlawful homicides, though, of course the principles apply to other areas.

If the intervening event is foreseeable then the accused will remain liable for the resulting death. For example if the accused were to render X unconscious and then leave him lying across a busy railway track, A would be liable for X's resulting death at the wheels of the express train. If on the other hand the intervening act is totally unforeseeable then the accused will escape liability. If the accused were to render X unconscious and leave him in a building which was then gutted by a gas explosion the accused would remain liable for the initial assault, but not for the death.

A particular application of this type of principle occurs where the accused has acted in such a way as to lead another to take avoiding action, thereby injuring or killing himself. In *Pitts* (1842) it was held that an accused could be held responsible for the death of a victim who had thrown himself into a river to escape harm he reasonably apprehended to be forthcoming from the accused. (Should the same result follow if the victim's response is unreasonable? See *Blaue,* below.) In *Pagett* (1983) the accused had held a girl in front of himself as a shield and had then fired shots at armed police officers. The officers had instinctively returned the fire and the girl had been killed. The Court of Appeal held that in these circumstances it was perfectly proper to say that the accused's actions caused the death of the girl. The court would almost certainly reach the same conclusion if the police, in returning the shots, had hit and killed an innocent passer-by. In all such cases the accused's eventual liability will depend upon his state of mind at the time that the action occurred.

It seems also to be generally accepted that the accused must take the victim as he finds him. For example if the accused were to hit X over the head, but because of a brain condition X died, although the blow on the head was very light, the accused would be held liable for X's death. Whether he will be convicted of murder or manslaughter will, of course, depend on his intentions. Clearly also in many cases, whether the resulting charge is one of unlawful homicide or some form of assault will depend on a host of factors such as the distance to the hospital and the competence of the surgeons and equally clearly this is a risk you take when you injure someone. However the law has gone further than this. It would appear that if you seriously injure a person who, because of some religious beliefs, refuses to accept the necessary medical treatment you will remain liable for the resulting death. In centuries gone by it was probably quite reasonable for any citizen to live in fear of hospital treatment and possibly today it may be reasonable for an assault victim who faces major surgery to refuse to undergo treatment and in this case it would be reasonable to hold that the accused's initial assault could be held to be the cause of the resulting death. Where, however, the surgery is minor or where the objection is based solely on a religious belief, it seems very hard to hold that the accused remains responsible for the resulting death, but this was precisely the decision reached by the Court of Appeal in *Blaue* (1975), where the accused stabbed V and penetrated her lung. V, being a Jehovah's Witness refused a blood transfusion which might well have saved her, and she died. In cases where the victim is injured while trying to escape from the accused, the test of causation used is whether the resulting injury would be something a reasonable man would have foreseen, and this test could have been applied in *Blaue*, but the Court of Appeal chose to base its decision on the idea that the accused takes his victim as he finds him and this includes his mental as well as physical make-up. So far the cases have drawn a distinction between cases in which the victim has been only slightly injured where the doctrine used by the Court of Appeal in *Blaue* has not been applied and those such as *Blaue* where the injury is serious and medical treatment is refused. However the principle of taking your victim as you find him would be equally applicable to a situation in which the victim received a cut on his finger yet takes no medical treatment and dies from blood poisoning. Should the rapist be liable for the death of his victim who commits suicide while her mind is unhinged by the rape?

Outside the cases dealing with unreasonable refusal of medical treatment there are cases which hold that the accused would remain liable for the death of a victim where the death of the victim is attributable to his own stupidity following the initial attack. In one case the victim of an illegal 800 lash flogging drank spirits, probably to ease the pain. It was held that the drinking of the spirits probably contributed to his death, but Governor Wall who had imposed the flogging was nonetheless held legally responsible for the death and executed (1802). It is suggested by Professor Williams that the best test to apply in this type of case is whether the subsequent action by the victim was reasonably foreseeable, and only if it was should the accused be held liable for the subsequent death. However, following *Blaue* it is not clear what sort of test the court would apply.

The final group of situations we should consider are those involving medical treatment. The situation envisaged here is one in which the victim of an assault dies while in the hands of the medical profession. Really this is an application of a principle mentioned before, that the accused will be held liable for the death where the intervening event is foreseeable, but since hospital cases seem to have developed an identity of their own we can consider them separately.

In the case of *Jordan* (1956) the accused was charged with

murder. Following an assault in a cafe in which he had been seriously injured, the victim was taken to a hospital where thanks to good medical treatment he was making a satisfactory recovery. What happened then can only be regarded as a very bad series of mistakes. It was quite clear that this patient was allergic to a certain drug and that his treatment required that he not be given large intakes of liquid. Unfortunately the medical staff administered this drug to him and gave him large quantities of liquid. As a result of this treatment he died and Jordan was held liable for his death. On appeal, evidence was given by two doctors that in their view the medical treatment and not the initial stab wound was the cause of the victim's death; the medical treatment, they said, was palpably wrong. As a result Jordan's appeal was allowed. The court was disposed to find that where the death resulted from any normal treatment employed to deal with a felonious injury, the death should be held to be caused by the felonious injury, but not where the treatment was not normal.

Not surprisingly this case caused consternation in the medical field among doctors who did not relish the idea of being held to be the factor which relieved the accused of liability for the subsequent death because the treatment employed was "not normal," whatever that meant. In the later case of *Smith* (1959), in the midst of a barrack room brawl the accused bayonetted another soldier who was then carried rather roughly to the Medical Officer's reception station where the Medical Officer failed to diagnose the fact that the soldier's lung had been pierced. As a result of this poor treatment the soldier died some two hours later. At Smith's trial, evidence was given that, had the Medical Officer diagnosed the injury correctly, the victim might well have survived. This time however the resulting conviction was upheld and *Jordan* was distinguished. The court held that if at the time of death the original wound is still an operating cause and a substantial cause, then the death can properly be said to be a result of the wound, albeit that some other cause of death is also operating. Only if it can be said that the original wound is merely the setting in which another cause operates can it be said that the death does not result from the wound. Putting it another way, only if the second cause is so overwhelming as to make the original wound merely part of the history can it be said that death does not flow from the wound.

The problem may well arise today where the victim of an assault has suffered irreparable brain damage, but is being kept "alive" on a respirator. If the doctors decide that the victim cannot recover and switch off the respirator, the defendant will nonetheless remain responsible for the victim's death. It may be possible to argue that the doctors are also partially responsible for the victim's death; but it is absurd to imagine that they would be charged with murder. (*Malcherek* (1981)).

The role of judge and jury in causation issues

In *Pagett* (1983) the Court of Appeal gave extensive consideration to the part to be played by judge and jury in determining issues of causation in homicide cases. The Court was mindful of the statements by the House of Lords in *D.P.P* v. *Stonehouse* (1978) where it was said that trial judges should be wary of usurping the right of the jury to determine issues of fact. The Court held that the proper approach was for the trial judge to direct the jury on the relevant principles relating to causation, and that the jury should then be left to decide whether, in the light of those principles, the relevant causal link had been established. Generally in homicide cases there would be little need for the judge to say much about causation since the causal link would usually be obvious. Even where it was necessary to say something, it would usually suffice if he told them that it was sufficient that the accused's act had contributed significantly to the death of the victim; it did not have to be the sole or even the main cause of it. Sometimes specific questions of causation would arise and then the judge would have to direct the jury on the principles to be applied. Such a case would be where it is alleged that intervention by a third party had broken the chain of causation between the act of the accused and the death of the victim. However neither a reasonable act done for the purpose of self-preservation nor an act done in the execution of legal duty constituted such an intervening act.

2. MENS REA

Not only must the prosecution show that the accused brought about the *actus reus* of the crime, but they must also, in most cases, prove that he caused the *actus reus* with *mens rea*. Literally translated *mens rea* means "guilty mind," but the expression "guilty mind" is both misleading and too imprecise as a yardstick of liability. This is well demonstrated by the case of *Cunningham* (1957). In this case a building which had previously been one house had been converted into two; the cellar had been divided by a wall of loose stone rubble. Cunningham's prospective mother-in-law lived in one of these houses and the other was unoccupied, being the house in which Cunningham would live after his marriage. On the occasion in question he entered the empty house, wrenched the gas meter off the wall in the cellar in order to steal its contents and in so doing he fractured the gas pipe, causing gas to seep through the rubble and into the adjoining house. As a result Mrs. Wade, his prospective mother-in-law, was partially asphyxiated. He was charged with "unlawfully and maliciously" administering a noxious thing to Mrs. Wade contrary to section 23 of the Offences Against the Person Act 1861. The judge directed the jury that "malicious" meant "wicked—something which he (Cunningham) has no business to do and perfectly well knows it." In this sense Cunningham undoubtedly had a guilty mind. He knew that he was up to no good and there was no doubt that he had committed the crime of theft and possibly burglary into the bargain. Nonetheless this was held, on appeal, to be a misdirection. "Malicious," said the Court of Criminal Appeal, required either that (i) Cunningham intended to administer the noxious thing or (ii) without intending to administer it, he foresaw that by fracturing the pipe he might cause gas to seep through the house to the injury of Mrs. Wade. In *Sheppard* (1981) Lord Diplock held that the word "wilfully" imported the same notions.

Cunningham shows that *mens rea* must not be confused with having a bad motive. Conversely the fact that the accused has the best of motives does not mean that he cannot have *mens rea*. In a tragic case (*The Times*, October 7, 1965), Mr. Gray killed his 11–year-old son by administering an overdose of drugs and then gassing him while he was asleep. Mr. Gray was a devoted father and had done this because his son was dying from an incurable cancer and was in such pain that he could not even bear the weight of his bed sheets. On Mr. Gray's conviction for manslaughter (the charge was murder but this was reduced to manslaughter on account of diminished responsibility; see below p. 157) the judge said to Mr. Gray, "I am perfectly certain that there is not a single person inside this court who will feel that you are in any sense a criminal." One can see what the judge meant but, as the conviction for manslaughter proved, Mr. Gray had committed a crime; he had caused the *actus reus* of an unlawful homicide and in intending to kill his son he had the necessary *mens rea* for murder or manslaughter.

What then precisely does *mens rea* mean? Basically it is the term given to the accused's state of mind which is required to be proved in relation to each of the elements of the *actus reus*. In Chap. 2 we illustrated this by pretending that in the crime of murder intention was required on each of the elements of the *actus reus* (see above, p. 20). Unfortunately the reality is not quite as straightforward. *Cunningham* shows us that criminal liability is not restricted to intentional conduct, at least as far as section 23 of the Offences Against the Person Act 1861 is concerned and, indeed, liability is rarely so restricted.

It may help to start by taking a fairly simple factual situation. Peter has been working as a builder at the top of a tall block of flats when he causes a brick to fall from the building to the street below where it kills Henry who happens to be walking past. Most would probably agree that without more information they could not decide whether Peter deserves to be punished by the criminal law for his act. Clearly the prosecution will have to prove as part of its case that Peter actually caused the stone to fall and that it was the fact of being hit by the stone that led to the death of Henry and these matters have already been considered. What we need to examine now is Peter's state of mind in relation to the incident. Of course, if it turns out that Peter had nothing to do with the brick falling from the building, then it would be totally irrelevant that as he watched it fall and saw Henry below, he thought to himself that he hoped it would hit him. If, however, the brick was caused to fall by Peter then we need to know whether this was done deliberately and with what purpose in mind. The following is a list of possible states of mind—though it in no way purports to be an exhaustive list.

1. Peter had slipped on a patch of grease and in an attempt to save himself from serious injury he had dislodged the brick which had then crashed to the ground. In other words, this is what most would describe as an accident; Peter was in no way culpable.

2. Peter had shied the brick at a tin can on the roof without thinking that it could possibly go over the edge. It may well be that most people would see this as an irresponsible act on Peter's part in that they would see that there was a good chance that the brick would go over the top.

3. Peter has been left with a load of bricks after completing his task and rather than laboriously carry them down, he simply

throws them to the street below. It never enters his head that they might injure somebody below. A situation rather like that in number 2, but probably just that little bit more irresponsible.

4. As in 3, but in this situation Peter has actually thought about the dangers to people below, but has dismissed them as non-existent. The difference here is that he has though about the risks but has reached the wrong conclusion. Is this worse than not seeing the risk in the first place?

5. As in 3, but in this example Peter realises that there is a chance of hitting people below, but thinks that it is a chance worth taking, in order to save himself a lot of work. Most would see this as more reprehensible than any of the earlier examples.

6. Peter throws the brick down in the attempt to scare the life out of Henry, one of his work mates, but without any thought that he might injure him.

7. Peter throws the brick down deliberately trying to hit and seriously injure Henry.

What we are discussing here is culpability. The real question is where should we draw the line between conduct which should attract criminal liability and conduct which should not. If you were to draw the line above 7 and say that only the situation in 7 should attract criminal liability you would have taken an extremely narrow view of liability. On the other hand if you were to draw the line above 1, then you would, in effect, be saying that culpability formed no part of criminal liability. Indeed some have argued that this should be the position. Where the accused has caused the prohibited act he should be guilty irrespective of his state of mind; that should be relevant only in relation to the penalty. Such an approach would undoubtedly simplify the law, but would be totally unacceptable to most as a general basis for criminal liability. We shall see, however, that in practice the degree of culpability required varies from crime to crime and from element to element within a given crime. In some crimes the courts have adopted the extreme position just described in which the prosecution is exempted from the need to establish any form of guilty mind (see, *e.g. Larsonneur,* p. 37 above).

Now that we have seen that in relation to a given incident it is possible to detect a whole range of mental states, we should turn to the classification the lawyers have made of these various states. After that we can examine the question of how one determines what mental state is required for a given crime.

(1) Intention

We saw in Chapter 2 that in the crime of murder the prosecution must prove that the defendant intended either to kill or to seriously injure another human being; here nothing short of intention will suffice. Most crimes, however, can be proved if the accused has acted *maliciously* as defined in *Cunningham* (above p. 50). In such cases there is no need to pursue a refined distinction between intention and the second state of mind outlined in that case which, for the moment, we will refer to as *Cunningham recklessness*. Where, however, proof of intention is required on at least one aspect of the *actus reus* or where the crime requires proof of what is sometimes called an ulterior intention (see below p. 74) it will be necessary to distinguish between intention and recklessness. Apart from murder, examples of these crimes include any charge of attempting to commit a substantive offence (see below, p. 195), wounding with intent to cause grievous bodily harm contrary to Offences Against the Person Act 1861, section 18 (see below, p. 244) and burglary contrary to Theft Act 1968, section 9(1)(*a*) (see below, p. 322). The word *intention* has caused much difficulty in recent years and this is largely due to a reluctance by the courts judicially to define what is, after all, a word in everday use by ordinary citizens. The problem has been particularly acute in relation to the crime of murder. Until the decision of the House of Lords in *Moloney* (1985) it was generally assumed that the prosecution would succeed on a charge of murder if it could prove one of four states of mind:

(i) intention to kill
(ii) foresight that what you were doing was likely (or according to some judges highly likely) to kill
(iii) intention to cause grievous bodily harm
(iv) foresight that what you were doing was (highly) likely to cause grievous bodily harm (grievous means serious).

There was some confusion as to whether categories (ii) and (iv) were a form of intention or whether it was the case that *Cunningham recklessness* sufficed for murder. In practical terms, however, it meant that the *mens rea* of murder was widely drawn. Thus suppose that the accused was charged with planting a bomb on board a transatlantic airliner intending that it should explode when the aircraft was over the sea. The motive behind this was to send some worthless cargo to the bottom of the sea so that the accused could claim on a bogus insurance policy.

The aircraft duly exploded and all the passengers and crew were killed. The accused tells the court that he did not want anyone injured. He had hoped that the aircraft would make a forced landing in the sea and that everyone would get into the life rafts before the plane sank. Did he intend to kill the passengers and crew? Under the law of murder defined above, this does not really matter. The jury would have little difficulty in holding that he foresaw that what he was doing was likely, at least, to cause serious bodily harm to those on board and this is sufficient. However, in *Moloney* (1985) the House of Lords held that the case which was thought to lay down the four categories of *mens rea* for the murder, *Hyam*, had been misinterpreted. The law of murder requires that the prosecution proves that the accused either intended to kill or to cause serious bodily harm and that for this purpose foresight that what you are doing is likely (or even highly likely) to cause death or serious bodily harm is not the same as intending those ends. Thus the House of Lords has, in effect, removed categories (ii) and (iv) from the list. This means we now have to ask whether our bomber intended to kill or seriously injure the crew and passengers; it is not enough that we can say he foresaw that he was likely to kill or seriously injure them. So, if you believe what the bomber has said, do you find that he intended to kill or seriously injure the passengers? If your answer was "yes" then would it differ if the bomb had been placed, not in an aircraft, but on a ship, or if it was a terrorist bomb planted in a pub, a short warning having been given to the drinkers to get out? What would the average person in the street answer if you asked "what is meant by saying that a person intends to kill another?" The answer would probably be that you intend to kill someone when you deliberately set about to produce that result. The strongest situation is where the accused desires to produce a given result. Thus if the accused wants to kill his uncle because his uncle has ill-treated him and to this end holds a gun against his uncle's head and pulls the trigger, we would have little difficulty in finding that the accused intended to kill his uncle.

There is also no difficulty where the accused wishes to bring about a given result but uses a method which he knows has only a limited chance of success. For example if he lies in wait for a victim, intending to shoot him at close range only to find that the victim will pass by on another road which is a lot further away. He fires the gun, knowing the chances of hitting the victim are remote, but he is lucky and the victim is killed. Clearly he has intended to kill the victim.

Difficulties begin to arise when the consequence is not wanted for its own sake. In *Steane* (1947) the accused, who had given broadcasts for Germany during the Second World War because of threats to the safety of his family if he did not do so, was charged under regulation 2A of the Defence (General) Regulations with "doing an act likely to assist the enemy with intent to assist the enemy." Delivering the judgment of the court Lord Goddard C.J. referred to British prisoners-of-war who had been forced by their brutal Japanese captors to work on the Burma Road, and considered what the position would have been had they been charged under the same regulation. In such a case, said Lord Goddard, "it would be unnecessary surely . . . to consider any of the nicetics of the law relating to duress, because no jury would find that merely by doing this work they were intending to assist the enemy." He concluded, allowing Steane's appeal, that the jury should have been instructed that they could find that Steane lacked the necessary intent if they found that he did what he did in subjection to the power of an enemy.

It is easy to sympathise with Lord Goddard's conclusion. No one would want to see those British prisoners-of-war subject to the risk of even a charge, much less a conviction. However, it is an old adage that hard cases make bad law. It is tempting, but wrong, to say that a man who acts under duress does not act intentionally. The prisoners did not choose to build the road but they did build it and they knew that their acts would undoubtedly assist the Japanese. It would certainly be odd to say that they acted unintentionally. What Lord Goddard did was to confuse intention and motive; he talked of an "innocent" and "criminal" intent, but whether conduct is intentional is not determined by the motive with which it is done. The exculpation of such prisoners, and Steane, should be sought in the defence of duress, not in lack of intention.

The same is true where A desires to take an inheritance under the will of his grandfather. He knows the money will be coming to him sooner or later but is desperate to get his hands on it immediately. He is very fond of his grandfather and if there was a way of getting the money without killing the old man he would take it, but there is not and so he poisons him. On a subsequent charge of murder it would be of no avail for him to say that he did not intend to kill his grandfather, because he did not desire the old man's death. He deliberately killed his grandfather and the killing was an intentional one.

Further problems exist where the accused intends to bring

about consequence A but realises that in doing so he may well bring about consequence B, which he does not desire. He nevertheless takes the risks and consequence B occurs. Can we say that he intended, to bring about consequence B? Clearly he is reckless within the meaning given above, (p. 53), but if the crime requires proof that the accused intended consequence B this will not be enough. If we return to our example of the bomb on the aircraft, we might be tempted to say that the accused intended to kill the people on board because he knew that it was virtually inevitable that all must die. But the same could not necessarily be said if the bomb were on board a ship or if it had been planted in a pub and a warning, albeit short, given.

These problems can arise in any crime where intention is required on at least one aspect of the *actus reus*. They present a special problem in murder because of the House of Lords' insistence that murder is a crime which requires an *intention* to kill or cause grievous bodily harm while at the same time trying to ensure that the word is not given a meaning which would result in the exclusion of many heinous killings from the category of murder.

In *Moloney* Lord Bridge said that in the vast majority of cases where the prosecution had to establish that the accused intended a given consequence it would be sufficient for the trial judge to invite the jury to consider whether the prosecutor had satisfied them that the accused did so intend. The word "intend" is a word in normal everyday use and should need no lengthy explanation. However there would be cases, though these would be rare, where some further guidance would be necessary. These are presumably cases where the jury might need some guidance on the distinction between motive and intention. He said that this can usually be explained by reference to the facts of the case or to some homely example. "A man who, at London Airport, boards a plane which he knows to be bound for Manchester, clearly intends to travel to Manchester, even though Manchester is the last place he wants to be and his motive for boarding the plane is simply to escape pursuit. The possibility that the plane may have engine trouble and be diverted to Luton does not affect the matter. By boarding the plane the man conclusively demonstrates his intention to go there, because it is a moral certainty that that is where he will arrive." In other words a man can intend certain consequences even though he does not desire them. In order to assist a jury in such deliberations Lord Bridge suggested that they be invited to consider two questions.

"First, was death or really serious injury in a murder case . . . a *natural* consequence of the defendant's voluntary act? Secondly, did the defendant foresee that consequence as being a *natural* consequence of his act? The jury should then be told that if they answer yes to both questions it is a proper inference for them to draw that he intended that consequence."

As is often the case, one of those "rare" cases in which this further guidance will be necessary arose almost immediately. Indeed, it is clear that such cases will not be all that rare. You will recall the case of *Hancock and Shankland* ((1986) above, p. 22) where two Welsh miners were tried for the murder of a taxi driver after they had dropped concrete blocks from a bridge into the path of his oncoming taxi. They maintained that they had only meant to prevent the driver from taking a strike-breaker to his mine. The trial judge rightly identified this as one of those exceptional cases which would cause the jury difficulties and so he gave them a direction in the terms suggested by Lord Bridge in *Moloney*. The accused may indeed have intended to kill or seriously injure someone in the car, but as in most cases there was no direct proof of their actual state of mind. The jury may well have found it easy to infer that the accused had deliberately taken the risk of causing serious bodily harm and that this was more than a slight risk, but *Moloney* has made it clear that this is not the same as intending to cause that serious bodily injury. The trial judge, not unreasonably tackled this problem by directing the jury in the terms suggested by Lord Bridge (outlined above). The jury convicted the two men of murder. Their convictions were quashed by the Court of Appeal and the prosecution's subsequent appeal was dismissed by the House of Lords. So what had gone wrong?

The House of Lords agreed that a conviction for murder could be based only upon a finding that the accused intended to kill or seriously injure another; that foresight by the accused that what they were doing was likely to cause death or serious bodily harm was not the same thing. However, Lord Scarman said that Lord Bridge's guidelines in *Moloney* were defective in that they referred only to natural consequences and did not advert to the probability of a consequence occurring. A juror might be misled into thinking that it was sufficient that a consequence flowed naturally from the act of the accused. It was clear that Lord Bridge intended the issue of probability to be considered since elsewhere in his speech he said that the probability of the consequence must be little short of overwhelming before it will suffice to establish the necessary intent. His mistake was in thinking that such reasoning was conveyed by the word "natural." Lord Scarman thought, however, that jurors needed specific guidance on the probability issue. He said that they needed to be told that the greater the probability of a consequence, the more likely it is that the consequence was foreseen and that if that consequence was foreseen the greater the probability is that that consequence was intended. Unfortunately even here there is a problem. In *Moloney* Lord Bridge said that the awareness had to be of a probability that was little short of overwhelming—or a moral certainty, whereas the Court of Appeal in *Hancock and Shankland* spoke of the high likelihood of the consequence occurring. There would seem to be a substantial difference of degree between the two approaches, and it is unfortunate that the House of Lords in *Hancock and Shankland* did not resolve the matter.

So it would seem that the judge should, in these cases where extra guidance is necessary, tell the jury that in the end it is up to them to decide whether or not the accused intended the consequence in question; that nothing short of intention will do. That it is perfectly proper for them to ask themselves about the probability of a consequence occurring. That if they felt that there was (at least) a high likelihood of the consequence occurring this was evidence from which they might infer that the accused foresaw the occurrence of that consequence and from that they might infer that he intended it.

In the Court of Appeal in *Hancock and Shankland* Lord Lane C.J. tried to give some guidelines for use by trial judges. Lord Scarman, however, in the House of Lords said that while they were not inaccurate they were probably too complex for use by a lay jury. In the subsequent case of *Nedrick* (1986) Lord Lane had another go. He said that "where a man realised that it was for all practical purposes inevitable that his actions would result in (death or serious harm), the inference might be irresistible that he intended that result, however little he might have desired or wished it to happen." It seems eminently sensible for Lord Lane to try to provide help for the poor beleaguered trial judge, who after all has had very little help from the House of Lords. There is nothing to tell us what "intention" is, only how it may be proved. There is nothing to assist the jury make that leap of reasoning. It would surely make more sense simply to say that for purposes of criminal liability a man intends a consequence if (i) he desires to bring about that result or (ii) he is aware that the probability of its occurrence is little short of overwhelming.

As we have seen earlier the *actus reus* of an offence may consist of conduct, prohibited result and circumstances. Whereas it is perfectly possible to say that the defendant intended to act in a certain way and that he intended to bring about the prohibited result, it sounds wrong to say that the accused intended that certain circumstances existed. For example, in the crime of rape it would not be good English to say that the defendant intended that the woman did not consent. In relation to circumstances the equivalent of "intend" is "know." We should therefore say that the defendant "knew" that the woman was not consenting. (See *Panayi and Karte* (1988).)

(2) Recklessness

You will remember that in *Cunningham* (above, p. 50) the Court of Criminal Appeal said that the jury should have been directed that in order to convict the accused they should be satisfied that either (i) he intended to administer the noxious thing or that (ii) he had foreseen that, by fracturing the gas pipe, he might cause gas to seep through the house to the injury of Mrs. Wade. This second state of mind is traditionally known as recklessness and it normally serves as the basis of most, but not all, crimes. It is often referred to as deliberate risk taking. This type of *mens rea* suffers from the fact that the word "recklessness" is an everyday word often used to mean negligence (failure to see risk that reasonable people would have seen—see below, p. 65). The word is to be found in several modern statutes (Theft Act 1968, Sexual Offences Amendment Act 1976, Criminal Damage Act 1971) until 1982 decisions of the Court of Appeal had tended to support the definition given in *Cunningham* of conscious risk taking (see, e.g. *Stephenson* (1979)).

That recklessness involved conscious risk taking appeared to be settled until the decision of the House of Lords in *Caldwell* (1982), where Lord Diplock, stated that where the word "recklessly" or "reckless" was used in a modern statute it ought to be given a wider, less artificial meaning. Speaking in the context of the Criminal Damage Act 1971, Lord Diplock said that it means that (i) the accused does an act which, in fact, creates an obvious risk that property will be destroyed or damaged and that (ii) he *either* has not given any thought to the possibility of there being any such risk *or* he has recognised that there was some such risk and yet has carried on with his actions.

If we examine this definition we can see that it embraces two distinct tests. The prosecution will succeed if it can establish that D created an obvious risk of damage or destruction and, having recognised the existence of such a risk nonetheless went on with his activity. This, of course, is basically *Cunningham* recklessness described above. Under the second test the prosecution will succeed if it can establish that the accused created an obvious risk of damage or destruction and continued with his activity not having given any thought to the existence of such a risk. The main point to understand in this test of recklessness is that we are no longer concerned to establish that the accused has appreciated the risks of his conduct. It is sufficient that they are obvious risks. In *Lawrence* (1982) which was decided on the same day as *Caldwell*, the phrase "obvious risk" became "obvious and serious risk." Whether the addition of the word "serious" makes any real difference is open to debate. The phrase clearly means that the risks must be more than an outside chance. It is equally clear that both the words "serious" and "obvious" qualify the word "risk" and not the damage or destruction, the risk of which has been caused by the defendant. It is not altogether clear from *Caldwell* to whom the risks must be obvious. On the one hand it could mean that the risks would have been obvious to the accused had he only stopped to think; on the other hand it could mean that the risks must have been obvious to reasonable people. Could this ever be a meaningful distinction? Admittedly there will be few cases in which the risks which would be obvious to reasonable people would not also be obvious to the accused given a moment's thought. In *Elliott* v. *C.* (1983), however, a young 14 year old girl had spent the evening with a friend and being unable to stay the night with the friend had stayed out of doors. During the night she entered a shed and found a bottle of white spirit and some matches. She poured the spirit on the floor of the shed and set fire to it. According to her story she thought it might ignite, but had no idea that it would get out of control and destroy the whole shed. The magistrates took the view that in all the circumstances including the fact that she was somewhat backward, the risk of destruction of the shed was not one which was obvious to her and therefore she did not fall within the meaning of recklessness given by Lord Diplock. On appeal against her acquittal the Divisional Court took the view that the risk had only to be obvious to a reasonably prudent person. It did not have to be a risk which could have been obvious to the defendant had she given any thought to it. However harsh this may seem to be it must be taken as representing the current position.

A further attempt to mitigate the severity of the rule was made by the defence in *Stephen Malcolm R.* (1985). It was conceded that it was now well established that the jury should not be invited to consider whether the risk was obvious to the particular defendant. However, defence counsel suggested that it would be correct to ask whether the risk would be obvious to a person of the defendant's age with such characteristics of the defendant as affect his ability to appreciate the risk. The Court of Appeal, again reluctantly, held that this was not the approach envisaged by Lord Diplock. It is clear, therefore, that the prosecution merely have to show that the risk would have been obvious to the reasonable man.

In *Sangha* (1988) the Court of Appeal held that the test of what constitutes an obvious and serious risk is "is it proved that an ordinary prudent bystander would have perceived an obvious and serious risk that property would be damaged and that life would thereby be endangered." In the case itself the court found that there was, in fact, little chance of a fire spreading to an adjacent building so as to endanger life. The reason for this was the construction of the building—a factor which would only be appreciated by a building expert. This was irrelevant. As far as the ordinary prudent bystander was concerned, the accused had created an obvious and serious risk that property would be damaged and that life would thereby be endangered.

In *Miller* (1983) (above) Lord Diplock said that where recklessness was being used as the basis for liability in a case in which the accused was being charged for his failure to avert a danger he had unwittingly created, he thought that the jury should be directed that the accused was liable "if, when he does become aware that the events in question have happened as a result of his own act, he does not try to prevent or reduce the risk of damage by his own efforts or if necessary by sending for help . . . and the reason why he does not is either because he has not given any thought to the possibility of there being any such risk or because, having recognised that there was some risk involved, he has decided not to try to prevent or reduce it." This is a complex direction. It seems to be saying that the prosecution must prove, at least, that the accused had become aware of the event which had occurred because of his own, albeit unwitting, action. It is not necessary that he realises that he must take action to prevent further harm, merely that there was a risk of damage or further damage happening if nothing was done and that he either gave no thought to this or deliberately decided to do nothing about it. Thus on the facts in *Miller* once he perceived that his cigarette had set fire to this bedding the prosecution simply had to prove that his conduct had created an obvious risk of damage to property which needed attention and that his failure to (for example) call the fire brigade was due either to the fact that he realised that without attention the fire would get worse and deliberately decided to do nothing about it, or that he gave no thought to whether the fire needed attention.

Cunningham or Caldwell Recklessness

Until the decision of the House of Lords in *Caldwell* it was fairly safe to say that the requirement of *mens rea* for most crimes was satisfied if the prosecution could establish intention (or knowledge) or *Cunningham* recklessness in relation to each aspect of the *actus reus*. We must now consider what impact the decision of the House of Lords in *Caldwell* has had upon this proposition. Since *Caldwell* extends rather than restricts liability, it follows that the above proposition remains true. What has happened is that in some cases the prosecution will succeed by establishing something less than *Cunningham* recklessness. In which crimes will this be true?

In *Lawrence*, a decision of the House of Lords on the same day as *Caldwell* concerning reckless driving, Lord Diplock said that his definition of recklessness should apply to any modern statute which contained the word recklessness. This clearly covers the Criminal Damage Act 1971 and reckless driving contrary to section 2 of the Road Traffic Act 1988. The word reckless also appears in section 15 of the Theft Act 1968 but for reasons which will be described later it can have no application there (see below, p. 307). Possibly the most contentious area has been in relation to the offence of rape. In section 1(1) of the Sexual Offences (Amendment) Act 1976 the *mens rea* of rape is stated to be that at the time when the accused had intercourse with the woman against her will he either knew that she did not consent or was reckless as to whether she consented to it. This section was passed with the express purpose of giving statutory effect to the decision of the House of Lords in *Morgan* (see below, p. 82) where it was held that a man was not guilty of rape if he honestly but unreasonably believed that the woman was consenting. However, in *Pigg* (1983) the Court of Appeal held, *obiter,* that the extended definition of recklessness should apply to the offence of rape. In other words the prosecution would succeed if it could establish that the defendant had given no thought to the obvious and serious risk that the woman was not consenting. Later cases, in particular *Satnam and Kewal* (1984) held that a direction in such terms was more likely to confuse a jury. A man should not be convicted of *reckless* rape unless his attitude towards the woman was one of "couldn't care less whether or not she is consenting." Since you cannot "care less" about something you have not thought about, this ruling means that the extended form of *recklessness* does not operate in rape. The jury must be satisfied that the accused deliberately took the risk that the woman was not consenting. This approach, it is submitted, is far more in keeping with the spirit of *Morgan* and the Sexual Offences (Amendment) Act 1976 which is based upon that case.

In *Caldwell* itself, Lord Diplock conceded that the Court in *Cunningham* had been concerned with the word "maliciously." He said that in that context the more restricted definition was probably appropriate. In *Morrison* (1988) a woman detective constable, in an attempt to arrest the defendant, had grabbed hold of his clothes. In trying to get away the defendant had dived through a window shattering the glass. The arresting officer had been pulled into contact with the glass and her face had been severely lacerated. The defendant was charged under Offences Against the Person Act 1861, section 18, with unlawfully and maliciously wounding the officer with intent to resist arrest. There was no doubt that the defendant intended to resist arrest, but the trial judge had directed the jury in terms that suggested that *Caldwell* recklessness would suffice in relation to the wounding where the *mens rea* is defined in terms of "maliciously." The Court of Appeal, while regretting the existence of two forms of recklessness, said that in crimes such as section 18 where the word "maliciously" was used, the right test to apply is that of *Cunningham* recklessness, (see also *W.* v. *Dolbey* (1983) and *Farrell* (1989)).

A particular problem is posed by offences such as assault which have traditionally been held to be offences which can be committed recklessly, though there is no statutory definition containing the word reckless. Here it must be said that recklessness has meant that the accused must have foreseen the likely consequences of his actions. In *Seymour* (1983) Lord

Roskill said that the *Caldwell* test should be used wherever reckless suffices as a basis for liability. Taken literally this could mean that in future the *Caldwell* test would control liability in offences of assault. On the other hand Lord Diplock did say that his definition should apply where the word "reckless" appeared in modern statutes, and so it is suggested that liability in assault remains founded upon the *Cunningham* test.

The position in manslaughter is rather obscure. It is possible that as a result of the decisions in *Seymour* and *Kong Cheuk Kwan* (see below, p. 231) that there now exist only two forms of involuntary manslaughter namely unlawful act (or constructive) manslaughter and reckless manslaughter. It would appear that the test of recklessness in this latter category is that of *Caldwell*. In unlawful act manslaughter the prosecution has to establish that the killing was the result of a separate criminal offence for which the accused has the appropriate *mens rea*. In so far as this offence is normally some form of assault the position depends upon the approach taken to the *mens rea* of assault as outlined in the preceding paragraph.

Whatever the eventual outcome of the present debate, recklessness will, in the foreseeable future, continue to be risk taking (either conscious or unconscious), and we should finally note that the risk must be a risk you are not justified in taking. Whether or not the risk is one you are justified in taking will depend upon how the court measures the social utility of the accused's actions. Many doctors operate knowing that the patient might die as a result of the operation. They are therefore taking a conscious risk of killing the patient. But in nearly every case the risk is a justifiable risk, and thus if the patient dies the doctor will not face a charge of manslaughter. On the other hand, if X drives his car down a High Street at 90 m.p.h. in order to evade police capture he risks killing pedestrians and this risk is not one he is justified in taking since there is no social utility in his action. Nor would it be a justifiable risk for the driver of an ambulance to risk killing pedestrians in order to get his patient to hospital quickly.

Conclusion

Where, therefore, you see that the *mens rea* required in a particular crime is recklessness, you must consider which of the two forms is meant. Eventually this tangle will have to be sorted out by legislation, but this will not be easy. Following the work of a Committee under the Chairmanship of Professor J.C. Smith the Law Commission has recently published a Draft Criminal Code for England and Wales [Law Comm. No. 177; April 1989]. Under such a Code, the mental states would be defined, and future legislation would be construed in accordance with these definitions. It is quite certain that conscious and unconscious risk taking, will have to be included in such a code. A major problem, however, will be finding names for these states of mind which will not cause problems for lay juries. It is possible that Parliament may decide that "reckless" should cover a state of mind in which the accused deliberately takes an unjustified risk (as in *Cunningham*), but doubts must remain as to whether this would be wise. The word "reckless" to most laymen probably conotes a high degree of carelessness; it probably does not signify that the person so described had thought about the possible consequences of his actions. If this is correct then the use of the word "reckless" to mean conscious risk taking would be unsafe in jury trials because the jury, in the sanctuary of the jury room, would probably soon forget that they had been instructed that in criminal liability the word had a different meaning from that in every day usage. Having said that, it is not easy to think of a word which does signify conscious risk taking.

(3) Other mental states

Although the term "*mens rea*" was traditionally used to indicate that the prosecution had to establish intention or recklessness on the part of the accused, it has come to include "negligence" which is not really a state of mind of the accused at all. Further we have already mentioned that there are now a great many crimes where the accused may be convicted in the absence of intention, recklessness or negligence on his part. Thus it is important to explain two further "states of mind" which an accused might possess in relation to a particular *actus reus*. These are negligence and blameless inadvertence.

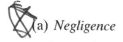 (a) *Negligence*

In the civil law the classic definition of negligence is that given by Alderson B. in *Blyth* v. *Birmingham Waterworks Co.* (1856). "Negligence is the omission to do something which a reasonable man, guided upon these considerations which ordinarily regulate the conduct of human affairs, would do, or doing something which a prudent and reasonable man would not do."

It is thus not a defence in a civil action for the defendant to show that he did not foresee the harm if a reasonable man would have done so; nor even to show that his failure to foresee was due to physical or mental limitations not shared by the reasonable man. Nevertheless it seems probable that the defendant's physical and mental defects may be taken into account in determining whether he is negligent to the extent that they make it impossible for him to take the necessary precautions. Thus it would not avail a man with defective eyesight to attribute a car accident to his inability to judge distances, but if the same man were to fall over and injure the plaintiff's prize poodle when walking along the pavement, the appropriate test would be whether, for a man with defective eyesight, he had taken reasonable care.

So far as the criminal law is concerned there is, of course, no general crime of negligently causing harm. There are, however, particular crimes of neligence. At common law the only instance of a crime of negligence appears to have been manslaughter, though in this type of manslaughter the negligence had to be gross. It is not entirely clear whether this form of manslaughter still exists (see below, p. 231). Parliament, has, however, thought it appropriate to create certain crimes of negligence. Possibly the best known of such crimes is careless driving contrary to section 3 of the Road Traffic Act 1988.

Where the crime is one of negligence the test to be applied is probably the same as that in civil cases though in a criminal case (a) the standard of proof required is more stringent (see below, p. 89); and (b) generally there is no need to prove actual harm to person or property. Thus on a charge of careless driving where the accused is a learner driver his driving will be considered careless if he fails to measure up to the standard of the reasonably experienced driver and no allowance is made for the fact that he is a learner; *McCrone* v. *Riding* (1938). In that case Lord Hewart C.J. said "That standard is an objective standard, impersonal and universal, fixed in relation to the safety of other users of the highway. It is in no way related to the degree of proficiency or degree of experience attained by the individual driver" (*cf. Lamb,* below p. 233).

Crimes of negligence are exceptional in our law. Sometimes, however, Parliament will create a crime and then make the absence of negligence a defence. Under section 7 of the Sexual Offences Act 1956 it is an offence for a man to have intercourse with a mental defective but by section 7(2) it is provided that the accused does not commit the offence if he does not know and has no reason to suspect the girl to be a defective; the Court of Criminal Appeal made it clear that the accused bore the burden of proof on this defence. Construing this provision in *Hudson* (1965) the Court of Criminal Appeal said that the trial judge was wrong to direct the jury that the test was wholly objective (*i.e.* would a reasonable man have believed that the girl was mentally defective?); the jury should have been instructed to consider whether it was reasonable for Hudson not to have realised that the girl was a defective. This is different from the wholly objective test approved for careless driving in *McCrone* v. *Riding*. The test in *Hudson* is still objective in the sense that it would not avail an accused to show that he was in fact unaware that the girl was a defective, but it will avail him to prove that persons sharing his limitations, whether physical or mental, would not have realised that the girl was a defective. Under section 7, therefore, a conviction is possible only if the jury concludes that the relevant standard could have been attained by the accused; with careless driving the accused may be convicted even though the relevant standard was unattainable by him.

It must not be though that whenever a statutory offence is defined with a defence of no negligence, it inevitably follows that the court will adopt the subjective-objective form adopted in *Hudson*. The precise wording of the provision is all important. Under section 7 it is a defence if *"he* does not know and has no reason to believe" (italics supplied) that the girl was a defective. Had the provision been worded, for example, "it shall be a defence to prove that a reasonable person would not in the circumstances have realised that the girl was a defective" the trial judge's direction would almost certainly have been upheld.

Although, manslaughter apart, there are no crimes of negligence at common law, negligence has, at least in the past, had relevance in connection with the defence of mistake of fact. Sometimes courts have held that a mistake of fact is a defence only if it is honestly made *and* that there were reasonable grounds for making it. The result of this can be, in effect, to make negligence a ground of liability even in connection with serious crimes. The matter of mistake is a highly complicated one and is dealt with more fully below (p. 78).

(4) The relationship between recklessness and negligence

We have seen that under the wider definition of recklessness in *Caldwell*, the accused can be held to be reckless not only if he deliberately takes an unjustifiable risk (*i.e.* *Cunningham* recklessness), but also if he fails to give any thought to an obvious risk which he has created. Negligence is often described as failing to foresee that which a reasonable man would foresee. Is there any real difference between the concept of negligence and the second limb of the *Caldwell* test for recklessness; it would, after all, be strange if we were using two names for the same concept?

In the first place it is possible to say that even if *Caldwell* recklessness is a form of negligence, the use of the phrase "obvious risk" (in *Lawrence* it became obvious and serious) in the *Caldwell* test suggests that we are dealing with a high degree of negligence and not just the sort of negligence which would suffice for a charge of careless driving (see above, p. 66). So it might be that *Caldwell* recklessness could be likened to "gross negligence"—a high degree of negligence that was thought to be required for some forms of manslaughter (see below, p. 226). But is this an accurate statement of the law? Let us consider an illustration. Suppose that Mike is driving his sports car behind a slow moving lorry which he wishes to overtake. He pulls out from behind the lorry to get a clear view of the road ahead. He notices, in the distance, a car coming in the opposite direction towards him. He pulls out to overtake the lorry and is involved in a head-on collision with the oncoming vehicle. Was he reckless or negligent as to causing the collision.? This will depend upon an assessment of all the surrounding circumstances, including his assessment of the situation.

If he recognises that there is a risk that he may not get past the lorry in time, he will be reckless within the *Cunningham*, meaning of this word (and also within the subjective limb of the *Caldwell* test). Presumably it would not matter whether he foresaw the risk as a large or small risk, since any risk in these circumstances would be unjustifiable.

If, on the other hand, it never entered his head that there was a risk of a collision, then he clearly cannot be held to be reckless under the *Cunningham* test. However, if the risk he had, in fact, created was an obvious risk, then he would be reckless within the *Caldwell* wider definition of recklessness. He would also be grossly negligent as to causing the collision.

Suppose, however, the court reached the conclusion that he

had given careful thought to the possibility of there being such a risk and had honestly come to the conclusion that there was no such risk? He would clearly not be reckless within the *Cunningham* test. He might well be grossly negligent, but would he be reckless within the *Caldwell* meaning of the term? It could be argued that he would not fall within Lord Diplock's test since he had given thought to the existence of the risk, but had (probably negligently) reached the wrong conclusion. (This is sometimes referred to as the *Caldwell* loophole). Is there anything to choose between the person who never gives any thought to whether or not there is a risk and one who having thought about it wrongly concludes that there is no risk? There is clearly little to choosen between them. However, if we say that the man who considers the risk and concludes there is none falls within the *Caldwell* test of recklessness, then we are forced to the conclusion that *Caldwell* recklessness and gross negligence are the same thing. The matter was recently considered by the Divisional Court in *Chief Constable for Avon and Somerset* v. *Shimmen* (1986). In that case the defendant had been attempting to demonstrate karate blows. He was standing near a plate glass window. When it was pointed out he might hurt someone he assured his friends that he was in control. He made as if to kick the window. Unfortunately his foot shattered the window and he was charged with destroying property contrary to section 1(1) of the Criminal Damage Act 1971. The Court accepted that he had not intended to destroy the window. The question was whether he was reckless in this regard. It appeared that the defendant recognised that there was some risk, but that he considered he had reduced this to a minimal level. The Divisional Court held that in these circumstances this amounted to recklessness. Now it is clear that this was *Cunningham* recklessness. Although he had taken precautions to minimise the risk he still recognised that there was risk, albeit very slight. But since he was not justified in placing the window under even the slightest risk of harm, this amounted to deliberate risk taking. The Divisional Court considered that where the defendant considers the risk but completely dismisses it, he might well be outside the *Caldwell* test; but *Shimmen* was not such a case.

It is thus possible that there is a difference between gross negligence and *Caldwell* recklessness. This is where the defendant has given thought to the possibility of there being a risk, but has concluded that no risk whatsoever exists. This however may well amount to gross negligence.

(b) *Inadvertence*

On principle, it might be thought, a man who causes harm inadvertently and without a scintilla of fault on his part ought not to be convicted of a crime. Thus A should not be guilty of homicide when in driving his car with every care he causes the death of a pedestrian who suddenly steps into the path of his car. Nor should B be guilty of receiving goods which are, in fact, stolen, which he buys in good faith from a reputable dealer. Nor should C be guilty of abducting a girl under 16 if he reasonably believes that she is 18; nor D guilty of selling unsound meat if he has employed a qualified analyst who certifies the meat to be sound. In all these situations the accused would lack *mens rea*, at least as we have defined it, in that he does not intentionally or recklessly bring about the elements which constitute the crime.

In reality the position is not quite so straightforward. In the illustrations given A would not be guilty of unlawful homicide; B would not be guilty of receiving stolen goods; but C can be convicted of abduction and D of selling unsound meat. On the face of it this is very unfair to C and D and so some explanation is called for.

It is worth considering whether it is necessarily unfair to impose criminal liability even though the accused lacks *mens rea* in the strict sense. Let us consider a rather fanciful illustration. Suppose that H poisons W, his wife, using a poison that a brilliant chemist had assured him would take 18 months to take effect. In fact, owing to W's curious metabolism, W dies just inside the year and a day period. Is it to be said that H ought to be acquitted of murder or manslaughter because he did not intend or forsee that death would occur within a year and a day? On a strict application of the *mens rea* doctrine he must be acquitted of murder. But should we go this far? After all, H does intend to kill—he intends the prohibited act—and is merely inadvertent to a circumstance. Moreover that circumstance has no moral content; it does not alter the fact that H deliberately killed W and there is much to be said for the view that H should take his chances on the death occurring inside or outside the stated period.

Although the above problem might be thought to be far fetched, it was essentially the problem that arose in *Prince* (1875). William Prince eloped with Annie Phillips, who was aged 13, and was subsequently charged with an offence under section 55 of the Offences Against the Person Act 1861 which provided "Whosoever shall unlawfully take or cause to be taken any unmarried girl, being under the age of sixteen years, out of the possession and against the will of her father or mother or of any person having the lawful care or charge of her, shall be guilty . . ." (see now Sexual Offences Act 1956, s.20). The jury concluded that Prince honestly and reasonably believed that Annie was 18 years old but a conviction was directed by the trial judge and that conviction was affirmed by the Court for Crown Cases Reserved. One view that was taken, expressed by Bramwell B., was that Prince did intend to do the prohibited act. He intended to take a girl, not a woman, whom he knew to be in the possession of her parents and further he was aware that he had no lawful authority for the taking. The only factor he was unaware of was the circumstance that she was under 16. Bramwell B. accordingly felt able to hold that Prince had *mens rea*. It is worth noting that when Prince eventually came up for sentencing he was given six months' imprisonment with hard labour; evidently the trial judge was of the opinion that, despite his mistake as to Annie's age, Prince had acted wrongly.

Did Prince get justice? Does not the fact that Prince believed Annie was over 16 take the carpet out from underneath Bramwell B.'s argument? Had Annie been, as Prince supposed she was, 18, Prince would have needed no one's consent—other than Annie's which had been readily given—to take her away. On the other hand Prince knew that her parents would disapprove—why else did he elope with her without telling them? Whether you approve or disapprove of Prince's conviction indicates what you think *mens rea ought* to mean.

In *Lemon* (1979) the editor and publishers of *Gay News* were charged with the offence of blasphemous libel. They had published a poem which purported to describe in detail certain homosexual acts carried out on the body of Christ shortly after his death. It also suggested that Christ took part in promiscuous homosexual practices with the disciples and others. The trial judge directed the jury that the prosecution need only prove that the defendants intended to publish the article which, in the jury's mind was, in fact, blasphemous. There was no need to prove that the defendants intended to blaspheme. As in *Prince* the trial judge relieved the prosecution of the need to prove even negligence as to one vital element of the *actus reus*. The result was that so long as the defendants intended to publish they might be blamelessly inadvertent in respect of whether or not the material was blasphemous—the House of Lords accepted as blasphemous an article which would tend to vilify

Christ in his life and crucifixion. Again, one might ask whether the defendants received justice in *Lemon*. Of course, it is more difficult to believe in *Lemon* that the defendants did not at least know that the poem was likely to shock and cause resentment amongst Christians, whereas Prince might well have never imagined that Annie Phillips was under 16. Yet in both cases the courts have held *mens rea,* in the sense of intention or recklessness (or even negligence) to be irrelevant as to, at least, one aspect of the *actus reus*.

It is, however, important to remember that even in crimes of strict liability some mental element will be required. Had Prince believed that Annie was a prostitute and thus not in the care of her parents, he would have been acquitted since in *Hibbert* (1869) the Court for Crown Cases Reserved held that *mens rea* was required on the aspect of the girl being in the control of her parents or guardian. So *Prince* and *Lemon* do not decide that no *mens rea* at all is required, only that, in the case of *Prince,* once the prosecution established that he intended to take a girl out of the possession of her parents, then a conviction was possible even though he reasonably believed that she was 18. You may well wonder why such a distinction was drawn between the various elements of the *actus reus* in *Prince.* The answer is probably that these two elements came for discussion at different times and a different mood existed amongst the judges. There can be no logical defence of the distinction (see further Offences of Strict Liability, Chap. 4).

(5) So what do we mean when we say that a crime requires mens rea?

Often, you will see the phrase "...is a crime which requires *mens rea.*" So what exactly is meant by the phrase? Traditionally it was used to signify a crime which at least as to the major elements of the *actus reus,* required intention or *Cunningham* recklessness. Thus it drew a line between *Cunningham* recklessness and negligence indicating that *mens rea* really described those crimes in which the jury would need to be satisfied that the accused actually foresaw the prohibited result as opposed to those crimes which are established by proof only that the accused ought to have foreseen the prohibited result. But even in arguably the most heinous crime, murder, this was a gross oversimplification. Clearly in murder the central feature of the *actus reus* is an unlawful killing of a human being, but we have already seen from *Moloney* (above, p. 22) that the prosecution do not have to prove that the accused even foresaw death, let alone that he intended to kill. It suffices that the prosecution establish that grievous bodily harm was intended. Further *Cunningham* recklessness cannot be required in relation to the element of death occurring within a year and a day since it must follow that if the accused does not have to foresee that death will occur, it cannot be necessary for the prosecution to prove that the accused foresaw that death would occur within a year and a day. The most that could be required on this element is that the prosecution should establish that the accused should have foreseen that death would occur within a year and a day— *i.e.* negligence. It is more likely that a court faced squarely with this question would hold that not even negligence was required, yet no one would describe murder as a crime of strict liability.

The position has been further blurred by the decision in the *Caldwell* line of cases. Criminal damage (see below p. 344) has traditionally been regarded as a crime requiring *mens rea*, but following *Caldwell* this in nearly every case would be satisfied by something barely distinguishable from negligence.

In truth the phrase "the crime requires *mens rea*" has very little meaning. It is safer to understand the term *"mens rea"* as the overall term used to describe the mental state the prosecution will have to prove in order to get a conviction in a given crime. There are very few crimes in which no *mens rea* at all is required; *Larsonneur* is one example (see above p. 37). Even in crimes of strict liability some mental element will be required. Thus if a butcher is charged with selling unsound meat, the prosecution will have to prove that he intended to make a sale—though they will be relieved of the necessity of proving that he knew or even ought to have known that the meat was unsound.

However we can possibly make certain general propositions:

1. Intention will always suffice as the basis of liability, but is rarely the only possible basis. It is an essential feature of attempted crimes and of crimes such as section 18 of the Offences Against the Person Act 1861 which use expressions like "with intent to. . . ." Since *Moloney* (1985) it is also an essential feature of murder.

2. In other crimes it will generally suffice to prove intention or *Cunningham* recklessness as to each element of the *actus reus*.

3. Following *Caldwell* a wider definition of recklessness will apply to crimes defined in a modern status where the word "recklessness" or its derivatives is used—with the exception of rape and offences under the Theft Acts of 1968 and 1978 where *Cunningham* recklessness still operates.

4. In certain crimes the prosecution must establish what is sometimes referred to as an *ulterior intention*. The word *ulterior* is used because this intent does not relate to any element of the actus reus. Thus in the offence of burglary contrary to Theft Act 1968, section 9(1)*(a)* the prosecution must prove that the defendant entered a building...as a trespasser and with intent to commit one of four specified offences, the most usually alleged being to steal. Theft does not form any part of the *actus reus* of burglary contrary to section 9(1)*(a)* and so the intent is said to go "beyond" the *actus reus*. Other examples of crimes of ulterior intent include theft and wounding with intent.

5. Crimes where intention or recklessness (in either sense) suffice as the basis of liability on each element of the *actus reus* are often called crimes of *basic* intent. Crimes in which, on at least one aspect of the *actus reus,* intention alone suffices and crimes of ulterior intent are referred to in this context as crimes of *specific* intent. We shall see later that the real and possibly only significance on this terminology relates to the defence of self-induced intoxication. Voluntary intoxication is a defence only to crimes of specific intent. You must not, however, for one moment suppose that this is a clearcut and logical classification. Murder, as it was defined in *Hyam* (above, p. 53), would seem to have been a classic example of a crime of basic intent. However since it was accepted that voluntary intoxication provided a defence to a charge of murder, murder had to be classified as a crime of specific intent. In *Moloney* the House of Lords seems to use this classification of murder as a crime of specific intent as a reason for saying that only an *intention* to kill or cause serious harm will suffice. In truth what the courts have done is to decide as a matter of policy that drunkenness shall operate as a defence only for certain crimes, and then they have tried to rationalise this decision by reference to a supposed classification of crimes into those requiring basic and those requiring specific intent. It is far safer to say that a crime of specific intent is one in which self-induced drunkenness has been held to provide a defence and a crime of basic intent is one in which the defence does not operate. (see below p. 161).

A point which, by now, should be obvious, but which is worth re-inforcing, is that the required *mens rea* varies not only from crime to crime, but also from element to element within a given crime. The most obvious example of this is to be found in strict liability crimes as in the case of *Prince* and *Hibbert* (above, p. 70), where we saw intention or *Cunningham* recklessness required on one element of the *actus reus* but no *mens rea* whatsoever was needed in relation to the age of the girls (see also mistake, below, p. 78).

3. ACTUS REUS AND MENS REA: HOW DO THEY RELATE TO EACH OTHER?

Where *mens rea* is required the prosecution must establish that the *actus reus* and the *mens rea* were concurrent. Suppose that the accused intended to shoot X on Friday afternoon, but, for some unforeseen reason, failed to do so, and then on Saturday morning ran over and killed X completely accidentally without realising whom he had hit. Should we allow the prosecution to say that he had the necessary *mens rea* on Friday and performed the *actus reus* on Saturday morning and thus he should be convicted of murder? Clearly not. The prosecution must show that the accused perpetrated the *actus reus* and at that time possessed the necessary mental state. The courts have allowed a certain degree of flexibility, though not sufficient to cover the above case. In *Fagan* (1969) the accused accidentally drove his car onto a policeman's foot and when asked to remove his car from the foot refused to do so immediately. The objection to any charge involving an assault on the policeman is that in this case the *actus reus* would consist of the infliction of unlawful personal violence by Fagan upon the policeman, and the *mens rea* would be that the accused intentionally or recklessly applied force to the person of another (see below, p. 237). Now it is clear that unlawful personal violence was inflicted by Fagan upon the policeman, but at the time when he drove onto the foot he neither intended to do so nor did he realise that there was any risk of so doing. When he realised what he had done and decided to get some fun out of it, it could be argued that the act of inflicting violence was already over. However the court took a commonsense view of the situation and resolved that an assault was a continuing offence, in this case beginning when he drove onto the policeman's foot and continuing up to the time when he drove off, and that if *mens rea* was proved to exist at any time during the continuance of the assault, the prosecution had made out its case.

A similar result could be obtained by holding that Fagan, having inadvertently caused harm to the constable, was now under a duty to take reasonable steps to prevent further injury. (See *Miller*, above, p. 41). The approach used in *Fagan* should only be adopted where the *actus reus* is of a truly continuing nature: see further *Kaitamaki* v. *The Queen* (1985).

The courts have also held a charge to be proved where the accused in order to gain Dutch-courage for the killing of his wife, drank a large amount of scotch and then killed his wife (*Att.-Gen. for Northern Ireland* v. *Gallagher*, see below, p. 171).

A more extreme example is provided by those cases where the accused has attacked another with the appropriate *mens rea* for murder but has failed to kill the victim and has then disposed of the "body," the act of disposal in the end killing the victim. In *Thabo Meli* v. *The Queen* (1954) the two accused had attempted to kill the deceased by beating him over the head. They had then rolled his "body" over a cliff in an attempt to make it look as if he had died from accidentally falling over a cliff. Medical evidence, however, revealed that he had in fact died from exposure and not from the beating. The problem facing the court was the fact that at the time the accused possessed the necessary malice aforethought for murder they failed to achieve their objective and when they rolled the body down the cliff they believed that the victim was already dead. However the court held that it was impossible to divide up what was really one series of acts in this way. The court seemed to base its decision upon the idea that there was an antecedent plan and that the victim died as a result of that plan, albeit in a way not anticipated by the accused. However, in subsequent cases the doctrine has been applied in situations where there was no antecedent plan. It has been suggested that the answer is possibly that the accused will be liable if he kills during the continuance of the "transaction" in which he acted with *mens rea*; and that transaction is continuing as long as D is covering up the homicide or other offence he believes he has committed. In *Thabo Meli* the court was concerned with a charge of murder; the principle has been held to apply also in cases of manslaughter (*Church* (1966)).

It was clear in *Thabo Meli* and *Church* that the victim had been killed as a result of the second of the two acts. In *Att.-Gen.'s Reference* (*No. 4 of* 1980) (1981) the Court of Appeal was faced with a variant on the problem. There the accused had slapped his girlfriend on the face and this had caused her to fall down the stairs, banging her head. He then put a rope around her neck and dragged her up the stairs, placed her in the bath and then drained off all her blood. Finally he sawed up her body into disposable pieces. The victim died either from the fall, or due to being strangled, or due to having her throat cut; it was not, however, proved exactly how she died as very little of her body was found. The Court of Appeal held that if the jury were satisfied that culpability had been established in respect of all the acts which might have caused the victim's death, then they were entitled to convict him of manslaughter. If, however, they were not satisfied that culpability had been established on all of the acts which might have caused death then they would be bound to acquit. (See also *Fisher* (1987)).

However, these rare cases aside, the rule remains that the prosecution must prove that the accused caused the *actus reus* with the necessary *mens rea*.

4. TRANSFERRED MALICE

Let us imagine a situation in which X intends to kill Y and to this end shoots at him. The bullet misses Y but hits and kills Z. What view should the law take of this? On the one hand you might argue that he only intended to kill Y and that unless you could find the necessary *mens rea* for a charge in relation to Z (for example that he was reckless or grossly negligent as to the fact that his shot might kill others) there should no conviction. On the other hand in deliberately trying to kill one man he has unlawfully caused the death of another and should therefore be treated as if he had killed Y. We have already mentioned the fact (above, p. 22) that the law adopts the second approach. It is said that the malice X bears towards Y is transferred to Z. X can therefore be convicted of murdering Z even though he only intended to kill Y and was possibly even unaware of Z's presence (see *Latimer* (1886)). But suppose that the bullet had missed Y and had struck, not Z, but Z's pet labrador, killing it. Clearly the killing of a dog does not constitute any offence against the person, though it might constitute an offence of criminal damage to Z's property. Can we still join X's *mens rea* against Y to the *actus reus* of destroying Z's property? In *Pembliton* (1874) in the course of a fight outside a public house the accused picked up a stone and threw it at someone, but succeeded only in breaking a window behind his intended victim. He was charged with (the then equivalent of) the offence of criminal damage to property, but his conviction was quashed on the ground that you cannot join the *mens rea* of an offence against the person with the *actus reus* of an offence against property. Does this mean that Pembliton and X in our hypothetical example must go free? In our hypothetical example it is quite probable that you would be able to bring a successful charge against X for attempting to murder Y. Alternatively you might be able to charge X with criminal damage to Z's dog, but on the basis that he gave no thought to an obvious risk of damage to the dog and not on the basis that he intended to kill a human being.

Suppose that X is about to shoot at Y, and so Y, in self-defence, fires a shot at X but misses X and hits Z a totally innocent by-stander. In such a case the defence that would have been available to Y on a charge of murdering X will be available to him on a charge of murdering Z.

5. MISTAKE: ITS EFFECT ON MENS REA

In some respects the question of mistake ought to be left to the general chapter on defences to criminal charges. On the other hand the defences of mistake and of accident are so closely bound up with the *mens rea* of the crime in question, that discussion of them will be included in this chapter (accident will be discussed at p. 91). A lot of confusion is caused in relation to the defence of mistake by rather ill-defined use of terminology. The basic rule is, it is suggested, fairly simple. If the accused makes a mistake, the effect of which is to deprive him of the necessary *mens rea* required for that crime, then the mistake is capable of affording him a defence. From this it follows that if the accused makes a mistake as to an issue for which no *mens rea* is required then the mistake will not afford him a defence. Thus, for example, we have seen that the offence of abducting unmarried girls under the age of 16 (Sexual Offences Act 1956, s.20) does not require that the prosecution prove that the accused knew, was indifferent as to the fact or even ought to have known, that the girl was under 16. Thus a mistaken belief, however reasonably held, that the girl was 17 would afford no defence. On the other hand a mistake by a man charged with murder to the effect that he thought he was shooting at an escaped bear would mean that the prosecution would not be able to prove that he intended to kill a human being. We shall see later that complications are caused by the fact that the courts do not seem to be able to make up their minds as to whether the mistake must be an honest mistake or an honest and reasonable mistake (see p. 81). Another type of mistake often made is the fact that the accused did not know that what he was doing was a criminal offence. For example, in one case the accused told the court that buggery was not an offence in his country and that as a result he was unaware that it was here (*Esop* (1836); but see now Sexual Offences Act 1967, s.1). Clearly the accused made a mistake, but it was not a mistake that would affect the necessary *mens rea* of the offence. The prosecution would have to establish that the accused had sexual connection with the other man and that was what he intended to do. It is not part of the prosecution's case to establish that the accused knew that buggery was an offence. It is often put in the form that the prosecution must prove that the accused was aware of the facts which made the action criminal, but not that he knew that it was criminal. For example in the crime of handling stolen property the prosecution would have to prove that the accused deliberately received the goods knowing or believing that they were stolen. The prosecution do not have to prove that the accused knew that the handling of stolen goods is a criminal offence. Unless it were part of the offence that the accused knew he was committing a crime, this type of mistake will not suffice since it does not relate to the *mens rea* of the crime. Consider, however, a situation in which the defendant, a foreign prince, is charged with stealing a pullover from a large department store. He says that in his country members of the Royal Family of any country are expected to take what they want without payment. He simply assumed that this would be the case here. Is he in the same position as *Esop* who believed that buggery was legal in this country? The cases look very similar. However, in the crime of buggery the prosecution simply have to establish the intention to have sexual connection. In theft the prosecution must establish that the defendant acted dishonestly and the foreign prince's belief would make it unlikely that a court would hold him to be dishonest. The illustration hopefully reinforces the rule that mistake will only succeed as a defence if it can negative all or part of the *mens rea* required for the offence. It is probably preferable to refer to the mistake in *Esop* as ignorance of the law rather than mistake of law for reasons which will soon be apparent. Whether or not ignorance of the law should provide a defence is a question beyond the realms of an introductory book; suffice it to say that it does not.

If then, it is appreciated that the mistake is one which affects the *mens rea* of the accused, then it will be possible to appreciate that the mistake may take several forms. In the first place it may be one that clearly relates only to factual issues. For example in *Rose* (1884) the accused was charged with the murder of his father. He said he had thought that his father was about to kill his mother and that was why he had killed him. The court found that the accused's belief was an honest one (and indeed a reasonable one). If the facts were as the accused believed them to be he would have had a good defence to the killing (see now Criminal Law Act 1967, s.3, below p. 174. This was purely a mistake of fact; there was no mistake as to any legal issue whatsoever. On the other hand the accused's mistake might refer to some legal concept which relates to the *actus reus* of the crime. For example in the crime of theft the prosecution must prove that the accused appropriated property belonging to another. It would be a defence that the accused believed that it was his property and not that of another. His mistake may be purely factual in the sense that he picked up an item of property thinking that it was his own, or it may be that due to a misunderstanding of certain rules relating to the transfer of property he thought the item, which previously belonged to Y, now belonged to him. Another such case would be where the accused is charged with bigamy (Offences Against the Person Act 1861, s.57); this requires that the prosecution prove that, being married, he married another. It would be a defence for the accused to show that he believed that his first wife was dead, and this would be a mistake of fact. On the other hand he might say that he had been through certain procedures at a solicitor's office and that he believed that as a result his marriage had been dissolved or annulled. Such a belief may be a defence. The mistake, in one sense, is a mistake of fact, namely that he believed that he was a single person. On the other hand it is a mistake as to the effect of certain legal processes and to that extent is a mistake of law. Whichever view is taken the mistake means that the accused did not intend, being a married person, to marry another; his intention was, as a single person, to marry. To reiterate a point made earlier, a mistake that bigamy was not a criminal offence would be no defence whatsoever. Both these mistakes are in a sense mistakes of law; the difference being that one affects the *mens rea* that has to be proved by the prosecution, the other does not. It is for this reason that it is suggested the second type of mistake, that is "I did not realise bigamy was a crime," be called ignorance of the law.

Once it is appreciated that the effect of mistake is to negative *mens rea,* then the answer to the question "does it have to be a reasonable mistake?" should be straightforward. You will recall that in murder the prosecution must prove that the accused intended to kill or seriously harm a human being. If the accused *honestly* believed that he was shooting at a bear, then the prosecution will be unable to establish the necessary *mens rea.* The same would be true if *Cunningham* recklessness is required. An assault requires that the prosecutor prove the accused intended to place the victim in fear of immediate harm or foresaw that his conduct would this effect. An *honestly* held belief that the other person will not be put in fear is therefore totally inconsistent with the necessary *mens rea.* It follows that an honest but totally unreasonable mistake should suffice. On the other hand if we take the crime of driving without due care and attention where the prosecution need show only that the accused's driving did not reach the standard of a reasonable driver, then it will not avail him to say that he honestly thought that the road was clear; if the prosecution can show that reasonable motorists would not have made the mistake, then they have made out their case. Thus where the crime is one of negligence, it follows that a reasonable mistake is required. Unfortunately the courts have not, until recently, followed this simple approach. Problems of proof have become entangled with questions of substantive liability. If we return to the man who said he thought that he was shooting at a bear, how does the prosecution prove that he intended to shoot a human being? On what basis can a jury accept that he honestly thought that he was shooting at a bear? In practice, in the jury room, the jurors will inevitably ask themselves whether they, as reasonable persons, could have made such a mistake. If the answer is "no," then they will probably come to the conclusion that the accused did not, in fact, make such a mistake. There is nothing wrong in this type of reasoning. Unfortunately, however, judges in directing juries seem to have strayed into telling them that the mistake must be one which the accused honestly and reasonably held. So what was a perfectly acceptable method of assessing whether or not a mistake was honestly held, becomes an essential part of the defence. Over the years a very uneven pattern emerged; in some cases the judge would tell the jury that the mistake must be one which a reasonable person could have made; in others he would tell them that it sufficed that the accused honestly made such a mistake. Attempts were made by writers to try to find some logical analysis of the decisions, but with little success.

In *D.P.P.* v. *Morgan* (1976) the House of Lords appears to have laid the basis for a more realistic approach. In that case Morgan returned home with several friends after an evening's drinking. He invited them to have sexual intercourse with his wife, saying that they should not be put off by any protests she might make as these would only be her way of increasing her sexual pleasure. The facts show that the wife put up tremendous resistance, but was eventually overcome by the men who then had intercourse with her. They were charged with raping her, but pleaded that they believed that she was consenting. The trial judge directed the jury that the accused men would have a defence if they honestly believed that she was consenting to intercourse and furthermore that there were reasonable grounds for such a belief. Not surprisingly the jury convicted the accused and their appeals eventually reached the House of Lords. Their Lordships held that the trial judge should have directed the jury that if the men honestly but unreasonably believed that the wife was consenting to intercourse, then they were not guilty of rape. However, the appeal was dismissed by application of the proviso; in other words their Lordships took the view that on the evidence before the court the jury would have reached the same conclusion even if they had been properly directed. At that time rape was an offence covered only by section 1 of the Sexual Offences Act 1956 which merely provided that "it shall be an offence for a man to rape a woman." The House said that this was clearly an offence requiring *mens rea*. Lord Hailsham said "the prohibited act in rape is non-consensual sexual intercourse, and . . . the guilty state of mind is an intention to commit it." It is thus totally contradictory to tell the jury that the prosecution must prove that the accused intended to have intercourse with a woman who he knows or believes is not consenting, while at the same time directing them that if he honestly believed that she was consenting it would still not be a defence unless a reasonable man would have so believed.

The House considered the line of authority relating to bigamy. We have seen that it is an offence for a person "being married to marry." It is a defence for the accused to show that at the time of the second marriage he believed that, in fact, he was a single person. However the courts have traditionally held that this must be a belief held on reasonable grounds. Were these cases, therefore in conflict with the decision the House had reached in rape cases? Their Lordships held that the bigamy cases were distinguishable. Lord Cross said "If the words defining an offence provide either expressly or impliedly that a man is not to be guilty of it if he believes something to be true, then he cannot be found guilty if the jury think that he may have believed it to be true, however inadequate were his reasons for doing so. But, if the definition of the offence is on the fact of it "absolute" (this means the offence requires no *mens rea*—see p. 70) and the defendant is seeking to escape his prima facie liability by a defence of mistaken belief, I can see no hardship to him in requiring the mistake—if it is to afford him a defence—to be based on reasonable grounds." Rape, held Lord Cross, comes into the first category and bigamy into the second. In other words he is saying that in law bigamy is a crime requiring only that the prosecution proves that the accused deliberately contracted the second marriage and that a reasonable person would have realised that an earlier marriage was still subsisting. Negligence suffices on this aspect of the *actus reus* and negligence can only be displaced by a reasonable mistake.

The actual decision in *Morgan* led to a great public outcry; the House of Lords, it was said, had published a rapist's charter. A committee under Mrs. Justice Heilbron was established and on the basis of its report the Sexual Offences (Amendment) Act 1976 was passed, which, in effect, gave statutory effect to *Morgan*. By section 1 it provided:

> **1.**—(1) For the purposes of section 1 of the Sexual Offences Act 1956 (which relates to rape) a man commits rape if—
>> (a) he has unlawful sexual intercourse with a woman who at the time of the intercourse does not consent to it; and
>> (b) at the time he knows that she does not consent to the intercourse or he is reckless as to whether she consents to it;
>
> and references to rape in other enactments (including the following provisions of this Act) shall be construed accordingly.

The use of the word "reckless" is perhaps unfortunate in the light of recent developments, but it seems that it will now receive its older *Cunningham* meaning and the section will be interpreted in a way to preserve the decision in *Morgan*. (See above, p. 63).

The use of the proviso in *Morgan* demonstrates that it is likely to be a rare case in which a jury will be willing to hold that the accused honestly held a mistaken belief which appears to them to be unreasonable. In *Cogan and Leak* (1976), however, on facts very similar to those in *Morgan*, the trial judge, aware that *Morgan* was on its way to the House of Lords, took the precaution of asking the jury to indicate whether they had formed the conclusion that the men honestly believed that the woman was consenting and, if so, whether they thought that the belief was reasonable. The jury said that they thought that the belief had been honestly held by the men but that it was an unreasonable belief. The men's conviction was subsequently quashed following the decision in the House of Lords in *Morgan*. (In *Cogan and Leake*, the husband who had invited the men to have intercourse with his wife clearly knew she was not consenting, but as the law provides that a man cannot rape his wife, he could not be convicted as a principal offender. For his position following the acquittal of his friends see post, p. 133).

It would thus appear that where the prosecution is required to prove intention or *Cunningham* recklessness, it will fail unless it can prove that the accused did not honestly believe that the facts were as he alleges he believed them to be. Where, however, *Caldwell* recklessness suffices, or where the crime is one of negligence, then the prosecution need only show that a reasonable man would not have made such a mistake. Where the offence is one of strict liability then even a reasonable mistake affords no defence. Since the decision in *Morgan*, there have been suggestions that the decision is not to be taken as anything more than a decision on the law relating to rape (*Pheekoo* (1981)) but this has been rejected by the Court of Appeal (*Kimber* (1983)).

One area that has caused some confusion since the decision in *Morgan* relates to the issue of unlawfulness in relation to offences against the person. In these crimes the *actus reus* will require that the defendant's action was unlawful. Assault, for example, can be described as the unlawful application of the slightest amount of force against another (see further p. 237 below). In the context of assault the word *unlawful* means that the prosecutor must prove that there was no consent by the victim to the force, and that it was not done for the purpose of preventing a crime or in self-defence. The prosecution will also have to establish the necessary *mens rea* on each of these elements. In *Albert* v. *Lavin* (1982) the Divisional Court appeared to say that an honest but mistaken belief that the victim was consenting would be a defence, but that a mistaken belief that there was a need for self-defence or action to prevent a crime would have to be based upon reasonable grounds. The effect of this would be that the prosecution would succeed if it could prove that the defendant realised that the victim might not be consenting (*i.e. Cunningham recklessness*) and that a reasonable person would have realised that there was no reason to act in self-defence or to prevent a crime (*i.e.* negligence). In *Kimber* (1983) Lawton L.J. said that there could be no justification for such a distinction and, in *Gladstone Williams* (1984), the Court of Appeal finally took the opportunity to resolve the muddle. In that case W had witnessed what he considered to be a man, M, beating up a coloured youth. In fact M was trying to arrest the black youth for the mugging of an old lady. M told W, falsely, that he was a police officer effecting an arrest. He could not produce his warrant card and W thereupon tried to protect the black youth. In the course of the struggle M received several injuries. W was charged with an assault and pleaded that he believed that he was acting properly to protect a youth from a beating. The Recorder at the trial directed the jury that the appellant would have a defence only if he honestly and reasonably believed that his intervention and action was needed to save the youth from an unlawful beating. The Court of Appeal held that the mental element necessary to establish guilt was an intention to apply unlawful force to the victim. Force may be applied lawfully where the victim consents, where the defendant is acting in self-defence and where the defendant is using reasonable force either to prevent the commission of a crime or to assist in a lawful arrest. It is for the prosecution to prove that the accused intended to apply the force unlawfully. If the defendant mistakenly believes that the victim is consenting or that it is necessary to defend himself or that a crime is being committed which he intends to prevent, the prosecution have not made out the charge. It is neither here nor there whether the mistaken belief was formed on reasonable grounds except insofar as it helps the jury to decide whether or not the belief was actually formed. The Court of Appeal also stressed that in these cases trial judges must be very careful that they direct the jury properly on the burden of proof. It is very easy to leave the jury with the impression that it is up to the accused to prove that he honestly believed that *i.e.* the victim was consenting or that he needed to defend himself. The judge must make it quite clear that it is for the prosecution to prove that the defendant did not hold such a belief.

This approach has been recently confirmed by the Privy Council in *Beckford* v. *R.* (1987). There, in a murder case, Lord Griffiths gave approval to a model direction on self-defence prepared by the Judicial Studies Board and which is presently widely used by trial judges. The direction contains the following guidance.

"Whether the plea is self-defence or defence of another, if the defendant may have been labouring under a mistake as to the facts, he must be judged according to his mistaken view of the facts: that is so whether the mistake was, on an objective view, a reasonable mistake or not."

Lord Griffiths commented that some people were concerned that the abandonment of the objective approach (*i.e.* reasonable belief) would result in the success of too many spurious self-defence claims. This simply had not happened. If a jury feels that the belief is unreasonable, they may well conclude that the defendant did not in fact hold that belief. (See *Cogan and Leak* (1976); but see also *O'Grady* (1987) below, p. 166, where the mistake was induced by voluntary intoxication).

Mistakes and intoxication

It will be appreciated that even where an honest but unreasonable mistake suffices to negative the *mens rea* required, the jury will have to ask themselves whether they believe that the defendant actually held such a belief or whether he invented it at the trial in the realisation that it would give him a good defence. In reaching its conclusion on this question the jury will have to examine all the circumstances. One factor which is likely to make it seem more probable that he actually held such a belief is evidence that at the time of the offence he was in a drunken state (or under the influence of drugs). However for policy reasons the defendant may not be permitted to rely on a mistake which owed its origins to intoxication. (See below, p. 161 and *O'Grady* (1987); below, p. 166).

6. Problems of Proof in the Criminal Law

Probably more than with any other branch of substantive law

the student of criminal law finds it difficult to keep theoretical problems of criminal liability apart from the practical problems of proving a case in a court. Very soon he will ask the question, "this is all very well, but how do you prove that he intended to kill?" It could be argued that in some ways it is the failure to keep these two issues apart that has led to so much of the uncertainty in, for example, the cases on mistake. We will conclude this chapter with a look at two of the problems of proof; the questions how do you prove and who has to do the proving?

Proof of actus reus and mens rea

By and large the proving of the elements of the *actus reus* presents little problem. The basic *actus reus* of most crimes consists of elements which can be perceived by the senses and can therefore be testified to in court by witnesses. Even where the *actus reus* includes a mental element such as the lack of consent on the part of the victim, this will rarely cause difficulties since the victim will be ready to testify. However, proof of the *mens rea* of a given criminal offence is, on the face of it, an impossibility without the confession of the accused. How can you decide whether the accused intended permanently to deprive the victim of his wallet in the crime of theft? The answer is that, in the absence of a confession by the accused, the *mens rea* will have to be proved by circumstantial evidence; the jury will be given factual evidence which has been perceived by a witness and will be asked to draw the necessary conclusions from that evidence. For example if the accused has been charged with murdering Z by shooting him, then if a witness testifies that he saw the accused level the gun at Z and pull the trigger, this will be direct evidence that the accused committed the *actus reus* of murder. It will also be circumstantial evidence that the accused intended to kill Z. Of course we will never know that he did intend to kill Z, but if the witness says that the accused took careful aim and did not appear surprised when the gun went off, the jury would be entitled to draw the conclusion that the accused intended to kill. If the accused were to take an axe and decapitate Z, the natural consequence would be that Z would die. There grew up a maxim that a man must be taken to intend the natural and probable consequences of his actions. Clearly it is permissible for a jury, in trying to decide what was going through the mind of the accused at the time he brought about an *actus reus* to, use a principle of common sense that if a certain act normally has a certain result, then in the absence of evidence to the contrary a person who did that act probably intended to produce that result. Unfortunately the courts began to direct juries that, if the results were the natural and probable consequences of the accused's actions, they were bound to infer that the accused intended those results. Once again what was a useful tip for juries as to how to decide what a man intended became a mandatory direction.

In 1967 by section 8 of the Criminal Justice Act, Parliament provided:

"A court or jury in determining whether a person has committed an offence,

(a) shall not be bound in law to infer that he intended or foresaw a result of his actions by reason only of it being a natural and probable consequence of those action; but;

(b) shall decide whether he did intend or forsee that result by reference to all the evidence drawing such inferences from the evidence as appear proper in the circumstances."

It is important to understand the effect of this section. It is concerned only with those crimes where the law requires that the accused be proved to have intended or foreseen a given result or consequence. The law of murder requires that the accused intend death or serious bodily harm; section 8 thus applies and controls the question of how the jury shall decide that issue. The law of reckless manslaughter (see below, p. 233) does not require that the accused foresaw death or any other result and so section 8 has no application. It certainly does not alter the substantive law of murder and manslaughter.

If the given crime does require that the accused has intended or foreseen a particular result then section 8 does not prevent the jury from drawing the conclusion that people generally intend the natural and probable consequences of their acts, it merely prevents the judge from forcing them to draw that conclusion. They are entitled to consider any relevant evidence which they feel may help them decide what the accused actually intended. Another relevant piece of evidence would be motive; we have seen that motive is rarely directly relevant, but indirectly it may help the prosecution to prove that the accused actually intended a certain result.

It might have been arguable that the jury should be entitled to consider the fact that the accused was under the influence of alcohol, since this is likely to be a factor relevant to the assessment of what the accused actually intended. However, special policy considerations have led the courts to adopt a harsher attitude towards self-induced intoxication (see below, p. 161).

The burden and standard of proof

During the course of a criminal trial the court will be guided by the rules of evidence. These rules are designed to ensure that the accused receives a fair hearing while at the same time ensuring that the jury or magistrates are not confused by irrelevant issues. While an understanding of these rules together with the rules of criminal procedure is essential for an all round grasp of criminal law and practice, it would not be possible to undertake any meaningful examination of them in a work of this size. However, no study of the principles of criminal law would be complete without an understanding of the rules of evidence relating to the burden and standard of proof.

We can start by asking some rather basic questions. Who has to prove what at a criminal trial? Does the prosecution have to prove that the accused is guilty or does the accused have to show that he is innocent? When we get to court who has to start the ball rolling? What would happen if neither side called any evidence? How satisfied does the jury have to be of guilt or innocence before it returns a verdict?

If we take the well-known saying "a man is innocent until he is proved guilty" (sometimes called the presumption of innocence) this is merely another way of stating the legal rule that the prosecution must prove the guilt of the accused. In terms of a criminal trial it means that the prosecution bears the burden of proving each element of the *actus reus* and *mens rea* of the crime in question (this burden is sometimes called legal burden or burden of proof). Thus in a case where X is charged with murder the prosecution bears the burden of proving that X unlawfully killed another human being within the Queen's Peace and that he intended to kill or cause grievous bodily harm. If the prosecution fail to satisfy the jury of any of these elements then the jury must acquit. The next question that occurs is, just how satisfied do the jurors have to be on each of these elements before they can convict? The traditional answer is that the prosecution must satisfy them beyond reasonable doubt. But what does that mean? The Court of Appeal has in the past said that it is probably safer not to try to explain this phrase to the jury, on the basis that most people probably have a good understanding of it and that explanations are only likely to confuse. It means literally that if the jury are left with any doubts which are not just fanciful they should acquit. Thus if the jury comes to the conclusion that the accused is probably guilty, but they still have serious doubts about the major piece of identification evidence they should acquit. Today judges tend to direct the jury that they should acquit unless they are sure of the accused's guilt. This is probably rather generous to the accused, but it undoubtedly states the high standard of proof expected of the prosecution.

The rules relating to the burden of proof also answer another of our opening questions, namely, what would happen if neither side produced any evidence? The prosecution would fail to discharge its burden of proving the elements of the *actus reus* and *mens rea* and so the accused would be acquitted. It therefore follows that at a criminal trial the prosecution will have the task of starting the proceedings since if no evidence is introduced the accused will be acquitted.

It will be convenient at this stage to introduce a second burden, the evidential burden. Just as on every issue in the trial there is a legal burden resting on one side or the other so there is an evidential burden. Whereas the legal burden indicates which side will win on any given issue if sufficient proof is not adduced, the evidential burden determines which side has the duty to introduce evidence on that issue. Normally the party with the legal burden on an issue will also have the duty to introduce evidence on that issue. So in a criminal trial the prosecution will have the duty to introduce evidence that the accused committed the *actus reus* of the crime with the necessary *mens rea* (evidential burden) and at the end of the trial will fail if they have not satisfied the jury beyond reasonable doubt on these issues (legal burden).

Does the side with the evidential burden on an issue merely have to say that they want that issue considered? It is not quite as simple as that. The effect of failing to discharge an evidential burden is that the judge will not leave the issue to be considered by the jury. In terms of a criminal trial this will mean that the prosecution, by the close of its case, will have to have adduced sufficient evidence of *actus reus* and *mens rea* that the trial judge can find there is evidence upon which a jury could reasonably convict the accused. If at this stage he feels that no reasonable jury could convict the accused then he must direct the jury to acquit.

As a matter of practice the prosecution will expect at the end of their case to have proved the accused's guilt beyond reasonable doubt. They may hope to strengthen their case by cross-examining defence witnesses, but they should not rely on this since, for example, the defence may decide to call no evidence in the light of a very weak prosecution case.

We shall see shortly that occasionally the accused bears an evidential burden on a given issue, even though the prosecution bears the legal burden (*e.g.* automatism). Here the accused must adduce sufficient evidence which could create a reasonable doubt in the mind of the jurors. If he fails to do this then the judge will not leave that issue for consideration by the jury.

The next question we must ask is whether the accused who raises a defence, such as self-defence, to a criminal charge will have to prove that defence; will he have the legal burden on that defence? It is very easy to say the accused must prove he was acting in self-defence, but a moment's thought will reveal a difficulty. We have already said that the prosecution must prove all the elements of the *actus reus* and the *mens rea* or the accused will be acquitted. Most defences are, in effect nothing more than denials of one element of the *actus reus* or *mens rea*. For example the defences of mistake and accident are another way of saying that the killing was not, in the circumstances, intentional or reckless. Such reasoning applies to most defences. It would therefore be illogical to say that where the accused claimed the killing was an accident, the prosecution must prove that the accused intended to kill the victim while at the same time saying that it is up to the accused to prove that he did not intend to kill the victim. Where the accused raises the defence of self-defence he is saying that the prosecution have failed to prove that the killing was unlawful—*i.e.* he is denying the *actus reus*. In the famous case of *Woolmington* v. *D.P.P* (1935) the accused had gone armed with a shot gun to persuade his wife to return home to live with him. The gun went off and his wife was killed. The prosecution charged Woolmington with murder and he claimed that it was an accidental death. At first instance the trial judge told the jury that if the prosecution had satisfied them that the accused had unlawfully killed his wife, then they should return a verdict of murder unless he could show that it was something less; for example that it was an accident. The trial judge was in effect placing the legal burden of disproving *mens rea* on the accused. The case eventually reached the

House of Lords where Viscount Sankey L.C. said that the trial judge had been mistaken in his direction to the jury. It was a prime rule of English criminal trials that the prosecutor had to prove the guilt of the accused and not the accused his innocence. It was therefore up to the prosecutor to prove to the jury beyond reasonable doubt that it was not an accidental death; in other words to prove that the accused intended to kill his wife.

Does this mean that the prosecutor must raise and rebut all possible defences open to the accused? Wouldn't that make the trial rather lengthy? Let us consider the *Woolmington* case further. The prosecution were able to establish that the accused was holding the gun when it went off and that the shot caused the death of the wife. There was also the evidence of bad relations between Woolmington and his wife. From evidence such as this the prosecution would ask the jury to conclude that the killing was deliberate. From a tactical point of view if the accused wants the jury to examine the possibility of the killing as an accident he would be advised to tell them how the accident happened (thus the accused here is sometimes said to bear a tactical burden). But this does not mean that the accused bears even an evidential burden of adducing some evidence. If he did bear such a burden, failure to adduce sufficient evidence capable of creating a doubt in the mind of a jury would mean that the issue of accident would be withdrawn from the jury, and this would be tantamount to withdrawing the need to find *mens rea* from them.

It is suggested that only a tactical burden exists in all defences which are so central that they are nothing more than denials of *actus reus* and *mens rea*; defences such as mistake, mistaken identity, accident, and consent for a charge of rape.

On the other hand there are defences where the courts have taken a stricter line. If the accused wishes to rely on the defence of automatism (see above, p. 34) then it has been held that he must adduce sufficient evidence of automatism which is capable of creating a reasonable doubt about the voluntariness of his conduct in the minds of the jury. He will probably be expected to produce some form of medical evidence to support the credibility of the defence. If such evidence is not produced then the trial judge will not leave the question of automatism to the jury. If, on the other hand, he concludes that the defence has submitted sufficient evidence to create a doubt then he will leave the issue to the jury, but he will direct them that it is for the prosecution to prove beyond reasonable doubt that the accused was not acting in a state of automatism. Thus this is a case where the accused bears an evidential burden, while the prosecution retains the legal burden. In the case of automatism the reason would appear to be that allegations of blackouts are easy to make but hard to rebut and so the accused should at least have to provide the basis for such a plea before the prosecution should be expected to rebut it. Another reason for laying the evidential burden on the accused in such a case is that unlike the defences of mistake and accident, automatism is not so immediately recognisable as a mere denial of the *actus reus* and *mens rea*. Thus it is suggested that the accused will also bear an evidential burden when he raises such pleas as self-defence, provocation, duress, necessity and drunkenness.

Finally we should note that in one or two instances the accused bears not only an evidential burden, but also the burden of proof;

(1) Where the accused raises the defence of insanity (p. 151, below) he must prove that he falls within the terms of the *McNaghten Rules*.

(2) Certain statutes specifically place the burden of proof on the accused. This is the case in the defences of diminished responsibility (Homicide Act 1957, s.2) and suicide pacts (Homicide Act 1957, s.4). A recent example of such express provision can be found in Public Order Act 1986, section 6.

(3) Even where the statute does not expressly place the burden of proof on the accused, the courts may decide that the correct interpretation of the wording of the statute indicates that this was the intention of the legislature. (See *Hunt* (1987).)

However in all cases where the accused bears the burden of proof, the standard of proof is lower than that required of the prosecution. Thus, if the accused relies on the defence of insanity, he need prove only that it is more likely than not that he is insane. This is sometimes referred to as the civil standard of proof—proof on a balance of probabilities.

CHAPTER 4

STRICT LIABILITY

IN the last chapter we saw that in some situations the courts have imposed what is known as strict liability; in other words they have dispensed with the need for *mens rea* as to at least one aspect of the *actus rea*. Thus in *Prince*, the accused's honest and even reasonable mistake did not provide any defence to the charge of abduction (above, p. 70). In this chapter we shall examine in more detail the phenomenon of strict liability and try to discover whether there is any way of predicting whether a court will find strict liability in a given piece of legislation.

It is an offence under section 5 of the Road Traffic Act 1988 to drive or attempt to drive a motor vehicle on a road or other public place having consumed alcohol to such an extent that the amount of alcohol which has passed into the blood stream at the time a specimen of breath is taken exceeds the prescribed limit, which is at present 35 microgrammes of alcohol per 100 millilitres of breath (the offence is commonly called OPL—over the prescribed limit). Most readers will immediately recognise this as the breathalyser legislation under which the motorist who fails a preliminary breath test at the side of the road will be asked to provide a specimen of breath for analysis on an intoximeter. If this analysis proves positive the motorist will be charged with an offence which carries with it the mandatory penalty of disqualification for at least a year. But what *mens rea* must the prosecution establish in order to gain a conviction? The accused might know he is over the prescribed limit—unlikely but possible; more likely he is aware of the risk but nevertheless drives. Possibly he honestly believes that ten pints of beer will not take him over the limit—this would be a negligent even if not a grossly negligent belief. In some cases he may honestly and totally reasonably believe that he is not over the limit—for example in the cases where his orange juice has been laced by a "friend." Which of these should we catch and convict? Probably the man in the street would say that the first three ought to be guilty, but not the man who has had his drink

94

laced. This would be based upon the notion that if you know you have had some alcohol you should know that you may be breaking the law, but the man with the laced drink may be totally unaware of the risk he is taking.

However the courts have held that even the laced drink man should be convicted, though he may have a chance of avoiding the disqualification penalty. In other words the courts are saying that not only does the prosecution not have to establish that the accused knew or even should have known that he was over the limit, but also that there is no need to show that he was even aware that he had consumed alcohol. In the language of the previous chapter we have imposed liability for blameless inadvertence.

This raises further questions. Who is responsible for the development of such crimes? How do we know which offences and which elements of those offences will attract strict liability? Is there any defence to such crimes? What justification can there be for such a development?

1. WHO CREATED THIS GENRE OF CRIMES?

The fact that in almost every case on which strict liability is imposed the offence is created by statute would tend to suggest that it was Parliament who created strict liability, and indeed in many cases the judges have said it was clearly the intention of Parliament to impose strict liability. In some ways this may be true. The courts are expected to give effect to the will of Parliament as expressed in the statutes but it is extremely unlikely that the drafters of nineteenth century legislation had any clear cut views that the use of certain words in statutes would lead the courts to impose strict liability. Today Parliamentary draftsmen will be, or should be, aware that the use of certain expressions will lead the courts to impose strict liability and so their use can be taken to express Parliament's intention to impose strict liability; if the Draft Criminal Code (above, p. 65) or something akin to it is passed the legislators will have clear guidance as to how various forms of legislation will be interpreted. In the nineteenth century, however, it would be wrong to suggest that the legislators had any such clear cut ideas. The truth is that it was the nineteenth century judges who began to develop the concept of strict liability, and since that time much has come to depend upon the outlook of the senior criminal judge, the Lord Chief Justice. The haphazard system of the common law has also meant that since courts tend to interpret only that part of the *actus reus* which is necessary for the decision in the particular case, completely irrational differences can exist in the *actus reus* of the same crime. For instance in *Hibbert* (see above, p. 72) the court held that the prosecution had to establish that the accused was aware that the girl was in the possession of her parents, while on the same statute in *Prince*, the differently constituted Court for Crown Cases Reserved held that the prosecution did not have to prove that the accused was aware that the girl was under 16. Thus *mens rea* was attached to one part of the *actus rea*, but not to another, and there is no truly logical reason to justify this.

2. How Can You Identify Crimes of Strict Liability?

With very few exceptions (public nuisance, blasphemous libel, criminal defamatory libel and parts of contempt of court) crimes of strict liability are statutory offences. It is highly unlikely that we shall see the creation of any new common law crimes of strict liability. Since, in reality, we can say that strict liability operates only in respect of statutory crimes, the principles of statutory interpretation operate and the courts are supposed to try to discover the intention of Parliament from the wording of the statute. One principle of statutory interpretation is that in statutes creating criminal offences there is a presumption that *mens rea* will be required even where it is not specifically mentioned. An example of a crime which expressly provides for *mens rea* is section 1 of the Sexual Offences (Amendment) Act 1976 where in the crime of rape it is expressly provided that the accused must either know that the woman was not consenting to sexual intercourse or be at least reckless as to this fact. On the other hand many offences contain no reference at all to the requirement of *mens rea* and here the courts should start from the principle that *mens rea* is required. Thus common assault under section 47 of the Offences Against the Person Act 1861 is punishable with six months' imprisonment and or a fine not exceeding £2,000. The courts have interpreted this to mean that the prosecution must prove that the accused either, intended to cause the victim to apprehend immediate and unlawful violence or that he foresaw that his actions would have this effect.

However this presumption in favour of *mens rea* is rebuttable and we must now examine the factors which are likely to cause its rebuttal.

(1) The wording of the act

As with any other statute the court's first duty is to try to ascertain the intention of Parliament, not from any extraneous sources, but from the wording of the Act itself. If the Draft Criminal Code is enacted then the courts will know that certain wording indicates that Parliament intended the crime to be one of strict liability. At present there is no guarantee that any given form of wording will create an offence of strict liability. On the other hand there are one or two discernible patterns. Thus certain words have received fairly consistent interpretation as requiring or dispensing with the need for *mens rea*. We will now have a look at some of these "key" words.

"Permitting or allowing"

Where it is an offence to permit or allow another to do a certain act, the prosecution will normally be expected to prove that the accused was aware of the circumstances which made the act unlawful or deliberately avoided finding out (but *cf. Gammon* v. *Att.Gen.* below, p. 103). Thus under a statute creating an offence of permitting or allowing another to drive a motor vehicle with defective brakes, the prosecution would have to prove that the accused knew that his vehicle's brakes were defective before he could be said to have permitted or allowed the other to drive it (see for example, *James & Son Ltd.* v. *Smee* (1955)). You must remember, however, that he does not have to know that it is illegal to permit or allow another to drive a vehicle with defective brakes (see above, p. 79). On the other hand where the statute makes it an offence to *drive* or *use* a vehicle with defective brakes the courts have tended to say that the prosecution need not prove that the driver or user knew that the brakes were defective (see, for example, *Green* v. *Burnett* (1955)).

Cause

Where statutes create an offence of causing something to happen the courts should, according to the House of Lords in *Alphacell* v. *Woodward* (1972) adopt a common sense approach

—if reasonable people would say that the accused has caused something to happen then a conviction is appropriate without the need for *mens rea*. Thus in *Wrothwell Ltd.* v. *Yorkshire Water Authority* (1984) it was held that where the accused had poured a toxic chemical down a drain believing, wrongly, that it would find its way into the main sewer when, in fact, it entered a local stream, it was right to say that he had caused a poisonous matter to enter a stream.

Of course, there are many crimes requiring a prohibited result where the prosecution must show that the accused either intended to cause or foresaw that his actions would cause the prohibited result. What the present line of cases shows is that the express use of the word *cause* in a statute is not likely to lead the court to require *mens rea*.

Possession

The word possession has caused many problems for the courts over the years. It is the basis of many offences that the accused be *in possession* of a prohibited substance. Since many of the offences involved the possession of prohibited drugs and since these offences were often interpreted as imposing strict liability, the courts from time to time attempted to mitigate the severity that would be caused by strict liability by holding that the word "possession" had a mental as well as physical aspect. For example, would we wish to convict an innocent shopper of being in possession of cannabis when the cannabis had been placed in her shopping bag by a drug supplier who believed that he was just about to be arrested? Is she in possession of the drug? Suppose that just before she left home, and without her knowledge, her husband slipped the keys to the house into her raincoat pocket; is she in possession of these keys while she is walking round the shops? If a pickpocket took the keys out of her pocket, would he not have stolen them from her? Yet is she any more in possession of the keys than the cannabis?

In the realms of possession of drugs the House of Lords in *Warner* v. *Metropolitan Police Commissioner* (1969), a case under previous legislation but still applicable to the definition of possession, accepted that A would not be in possession of a drug which had been slipped into his pocket or shopping basket without his knowledge. In these types of case we are saying that the prosecution have failed to establish possession. What then of the situation where the accused knows he is in possession of a substance, but is genuinely unaware of the nature of the substance? Suppose A has been given some tablets and told they are aspirin when they are, in fact, heroin. He is clearly in possession of the tablets and this is as far as the mental element in possession goes. Unless the controlling legislation provides that it is an offence knowingly to possess heroin or unless the statute provides a defence of mistake of fact (see, *e.g.* the Misuse of Drugs Act 1971, s.28 below) he is guilty of possessing the prohibited substance. In other words the word "possession" does not involve knowledge of the nature of the thing one possesses.

Does this mean therefore that if you know you possess a substance, but you do not know what it is because it is in a locked container, you are in possession of that substance. Suppose that you believe that it is some photographic equipment, but in fact it is heroin tablets. Can you be said to be in possession of heroin for purposes of section 5 of the Misuse of Drugs Act 1971? The House of Lords took a more lenient view of such container cases. They said that if you were completely mistaken as to the nature but not the quality of the contents, have had no opportunity to examine the contents and do not suspect that there is anything wrong with the contents, then you are not, for the purpose of offences as in section 5, in possession of the contents. The reference to a distinction between nature and quality means that if you believed the contents to be photographic equipment and it was heroin, then this would be a mistake as to the nature of the contents. On the other hand if you thought the package contained aspirin and it turned out to be heroin, then this is a mistake as to quality; you thought it was a drug—and it was, you were merely mistaken as to what sort of drug. Although cases such as *Warner* must now be read subject to the provisions of the Misuse of Drugs Act 1971, *Warner* remains as general authority on the meaning of the word "possesses" in situations where the proscribed goods are in a container. Where, however, there is no container, stricter provisions apply. In *Marriott* (1971) the accused possessed a penknife to the blade of which adhered 0.03 grains of cannabis. On appeal against conviction the court held that the proper direction to a jury in such a case would be that the accused was guilty of possessing cannabis if he knew that there was a substance on the penknife even if he did not know what that substance was. It was not, however, sufficient to prove that he knew he was in possession of the penknife (see also *Searle* v. *Randolph* (1972)).

These cases dealt with the meaning of the word "possess." Section 28 of the Misuse of Drugs Act 1971 provided certain defences for those charged with the possession of controlled drugs. For example, section 28(3)(b)(i) provides that the defendant shall be acquitted if he proves that he neither believed nor suspected nor had reason to suspect that the substance or product in question was a controlled drug. The court of Appeal in *McNamara* (1988) appears to have used this provision to find a simpler approach to the container situations which avoids the need to distinguish between differences in kind and quality. The court held that it was for the prosecution to prove that the defendant (i) had control of the container, (ii) knew that he had control of the container and (iii) that the box contained something which was in fact the drug alleged. It was then up to the defendant to bring himself within the provisions of section 28(3)(b)(i) by proving that be neither believed nor suspected nor had reason to suspect that the substance or product in question was (any sort of) controlled drug. *Lewis* (1988), however, shows that the word possession will continue to cause problems).

Knowingly

One would think that the word knowingly could cause few problems and that it would indicate an express requirement for *mens rea*. This is true to the extent that it clearly requires *mens rea* as to the clause it qualifies, but it is not always easy to identify the clause it does qualify. For example in *Hallam* (1957) the accused was charged with knowingly possessing explosives. Does this mean that the accused knows that he is in possession of a substance which is later identified as an explosive even though he thought it was soap powder, or does it mean that he must be both aware that he possesses a substance and that he further knows the substance to be an explosive? In the case cited the court held that the prosecution must prove that the accused knew that the substance was an explosive. Indeed to have held otherwise would have been to render the word "knowingly" superfluous since, as we have seen, the word "possess" is usually held to require at least the knowledge that the accused has something in his possession. It would have been better had Parliament defined the offence as possession of goods knowing them to be explosives. A similar result was reached in *Westminster City Council* v. *Croyalgrange Ltd* (1986) where the offence was knowingly to use or knowingly to cause or permit the use of premises as a sex establishment without a licence. The Court held that the prosecution must establish that the defendant both knew that the premises were a sex establishment and that they were being so used without a licence.

The word "knowingly" has been used by the courts indirectly to indicate strict liability. In certain offences the word knowingly appears in one section but not in the next, or in some but not all subsections of a given section. Where this happens it is tempting to say that this is a clear indication that Parliament must have intended those sections which do not contain the word "knowingly" to impose strict liability. Thus in *Neville* v. *Mavroghenis* (1984) the accused was the landlord of rented premises and was charged with an offence under section 13(4) of the Housing Act 1961—failure to maintain premises in a proper state of repair. The stipendiary magistrate who tried the case held that since he was unaware of the defects he could not be liable. The prosecutor appealed. The Divisional Court held that section 13(4) could be divided into two limbs. The first limb contained the phrase "knowingly contravenes" and thus clearly required that the prosecution proved that he had knowledge of the defects. The second limb was in the form "without reasonable excuse fails to comply with any regulations." The word "knowingly" did not appear, and thus it was irrelevant that he was unaware of the defects. (See also *Cundy* v. *Le Coq* (1884) which is to the same effect.) It should, however, be noticed that in *Neville* v. *Mavroghenis* that the words "without reasonable excuse" in the second limb did at least provide the accused with a "no negligence" defence which is a decided improvement on strict liability with no such defence; see below, p. 108. In the *Pharmaceutical Society of Great Britain* v. *Storkwain* (1986) the House of Lords followed similar reasoning to hold that a provision of the Medicines Act 1968 which made it an offence to sell certain medicines without the prescription of an appropriate medical practitioner, created an offence of strict liability. The result was that an offence was committed by a pharmacist who had sold medicines on the strength of a forged prescription believing it to be genuine. However you must remember that although the presence of the work "knowingly" in one section and its absence in the next is a pointer in the direction of strict liability it must not be taken to be conclusive. In *Sherras* v. *De Rutzen* (1985) the accused was charged with selling alcohol to a police constable on duty. The defence submitted that the constable had removed his duty armband and so it was impossible for the accused to know that he was on duty. Against this it was argued that whereas other surrounding provisions of the statute used the word knowingly, section 16(2) of the Licensing Act 1872 did not. The Divisional Court quashed the conviction largely on the basis that without the requirement of knowledge the accused would be defenceless, since he would be convicted even if he had asked the constable whether he was on duty and the constable had told him falsely that he was not.

Wilfully and maliciously

We have already seen that the word "maliciously" generally connotes some degree of subjective awareness as defined in *Cunningham* (above, p. 59). This interpretation of the word would seem to survive the decision in *Caldwell*, though it is unlikely that any new statutes will use the word "maliciously."

"Wilfully," on the other hand, which suggests a full *mens rea* requirement, has been interpreted less consistently by the courts. Thus in *Cotterill* v. *Penn* (1936) D. was held unlawfully and wilfully to have killed a house pigeon when he shot a bird honestly thinking that it was a wild pigeon. Clearly the court took the work "wilfully" to mean that the prosecution must prove that the accused deliberately shot at the bird in question, but that it did not require the prosecution to prove that the accused knew that the bird was a house pigeon. However, in *Sheppard* (1981) the House of Lords held that where an accused was charged with an offence of wilfully neglecting a child in a manner likely to cause him unnecessary suffering or injury to health (contrary to section 1 of the Children and Young Persons Act 1933) the word wilful must be taken to apply both to the prohibited act (*i.e.* neglect) and to the consequences (*i.e.* unnecessary suffering). This was not, therefore, an offence of strict liability. Although the word "wilful" was held to apply to both parts of the offence, it was satisfied by what, in effect, amounted to *Caldwell* recklessness.

Conclusion

It is important to stress that these sort of "Key" words are useful guidelines, but you must not expect complete consistency from the courts.

(2) Crimes and quasi crimes

In *Warner* v. *M.P.C.* (1969) the issue of strict liability received attention for the first time from the House of Lords in a case relating to possession of drugs. The House of Lords gave its approval to the notion of strict liability. In *Sweet* v. *Parsley* (1970) four of the same Law Lords appeared to be suggesting a much stronger adherence to the presumption of *mens rea*. The *Sweet* case was not, however, in any sense a denial of strict liability. What their Lordships said was that there were two types of criminal offence: the first were those which could truly be said to be criminal such as murder, rape, theft and assault. These were to be distinguished from those which are not criminal in any really sense, but are acts which in the public interest are prohibited under a penalty. Crimes of this second type have been called regulatory offences, quasi crimes or crimes *mala prohibita*. In other words when Parliament makes regulations to govern the better running of society—such as regulations to ensure that food and drink are sold and served under hygienic conditions or regulations to prevent industry from polluting the environment—then it is common to sanction breaches of such regulations with a penalty, though no one really thinks of the offenders as criminals. The significance of the distinction is that in the former category (true crimes) the presumption in favour of *mens rea* should rarely, if at all, be rebutted, whereas in the second category it is easier to infer that Parliament intended the presumption to be rebutted. Thus whereas in *Sweet* v. *Parsley* the offence of "being concerned in the management of premises which are used for the purpose of smoking cannabis" was treated as a true crime (*mala in se*) which thus required *mens rea*, in *Alphacell Ltd.* v. *Woodward* (1972) the House of Lords treated the offence of "causing polluted matter to enter a river" as a regulatory offence and dispensed with the requirement for *mens rea*. The result was that the defendants in *Alphacell*, who has taken great care to ensure that they did not pollute the river, were convicted.

Recently in a case before the Privy Council concerning building regulations in Hong Kong, Lord Scarman found that the law could be summarised thus: "(1) there is a presumption of law that *mens rea* is required before a person can be held guilty of a criminal offence; (2) the presumption is particularly strong where the offence is "truly criminal" in character; (3) the presumption applies to statutory offences, and can be displaced only if this is clearly or by necessary implication the effect of the statute; (4) the only situation in which the presumption can be displaced is where the statute is concerned with an issue of social concern; public safety is such an issue; (5) even where statute is concerned with such an issue, the presumption of *mens rea* stands unless it can also be shown that the creation of strict liability will be effective to promote the objects of the statute by encouraging greater vigilance to prevent the commission of the prohibited act." (*Gammon* (*Hong Kong*) *Ltd.* v. *Att.Gen.* (1985)).

It is thus important that we are able to identify these crimes which are classified as "quasi crimes" or "offences of social concern." Clearly no definitive list could be provided, but the following areas should serve to provide some indication.

Sale of food and drink

Here there are many complicated regulations designed to ensure that hygiene prevails and also to ensure that customers are not given short measure. This area extends to the rules concerning the licensing of public houses. These crimes are prime examples of "regulatory offences" (see *Meah* v. *Roberts*, below, p. 108).

Laws governing the environment

Like clothing, strict liability has its fashions. At times of economic crises we see strict liability being applied in regulations designed to help the economic situation. In the sixties the concern seemed to be with drugs, while in the seventies pollution of the environment became one of the main topics concern. The argument here seems to be that there is a form of activity which is causing grave public concern and that breaches of the regulations designed to help the community should be subject to sanctions irrespective of whether the transgressor did it innocently or culpably. Such severe action, it is said, will serve to keep people on their toes.

Drugs

As mentioned in the previous paragraph increasing concern over drugs led to strict liability being imposed in the field of possession, etc., of dangerous drugs, but the recognition by the House of Lords that some of these offences fall into the category of true crimes has led to a softer approach being adopted by the courts and by the legislature in the Misuse of Drugs Act 1971.

Road traffic

Many road traffic offences are created by regulations and provide sanctions for beaches of rules designed to ensure that the vehicles are in a roadworthy condition; it is a good bet that most of these offences will be interpreted as imposing strict liability. Another group of offences deals with the way in which the vehicles are actually driven on the road. Into this category fall the offences relating to driving whilst under the influence of alcohol. Although these latter offences are now purely summary, the penalties can be severe and nearly always include a year's disqualification; but as we have already said, the courts have interpreted these offences as imposing strict liability. Speeding is clearly a crime of strict liability, careless driving is a crime of negligence and reckless driving and causing death by reckless driving which carries up to five years' imprisonment are crimes requiring some form of *mens rea*. Thus it would seem that as the maximum penalty increases the less likely the courts are to impose strict liability.

(3) Arbitrary lines

In many offences arbitrary lines are drawn. For example it is an offence for a man to have sexual intercourse with a girl who is a few minutes off her sixteenth birthday, whereas on the stroke of midnight the act would become perfectly lawful. Now it is quite clear that this law is based on the philosophy that young girls are not capable of giving meaningful consent either to older men who may be seeking to corrupt them or even to boys of their own age. Rather than expecting courts to try to determine whether or not a girl was capable of giving true consent, Parliament decided that all girls under 16 should be deemed incapable of giving consent to intercourse (hence in the United States this is called statutory rape). No one is suggesting that the few minutes between 11.55 pm and midnight are going to invest the girl with the wherewithal to make a true consent; the line that is drawn is totally arbitrary. However, where such lines are drawn one can expect the courts to dispense with the need for *mens rea* on that element.

(4) Smallness of the penalty

Another pointer to the way in which a court will interpret a given offence is the size of the penalty available. As a general rule the larger the penalty the less likely the court is to treat it as a crime involving strict liability. The reasoning behind this is that a heavy maximum penalty is an indication of Parliament's intention that the accused should be shown to be blameworthy. Whereas you can impose fines on blameless individuals, imprisonment should be reserved for those who are at least negligent. In *Gammon* (*Hong Kong*) *Ltd.* v. *Att.Gen.* (1985), however, Lord Scarman held that where the regulations were concerned with a matter of public safety it was quite proper that severe penalties could be imposed even for strict liability offences. He thus took the view that strict liability was needed in order to promote greater vigilance among builders and continued, "It must be crucially important that those who participate in or bear responsibility for the carrying out of works in a manner which complies with the requirements of the ordinance should know that severe penalties await them in the event of any contravention or non compliance with the ordinance by themselves. . . . "

At the end of the day there is no sure test to discover whether a statute has imposed strict liability. The above principles have been taken from cases. They are not applied consistently but provide some indication of how the courts will react when confronted with a new criminal offence.

3. DEFENCES TO OFFENCES OF STRICT LIABILITY

If we say that the offence is one of strict liability does this mean that the accused can have no defence to it? No, for that would be going too far. We have already said that where an offence is held to be one of strict liability, this usually means that the court has dispensed with the need to prove intention, recklessness or negligence as to one element of the *actus reus*, usually the central element. The practical effect is that on that one element the accused cannot raise the defence of mistake of fact, *even if his mistake was reasonable*. It possibly also means that the defence of impossibility will not apply to that element; thus where the accused is charged with failing, as the owner of a vehicle, to display the excise licence, it will be of no defence to show that it happened without any default of his own while he was away from the vehicle. However mistake of fact may well apply to other elements of the *actus reus* and the remaining general defences such as infancy, duress, necessity and automatism are possible defences to a charge. Let us consider a hypothetical example. The offence of driving having consumed too much alcohol requires that the prosecution prove that the accused was driving on a road or other public place. The notion of driving involves a mental element or at least the concept of voluntary conduct. Thus if the accused were to show that he had received a blow on the head immediately before he started to drive and this had produced a state of automatism, then he would be able to say that he was not "driving" the car. On the other hand a defence that he was unaware that he had consumed any alcohol since a friend had laced his drink would fail; liability on this element is strict and mistake of fact is no defence.

In Australia the courts have made attempts to lessen the rigours of strict liability by allowing the accused to plead by way of defence that he had taken all reasonable care. If we consider the example of a butcher who sells bad meat (an offence contrary to the Food and Drugs Act 1955, s.8), if such an approach were to be adopted, the prosecution would at first prove that the butcher had sold meat and that this meat had turned out to be bad. If nothing further is said then the butcher will be convicted. However if he can prove, on a balance of probabilities, that he had taken all reasonable precautions to ensure that the meat sold in his shop was sound, then he would be acquitted. Of course, this would be another exception to the rule in *Woolmington's* case which says that it is for the prosecution to prove guilt and not for the accused to prove his innocence. However if the alternative is strict liability with no such defence, then it is clearly an improvement from the point of view of the butcher. It would be an even greater improvement if the butcher merely had to introduce evidence that he had taken all reasonable care, leaving the prosecution to prove that he had taken all reasonable care.

We have not adopted such a general midway position in offences in strict liability. Occasionally the courts have held that a statute, which might have been expected to impose strict liability, did not, in fact impose strict liability, because there was nothing the accused could have done to protect himself. Thus in *Sherras* v. *De Rutzen* the court held that a statute making it an offence for a licensee to sell alcohol to a policeman on duty did not impose strict liability since this would have left him defenceless had the constable deliberately lied about being off duty. Similarly in *Lim Chin Aik* (1963) the Privy Council took the view that the imposition of strict liability is pointless unless there is something that the accused can do to prevent himself breaching the regulation.

It is becoming more common today for statutes which impose strict liability to contain express defences. Thus one type of defence consists of allowing the accused to escape conviction if he can prove that the contravention of the regulation was due to the fault of a third party and that he, the accused, took all reasonable precautions against breaking the regulations (see, *e.g.* the Food and Drugs Act 1955, s.113). More generally statutory defences take the form of casting the burden on the accused to prove that he was not negligent; thus we do specifically for some crimes what the Australian approach would suggest we should do for all crimes of strict liability. (See for example Trade Descriptions Act 1968, s.24; also *Neville* v. *Mavroghenis* above, p. 101).

An illustration

It will be useful at this point to consider a case in which many of the principles of strict liability were demonstrated. In *Meah* v. *Roberts* (1977) a family visited an Indian Restaurant in Canterbury. The father ordered lemonade for his two children which was served in glasses. After they had drunk some of the lemonade they began to scream and complain of burning in the mouth. The waiter examined the bottle from which he had poured the drink and discovered the word lemonade had been crossed out and the word "cleaner" had been printed in small letters underneath. It transpired that L, a fitter from Carlsberg Ltd., had recently been to the restaurant to clean the lager equipment for which he had used caustic soda. When he had finished he called over a waiter and explained to him the cleaning process and then left some of the cleaning fluid in an empty lemonade bottle which he placed under the bar. This bottle had been moved to the area where the lemonade bottles had been kept. It was also clear that Meah the manager had never taken any steps to acquaint himself with the cleaning process.

Meah was charged with selling food (lemonade) (i) which was intended for but was unfit for human consumption (contrary to section 8(1)(*a*) of the Food and Drugs Act 1955) and (ii) which was not of the nature of the food demanded by the purchaser (contrary to section 2(1) of the Act). Meah then brought third party proceedings (under section 113 of the 1955 Act) against L who he claimed was responsible for the breaches under sections 2 and 8, while Meah had used all due diligence to secure compliance with the terms of the Act.

At the trial Meah said that although it was obvious that caustic soda had been given to the children, sections 2 and 8 required a sale of the offending produce. (Section 2(1) provides 'If any person sells to the prejudice of the purchaser any food or drug which is not of the nature, or not of the substance, or not of the quality, of the food or drug demanded by the purchaser, he shall...be guilty of an offence." Section 8(1) provides "...any person who (a) sells...any food intended for, but unfit for, human consumption shall be guilty of an offence.") He argued that since the purchaser had ordered lemonade and had been mistakenly supplied with caustic soda, there was no sale of what was actually supplied. It is clear that although the sections impose strict liability, the prosecution must still prove a sale, and one might, as Meah, argue "how could you say I sold him the liquid. The mistake surely means that, in law, there was no sale." However the Divisional Court took the view that "sells...any food" in the two sections meant supplies, pursuant to an agreement to sell food, something purporting to be the food demanded by the purchaser. The fact that the article supplied was wholly different from the article demanded did not prevent there being a sale of the article demanded for the purpose of sections 2 and 8. Thus Meah had sold the offending liquid to the children and, of course, once a sale was proved, it was no defence to say he had made a mistake as to its nature. It would seem to follow that if X goes into a shop and asks for a bag of putty and is given in mistake, a pound of mouldy cheese, there would be no sale of food—since the product asked for was not food at all. Section 8(1)(a), however, also covers "offers or exposes for sale, or has in his possession for the purpose of sale..." and this would cover the mouldy cheese example.

Meah fared no better with his section 113 defence. This section provides that a person charged under the Act may bring before the court in the proceedings any person whom he claims was responsible for the default. The court was satisfied that L was responsible for Meah's breach of the regulations and so his conviction was upheld. L had argued that the third party proceedings could only be taken against somebody employed in the sale of the food, but the Divisional Court took the view that section 113 applied to any person who caused the contravention. However section 113 goes on to provide that if the original defendant, in addition to providing a scapegoat can also prove that he used all due diligence to ensure that the provisions in question were complied with he is entitled to an acquittal. The Divisional Court upheld the finding by the magistrates that although L was rightly convicted. Meah had not proved he had taken all due precautions, since he had failed to take steps to ensure that his staff did not get the cleaning fluid mixed up with the drinks. Meah's conviction, therefore, was also upheld.

4. Why Do We Have Crimes of Strict Liability At All?

Clearly from the point of view of the police and the prosecution, strict liability is an attractive proposition. It relieves them of the duty of proving *mens rea* on what is normally the most troublesome aspect of the *actus reus*. In our hypothetical butcher case, it will rarely trouble the prosecution that they have to prove that the accused intentionally sold a given piece of meat. Proof, however, that he knew or had reason to believe that the meat was bad would be far more difficult to find. Those who support the notion of strict liability would probably argue that to allow the butcher a defence of an honest or even an honest and reasonable mistake would surely undermine the efficacy of the legislation. Regulations relating to food and drink, public hygiene, road safety and pollution are designed for the benefit of the public and strict liability is essential to keep those involved in these areas on their toes by ensuring conviction for any breach however innocent. It was once said that if a town has built and is maintaining defences against a flood, if X does anything which causes the barrier to fall, it matters not whether he did it innocently or not.

Those who support strict liability would also say that the offences are by and large less serious offences and the penalties imposed are normally very light. In any event where the court is satisfied that the accused took all reasonable care this can be reflected in the sentence—he can be given an absolute discharge. How strong are such arguments? Do we really need crimes of strict liability?

The argument that it might be difficult to prove *mens rea* on a given element can be taken to extremes. The prosecution often find it extremely difficult to prove the *mens rea* of a murder charge, but rarely is the argument advanced that therefore murder should be a crime of strict liability.

Secondly, it is not very comforting for a butcher, who relies on his reputation to know that the court is sorry for his conviction and has awarded only an absolute discharge. The fact remains that he has been convicted and his conviction will probably be reported in the local press. The reader who may have been a customer of the butcher will not be concerned with the butcher's lack of culpability, merely with the fact that he sold bad meat.

This leaves the argument that strict liability is necessary to keep people on their toes. Such was clearly the major argument used by the Privy Council in the *Gammon* case (above p. 104) to support the imposition of strict liability. This has always appeared to be taking a sledge hammer to crack a nut. Clearly we want to do everything possible to ensure that butchers and those concerned in the sale of food and drink, for example, should take every precaution to ensure that their wares are fit for sale, but does this mean that we need strict liability to achieve it? Obviously the existence of strict liability makes a trader aware that he will need to exercise great care in his trade, but surely so would a defence that allowed him to prove (or raise evidence) that he took all reasonable care. Let us return finally to our neighbourhood butcher. He has sold a piece of meat which an inspector has found to be bad. There are several possibilities as to his mental state in relation to this sale. (i) He may have known that the meat was bad, and yet deliberately sold it. (ii) He may have suspected that the meat was bad, and yet taken the risk in selling it. (iii) He may not have suspected the meat to have been bad, although reasonable steps would have shown this to be the case. (iv) He may not have suspected the meat to be bad and reasonable steps would not have revealed this to him. Clearly we would want to convict those in categories (i) and (ii). In this area we may want to convict in situation (iii) since we would want butchers to take reasonable steps and we would probably not complain if a sloppy butcher was fined. However what do we achieve by convicting number (iv). By our very definition we have said that even the taking of reasonable steps would not have revealed to him that his meat was bad. Knowledge that he would be convicted however much care he has taken would keep him on his toes, but so would knowledge that he would be convicted if he could not prove that he had taken all reasonable steps. Common sense would seem to suggest that the line should be drawn between (iii) and (iv) and that nothing is gained from convicting the accused in case (iv).

It may well be, as the Court said in *Sheppard* (1981), that in recent years the climate of judicial opinion has grown less favourable to the recognition of strict liability offences. It remains equally true, however, that this category of offences remains far from being dead and buried.

CHAPTER 5

PARTIES TO CRIMINAL OFFENCES

I. *PRINCIPAL AND SECONDARY OFFENDERS*

WHEN a criminal offence is committed attention is primarily focused on the perpetrator. In a case of murder the police will look for the killer, in a case of burglary the person who entered the building as a trespasser, in a case of criminal damage the person who caused the damage and so on. However a moment's reflection tells us that if the criminal law were concerned only with the perpetrator it would be seriously defective. Someone who helps the perpetrator (for example by providing the gun for a killing, or a key for a burglary) ought also to incur liability for the crime. In some cases the helper may indeed have played a much more significant part than the perpetrator for he may have been the one who conceived and planned the offence. On the other hand a point is reached at which the assistance given is so remote that it would be unfair or unrealistic to make the helper a party to the crime. In a well-known civil case (*Lloyd* v. *Johnson* (1798)) it was held that a laundress could recover from a prostitute the cost of washing expensive dresses and some gentlemen's nightcaps though the laundress knew well that the dresses were used for the purpose of enticing men in public places. In such circumstances the laundress could hardly be regarded as a party to the prostitutes's offence of soliciting. Once again the task of the law is to draw the line at the appropriate place.

Our starting point should be section 8 of the Accessories and Abettors Act 1861 (as amended by the Criminal Law Act 1977). This provides "Whosoever shall aid, abet, counsel or procure the commission of any indictable offence whether the same be an offence at common law or by virtue of any Act passed or to be passed, shall be liable to be tried, indicted and punished as a principal offender." There are similar provisions in relation to summary offences. Until 1967 offences were either felonies or misdemeanours and in the case of felonies various degrees of

112

participation were identified. The actual perpetrator of the offence was known as the principal in the first degree, anyone who was present at the scene of the crime and gave assistance was known as the principal in the second degree, while anyone who gave assistance before the commission of the crime but who was not present at the scene was designated an accessory before the fact. A person who gave assistance to the felony after the offence was called an accessory after the fact. With the passing of the Criminal Law Act 1967 the distinction between felonies and misdemeanours was abolished and section 8 of the Accessories and Abettors Act became applicable to all indictable offences, with the resulting disappearance of the above classifications. Today it is more normal to refer to the actual perpetrator of the offence as the principal offender and all the others who assisted in the commission of the offence as the secondary parties, or accessories, and these are the terms we shall use in this chapter.

From a procedural point of view it is not necessary to distinguish in the indictment between principal and secondary offenders—all can be indicted as having committed the offence—provided that at the trial the prosecution can prove that the offence was in fact committed by someone and that those on trial are either principal or secondary parties. However, the House of Lords has indicated that it is desirable that in the particulars of the offence given in the indictment the prosecution should indicate whether he is charged as a perpetrator or secondary party so that he is better able to meet the evidence to be brought against him. Once convicted they are all liable to the same penalty. This was brought home in a dramatic way by the case of *Craig and Bentley* (1952) where following a rooftop chase Bentley was arrested by police officers following a robbery. He called out to Craig "Let him have it Chris" and Craig shot and killed a police officer. Both were indicted and convicted of murder. Craig was too young to face the death penalty and he was sentenced to life imprisonment, but Bentley, who was in police custody at the time of the killing, was hanged.

Three points should be noted before we go any further: (i) a person does not become a secondary party to a crime until that crime is either committed or attempted by the principal. If B supplies A with a gun in order to kill X, B becomes a party to the murder only when A kills X, though he will be a party to an attempt if A attempts to kill X and fails; (ii) both section 8 of the Accessories and Abettors Act 1861 and the Criminal Law

Act 1967 were designed to improve criminal procedure and not to affect substantive criminal liability. Thus the old cases are authoritative on the question of who is a participant in a given crime. Today, however, we do not need as a general rule to distinguish between the various types of secondary participation; (iii) With the abolition by the Criminal Law Act 1967 of felonies, the old offence of being an accessory after the fact to a felony automatically lapsed. However section 4 of the Act introduces a new offence of assisting arrestable offenders which has similar features to the old offence (below, p. 136).

1. The Principal or Perpetrator

Suppose that A, B and C are charged with the murder of X. The evidence establishes that they had agreed to kill X, that all were present at the time of the killing, and that X was killed by a single stab wound. All deny striking the fatal blow and the evidence does not establish which was the perpetrator though it was clearly one of them. It would be the height of absurdity if the law provided in such a case that all three should be aquitted and of course they are not. All three may be convicted of murder and on conviction all three must be sentenced to imprisonment for life.

In this illustration there is no need to isolate the principal, but sometimes this is necessary because the rules relating to his liability differ from those of secondary parties. One situation in which it is necessary to draw a sharp distinction between the principal offender and secondary party is where the offence is one of strict liability (see above, p. 94). We have seen that a person may be made liable for certain offences even though he lacks *mens rea*. But strict liability is imposed only on the principal offender and is not imposed on secondary parties. In *Callow* v. *Tillstone* (1900) the principal offender was a butcher who was charged with exposing bad meat for sale. He had got a vet to examine a carcase of a heifer which had eaten yew leaves. The vet passed it fit for sale and relying on the vet's certificate the principal offender put it up for sale. The offence was one of strict liability and the principal offender was therefore convicted. The justices also convicted the vet as they found that he had been negligent in issuing the certificate. On appeal the vet's conviction was quashed since he did not know nor was he reckless as to the meat being bad. It may strike the reader as a trifle odd that the principal offender was held liable even though he was entirely blameless while the secondary party (the vet) was not liable though he was at fault in the sense that he was negligent. However the courts have taken the view that strict liability applies only to the principal offender. The reason for all this is that liability for secondary participation arises at common law and criminal liability at common law generally requires *mens reas* in the form of intention, knowledge or *Cunningham* recklessness. You could argue that this is illogical since if there are good policy reasons for imposing strict liability on the principal there are equally good reasons for imposing it on the secondary offenders—but the law is not always logical.

A similar situation may arise in relation to vicarious liability (see below, p. 138). Under this doctrine the licensee of a public house who is away from the premises may be held liable for the crimes committed by his employee whom he has left in charge at the pub. However, if the employee is only liable as a secondary party, for example he has aided and abetted customers consuming alcohol after hours, the licensee cannot be vicariously liable (see below, p. 142). Thus in this situation we need to know whether the employee is a principal or secondary party.

So how is the principal to be marked off from the secondary parties? Normally this presents no problems. A shoots and kills X with a gun provided by B. A is the perpetrator or principal and B is a secondary party to it. C enters a building to steal while D keeps a watch outside; C is the principal offender in the burglary and D is the secondary party. However it is not always as clear as this. Suppose that E holds Y while F stabs him and Y dies as a result. Is E a principal offender or a secondary party? (It is possible to have more than one principal offender). If E had merely decoyed Y to the place where F stabbed him, then E would clearly only be a secondary party. Does he become a principal by holding Y so that Y cannot defend himself against F's murderous attack? This case is clearly right on the borderline. If the crime had been rape and E had held Y down while F had intercourse with her, you could hardly say that E was the perpetrator of the rape—you could not really say that E raped Y. On the other hand if E holds Y while F punches him you could say that E and F are co-perpetrators of an assault since for E to hold Y against his will is in itself an assault. But where E holds Y so that F can stab him it may be unrealistic to say that E killed Y: what he has done is to help F kill Y.

The principal offender is, therefore, any person (or persons) who by his own conduct directly brings about the *actus reus* of the crime. This formulation may not, however, suffice for all cases. Suppose that A puts poison in X's medicine knowing that B a nurse will innocently administer the poison to X in the course of her duties. Or suppose that C persuades D, a nine year old boy, to steal from Y. Neither B, since she lacks *mens rea,* nor D, since he is under the age of criminal responsibility (see below, 188) can be charged as parties either to the killing of X or the stealing from Y. In both cases it might be said that A and C did not directly bring about the *actus reus* of the respective crimes. Common sense, however, tells us that A killed X and C stole from Y and the formulation at the beginning of this paragraph should be taken to include such cases. (In the cases, B and D are often referred to as innocent agents; thus we say that A killed X through the innocent agency of B. It is probably safer and simpler to say—can we drop B out of the picture and say A killed X?)

2. SECONDARY PARTIES

From the discussion in the preceding section we can say that a secondary party (sometimes called an accessory) is, broadly speaking, someone who helps to bring about the crime without being the actual perpetrator. Such a broad definition, though it will probably suffice for most cases, is not sufficiently refined to deal precisely with all the cases that can arise.

It might be thought that the position of a secondary party was exactly the same as that of a principal. After all section 8 of the Accessories and Abettors Act 1861 provides that he is liable "to be indicted and tried as if he were a principal offender." However this is not really so and the liability of the secondary party turns out to be rather more complex than that of the principal. Suppose that A and B are charged with a crime and it is alleged that A is the perpetrator and that B is the secondary party. Against A it has to be proved that he by his own conduct directly caused the *actus reus* with the appropriate *mens rea.* Against B it has to be proved that:

    (i) he knew that A would cause the *actus reus* with the appropriate *mens rea; and*

    (ii) that he helped A to commit that crime knowing that his conduct would be of assistance to A.

You may say that the proposition (ii) includes proposition (i), but this way of setting out the requirements in relation to B serves to emphasise that the *mens rea* of a secondary party extends not only to knowledge of the principal's *mens rea* but also requires a further intention to help the principal; and, in the case of the secondary party, not only has it to be shown that the *actus reus* of the crime was brought about but also that there was some conduct of the accessory which helped the commission of that crime.

It follows, therefore, that B cannot be convicted as an accessory to A's crime merely because he knows that A will commit the crime. B may learn that A plans to murder X or burgle Y's premises but this knowledge alone is not enough to make B a party to the killing of X or the burgling of Y's premises. It can make no difference that, on learning of A's intention, B is secretly delighted because he will inherit under X's will or because Y is someone he hates. An even more extreme illustration is provided by the case of *Allan* (1963). Allan was present when some of his friends became involved in a fight. He knew that his friends were committing a crime, but not only did he approve of their conduct, he had secretly resolved to help them should they require his aid. His conviction, however, as a party to the crimes committed by his friends was quashed because knowledge of the principal's crime coupled with an intention to aid is not enough unless there is also some conduct of the accessory which helps the principal.

So what exactly has to be proved against the accessory to make him a party to the principal's crime? Simply put it must be shown that with knowledge of the principal's crime the accessory did something to help in its commission with the intention of assisting; though in detail the position may be more complicated.

(1) Knowledge of the type of crime

First, the requirement of knowledge of the principal's crime does not require that B should know of every detail of A's planned crime. Take a case where A plans to steal money from a safe at a particular factory and needs cutting equipment for this purpose. He contacts B and purchases this equipment from him making no mention whatever of his plans. B, however, knows that A has a record for burglary, that he has no legitimate business for which such equipment could be required and guesses (correctly) that it is required to break into a safe on some premises or other. Nevertheless B supplies the equipment. B may be convicted as an accessory to the burglary committed by A though B has no idea when or where the crime is to be committed. The point is that he knows the essentials of the crime. But *Bainbridge* (1960) on which the last illustration was based shows that it is not enough to make B liable that he knew that A was up to no good—that would be far too vague. It was also accepted in that case that B would would not be liable if his only suspicion was that A planned to commit some different type of crime, such as receiving stolen metal and that the cutting equipment was to be used to break it up.

So the accessory will not escape liability saying that it was a case of no-questions-asked if he, in fact, realised what the principal was up to. Moreover, it is enough that the principal commits one of a range of crimes which was in the contemplation of the accessory. In *D.P.P for Northern Ireland* v. *Maxwell* (1978) Maxwell's task had been to lead Northern Ireland terrorists to a public house in a village where they left a bomb. He claimed that he could not be convicted as a party to the bombing since he did not know what the terrorists had planned to do. The House of Lords held that from his knowledge of the organisation he knew that the mission would take one of a number of forms and it was sufficient that the actual deed that night fell within the bounds of one of the offences he must have contemplated.

In most cases the test propounded in *Maxwell* will provide a ready answer. However one or two questions remained unanswered. For example if B suspects A is about to commit burglary and the equipment he has supplied will be used to force open the windows of the premises will he be liable if A's plan, which he carries out, is to rape a girl who lives there? Your immediate reaction will be to say that this is an entirely different crime from the one B contemplated. However where A enters the house as a trespasser with intent to rape someone inside this is burglary contrary to section 9(1)(*a*) of the Theft Act 1968 (see below, p. 323) and burglary is the very crime B contemplated. Perhaps the courts would take a common sense view in these sorts of case and hold that B should not be convicted as a party to a particular crime he almost certainly would not have supported. Another problem is that once B has supplied the equipment A can go on using it indefinitely for the type of crime B had in mind. Does B become a party to all the future crimes A commits with the equipment? This may seem rather hard on B but there is nothing technically to stop such liability arising.

We have said so far that the secondary party must know that the principal offender will commit a particular offence or one of a known group of offences. Knowledge here includes wilful blindness and so B would be liable if he guesses that A is about to commit a burglary with the equipment he is supplying and deliberately asks no questions so that he can say that he did not know what A is about. (Wilful blindness would seem to lie somewhere between intention and recklessness.) The court appears to have gone even further in *Carter* v. *Richardson* (1974) where A was a learner driver under the supervision of B. They were involved in an accident and it was discovered that A was over the prescribed alcohol limit. Here B was held to have knowledge of the crime even though he could not *know* that A was over the prescribed limit; he did, however, know that A might be over the prescribed limit and his recklessness constitutes sufficient knowledge for this purpose. So far as A in this case was concerned we have already seen that the offence is one of strict liability (above, p. 94) but as you are already aware *mens rea* must always be proved in a secondary party. Presumably what has to be shown against B is that he knew that A had been drinking and deliberately took the risk that A was over the prescribed limit.

(2) Liability for unforseen consequences

It follows from the foregoing discussion that while B may be liable for such crimes committed by A as were in B's contemplation, he is not liable for crimes committed by A that he does not contemplate at all. We have just seen that where B supplies cutting equipment to A knowing of its use in connection with a burglary that B becomes an accessory to the burglary. Suppose then, that as part of the burglary, A attacked X, a nightwatchman, and rendered him unconscious. B is not a party to the assault on X which was uncontemplated by him; the fact that B contemplated one crime (burglary) and that during the commission of that crime another (assault) was committed is not enough to make B liable as a party to the further crime. In relation to the assault B is totally lacking in *mens rea*.

In this example it is assumed that B supplies the equipment some days before the burglary and is not present at its commission. Does it, therefore, make any difference if B accompanies A on the burglarious expedition? The answer is that it makes no difference whether B is present or absent from the scene of the crime. B is liable only for such crime or crimes of A that he contemplates A will commit, intending to assist in their commission. Thus if B had accompanied A but had been totally unaware of the presence of the nightwatchman and had never contemplated that force would be used on any person, he could not be a party to A's assault.

Thus in *Jubb and Rigby* (1984) it was clear that the appellants had gone to the house of an elderly man in order to rob him. Six days later the man's body was discovered hidden under a carpet at the house. The appellants had been charged with the murder of the man and both sought to lay the blame for the violence on the other. Now it is quite clear that in such a case the jury must first be satisfied that the murder had been committed by at least one of the appellants. Once they are satisfied of this they may convict both appellants of the murder provided that they are also sure that the violence was within the scope of the concerted action of both appellants. Following recent guidance from the Privy Council in *Chan Wing-Siu* (1984) the Court of Appeal held that a trial judge should tell the jury that they may convict both parties provided the prosecution has proved that each knew that the joint venture would probably involve killing. Clearly it should also suffice if the prosecution have proved that each knew that the joint venture would probably involve grievous bodily harm. The use of the word "probably" is arguably too generous to the accused and certainly more so than the actual speeches of the Privy Council in *Chan Wing-Siu*. In *Siu* the Privy Council was seeking to exclude a situation where one party had given thought to the possibility that the other might use violence but had dismissed the possibility from his mind as being altogether negligible. Most bank robbers probably contemplate that occasionally they may have to overcome resistance by force, but that in the great majority of robberies no force will be needed because the sight of a gun will keep most people quiet. Thus we should want to say of these robbers that killing or grievous bodily harm was within the joint venture, but we cannot really say that they thought that their joint venture would probably involve killing or grievous bodily harm. It should suffice that the secondary party knew that there was a real risk that the venture would result in death or grievous bodily harm. In other words a risk greater than one which could have been dismissed as altogether negligible. It seems odd that provided the principal offender intended to cause death or serious harm, the secondary party can be held liable for murder provided he contemplated that there was a real risk that the gun would be used to cause death or serious harm (see *Moloney,* above, p. 22).

In *Smith* v. *Mellors and Soar* (1987) the two defendants were charged with driving a car over the prescribed limit (contrary to Road Traffic Act 1988, section 5 see above, p. 94). The evidence against them was that they were seen running away from a car and that later tests showed that the alcohol level in their blood was over the prescribed limit. The police were unable to identify which of them had been driving, but the magistrates found that the defendants were the only occupants of the car at a time when it was being driven on public roads. However, the magistrates were not prepared to find that each defendant knew that the other was over the prescribed limit and, since the police could not prove which was the driver, acquitted both. On appeal by the prosecutor the Divisional Court held that in the particular case, the decision was a reasonable one. On the other hand, in certain circumstances it would not matter who was driving. As long as the prosecutor could prove that two persons were going for a ride, each knowing that the other had consumed excess alcohol, the magistrates would be entitled to convict both. The Court did not answer the question whether the prosecutor would have to establish that a secondary party actually knew that the driver was over the prescribed limit; this would be almost impossible to prove. It is submitted that it would suffice if the secondary party deliberately took the risk that the driver was over the prescribed limit (*i.e. Cunningham* recklessness; see also *Foreman and Ford* (1988) and *Collins and Fox* (1988)).

In general terms, therefore, it can be said that B (even if he accompanies A for the purposes of carrying out the crime) is not a party to other crimes committed by A which were unforeseen by B. This does not mean that B escapes liability because A has deviated from the precise terms of that plan. If B counsels A to kill X by poisoning and A shoots X, B will be a party to the murder of X. If B counsels A to steal X's silver plate and A steals X's gold plate, B will be a party to the theft. Moreover B may be liable for a consequence unforseen by him if that consequence is one for which A is liable even though it was equally unforeseen by him. Suppose that B counsels A to kill X; A shoots at X, misses and kills Y. As we have seen, A will be liable for the death of Y (above, p. 77) by virtue of the doctrine of transferred malice. Since A is liable for the death of

Y even though that consequence was unforeseen by him, B will be liable as an accessory even though Y's death was also unforeseen by him. If however, B counsels A to kill C, but A deliberately deviates from the plan and kills D, B cannot be liable for that killing; if, however he had incited A to kill C (see below, p. 213) he can be charged with that offence (*Leahy* (1985)).

Now we can have a look at a rather more complex example. Suppose that A, B and C plan to burgle X's house in the night at a time when the occupants are expected to be asleep. They plan to steal certain valuable antiques. A and B are to enter the house and C is to remain outside in his car with the engine running. B knows that A carries a loaded revolver; C does not know this but knows that A has a reputation for violence. A and B enter the house. During the enterprise B commits various acts of vandalism by slashing furniture and furnishings with a razor. As they are about to leave they are surprised by X. A fires at him, misses and the bullet travels through the door killing Y, X's wife, who was standing behind it. If we consider the various crimes in turn:

(a) *The burglary*

This presents no problems. A and B are joint principals and C is an accessory. Though the point is unimportant A and B are also joint principals in theft. Could C say that he was not a party to the theft if some of the articles taken were not antiques? Probably not. (He could not deny liability for burglary since this arose the moment A and B entered the house with the intent to steal). He could do so if the compact was for the taking of antiques and nothing else but this is unlikely in the extreme. If C contemplated that other articles would be taken, and he would surely contemplate that A and B would appropriate any money they found lying about the house, he will be a secondary party to the theft of articles other than the antiques.

(b) *Criminal damage*

B is the principal offender here. Whether C will be held to be an accessory depends upon whether he knows of B's proclivities. It is not at all uncommon for burglars to be given to vandalising the premises they burgle; if C knows that B is given to this activity, he is a party to the criminal damage if he contemplates that B will commit it on this occasion—even if he hopes that B will not (see *C* v. *Hume* (1979)). If C has no such knowledge then he cannot be a party to the criminal damage. A's position as an accessory to criminal damage is essentially the same. (It should be noted that under s.9(1)(*b*) it is burglary, having entered premises as a trespasser, to commit criminal damage to the property. Thus the unresolved point discussed at p. 118 above could arise here. Both A and C contemplate burglary and this has occurred though in a form they did not contemplate).

(c) *Murder and manslaughter*

By virtue of the doctrine of transferred malice A is liable for the death of Y and will be liable to be convicted of murder or manslaughter depending upon his *mens rea*; murder if he intended to kill or cause serious bodily harm, manslaughter if he merely intended to frighten X. As for C, it is clearly not enough to make him liable in respect of Y's death that he knew that A was given to violence. But suppose that C contemplated that the householders might be awakened by the burglary and contemplated that A would use force against anyone who disturbed him. Here the fact that C is unaware of the gun is crucial. In *Davies* v. *D.P.P.* (1954) there was a fight between two rival gangs on Clapham Common. Basically what started as a punch-up ended with a member of one gang, Davies, stabbing to death a member of the rival gang. It was held by the House of Lords that Lawson, another member of Davies' gang, was not an accessory to murder since he did not know that Davies had a knife. It is clear that Lawson was not an accomplice in manslaughter either since it was said that he was not an accomplice "in the use of the knife." If, however, the death had occurred as a result of a blow struck by Davies' fist, then Lawson would have been an accessory to manslaughter. As we have seen a secondary party is liable for a consequence unforeseen by him if the crime is one in which the principal is liable for that unforeseen consequence. Manslaughter by an unlawful act is such a crime (below, p. 228) so that Lawson becomes party to manslaughter if he is a party to the form of violence which causes the death.

It follows in our example that C's ignorance of the gun insulates him from liability for the death of Y.

B's position is quite different because he knew that A had loaded the gun. If B realised that there was a real risk that A, if disturbed, would used the gun to seriously injure or kill another then B would be a party to murder. If B realised that there was a real risk that A would use the gun to frighten and A so used it, then B would be a party to manslaughter. In neither case does it make a scrap of difference that Y's death may have been unforeseen.

Suppose that B thought that A had taken the gun to give himself Dutch courage and that A would not use it. Strictly speaking B would not be a party to the death of Y. As a matter of fact, though, any jury is likely to give short shrift to such a claim by B when he knew of the loaded gun and knew that they were burgling occupied premises in the night. More realistically B may claim that he thought that the gun would only be used to frighten and that A would not use it with intent to kill. What then if it is accepted that B realised that the gun would be used to frighten and A then used it with a deliberate intent to kill or cause serious bodily harm? B cannot be guilty of murder because he does not share, and indeed is quite unaware of A's intent to kill. But surely, it might be said, that B is guilty of manslaughter because he had sufficient *mens rea* for that crime and there is an *actus reus*. *Anderson and Morris* (1966) however suggests otherwise. Following an attack by Welch on Anderson's wife, Anderson armed himself with a knife and, accompanied by Morris, went in search of Welch. When Welch was found he was attacked by Anderson who stabbed him to death. The judge instructed the jury that if they were satisfied that Morris took part in the assault they could convict him of manslaughter even if he was unaware that Anderson had a knife. This was clearly wrong and Morris's conviction was quashed but the Court of Criminal Appeal went on to indicate that even if Morris was aware that Anderson had the knife and that he planned to assault Welch, Morris would incur liability neither for murder nor manslaughter if, unbeknown to Morris, Anderson formed an intention to kill. This may seem a very generous result so far as Morris was concerned; after all if Anderson had used the knife with intent to frighten Welch and had accidentally caused his death, Anderson would have been convicted of manslaughter and Morris would have been an accessory. But the decision can be defended; Morris may have been prepared to help Anderson to assault Welch without being at all prepared to help Anderson to kill him.

In *Dunbar* (1988) the defendant was charged with murder along with two co-defendants whom, it was alleged, she had incited to kill her former lover. In her defence she said that she may have remarked that she would like to see him dead, and further that she suspected that the two co-defendants might burgle her former lover's house and that they might inflict some injuries upon him at that time. She was convicted of manslaughter. The Court of Appeal, however, held that a manslaughter verdict was not open to the jury. Either she was a party to the infliction of death or grievous bodily harm in which case she was guilty of murder, or she was a party to the infliction of some lesser harm, in which case the actual harm inflicted was not within the contemplated plan and she would not be a party to the unlawful homicide. The Court said that the law was correctly stated in *Anderson and Morris*.

(3) Aids, abets, counsels or procures

In addition to providing that the secondary party knew of the crime the principal intended to commit, the prosecution must prove that the secondary party helped the principal with intent to do so. In fact section 8 uses neither the words "help" nor "assistance" and imposes liability where the accessory "aids, abets, counsels or procures" the crime. Basically these verbs convey the idea of help or assistance but in the end we have to consider the precise interpretation of the words used in the statute itself. This was the important point made by the Court of Appeal in *Att.-Gen.'s Reference (No. 1 of 1975)* (1975) when it was said that these words must be given their ordinary meaning. Obviously the words overlap to some extent. If A and B meet X and B encourages A to assault X we may indifferently say that B aids, abets, counsels or procures A to assault X. On the other hand each word may contain nuances of meaning not conveyed by the others; *Att.-Gen.'s Reference (No. 1 of 1975)* illustrates the point. B added alcohol to A's drink without A's knowledge and A's subsequent driving of a car resulted in him being prosecuted under the breathalyser provisions. It was held that B had procured the commission of the offence by A. The court rejected an argument that the secondary participation always requires communication between the accessory and the perpetrator and held that a crime could be procured (*i.e.* brought about by endeavour) though there was no communication between the secondary and principal offenders. The court did not attempt an exhaustive definition of the remaining verbs but it would now be unwise to assume that they are synonymous. (See *Calhaem* (1985).)

(a) *Conduct amounting to aiding, abetting, counselling or procuring*

At all events there must be some conduct of the secondary party which can properly be said to amount to an aiding, etc. *Allan* (above, p. 117 shows that a secret intention to assist without any assistance in fact is not enough. (See also *Att.-Gen.* v. *Able* (1984) below p. 128.) On the other hand very little assistance may, in fact be required, and words alone may suffice. It would have been enough had Allan shouted encouragement to the principals or even if he had said "give me a call if you need a hand."

An interesting problem was posed by the speeches of their Lordships in the case of *Gillick* v. *West Norfolk and Wisbeach Area Health Authority and Another* (1986). It is clear that it is an offence for a man to have intercourse with a girl who is under 16 years of age. It is also clear that it would be an offence for another to aid, abet, counsel or procure that man to have intercourse with the girl. A doctor who prescribes contraceptive pills for a 15 year old girl knows that he is making it more likely that she will have intercourse. It ought to follow, therefore, that the doctor is a secondary party to that intercourse. Their Lordships recognised this possibility and said that a doctor may, in some circumstances, prescribe for a 15 year old girl without attracting secondary party liability. They did not, however, explain how this could be so. (See further the commentary by Professor Smith in [1986] Crim.L.R. 113.)

Presence as aiding, etc. If a shout or two of encouragement is enough to constitute aiding, why should not mere presence suffice? A may be just as much encouraged by the presence of B as by a word of encouragement. Clearly B's accidental presence cannot suffice but the reason for this is that B would then lack any intention to aid. But what if B then stays to watch? When terrorists seized the Iranian Embassy in London, their illegal activities were closely watched for some days by hordes of newsmen and, through the medium of television, by many millions of viewers. In a very real sense the terrorists drew encouragement from this for one of their primary aims was to secure publicity for their cause. Common sense tells us that the newsmen were not accessories to the continued imprisonment of the Embassy staff and the case of *Clarkson* (1971) strikingly bears this out. In that case B and C did not become secondary parties to rape merely because, to satisfy their prurient interest, they watched fellow soldiers repeatedly rape a girl in their barracks.

Presence, however, if it is not accidental constitutes some evidence of aiding, etc., though it must be considered along with all the other evidence. Thus presence coupled with evidence of a previous conspiracy between the parties to commit the crime will suffice. In *Coney* (1882), however, it was held to be a misdirection to direct a jury that (non-accidental) presence at a fight was conclusive evidence of aiding. No doubt his decision was right, but presence at an illegal activity which requires spectators if it is to prosper at all may more readily give rise to an inference of aiding and abetting than presence at other illegal activities. In *Wilcox* v. *Jeffrey* (1951) B was convicted of aiding and abetting A (the celebrated jazz saxophonist Coleman Hawkins) to play in public contrary to the conditions on which he was allowed to enter England. The Divisional Court thought it right in such a case to invite the jury to infer aiding from presence throughout the illegal performance together with the fact that B had met A at the airport and had written an account of the performance in the newspaper for which he worked. Suppose then that in *Allan* the trial judge had directed the jury that Allan's continued presence at the fight could be regarded as evidence of aiding, and that the jury had convicted him. Would the Court of Appeal have quashed his conviction?

Aiding, etc., by omission. The last question raises another problem. Is B liable for A's crime because he fails to intervene to prevent it or to put a stop to it? The general answer must be *No*, because there is no general duty to prevent the commission of crime by others. Exceptionally there may be circumstances where B is under a duty to take positive steps to prevent the commission of a crime by A. In an Australian case *Russell* (1933) it was held that a father was a secondary party to the homicide of his children where he stood by and watched the mother drown them (see also *Gibson* (1984)). In *Du Cros* v. *Lambourne* (1907) it was held that B could be convicted of aiding A to drive dangerously where A was driving B's car with his permission and was, to B's knowledge, driving it dangerously.

A difficult problem may be experienced where a group of people are sharing a flat and A discovers that B has possession of a controlled drug. Is A expected to leave the flat? If he stays will he be in danger of being held to have given passive encouragement to B? In *Bland* (1988) the Court of Appeal held that you could not get evidence of passive assistance merely from the fact that people live together. You would need evidence that A either encouraged B or that A had the right to control B's activities.

(b) *The mental element in aiding, etc.*

It has been pointed out that a secondary party's *mens rea,* in a sense, requires two elements: (i) knowledge of the principal's *mens rea* and (ii) an intent to aid the principal in the commission of his crime. The former of these requirements has been examined in some detail above; it is now necessary to say something more about the latter. Clearly B does not become a party to A's crime if, knowing of it, he accidentally helps in its commission as where B, knowing that A intends to steal from C's safe, absentmindedly fails to lock the safe. The words "aids, abets, counsels or procures" suggest purposive conduct on B's part.

In *Att.-Gen.* v. *Able* (1984) the Attorney General took civil proceedings to prevent further distribution of a booklet entitled "A Guide to Self Deliverance." The booklet had been published by the executive committee of a society designed to promote voluntary euthanasia. The aim of the booklet was to overcome the fear of dying and to reduce the number of unsuccessful suicides. In the book there were descriptions of various methods of suicide together with suggestions as to the most efficient and least painful methods of suicide. The booklet was available only to persons who had been members of the society for three months and who were over 25. The Attorney General sought a declaration that future supply of the booklet to persons who were known to be or were likely to be, considering or intending to commit suicide would constitute the offence of aiding, abetting, counselling or procuring suicide (Suicide Act 1961, s.2(1); below, p. 234). The Divisional Court made it clear that although it was permissible for the Attorney General to use the civil law in this way, it would only grant such a declaration if it was sure that the conduct in question would clearly be in contravention of the criminal law. Woolf J. said that the Attorney General had to establish three elements; (1) that the supplier intended the book to be used by, and to assist or otherwise encourage, a person actually contemplating suicide; and (2) that while so intending he supplied the book to such person; and (3) that the person then read it and was assisted or encouraged by reading it to commit suicide or attempt to do so. Since it would be for a jury to decide whether or not the necessary intent under head (1) existed, the Court was not in a position to say that the future supply of the book would, in every case, either be or would not be an offence; thus a declaration was inappropriate. (Would proof of heads (1) and (2) amount to an attempt to commit the offence under section 2(1)? See below, p. 197.

Suppose, however, that A plans to burgle X's house and he asks B to drive him to a specified destination. B does so and A burgles the house. B's liability may be considered on various hypotheses:

(1) If B believes that A's enterprise is an innocent one then B cannot incur criminal liability.

(2) If B knows what A plans and is willing to drive him to and from the scene of the crime he is evidently a party to A's crime.

(3) B is a taxi driver whom A has engaged at the normal commercial rates. B knows that A plans to burgle A's home but considers that this is none of his business. B reasons that if he refuses his services then another taxi driver (who does not have B's knowledge of A's intentions) will readily be found by A. Why, B asks himself, should he lose a fare when the crime will be committed anyway? A problem similar to this arose in *National Coal Board* v. *Gamble* (1959) where the defendants, the National Coal Board, had supplied X with coal. The procedure was that X's drivers filled up their lorries at the Coal Board's depot and then drove the loaded lorries on to a weighbridge. If the weight shown was correct the weighbridge operator issued the driver with a ticket at which time the court held that ownership of the goods passed to X. Under the Motor Vehicle (Construction and Use) Regulations it is an offence to drive a lorry on a public road when the load exceeds a certain weight. On the occasion in question the weighbridge operator saw that the lorry was overloaded and commented on this fact to the driver. The driver replied that he would take the risk and a ticket was issued. The driver committed the offence immediately he drove onto the road, but the difficult question was whether or not the Coal Board was liable as a secondary party (through the action of their employee). It seems clear that although the weighbridge operator did not want to help the driver commit an offence; he could not have cared less whether the driver was picked up for contravening the regulations or not. On the other hand he did know all the facts which constituted the offence and his action in issuing a ticket enabled the driver to commit the offence. The Divisional Court held that

this was enough to make the weighbridge operator (and therefore the Board) a secondary party. Thus it is sufficient that X performs an act which he knows will assist Y in the commission of a crime.

(4) Now suppose that B hopes that A will be unable to commit the burglary. Let us say that he hopes that on arrival at X's house they will discover that it is occupied and that A will thereupon call off the enterprise. It seems that this will not save B. In *D.P.P. for Northern Ireland* v. *Lynch* (1975) Lynch drove some terrorists to a place where they shot and killed a man. Lynch said that he was hoping that the crime—or any crime—would not be committed but it was said that this would be no defence. Would it make any difference that B spent the journey to X's house trying to persuade A not to burgle the house? *Fretwell* (1862) suggests that it might, for there B was held not guilty for the self-murder by A where he gave her (A) the wherewithal to procure an abortion whilst earnestly entreating her not to use it. This decision is, however, questionable. In *N.C.B.* v. *Gamble*, Devlin J. thought, surely correctly, that if B sold a gun to A knowing that A intended to murder his wife, B would be an accessory to the murder even though his interest was only in the profit he would make on the sale and was utterly indifferent to the fate of A's wife. It is unlikely that Devlin J. would take a different view of B's participation if B had sold the gun to A with a plea for matrimonial reconciliation. This brings us full circle to the case we were discussing at the outset of the laundress who washed and returned clothes to a prostitute knowing that she would use them to ply her trade in public. It seems unlikely that we should convict the laundress as a party to the prostitution and therefore a line has to be drawn. Of course cases B can always refuse to sell the gun or wash the clothes, but what if A is asking for the return of the gun he lent to B? If B refuses can he be sued for wrongful retention of A's property? It is unlikely that a civil court would uphold such an action and in any case *Garrett* v. *Arthur Churchill (Glass) Ltd.* (1970) would imply that such a plea would be no defence to B if he returns the gun. How then do we distinguish between the sale of the gun and washing of the clothes. The only really practical solution is to say that liability in these in these type of situations will depend upon the severity of the contemplated crime. Thus if B returns the gun to A knowing that he plans to shoot his wife he will be liable, but not if he knows that A plans a bit of illegal poaching. This seems hardly satisfactory but it is submitted it is the only practicable solution.

Thus far an attempt has been made to describe participation in crime and to show why we need to distinguish between the principal offender and secondary offenders and how the distinction is to be made. This does not exhaust all the problems which arise in connection with participation in crime and some mention must be made of these.

3. THE NEED FOR AN ACTUS REUS

It may happen that either the police have been unable to catch the principal offender but they have arrested the man they think aided the principal. Is it now permissible for them to bring the secondary party to trial in the absence of any principal offender? This raises several related problems which we can now examine.

(1) No principal offender

Provided that the prosecution is able to prove that the *actus reus* of the crime in question was caused by someone then the jury are entitled to convict B as a secondary party even though the prosecution have not been able to produce the principal offender.

(2) Previous acquittal of the principal offender

If the principal offender has already been tried and acquitted it is still possible for the prosecution to bring to trial the secondary offender provided that the evidence against him is not identical to the evidence upon which the previous jury acquitted the principal offender.

(3) Joint trial of principal and secondary parties

It is usual for the principal and secondary parties to the offence to be tried together. So the question then arises as to whether the jury could acquit the principal offender and convict the secondary party. This, to an outsider would look rather odd and indeed there are suggestions that this course is not open. However, such action is probably not as absurd as it may first appear. If the evidence against the parties is the same then it would be improper for the jury to acquit the principal and convict the secondary party. On the other hand, some evidence may only be admissible against the secondary party. For example, the secondary party may have made a voluntary confession to the police which he now denies. This, under the rules of evidence, would be admissible evidence against the secondary party who made it, but not against the others since in relation to them it would be inadmissible hearsay. In these circumstances there would be no illogicality in the jury convicting the secondary party even though they felt that they were not satisfied with the case against the principal offender.

One point needs to be remembered. In any of these cases if the acquittal of the principal is tantamount to a finding that the jury are not satisfied that the *actus reus* of the crime was committed by anyone, then obviously they cannot convict someone of being a secondary party. Thus in *Thornton* v. *Mitchell* (1940) the driver of a bus had been trying to reverse his vehicle with the help of signals on the bell from his conductor. On the given signal he reversed the bus and collided with two pedestrians. He was charged with driving without due care and attention and the conductor was charged with aiding and abetting. Now it is quite clear that the responsibility for what happened lay with the conductor, but he could not be charged with careless driving (even through the innocent agency of the driver) since he had not, in fact been driving the bus. Thus he was charged as a secondary party to the driver's careless driving. However the charge against the driver was dismissed, and this could only be on the basis that there was no careless driving, since the offence does not require any subjective *mens rea* on his part. The finding, therefore, was that no crime of careless driving had been committed. It was consequently impossible to convict the conductor as a secondary party to a non-existent crime. Was there any offence with which the conductor could have been charged? If he had intended or seen as likely the injury to the pedestrians then he could have been prosecuted for some form of assault (see below, p. 237). Had the pedestrians died he could probably have been prosecuted for manslaughter as the principal offender (see below, p. 226) but since there is, at present, no offence of negligently causing injury it seems that he committed no offence. If, however, the principal offence has been committed but, the principal offender is, for some reason, exempt from prosecution, then it is still possible to prosecute a secondary offender. This was the position in *Austin* (1981) where the Court of Appeal held that the effect of a statutory provision was that the perpetrator could not be prosecuted; it did not mean that he had not committed the offence.

In the case of *Bourne* (1952) where a husband forced his wife to have sexual connection with a dog, the wife would be the principal offender in the crime of buggery, but because of the duress factor she was not charged and would have been acquitted had she been charged. There was, however, the *actus reus* of buggery and it was held that the husband could be charged with and convicted of this offence.

In *Cogan and Leak* (1976) where the facts were similar to those in *Morgan* (see above, p. 82) the accused had invited a friend to have intercourse with his wife telling him that his wife was a willing partner. During the intercourse the wife lay passively with her face covered. The jury found that the friend had honestly but unreasonably believed that the woman was consenting and so, following the decision in *Morgan,* his conviction for rape was quashed. The husband, however, knew full well that his wife was not consenting, since he had terrorised her into consenting, but there is a rule in English law that a husband "cannot be convicted as a principal offender in the rape of his wife." Could he, however, be convicted as a secondary party to the rape of his wife by the friend who had now been acquitted on the ground of lack of *mens rea?* The Court of Appeal held that he could, but unfortunately based this decision largely upon the doctrine of innocent agency. In other words the Court was saying that the husband raped his wife through an innocent agent, namely his friend. Two objections can be taken to this. In the first place innocent agency should only be used where the innocent agent is being used as a sort of weapon by the real perpetrator of the crime. Thus X hands Y a poisoned apple to give to Z. Y hands it over to Z without any awareness of the poisonous contents and Z is killed. In that case it makes complete sense to say that X killed Z. It does not make any sense in *Cogan* to say that the husband raped his wife. He did not; his friend raped the wife assisted by the husband. Like the word "drive" in *Thornton* v. *Mitchell* (above) "intercourse" is another word which does not lend itself to the concept of innocent agency. Even if the husband were to be held to have raped his wife through an innocent agent, this would in effect make him the perpetrator of the crime and husbands cannot perpetrate the crime of rape on their wives. It would be much more sensible for the court to hold that although the friend had been acquitted of the charge of rape, the wife had nevertheless been raped and the husband had assisted in this offence.

Thus the overall effect of *Bourne* and *Cogan and Leak* would seem to be that if A gets B to commit the *actus reus* of an offence with the help of A, then A can be convicted as a secondary party to that offence even though B, the perpetrator has a defence to the charge.

Thus, it is submitted that provided that the prosecution can satisfy the jury that there was an *actus reus* of the crime in question, there can be a conviction of the secondary party even though the principal offender (i) is not known or (ii) is acquitted at the same time or subsequently, provided here that the evidence against the secondary party is not the same as that against the principal.

Can the secondary party be convicted of an offence greater than that of the principal?

Suppose that A and B return to A's house one night and discover A's wife in bed with X. Let us suppose that B sees that A is boiling over with rage and so he hands him a poker and urges A to smash in X's skull. If A were to do this, then he would be charged with murder and B would be charged as a secondary party. A, however, is likely to raise, probably successfully, the defence of provocation which will mean that he will be convicted only of manslaughter. B, however, cannot rely on such a defence. Can he therefore be convicted of murder while A, the principal, is convicted of manslaughter. Theoretically this would seem quite logical, but until recently it appeared that the Court of Appeal favoured a general rule that it was not open for a jury to convict the secondary party of an offence greater than that of the principal offender (*Richards* (1974)). However in *Howe* (1987) the House of Lords expressed its disapproval of *Richards* and, although the statements concerning *Richards* were *obiter dicta,* it seems fairly safe to assume that in our example of the adulterous spouse a jury could properly find A not guilty of murder but guilty of manslaughter on the ground of provocation, while convicting B, who cannot raise the defence of provocation, of murder. In this example both defendants have the same *mens rea*; the difference lies in a mitigating defence available only to A. The same result should follow in a case where A, the secondary party, has the *mens rea* of murder, while B, the principal offender has the *mens rea* only of manslaughter. For example, if A and B were escaping from the scene of the crime in a car driven by B, when a police officer stepped out into the road and signalled to B to stop. Suppose that A had urged B to run over the officer, but B had made an unsuccessful attempt to avoid hitting him. It may well be, if B's driving wee sufficiently bad, that B could be convicted of manslaughter (see below p. 226); he cannot be convicted of murder since he lacks the necessary *mens rea*. A, however, is a party to the *actus reus* of unlawful homicide (the *actus reus* for murder and manslaughter is the same, see p. 17) and since A possesses the *mens rea* of murder he should be convicted of that offence.

4. Victims as Parties to an Offence

When A is charged with raping B we can say that in a very real sense B is the victim of the crime and no one would suggest that B is a party to the rape. On the other hand, if A is charged with having unlawful sexual intercourse with his 15-year-old girlfriend, B is again the victim, but this time a very willing one and so why should she not be charged as an accessory to A's crime? The reason why B cannot be so charged is the rule in *Tyrell's* case (1894) which provides that where a statute is designed to protect a certain class of individual, then such an individual cannot be held to be a party to the crime however willing she was for the crime to be committed against her. The scope of the rule is uncertain but it has been applied mainly in the sexual area. It only protects, however, the victim of the particular crime. If B, a 15-year-old girl helps A to have intercourse with C, another 15-year-old girl, then B can be charged as a party to that intercourse, whereas C cannot.

5. Repentance by a Secondary Party Before the Crime is Committed

As we have said, the secondary party becomes liable only when the principal commits the offence in question or attempts to commit it. There may be, therefore, a fair amount of time between the act of assistance rendered by the secondary party and the commission of the offence by the principal. Is it therefore possible for the secondary party to escape subsequent liability by washing his hands of the crime?

It obviously makes sense to allow a person to avoid criminal liability by withdrawing from a criminal venture before it takes place. On the other hand, where an accused has given help to others who then commit a crime, it should not suffice that the accused has simply resolved to have nothing more to do with the venture. What therefore constitutes and effective withdrawal? This will depend upon the nature of the assistance given, the type of crime involved and the timing of the withdrawal? (*Becerra* (1975)). Where the accused's part in the crime has consisted solely in giving advice and encouragement, then he can effectively withdraw simply by telling the other parties that he is withdrawing his encouragement (*Whitefield* (1984)). Where the accused decides to withdraw long before the commission of the offence, it may suffice that he makes it very clear to the others that any further activity will go ahead without any further assistance from the accused. Where the offence is about to be committed it may well be that the accused must try, by force if necessary, to prevent the commission of the offence. If his assistance has been in the form of supplying a gun for a murder, then the court would certainly require something more than mere communication by the accused to the would-be killer that the accused wants nothing more to do with the offence. In such a case, or where communication with the other parties is impossible, it may be that the only effective action the accused can take to withdraw is to inform the police so that the crime can be stopped.

The mere fact that the police have already arrested the secondary party does not mean that he can no longer give assistance to the principal (see *Craig and Bentley,* above, p. 113).

6. Assistance Given After the Commission of the Crime

In this section we have been concerned with the situation in which someone has given help to the principal offender which has aided him in the commission of the offence. The giving of such assistance may, as we have seen, render the giver liable to be dealt with as if he were a principal offender. In other words, he may become a party to the actual crime. Help given after the offence has been committed will not normally render a person a party to the offence, but may nevertheless merit punishment insofar as it hinders the apprehension of criminals by the police. There are therefore offences to cover just this problem. We can briefly mention one or two of these offences here.

By section 4 of the Criminal Law Act 1967 it is provided that:

> "Where a person has committed an arrestable offence, any other person who, knowing or believing him to be guilty of the offence or of some other arrestable offence, does without lawful authority or reasonable excuse any act with intent to impede his apprehension or prosecution shall be guilty of an offence."

In order to gain a conviction under this section the prosecution must prove firstly that an arrestable offence (see above, p. 4) has been committed. It is not necessary that someone has been convicted of the offence and it would presumably be no defence that the principal offender was, for some reason, exempt from prosecution. Secondly, the prosecution must prove that the accused knew or believed that the principal offender had committed this or some other arrestable offence. This does not mean that the accused must know that what the accused has done amounts to an arrestable offence, but it suffices that he knows of the facts which, in law, constitute an arrestable offence. Thus it would suffice that the accused knew that the principal offender had forced a girl to have intercourse with him by threatening her with a knife. Thirdly, the prosecutor must establish that the accused has done any act with the intention of impeding the arrest or prosecution of the principal offender. It is clear that nothing short of intention suffices here. It is not sufficient that the accused realises that what he is doing will have the effect of impeding the arrest of the principal offender; this must be his motive in doing the act. Finally the prosecution must show that there was no lawful authority or reasonable excuse for the accused's action.

Under section 5 of the Criminal Law Act it is an offence to conceal information which may be of material assistance in securing the prosecution or conviction of an arrestable offender, where this has been done for any consideration (reward) other than the making good of the loss caused by the offence, or the making of reasonable compensation for that loss or injury.

We should conclude by saying that there are several other offences which might be used by the police against those who have, in some way, given aid to those who have committed criminal offences. Among these offences are; attempting to pervert the course of justice, obstructing the police in the execution of their duty, causing wasteful employment to the police and contempt of court. These offences are not confined to arrestable offences.

II. *VICARIOUS AND CORPORATE LIABILITY*

We shall conclude this chapter with a look at the way in which a master can be prosecuted for the crimes of his servants and a limited company can be prosecuted as if it were a human defendant.

1. VICARIOUS LIABILITY

In civil actions a master (usually covered today by the word "employer") is liable for the wrongs of his servants (employees) which were committed by the servants during the course of their employment. This usually enables the victim of the torts to sue a defendant who is more likely to be able to pay should liability be proved. But is such a concept really needed in the criminal law? After all in criminal law we are trying to attach liability to the person who is responsible for the commission of the offence. We are not normally concerned with trying to compensate the victim. Thus if X drives a lorry belonging to his boss and the lorry has defective brakes, X is the wrongdoer and should be punished. This is true, but by enabling the court to punish the employer it is thought that the law will keep him on his toes and ensure, for example, that he carries out regular safety checks on his fleet of lorries. This is an argument very similar to the one put forward in Chap. 4 for the justification of strict liability, and again much the same sort of effect could be achieved by carefully worded legislation based on liability for negligence. However, there is another reason for one form of vicarious liability, namely that under the Licensing Acts many offences can be committed only by the holder of the licence. Thus, for example it is an offence for a licensee to sell alcohol to a person under the age of 18. If there was no concept of vicarious liability it would mean that in order to obtain a conviction the prosecution would have to prove that the licensee personally sold the drink. Possibly had the courts not adopted a form of vicarious liability to cover these cases it would have forced Parliament to enact more sensibly worded legislation, but this is one area in which the courts have come to the aid of the legislature. We can now look at the forms of vicarious liability which have emerged.

(1) Express statutory vicarious liability

Occasionally Parliament provides expressly for the imposition of vicarious liability. For example, section 163(1) of the Licensing Act 1964 provides: "A person shall not, in pursuance of a sale by him of intoxicating liquor, deliver that liquor, either himself or by his servant or agent, from any van, barrow, basket or other vehicle or receptacle unless. . . . "

(2) Implied vicarious liability

Unlike the licensee cases which are discussed below, the statutes involved here do actually allow the police to prosecute the actual perpetrator of the offence, but the courts have allowed the police to treat the acts of the perpetrator as the acts of his employer. This they will do when the word used in the statute is one which, without too much of a strain on its meaning, can be interpreted to cover persons other than the actual perpetrator. Such words as "sell," "supply" and "use" have frequently received this extended meaning. Thus when a lorry driver takes a lorry out for his boss, it is not unreasonable to say that both the driver and the boss "use" the lorry. So both could be said to have used a lorry with defective brakes. This form of vicarious liability is found only in cases where the statute imposes strict liability. It cannot be used, in offences requiring *mens rea*, to transfer the *mens rea* of the actual perpetrator to his employer. Two cases will serve to show how this principle works.

In *Coppen* v. *Moore* (*No.* 2) (1898) the accused owned six shops which sold food supplies. In these shops he sold American ham, but he told all his managers that they were to call them "breakfast hams." Unfortunately a shop assistant in one of the shops without the knowledge of her own manager let alone the owner sold some of this ham as "Scotch Ham." Now clearly she committed the offence, but the Divisional Court held that the accused was also liable since he could in reality be said to be the seller of the wrongly described ham, even if he was not the actual salesman.

In *James & Sons Ltd.* v. *Smee* (1955) the offence in question was using, or causing or permitting to be used a vehicle in contravention of the Motor Vehicle (Construction and Use) Regulations 1951. The Divisional Court held that there were in effect three different crimes of which "permitting to be used" clearly required *mens rea* and "using" clearly did not. Thus if A, an employee, sets out in one of his employer's lorries which has defective tyres, the employer, B, can only be convicted of permitting the use of the vehicle if he knows that the tyres are defective whereas A can be charged with using the vehicle even if he is unaware of the defect. Furthermore, if the police rely on the "using" offence they can hold B vicariously liable—they can, in effect say that B was using the lorry. They may charge both A and B in which case they will be co-principals. If, however, the regulation had provided that it was an offence to drive a vehicle with defective tyres, then the police could charge only A as a principal offender. B could not be held vicariously liable since the word "drive" is not really capable of an extended meaning—you could not really say that B had driven the lorry. In this case it would only be possible to charge B as a secondary party and then only if he had knowledge of the defect.

(3) The licensee cases

Most people are aware that before a public house can sell alcohol to the public there will have to be a licence obtained from the local magistrates permitting such a sale. This licence has to be issued to a person and not to a company so it will be issued either to the tenant of the pub or, in most cases today, the manger who draws his salary from one of the breweries. The sale of alcohol is governed in the main by the Licensing Act 1964 under which there are many offences which can only be committed by the holder of the justices' licence. This means that he will have to be named as the principal offender and if he does not commit the offence then the offence is not committed which means that there is no chance of charging the actual perpetrator (*e.g.* a barman) as a secondary party (see above, p. 132). There are not many pubs or establishments operating under these licences where the licensee is the sole person working. Most places employ staff and so there is a good chance that it will be these staff that perpetrate the acts which if done by the licensee would be an offence. If the courts had not come to the Parliament's aid with a form of vicarious liability much of the legislation would by now have been rewritten in a more sensible way to cover offences committed by employees.

Some of the offences under the Licensing Act are offences of strict liability and where this is the case it may be possible to hold the licensee vicariously liable under the principles discussed in section (2) above. Thus it is an offence to sell drinks to a person under the age of 18 or to sell alcohol to a person who is already drunk. Both of these offences are offences of strict liability, and we have already seen the word "sell" is capable of an extended meaning. Thus if a barman sold a drink to a 17 year old, it would be possible to say that it was really a sale by the licensee through the agency of the barman.

On the other hand some of the offences are offences requiring *mens rea*. We saw in Chap. 4 (above p. 101) that the offence of selling alcohol to a policeman on duty requires that the offender knows that the policeman is, in fact, on duty. The offences of permitting drunkenness and permitting prostitutes to congregate also require *mens rea*. The courts have not allowed the type of vicarious liability we saw in the previous section to be used where the offence requires *mens rea*. Thus the courts have developed a second type of vicarious liability which is now used almost entirely to impute the guilty mind of the licensee's employees to the licensee himself. This operates only when the licensee has delegated general responsibility to his staff for at least part of the pub and is himself not present in that part when the offence is committed. (The principle is not restricted to the Licensing Act, but this is where it has been largely developed).

We can see how this type of vicarious liability works in practice by considering a hypothetical example. Suppose A is the landlord of the Fox and Hounds, a public house with both a bar room and a lounge. He employs B and C to look after the lounge and he is normally in charge of the bar room with the help of D. If, on one occasion E, who is 17 years old asks for a drink, it does not matter who serves him, in which bar or whether A is present or not. This is an offence of strict liability and the sale by any of the staff could, under the principles discussed in section (2) above, be regarded as the sale of the licensee. Since, however, the principal offender can only be a licence holder, if the sale was made by one of his employees, for example B, then B could only be liable as a secondary party and then only if he knew E was under 18.

Now let us consider an offence requiring *mens rea*. Let us suppose that members of the local rugby club are in the lounge celebrating a victory that day. They are now all well and truly drunk. It is an offence for the licensee to permit drunkenness on the licensed premises (Licensing Act 1964, s.172(1)). B who is the senior barman on duty in the lounge has been instructed by A that under no circumstances must he permit such behaviour. B, however, knows most of the players and consequently does nothing. Has an offence been committed? This will depend upon whether we can impute B's knowledge to A under the delegation principle. This raises two questions. Has A delegated authority for the general running of the lounge to B and A is absent? Of course, if he has gone out for the night he will have delegated authority to someone and he will not be present. But is it enough that he is simply in another room. Most of the cases on this topic suggest that it is sufficient that the licensee is not in the room in question at the time the offence is committed and that in his absence another is in charge (see *Howker* v. *Robinson* (1973)). However in *Vane* v. *Yiannopoullos* (1965) the House of Lords held that there had not been delegation when the licensee of a restaurant was not in the room in question, but had gone up onto another floor. Since there was no delegation the House of Lords did not give a final ruling on the delegation principle, but their comments suggested that they were not altogether happy about the idea of imputing *mens rea* to a licensee in this way. As Lord Donovan said "If a decision that 'knowingly' means that 'knowingly' will make the provision difficult to enforce, the remedy lies with the legislature." But the lower courts have continued to apply the delegation principle.

If the drunken men were in the room where A was clearly in charge then the delegation principle does not operate. So, in our example, if the drunken men were in the bar and only D is aware of their state, D's knowledge cannot be imputed to A. In such a case the prosecution will have to prove that it was A who personally permitted the drunken men to remain and that he knew that they were drunk.

Our final point can be made here. Suppose that various customers continue to drink after closing time with the knowledge of the bar staff. The point to remember is that the offence is drinking after hours and not permitting customers to drink after hours. Thus it is the customer who is the principal offender. Any of the staff who knowingly permit this to continue will be liable as secondary parties, but if A is absent the knowledge of his staff cannot be imputed to him under the delegation principle; you cannot be vicariously liable as a secondary party (*Ferguson* v. *Weaving* (1951)).

(4) Conclusion

It is to be hoped that under any future code of criminal liability the need for a concept of vicarious liability can be avoided. As we said earlier a properly drafted statute could impose liability for negligence on employers where this is thought necessary. Thus in the case where an employer is held vicariously liable for the use by an employee of a vehicle with defective breaks, the same result could be achieved by liability for failing to provide a proper system of vehicle maintenance.

2. CORPORATE LIABILITY

Limited companies possess what is known as legal personality. This means that the company can hold property as if it were an ordinary human being and that it can sue and be sued in the civil courts in its own name. The question for us to consider now is whether the company can be a party to criminal proceedings. Of course when a criminal offence is committed, the actual act must have been perpetrated by an ordinary human being and he will be liable as an individual for the criminal act, but the courts have held that in certain circumstances the limited company can also be held liable in the criminal law for the acts of one of the member individuals.

There are two ways in which a limited company can be held liable for criminal acts:

(i) The company can be held to be vicariously liable for the crimes of its employees in just the same way that a human employer can be held responsible for the crimes of his employee. Thus, as we saw earlier (above, p. 000) this will only apply in statutory crimes of strict liability where the court has been able to give an extended meaning to words such as "sell" or "use."

(ii) The company can be held liable by what is known as the doctrine of identification. What this means is that in each company the court recognises certain senior individuals as being the company itself and the acts of these individuals when acting in the company's business are treated as the acts of the company. It has been said that certain members of the company can be regarded as its brain and the others as its hands. This tells us that we are looking for people who have the power to control the company's actions. Thus in most companies we can say that the managing director and the other directors will be regarded as being in a position of control and this might even extend to the company secretary and non-director managers if they have sufficient executive power. But the line is not easy to draw with any degree of certainty and this was illustrated by the case of *Tesco Supermarkets Ltd.* v. *Nattrass* (1972). In that case an old age pensioner was trying to buy a packet of soap powder at the reduced price being offered by one of Tesco's shops. He could not find any packets priced at the lower price and the shop refused to sell him a packet at anything other than the full price. He complained to the inspector of weights and measures who brought a prosecution against Tesco Supermarkets Ltd. under the Trade Descriptions Act 1968, s.11(2). Tesco's sought to put the blame on the branch manager who had failed to ensure that packets at the reduced price were on display, despite the control exercised by the firm and its detailed instructions to managers as to how to deal with such matters. One of the issues confronting the House of Lords was whether or not the store manager could be identified as the company. If this was the case then Tescos would be liable for the offence. The House of Lords held that because of the strict controls exercised by the company over its branch managers they were left with so little power that they could not be regarded as part of the "brains" of the company. This meant that Tesco Ltd. was able to show that the offence was, in fact, committed by a third party—namely their manager—and thus it could rely on section 24 of the Act which provided that it would be a defence to a person charged under the Act to show that the commission of the offence was due to the act or default of another person and that he himself (*i.e.,* in this case, Tesco Ltd.) took all reasonable precautions to prevent the commission of such an offence by himself or any person under his control. (See defences to strict liability above, p. 108). This is not a true example of the third party defence since there is no need for the third party to be joined in the proceedings. It is sufficient that the defendant can give sufficient information to the prosecution to enable the true culprit to be prosecuted.

Liability of individual

If the firm is held to be liable because of the acts of one of its members, can the member be joined as a party to the proceedings? The answer to this is clearly yes. In both types of corporate liability he may be joined as a co-principal.

Are there any crimes a company cannot commit?

A company can be convicted of any offence provided that the sentence can be in the nature of a fine. You clearly cannot send a company to jail, let alone hang it. Thus the penalty must take the form of a fine which will fall upon the shareholders. The only crimes where this will not be possible are treason, murder and some forms of piracy where imprisonment is mandatory.

Theoretically this means a company can be convicted of all offences against the person except for murder. There is no reason why a company should not be liable for manslaughter, if, for example, its managing director electrifies its perimeter fence against vandals, killing a small child who accidentally touches the wire. It is however difficult to imagine that a company director acting in furtherance of his company duties could ever render the company liable for rape. However if Z, the managing director of X Co. Ltd., a film company, supervises the filming of intercourse between M, an 18-year-old male with N, a 15-year-old girl, there is no reason why Z and hence the film company should not be convicted as secondary parties to the unlawful sexual intercourse.

CHAPTER 6

GENERAL DEFENCES

ALTHOUGH specific crimes may be provided with special defences of their own, there are several defences which are of general application to criminal offences and these will be examined in this chapter. We saw in Chap. 3 that most defences are, in fact, allegations by the accused that the prosecution has failed to establish one or more elements of the *actus reus* or *mens rea*. In some cases the defence relates to a part of the *actus reus* or *mens rea* that is so central that the accused does not even have an evidential burden to discharge before the judge is bound to leave it for consideration by the jury. Thus if X is charged with the murder of Y and he says either that it was another man who shot Y or that the gun went off accidentally, he is doing nothing more than saying that the prosecution have failed to prove that he caused Y's death or that he had the *mens rea* needed for murder. Both of these issues are issues upon which the prosecution have the duty to introduce evidence and also the duty to prove to the court's satisfaction. It would obviously be advisable for the accused to introduce any evidence he possesses in support of such defences, especially where the prosecution appears to have a good case. On the other hand if the prosecution's case is weak he may be advised to say nothing, since the judge is bound to direct the jury that the prosecution must prove that the accused was the man who pulled the trigger and that he did so with the necessary *mens rea*. A second group of defences although relating to the *actus reus* or *mens rea* of the crime are not so central to the prosecution's case and here the accused may well bear an evidential burden, which means that unless, by the end of the case there is evidence which could create a reasonable doubt, the judge will not give the jury any direction on that issue. This is the case with the defences of self-defence, provocation, duress, necessity, automatism and intoxication. Finally there are those defences in which the accused bears not only an evidential but also a legal burden; here the accused will

146

not only have to introduce evidence of this defence, but he will also have to prove to the jury that it was more likely than not that factors amounting to such a defence existed. Under this category come the defences of insanity, and diminished responsibility (there are others but these are by far the best known).

If we discount for the moment those defences in the third category, it is probably not inaccurate to say that in order for the prosecution to secure a conviction, it must prove *actus reus, mens rea* and absence of a defence. Thus if X is charged with the murder of Y, the prosecution will have to prove the *actus reus* of the crime and this will include proof that the killing was unlawful. If X gives no evidence and the prosecution establish that X shot Y and that Y died as a result, the jury would conclude that the prosecution had also proved that the killing was unlawful. On the other hand if X believes that he acted in self-defence the judge will only direct the jury to consider whether the prosecution have failed to rebut self-defence beyond reasonable doubt if, by the end of the case for the defence, there is some evidence to support such a defence. It does not matter whether this has been raised specifically by the defence or whether it has emerged from various sources during the course of the trial so long as the judge feels that there is evidence upon which a jury could entertain a reasonable doubt.

It may be useful to survey the defences to which we shall be referring during the course of this chapter, and to which reference is made elsewhere. Let us suppose that X has been charged with the murder of Y. It is not contested that X fired the shot which killed Y and if X says nothing in his defence there is every chance that the jury will come to the conclusion that he had the necessary *mens rea*. Below are some of the defences that X may raise, together with a note of the burden of proof and the effect of a successful plea. X may plead:

(i) that it was an accident or that he thought that he was shooting at a wild animal; both of these defences were examined in Chapter 3. In both cases the accused is doing no more than asserting that he lacked the necessary *mens rea*, and he thus bears, at most, a tactical burden (above, p. 92). The result of a successful plea is an acquittal (above, pp. 78, 91).

(ii) that he was legally insane at the time of the killing. Such a plea would mean that the accused bears a legal burden of proving that he was insane on a balance of probabilities. If successful, the accused will gain a verdict of not guilty by reason of insanity (below, p. 151).

(iii) that he was suffering from diminished responsibility. This is a sort of modern version of insanity and is available only to those charged with murder. X will bear the legal burden of establishing the defence on a balance of probabilities. If he is successful the jury will return a verdict of not guilty of murder but guilty of manslaughter (below, p. 157).

(iv) that he was acting as an automaton. Here he will carry a burden of introducing evidence but not a legal burden of proof and a successful plea will lead to an acquittal (above, p. 34).

(v) that he was acting under the influence of alcohol or drugs. This is commonly known as the defence of intoxication and is normally raised to assert that that accused did not form the requisite *mens rea*. We shall see that it is not available as a defence to all crimes, but where it is the accused bears an evidential burden. Where the plea is successful it will result in an acquittal of the offence with which he is charged though, as we shall see, in many cases it will be possible for the jury to convict him of an alternative offence to which intoxication is no defence (below, p. 161).

(vi) that he was forced to kill Y in order to save the lives of many others. This would be a plea of necessity the existence of which has been the subject of several recent decisions (below, pp. 179 and 187).

(vii) that he was told by Z that if he did not help to kidnap Y, he and all his family would be killed. This is the plea of duress and X would bear the burden of introducing evidence on it. If it is successful then it would lead to an acquittal (below, p. 182).

(viii) that he was so outraged by what Y had done to him that he lost self-control. This is the defence of provocation, which is available only to those charged with murder, and places an evidential burden on X. If successful, this would lead to a conviction for manslaughter rather than murder (below, p. 217).

(ix) he did it to defend himself against an attack by Y—a plea of self-defence. Again this places an evidential burden on X, but unlike provocation a successful plea would lead to a complete acquittal (below, p. 176).

(x) that he is too young to stand trial (below, p. 189).

It is interesting to note the effect these defences have on criminal liability. Some of them are raised as a means of denying the mental state of mind required for a conviction; into this category fall those in paragraphs (i)–(v). In the other defences the accused may well admit the *mens rea*, but put forward some factor which he alleges excuses him from liability for deliberately causing the *actus reus*. We shall now examine these defences in turn. And the chapter will conclude with a brief summary of other defences of which space does not permit a fuller examination.

I. *THE MENTALLY ABNORMAL OFFENDER*

1. Unfitness to Plead

When we talk of the defence of insanity we normally mean a plea by the accused that at the time he was supposed to have committed the offence he was suffering from a state of mind which fell within the legal definition of insanity. Before we discuss that, however, we should first note that many of those who may well fall within the legal definition of insanity are not, in fact, tried at all. Where it is obvious that the person charged is suffering from a really severe mental abnormality which would make it impossible to conduct any sort of meaningful trial, he may well be committed to a mental institution by the Home Secretary using his powers under sections 47 and 48 of the Mental Health Act 1983. Clearly this should only be done where a trial is out of the question, and even then, if the accused later recovers he should be tried for the offence. Where the condition is not so obviously one in which no trial should be attempted, and the accused is brought before the court, a question might arise as to whether or not he is fit to stand trial. If the court comes to the conclusion that the accused cannot stand trial he is said to be unfit to plead.

What does unfitness to plead mean? A person is unfit to plead when he is unable to understand the charges that have been brought against him and is unable to appreciate the difference between a plea of guilty and a plea of not guilty. If he is able to understand these issues then he is fit to stand trial even if he is unable to recall any of the events to which the charges relate (*Podola* (1960)). This emphasises that it is the state of the person's mind at the time of the trial that is in issue. Podola by the time of the trial was clearly able to understand the charges that had been brought against him and knew the difference between pleading guilty and not guilty. In his case, if his claims were true, his difficulty lay in knowing whether to plead guilty or not guilty since he could not recall what had happened.

Who raises this issue, and when? Unfitness to plead can be raised by the accused, the prosecution or even the judge. Where it is raised by either the judge or the prosecution, it is then up to the prosecution to prove that the accused is unfit to plead and the standard of proof required is the criminal standard— beyond reasonable doubt. Where the accused claims that he is unfit to plead he bears the burden or proof and must prove on a balance of probabilities that he is unfit to plead. Like insanity, which will be considered below, this is a clearly recognised exception to the rule that the prosecution bears the burden of proof on all issues in criminal cases.

Where the issue of unfitness to plead is raised, the trial judge will empanel a special jury to determine whether or not it has been proved and the decision will normally be made right at the start of proceedings. However, where the question of fitness to plead is raised by the prosecution against the desires of the accused, in a case where the accused feels that he has a substantive defence or that the prosecution case is very weak, a decision that he is unfit to plead will have the effect of depriving him of the opportunity of clearing his name. Thus under section 4 of the Criminal Procedure (Insanity) Act 1964, the judge is given a discretion to postpone any decision on fitness to plead until after the case for the prosecution has been closed. If he then feels that there is no case to answer he can direct the jury to acquit the accused. It may still be that the accused's condition is so bad that he will need to be confined in a mental institution, but this will not then be under suspicion of having committed a crime.

What is the effect of a successful plea? The accused will not be tried. He will be committed to a mental hospital and his release can be secured only with the consent of the Home Secretary.

2. The Defences of Insanity and Diminished Responsibility

Now we can look at the true defence of insanity, under which the accused claims that because of his mental state at the time he allegedly committed the offence, he was not truly responsible for his actions. The defence of insanity is of common law origin and its requirements are to be found in the answers by the judges to a series of questions posed by the House of Lords. A man by the name of M'Naghten had tried to kill Sir Robert Peel but had killed his secretary by mistake. His acquittal on the ground of insanity provoked an outcry and the questions by the House of Lords to the judges were an attempt to clarify the position in relation to the defence of insanity. The questions and answers form what are known as the M'Naghten Rules 1843 and are the basis for the defence of insanity today. We shall see that insanity is a relatively narrow defence and does not provide for many mentally abnormal offenders. This led Parliament in the Homicide Act 1957 to provide a special defence, applicable only to murder, known as diminished responsibility which, when successfully pleaded, means that the accused will be convicted, not of murder, but manslaughter.

(1) Insanity

The word "insanity" is not a medically recognised term which describes a particular mental state; it is a legal term for a legally defined state of mind which will lead in any criminal offence to a verdict of not guilty by reason of insanity.

What must be proved in order to substantiate insanity?

There is a presumption that the accused is sane and the effect of this presumption is to cast upon the accused the burden of proving that he is insane. In other words he must prove that it is more likely than not that he is insane; he does not have to prove his insanity beyond reasonable doubt. (As to whether or not the prosecutor may raise the issue of insanity see below, p. 156). In order to establish insanity the accused must prove that, at the time he committed the act, "he was labouring under such a defect of reason due to a disease of the mind, as not to know the nature and quality of the act he was doing, or if he did know it, that he did not know he was doing what was wrong." Thus there are various elements which must be established.

(a) *Disease of the mind*

The first stage is for the accused to show that the defect of reason was caused by a *disease of the mind*. So the first question is "what is a disease of the mind?" You must remember that although this is referred to as the defence of insanity and although it is littered with medical sounding phrases, this is not a clinical definition which is recognised by doctors specialising in mental disorders. It is an attempt by the courts to establish in what circumstances an accused will be held not to be legally responsible for his actions. The term *disease of the mind* is clearly apt to cover any physical condition which is directly affecting the brain such as inflammation of the brain or a brain tumour. The case of *Charlson* in which the court held that a brain tumour was not a disease of the mind must now be regarded as questionable in the light of statements in subsequent decisions such as *Bratty* v. *Att.-Gen. for Northern Ireland* (1963). But the term has been given a far wider meaning; it has been held to cover conditions such as psychomotor epilepsy, arteriosclerosis and diabetes.

It has to be said that the average person in the street would most likely be amazed to hear such complaints classified as insanity and recently Lord Diplock said that it was with reluctance that he attached the label of insanity to a person suffering from psychomotor epilepsy, though he felt the law forced him to do so. So how does this position come about? In *Sullivan* (1984), in the House of Lords, Lord Diplock said:

" 'mind' in the M'Naghten Rules is used in the ordinary sense of the mental faculties of reason, memory and understanding. If the effect of a disease is to impair these faculties so severely as to have either of the consequences referred to in the latter part of the rules, it matters not whether the aetiology of the impairment is organic, as in epilepsy, or functional, or whether the impairment itself is permanent or is transient and intermittent, provided that it subsisted at the time of the commission of the act."

Thus any condition which produces these effects on the mind can and will be classified as a disease of the mind. In short, we are looking for a disease which affects the proper functioning of the mind. We can see from this statement of Lord Diplock that the impairment may be either temporary or permanent in nature. It must, however, arise from inherent factors and not from external factors such as a blow on the head or the administration of an anaesthetic for therapeutic purposes. Where the impairment had arisen from a blow on the head it would be totally improper to classify this as a disease of the mind. What, therefore, of the accused who is suffering from a condition, such as diabetes, which is not likely to lead to any impairment of the mind, unless the accused, for example, fails to follow his correct medication? In *Quick* (1973) the accused had inflicted actual bodily harm on a patient in the hospital where he worked as a nurse. He wished to plead that he suffered from diabetes and that as a result of a hypoglycaemic condition he was totally unaware of what he was doing. In other words he wanted to plead that he was acting in a state of non-insane automatism. The trial judge rule that the blackout had resulted from a disease of the mind and that the correct plea was, therefore insanity. At this point Quick, not surprisingly, changed his plea to one of guilty. He appealed against his conviction and the Court of Appeal held that the trial judge was wrong to treat the condition as a disease of the mind. The blackout had been caused not so much by his diabetes but by the effect of alcohol and the absence of a proper meal on the drugs he was taking. Thus it was caused by external factors and not by a disease of the mind. In *Hennessy* (1989), on the other hand, the defendant, a diabetic, was arrested after he was seen to have driven a stolen car. He was charged with taking a motor vehicle without authority (section 12 Theft Act 1968) and driving while disqualified (section 103 of the Road Traffic Act 1988). He pleaded that at the time of the offences he was in a state of non-insane automatism brought on by hypoglycaemia. He said that as a result of stress and depression caused by domestic circumstances he had neither eaten nor taken insulin for several days and this had led to the hypoglycaemia. The trial judge ruled that this constituted insanity, whereupon the defendant pleaded guilty and appealed against his conviction. The Court of Appeal held that, in *Sullivan*, Lord Diplock had been trying to distinguish between situations where the malfunctioning of the mind could properly be said to have been brought about by external factors and those in which it was brought about by an inherent disease. In *Quick* the drugs had acted like a novel feature or accident akin to a blow on the head and thus it was possible to say that the malfunctioning had been caused not by the disease but by external factors. In *Hennessy*, however, it was the disease itself, uncontrolled by insulin, which had produced the malfunctioning of the mind. Stress, anxiety and depression could, no doubt, be the result of external factors but they were not in themselves, separately or together, external factors of the kind capable in law of causing or contributing to a state of automatism. They constituted a state of mind which was prone to recur and which lacked the feature of novelty or accident, which was the basis of the distinction drawn by Lord Diplock in *Sullivan*.

Where the impairment is brought on by the voluntary consumption of alcohol or drugs for non-therapeutic reasons the courts will treat it neither as a disease of the mind nor as automatism. If, however, a permanent condition such as delerium tremens has been produced then this may well be treated as a disease of the mind.

The question of whether a given condition amounts to a disease of the mind is a question of law for the judge to decide.

(b) *Defect of reason*

The disease of the mind must have led to such a defect of reason that the accused did not know the nature and quality of the act he was committing or, if he did know, that he did not know that what he was doing was wrong.

The reference to nature and quality of his acts is basically another way of saying that the accused did not intend to do what he did nor was he reckless. Traditional examples given include the man who cut a woman's throat thinking that it was a loaf of bread and the nurse who put the baby on the fire, thinking it was a log of wood.

If the accused is relying on the second limb—that he did not know he was doing what was wrong—then he must prove that he did not know that it was legally wrong (*Windle* (1952)). Thus, even though the accused believed that what he was doing was morally abhorrent and that people in general would not approve, he is entitled to a verdict of not guilty by reason of insanity if he can show that he thought that it was legally permissible. (It is useful to remind you at this point that in the case of a sane adult, it is no defence to prove that he was unaware that his actions constituted a criminal offence, see above, p. 79). Thus if X's disease of the mind caused him to think that three of his friends, A, B and C were members of an assassination squad who had to be killed before they could kill him, then he would succeed on a defence of insanity, because his delusion caused him to think that he was legally entitled to kill A, B and C. If, on the other hand, his disease of the mind caused him to think that he was Jack the Ripper and so led him to go round killing prostitutes, he would not succeed with a plea of insanity because, as Jack the Ripper, he would know that he was not entitled to kill random prostitutes. (He would presumably be able to plead diminished responsibility.)

(c) *Insanity as a defence today*

We said at the beginning that insanity was a defence to criminal charges in general. So, in theory, it could be raised as a defence to even the most trivial assault. However the result of a successful defence of insanity is committal to a mental institution for an indeterminate length of time. In effect, therefore, insanity will rarely be raised by the accused on anything but a charge of murder and even there a plea of diminished responsibility would normally be preferred which could lead to a determinate prison sentence.

Although insanity is rarely raised expressly as a defence today, it may arise indirectly. This is because what can or cannot constitute a disease of the mind is a question of law for the judge to decide and occasionally an accused might find himself in trouble because he has attempted to plead that he did not possess the necessary *mens rea* for murder only to find that the judge has ruled that the reason he is advancing amounts to a disease of the mind. In *Clarke* (1972), the accused was charged with stealing from a shop. She pleaded that she had taken the items from the shelf absent-mindedly as a result of the depression from which she was suffering. If Mrs. Clarke had simply rested her case on absentmindedness, all would probably have been well. Unfortunately, medical evidence was called to support her statements and it was the effect of this evidence which led the trial judge to decide she was raising the defence of insanity. Understandably, Mrs. Clarke then changed her plea to one of guilty—only a complete fool would plead insanity in circumstances such as these. The Court of Appeal were not disposed to decide whether or not the trial judge was entitled to hold that the evidence pointed to a disease of the mind. The M'Naghten Rules required that the disease of the mind had led to a defect of reason which meant that she was unable to appreciate the nature and quality of her acts. Ackner J. said that the M'Naghten Rules were designed to cover persons who have lost the power of reasoning, not persons who retain the power of reasoning but in moments of stress fail to use these powers to the full. Since the trial judge's ruling had caused Mrs. Clarke to change her plea to one of guilty, the Court of Appeal felt bound to quash the conviction.

Such problems are even more likely to arise when the accused raises the defence of automatism. Indeed, in the recent case of *Hennessy* (1989), the Court of Appeal said that, although the M'Naghten Rules had, in many ways, lost the importance they once had, they were still relevant insofar as they might affect the defence of automatism. This is so, because once the trial judge takes the view that the defendant has put his state of mind in issue (as he does when putting forward a plea of automatism) he must decide whether it is truly a case of automatism or whether it is a case of legal "insanity" within the M'Naghten Rules. In making this decision he will apply the tests discussed above (p. 151). The result is of more than academic interest to the accused; for if the judge rules that it is insane automatism this will lead to a verdict of not guilty by reason of insanity, while non-insane automatism will lead to a complete acquittal. It will also affect the incidence of the burden of proof. If the trial judge rules that it is a plea of insanity it will be for the defendant to prove he is insane. If the trial judge rules that it is a plea of automatism it will be for the prosecutor to disprove it.

In *Dickie* (1984) the Court of Appeal said that courts should bear in mind the fact that insanity was a defence and as such should in most cases be raised specifically by the accused. However, there might be occasions on which it would be permissible for a judge to raise the issue of his own volition. But this should only occur where there was relevant evidence which goes to all elements of the M'Naghten test. It would seem that a judge ought only to do so where clear evidence of insanity has been produced in the court, but the defence has sought to avoid the consequences of such a plea by not classifying the evidence as insanity. Thus in *Sullivan* (1983) where the accused sought to avoid a charge of inflicting grievous bodily harm by adducing evidence that the attack had happened while he was in the last stages of a minor epileptic seizure, the trial judge was clearly right, on the evidence before him to rule that the defence amounted to one of insanity rather than automatism. Clearly, also, if the judge has doubts in his mind on the evidence before him, he should seek clarification from the witnesses to enable him to reach his conclusion. He should not, however, embark on a fishing expedition for further evidence. In *Dickie*, the Court of Appeal thought that the prosecutor should not raise the issue of insanity, but it must be the position that had the judge in *Sullivan* not raised the matter, the prosecutor would have been entitled to ask for a ruling. The court was clearly anxious that, as far as possible, insanity should be seen as a defence to be raised by the accused, and that we should not have the spectacle of the prosecution trying to get an acquittal on the grounds of insanity so that the accused will be shut away for an indeterminate period. A special provision allows the accused to appeal against such an acquittal (Criminal Procedure (Insanity) Act 1964, s.12).

Under section 6 of the Criminal Procedure (Insanity) Act

1964, it is clearly provided that if the accused raises the defence of insanity or diminished responsibility the prosecution shall be entitled to prove the alternative defence. But here the standard of proof required of the prosecution is the criminal standard—proof beyond reasonable doubt.

(2) Diminished responsibility

Such was the narrowness of the legal test for insanity that Parliament introduced a special defence which would apply to charges of murder only. This was known as diminished responsibility and a successful plea leads to the accused being convicted of manslaughter rather than murder. As with insanity, the burden of proof lies on the accused to prove that it was more likely than not that he was suffering from diminished responsibility at the time he committed the offence. In effect, it is rather like provocation in that it enables the jury to return a verdict of guilty of manslaughter but not a complete acquittal. Once the jury has returned a verdict of guilty of manslaughter, the judge then has a wide discretion over what should happen to the accused. He can commit him to prison for up to life, he can have him detained in a mental institution, he can put him on probation or even give him an absolute discharge. The net result is that diminished responsibility has almost entirely replaced insanity as a defence. In reality, insanity was only raised as a defence to a charge of murder and we shall see that any state of mind that can constitute insanity would also amount to diminished responsibility. With a finding of not guilty by reason of insanity, the judge is bound to commit the prisoner to an indefinite stay in a mental hospital such as Broadmoor whereas, following a successful plea of diminished responsibility, there is every chance that the judge will pass a determinate prison sentence. The more likely way for insanity to arise today is for the prosecution to claim that an accused who has pleaded diminished responsibility, is, in fact, insane. This produces the odd spectacle of the prosecution seeking to gain a verdict of not guilty (by reason of insanity) and the accused seeking to have himself convicted of manslaughter. There is, however, logic in this; the prosecution will be hoping to have an accused whom they consider to be a danger to society confined in a mental institution for an indefinite period.

What, then, must the accused prove in order to establish the defence? Section 2(1) of the Homicide Act 1957 provides:

"Where a person kills or is a party to the killing of another, he shall not be convicted of murder if he was suffering from such abnormality of mind (whether arising from a condition of arrested or retarded development of mind or any inherent causes or induced by disease or injury) as substantially impaired his mental responsibility for his acts and omissions in doing or being a party to the killing."

This looks all very technical. What is the judge supposed to do? Is he to try to define the terms of the section for the jury? The Court of Criminal Appeal eventually resolved that it was wrong for a trial judge simply to read the section to the jury and leave them to make what they could of it. He should give them whatever guidance they require to understand it (*Byrne* (1960)). Basically, three factors have to be established:

(a) *The accused must have been suffering from an abnormality of mind*

In effect, the judge should ask the jury whether the accused's mind seems normal—would they say that the appeared to them to be normal. If he appears "mad" or "insane" (as a layman would use these words) then he can be said to be suffering from an abnormality of mind. Thus it was apt to cover the accused in *Byrne* (1960) who had strangled a young girl and had then horribly mutilated her body. His defence was that from early years, he had suffered from overwhelming perverted desires which he found very difficult—if not impossible to resist. He submitted that he had killed the girl under the influence of such an urge. It is interesting to pause here for a moment. Could Byrne have successfully pleaded insanity? The answer is that he could not. Whether or not he could have established that he was suffering from a disease of the mind, the evidence suggested that not only did he appreciate what he was doing, but that he also realised that it was wrong. His trouble was that he found it very difficult to stop himself.

In *Seers* (1985) where the defendant had pleaded diminished responsibility on the basis of reactive depression the Court of Appeal said that *Byrne* (above) should not be taken as laying down an immutable rule that juries should, in every case where diminished responsibility is raised, be asked whether or not the defendant could be described in popular language as partially insane or on the borderline of insanity. Even if "insane" were given a broad meaning, it was inappropriate to describe every condition which might properly be described as an "abnormality of mind." The trial judge should always relate his direction to the jury to the particular evidence in the case.

(b) Cause of the abnormality of mind

The abnormality of mind must have arisen from a condition of arrested or retarded development mind or any inherent causes or must have been induced by disease or injury. This is clearly a very wide provision. Is it wide enough to cover an abnormality of mind caused by excessive drink or drugs? It would seem for this to be possible, the accused would have to argue that the alcohol had injured his mind; possibly, therefore, a condition such as alcoholism caused by long-term drinking might be covered, but not an accused who was simply drunk at the time he committed the offence. In *Gittens* (1984) the court was faced with a situation in which the abnormality of mind had been caused in part by inherent causes and in part by drink and drugs. In such a case it would seem that the jury should be asked whether they were satisfied, on a balance of probabilities, that if the accused had not taken drink (i) he would have killed as he in fact did? and (ii) he would have been under diminished responsibility when he did so. In other words the jury have to try to discount the effect of the voluntary consumption of alcohol. In *Tandy* (1988) where the defendant tried to prove that the diminished responsibility was caused by alcoholism, the Court of Appeal said that the issue for the jury was whether her abnormality of mind was induced by disease, namely the disease of alcoholism. She would have to prove that the drink taken on the day in question had been taken involuntarily as a result of her condition. If the jury found that she took the first drink of the day voluntarily, they should conclude that the defence of diminished responsibility was not open to her.

(c) Effect of the abnormality of mind

The accused must prove that the abnormality of mind substantially impaired his mental responsibility for his acts and omissions in doing or being a party to the killing. In *Byrne*, the accused had relied on perverted sexual urges which he alleged caused him to kill the girl. Clearly, if the evidence had shown that he found these urges to be irresistible, the defence would have been established. But this would amount to a total impairment of his responsibility and the Act says that he need only prove a substantial impairment. What, therefore, does the Act mean by "substantial?" This is clearly a question of fact and degree for the jury. If Byrne found his urges no more difficult to resist than the lusty male finds it to resist leaping on every attractive female he sees, then this would not be enough. In other words, his urges must be abnormally strong.

3. HOSPITAL ORDERS

We should mention here that when a person is proved to have committed a criminal offence (other than murder), the court has power, under section 37 of the Mental Health Act 1983, to make a hospital order under which he will be committed to the care of a mental hospital. Where the court, in such a case, feels that the accused is particularly dangerous, it can make a restriction order which has the effect of necessitating the consent of the Home Secretary before he can be moved or released.

4. CONCLUSIONS

It is interesting to note that one of the reasons for the introduction of the defence of diminished responsibility was the notion that the defence of insanity was not wide enough to cover all those mentally abnormal persons who were charged with criminal offences. It should be remembered that insanity is unlikely to be pleaded outside murder cases and diminished responsibility can be pleaded only in murder cases. However, it was to be expected that following the 1957 Act, the numbers of accused pleading some form of mental disorder as a defence would increase. In fact, the number has remained almost the same as before 1957. The major change is that those who, before 1957 pleaded insanity, now plead diminished responsibility, which tends to suggest that the courts before 1957 managed to subsume under insanity all those who are now found to be suffering from diminished responsibility. This whole area now seems ready for some far-ranging reform. A committee under the Chairmanship of Lord Butler made major proposals for reform (Report of the Committee on

Mentally Abnormal Offenders, Cmnd. 6244 (1975)). However, this seems yet another area in which governments are unwilling to find Parliamentary time and change seems as far away today as ever.

II. *THE INTOXICATED OFFENDER*

You will recall that under section 8 of the Criminal Justice Act 1967, where the definition of the offence requires that the prosecution prove that the accused intended or foresaw that a given result would be a consequence of his action (*i.e.* that sticking a knife into Y would cause Y's death) then the jury should be entitled to take into account any evidence which may help them reach a decision on the issue. The same should be true in relation to knowledge or foresight of circumstances. One such factor immediately springs to mind, namely that the accused has drunk so much alcohol or has taken such a large quantity of heroin that he really could not have been fully aware of what he was doing. Is this therefore a factor the jury are entitled to take into account? Why should it be any different from any other factor which might affect the accused's ability to form the necessary *mens rea* required? One reason is that many members of society would find it abhorrent that a person who has caused the *actus reus* of a criminal act should escape liability because he has got himself into such a state that he did not know what he was doing. Should the law, therefore, allow such a defence only if the court is satisfied that the accused was not at fault in becoming intoxicated or drugged; if, for example, his drinks had been laced? We shall examine first of all those situations in which the accused has knowingly consumed alcohol or drugs and seeks to adduce this as evidence that he should not be held responsible for the act he committed. After that we shall look at the situation where the intoxication was involuntary. (In this section we shall use the word intoxication to cover both drink and drug induced states).

1. VOLUNTARY INTOXICATION

If the basic common law principle, of requiring the *actus reus* to be accompanied by the necessary *mens rea* before there could be a conviction, were to apply in relation to defendants who had consumed vast quantities of alcohol, then it would follow that if the accused has consumed so much alcohol that he did not form the requisite *mens rea* for the offence he should be acquitted. But as we have already said, such a rule would be unacceptable to many. Objection could be taken on the ground that such a defence would be easy to raise and hard to rebut, or simply that people who get drunk should learn to accept the consequences, and possibly this last notion is at the base of the uneasy compromise that has been drawn by the courts in this area.

If there were no special rules relating to voluntary (or self-induced) intoxication, it would not necessarily follow that such intoxication would afford a defence of a criminal charge. It would only afford a defence if it negatived the requisite *mens rea* for the offence. Thus it would not have availed *Prince* (1875) (above, p. 70) to have said that he made his mistake about the girl's age because he was drunk. Liability in relation to her age was, and is, strict. It follows that a mistake about her age, however caused, is irrelevant. Where liability is based upon negligence, as in the offence of careless driving (contrary to section 3 of the Road Traffic Act 1988) it would be of no use for the defendant to say that had he been sober he would have seen the other car coming; the drunkenness affords all the evidence needed of negligence on the part of the driver. Also where liability can be established by the wider meaning of recklessness in *Caldwell* (above, p. 59) drunkenness will be irrelevant since the prosecution will merely have to prove that the defendant gave no thought to an obvious and serious risk; it matters not why he gave no thought. In fact in all these cases it will not matter whether the defendant was suffering from voluntary or involuntary intoxication.

Where, however, the prosecution has to establish intention or *Cunningham* recklessness (or the narrower meaning of recklessness within the *Caldwell* definition see above, p. 59), intoxication can clearly negative the *mens rea* required. Thus if X is accused of intentionally killing Y, the fact that he was intoxicated could explain why he thought Y was a wax works model. Also, if there is a *Caldwell* loophole (see above, p. 69) then D would be able to say that he gave some thought to the possibility of there being a risk, but, because of his drunken state, he concluded that there was no risk. The question, therefore, is whether the courts are prepared to allow the defendant to plead that he did not form the necessary *mens rea* in these cases because he was drunk. Section 8 of the Criminal

Justice Act 1967 (see above, p. 88) would seem to suggest that the jury should be entitled to consider any facts which might help them decide whether or not the accused possessed the necessary *mens rea*, and intoxication is a very relevant consideration. On the other hand many citizens would be gravely offended at the proposition that a person could escape criminal liability on the basis that he had got himself so drunk, he did not know what he was doing. Current public opinion is probably moving even more towards the condemnation of intoxication, and it is this which explains the law's approach to voluntary intoxication as a defence. We shall see later that the courts will probably be prepared to take a far more tolerant approach to cases where the accused is not responsible for his intoxication (see below, p. 171).

The general position can be stated thus. Where the prosecution has to establish intention or *Cunningham* recklessness (and probably to a case where the *Caldwell* loophole applies) the answer depends upon whether the crime is classified as one requiring *basic* or *specific* intent. In *Majewski* (1977) the House of Lords held that voluntary intoxication could be a defence only to crimes requiring *specific* intent; in relation to a crime of *basic* intent it was irrelevant. The question, therefore, is what do we mean by a crime of *specific* intent? As a general rule, these are crimes where, on at least one element of the *actus reus*, the prosecution will succeed only if it can establish intention, or crimes of ulterior intent (see above, p. 74). Crimes of basic intent are those crimes where the prosecution will succeed if it can establish either intention or recklessness on every aspect of the *actus reus*. However, it would be unsafe to suggest that this is a watertight definition or that the courts have adopted a consistent approach in this area. Before *Moloney* (above, p. 54) the above definition would have suggested that murder was a crime of basic intent, but the courts have always classified murder as a crime of specific intent. The crime of rape requires an intention to have intercourse, yet this is treated as a crime of basic intent. The safest answer is that crimes of specific intent are those crimes where the courts have permitted the defence of voluntary intoxication and crimes of basic intent are those in which the courts have refused to accept the defence of voluntary intoxication. We can safely say that the following have been held to be crimes of specific intent; murder, wounding or causing grievous bodily harm with intent, robbery, burglary with intent, theft and an attempt to commit any offence. There are others but these will suffice for our purposes. The following have been held to be crimes of basic intent: manslaughter, rape, maliciously wounding or inflicting grievous bodily harm, assault occasioning actual bodily harm, indecent assault, criminal damage (Criminal Damage Act 1971, section 1(1)). The recent case of *Hutchins* (1988) has added kidnapping and false imprisonment to this list. The effect of these rules is that where the defendant is charged with a crime of basic intent the court will not allow him to assert that he lacked the necessary *mens rea* for the offence when he is basing this claim upon the fact that he was suffering from self-induced intoxication. This is a rule of substantive law which, in effect, says that where there is evidence that the accused had become voluntarily intoxicated, the prosecution is relieved of the need to prove the *mens rea* of the offence; the result is that section 8 of the Criminal Justice Act 1967 is irrelevant.

Before we go any further it will be useful to illustrate the working of these rules in practice. Suppose that D has been charged with the murder of his wife. The prosecution must prove that D intended to kill or seriously injure his wife. Since murder is a crime of specific intent the defendant will be able to introduce evidence that because of his intoxicated state he did not know that the gun he was pointing at his wife was loaded; he just wanted to give her a scare. It will be up to him to adduce evidence of his intoxicated state, but once this is done it will be for the prosecution to prove that despite the alcohol the accused intended to kill or seriously injure his wife. If, however, D is charged with assaulting his wife thereby causing her actual bodily harm (contrary to Offences Against the Person Act 1861, section 47, see below, p. 240) not only will his plea that he lacked the necessary *mens rea* because he was drunk be held to be irrelevant, it will also have the effect of supplying the prosecution with all the evidence of *mens rea* that it needs. This is a crime of basic intent and if there was no question of intoxication, the prosecution would have to establish that D either intended to apply unlawful force against his wife or that he was reckless, in the *Cunningham* sense, to so doing. Once D relies upon intoxication as a means of showing he did not have the requisite *mens rea* the offence will be treated as one not requiring proof of *mens rea* at all or even that D acted in a voluntary manner.

Despite the outrage that these rules perpetrate upon the general principles of *mens rea*, it is possible to see some sort of logic, at least in relation to offences against the person. Where the defendant is charged with murder or an offence under section 18 of the Offences Against the Person Act 1861 (*e.g.* wounding with intent) he will be able to plead intoxication as a defence. This may mean that he escapes conviction for the offence charged, but the jury will in these cases be able to convict him of alternative offences which are crimes of basic intent where intoxication is irrelevant. In the case of our example of the husband who killed his wife, the jury may hold that he did not intend to kill her, but nevertheless convict him of manslaughter, a crime of basic intent where intoxication cannot be raised. The Courts in these cases take note of the public outrage that would be likely to follow if the defendants were totally exonerated. However, if this was the reasoning of the courts it would have made more sense had rape been classified as a crime of specific intent with indecent assault as its basic intent counterpart.

So far we have said that where the crime is one of specific intent, the accused may rely on self-induced intoxication to negative the *mens rea*, and where the crime is one of basic intent, he may not. Now we have seen in an earlier chapter (above, p. 32), that in most crimes there are several parts to the *actus reus* and the prosecution, must establish *mens rea* in relation to each. Thus in murder the prosecution must establish the unlawful killing of a human being within the Queen's Peace. Murder is a crime of specific intent because in relation to the killing of a human being the prosecution must establish an intention to kill or cause serious harm—nothing short of intention will do. In relation to the other elements it is fairly certain that *Cunningham* recklessness will suffice. Can the defendant rely on intoxication to negative the *mens rea* on these other elements? Rape is a crime of basic intent, but in relation to the act of intercourse the prosecution must establish that the defendant intended to have intercourse with the woman. Are we to say that self-induced intoxication could be relevant on that one aspect? In other words, does the labelling of a crime as one of specific or basic intent mean that intoxication is either relevant on every or no element of the crime?

In *Fortheringham* (1988) the defendant was charged with raping a 14 year old babysitter. He had returned home the worse for drink and had got into his bed. The babysitter had been instructed by the wife that if she and her husband were late home she was to sleep in the matrimonial bed with their child. The defendant had intercourse with the babysitter without her consent, but he maintained that because of the drink he had thought it was his wife. In a charge of rape the prosecution must prove that the defendant had intercourse with a woman who was not the defendant's wife and who did not consent to the intercourse. It has been held that where, because of intoxication, the defendant wrongly supposes that the woman was consenting, he is guilty of rape (*Woods* (1982)). The Court in *Fortheringham* said that the same principle should apply in relation to the issue of identity. This seems a logical decision since in relation to both consent and identity *Cunningham* recklessness would suffice as the basis for liability. However, if the husband had alleged that because of the drink he was totally unaware that he had had intercourse with anyone, a different argument might arise. On this aspect of the *actus reus* only intention will suffice. Is the court to say that it is irrelevant because rape is a crime of basic intent? The answer is, that the court almost certainly would so hold. However, where the crime is one of specific intent, the courts seem reluctant to allow intoxication to negative all aspects of the *mens rea*. This can be seen in the case of *O'Grady* (1987). You will remember that in crimes such as murder the prosecutor must establish that the killing was unlawful and that this means that the prosecutors must establish the absence of any circumstances of justification such as self-defence. In relation to this aspect of the *actus reus* the courts have held that a sober man is entitled to be judged on the facts as he believed them to be (*Williams* (1983) and *Beckford* (1987)). In *O'Grady* two friends who had been drinking heavily fought each other. O'Grady said that he could remember being attacked by his friend and that he had taken what steps he had considered necessary to save his own life. He had later fallen asleep and when he awoke he found his friend to be dead. On appeal against his conviction for manslaughter Lord Lane C.J. said that the issue of mistake should be kept apart from the issue of intent. Where the jury are satisfied that the defendant was mistaken in his belief that any force or the force which he in fact used was necessary to defend himself, and are further satisfied that the mistake was caused by voluntarily induced intoxication, the defence must fail. The question of basic or specific intent was irrelevant to this issue. Although the case involved a manslaughter conviction, Lord Lane indicated (*obiter*) that the same would be true of murder. If this is so then it means that a man who, because of voluntary intoxication, mistakenly believes he is shooting at a gorilla will have a defence to murder if he kills a human being, whereas a defendant will have no defence if he mistakenly believes, because of voluntary intoxication, that he is about to be violently attacked by a man whom he consequently shoots. It is hard to justify such a distinction or to see how you can keep the issues of mistake and intent apart since they are merely different ways of looking at the same issue. It would surely make greater sense to say that intoxication can be raised in relation to any element of the *mens rea* in a crime of specific intent and not at all in a crime of basic intent.

It is submitted that the effect of this case is to obscure an already muddied pond. Is the Court saying that even in a crime of specific intent intoxication is relevant only to certain aspects of the *mens rea*, namely the specific intent, or is it simply saying that it has no relevance simply to the issue of the defendant's belief in circumstances of justification? Suppose that D, a soldier in time of war, has shot and killed his sergeant; can intoxication be used to support his claim that

(i) he thought that his rifle was empty and he was only larking about?

(ii) he believed that the sergeant was making homosexual advances to him and that as a result he lost his self control (see below, p. 217)?

(iii) that he thought that the sergeant was about seriously to injure him?

(iv) that he thought the person at whom he was shooting was an enemy soldier?

It is possible that we have arrived at a position whereby the courts have held that intoxication can provide no defence to any aspect of a crime of basic intent, but that it may afford limited protection in crimes of specific intent.

As if to add injury to insult, the courts have further complicated matters by their approach to specific statutory defences in crimes of basic intent. It is an offence under Criminal Damage Act 1971 section 1(1), intentionally or recklessly to damage or destroy property belonging to another (see below, p. 344). Since *Caldwell* recklessness applies here it can be no defence that, due to voluntary intoxication, the defendant did not realise that he was damaging property or that he believed that the property was his own. (If the wider definition in *Caldwell* is used drunkenness is irrelevant, and if the narrower definition in *Caldwell* is relied upon a defence of drunkenness would be met by the classification of the offence as being one of basic intent). However, under section 5 of the Act it is provided that the defendant would have a lawful excuse if

he thought that the person entitled to consent to the damage
would have done so had he known the circumstances. In *Jaggard*
v. *Dickinson* (1981) the court held that her mistaken belief
amounted to a defence even though it was attributable to her
voluntary intoxication.

We have said earlier that where there is evidence of drunkenness in a crime of basic intent the prosecution is relieved of the
need to prove *mens rea*. This, however, raises further questions.
What do we mean by drunkenness? At what stage on the scale of
intoxication does the judge say that the prosecution is relieved of
the need to prove *mens rea*? Can the prosecutor seek to lead
evidence that the accused was drunk as an alternative to proving
mens rea? It would seem that the effect of *Majewski* is to make
drunkenness the basis for liability in crimes of basic intent where
it is raised, and so it would seem to follow that the prosecution
should be entitled to lead evidence which would establish such
liability. However, we should remember that *Majewski* was the
case of a defendant raising drunkenness by way of defence and
furthermore it was the case of a defendant saying that he was so
inebriated that he did not have the necessary *mens rea*. Most
adults are aware that it takes a lot of alcohol to reach the stage
where you simply do not know what you are doing. It is submitted that only where there is evidence that the accused had
reached this extreme state should the prosecution be relieved of
the need to prove *mens rea*. Equally, if the prosecution is to be
allowed to adduce evidence of intoxication instead of *mens rea*, it
should only be where there is evidence that the defendant had
drunk so much he did not form the necessary *mens rea*. We
should remember that the defence is the defence of drunkenness
or intoxication and although there is no definition of these terms,
they are not appropriate to cover the case of the defendant who
has had the odd drink. It would be absurd if a defendant, charged
with assault, could be convicted without any evidence of *mens rea*
simply because he admitted to having had a half pint of beer.
Unfortunately there is no clear answer to this issue and it may be
that the courts will eventually draw no distinction between the
defendant who has had a few beers and the defendant who is
completely intoxicated.

2. SELF-INDUCED AUTOMATISM

A similar problem may arise in relation to self-induced automatism. In *Bailey* (1983) the accused suffered from diabetes for

which he was receiving insulin treatment. On the day in question he complained of feeling unwell and drank a mixture of water and sugar, though he did not eat any food. Shortly afterwards he struck the victim a blow on the head. He claimed that he had been acting in a state of non-insane automatism caused by hypoglycaemia brought on by his failure to eat food. It was accepted that since the attack was caused more by the failure to eat rather than the diabetes itself, that this was not a disease of the mind. However the trial judge held that self-induced automatism was no defence either to wounding with intent nor to the alternative charge of unlawful wounding. The Court of Appeal took the view that since wounding with intent was an offence of specific intent to which voluntary intoxication would be a defence, by analogy the same must be true for self-induced automatism. His conviction for wounding with intent was, therefore, quashed. Unlawful wounding, however, is a crime of basic intent to which voluntary intoxication is no defence. Did it therefore follow that the accused's self-induced automatism should be equally inadmissable? The Court of Appeal thought there was a distinction between the two situations. Where the accused lacked the necessary *mens rea* in a basic intent crime because of voluntary intoxication, the court relieved the prosecution of the need to prove *mens rea*. It has been said that people should realise that they will react in violent and dangerous ways when they are drunk and so the necessary *mens rea* is supplied by their voluntary action in getting into the drunken state. But the same cannot necessarily be said of the man who fails to eat after taking insulin. If the accused realises that such a failure may lead to aggressive, unpredictable and uncontrollable conduct and nevertheless deliberately runs the risk or ignores it, this will amount to recklessness. However, there is no evidence to suggest that such consequences are common knowledge even among diabetics. It followed that his self-induced automatism should have been left to the jury on this basis, even on the basic intent charge of unlawful wounding.

3. Intoxication and Mental Abnormality

It is, of course, possible that the accused has consumed so much alcohol that, in the words of the M'Naghten Rules, he does not know the nature and quality of his acts, or if he does, then he does not know that he is doing what is wrong. But you will remember that before a jury is entitled to find that the accused is suffering from legal insanity they must find that his defect of reason was caused by a disease of the mind. Thus, in most cases of intoxication there will be no question of the accused being found to be legally insane. Where, however, the alcohol or drugs have produced a more than transitory effect on the accused's mind, it would be possible for the court to hold that he was insane. If such a finding is possible then the resulting insanity would be a defence to any criminal charge and not just to crimes of specific intent. The same sort of reasoning would apply to diminished responsibility. The abnormality of mind must have been caused by one of a specified list of causes and here injury would appear to be the only possible one. It does not seem unreasonable that the effect of a large quantity of alcohol or drugs might be held to injure the mind of the accused and in this case, on a murder charge, he would be able to plead diminished responsibility.

4. The Dutch Courage Cases

We have all heard of people having a drink in order to give themselves Dutch courage in order to be able to do something; for example, the candidate for a job who has a couple of whiskies in order to be able to face the interview. What is the position then when D, who has been planning to kill his wife for several weeks, has a few drinks to stiffen his resolve? We can look at this through a series of examples.

(i) D plans to kill his wife and he has half a bottle of whisky before he kills her. All the drink does is to remove a few of the misgivings that D has about his plan to kill his wife. It may even be that his plan is only a wild dream, and that one evening he has had rather a lot to drink at a party and suddenly finds the courage to do what he would never have done while sober. The answer to this type of example is quite simple. Since D still intends to kill his wife, the fact that the alcohol has given him the necessary courage to perform the task is totally irrelevant and provides no defence whatsoever.

(ii) D knows that alcohol or certain drugs produce in him a sort of Jekyll and Hyde transformation, and that while he is under the influence of the alcohol he is likely to make a violent assault on anyone nearby. He therefore deliberately gets drunk in the presence of his wife in the hope that he will attack her and kill her. In fact D does kill his wife whilst under the control of the alcohol, though he is totally unaware of what he is doing. It would seem that this would be no defence for reasons which will appear in example (iii).

(iii) D plans to kill his wife and so starts drinking a bottle of whisky to get Dutch courage. The effect of the alcohol is to deprive him of the ability to form the necessary *mens rea* for murder or to bring to the surface a mental condition from which he is suffering (*e.g.* psychopathy) which causes him to be unable to comprehend the nature and quality of his act or that what he is doing is legally wrong. In such a state he does, in fact, kill his wife. Can he now plead either drunkenness or insanity as a defence to the charge of murder? These were basically the facts of the famous case of *Att.-Gen. for Northern Ireland* v. *Gallagher* (1963). In that case the House of Lords held that if a sane and sober person, who is capable of forming an intent to kill and realises that such an act would be legally wrong, forms an intention to kill and gets himself so drunk that at the time he in fact kills he is uncapable of forming the intent to kill, he will not be able to rely on that self-induced drunkenness as a defence. Equally, if the drink he takes to give himself Dutch courage has the effect of bringing out a quiescent mental state under which he kills though he does not realise that the killing is unlawful then he will not be allowed to plead this drink-induced insanity as a defence.

Clearly, this ruling is sufficient to cover the example in number (ii) where the accused deliberately sets out to induce a state in which he thinks he will attack his wife. But it also covers situations in (iii) in which the accused, after forming the intent to kill, drinks merely to give himself courage and passes unwittingly into a psychopathic state during which time he kills his wife.

5. Involuntary Intoxication

Finally, we must consider the case of the person who commits a criminal act whilst under the influence of alcohol or drugs but where he was not responsible for that condition. He may have got into such a condition because his friend laced his drinks or got him to take drugs without his knowledge. Equally, the accused may have been forcibly injected with a drug or forced to consume alcohol. Finally, there are those situations in which the accused is on a prescribed course of medical treatment and he does not know the effect the drugs will have on him, and in particular, the effect it will have if combined with alcohol. In *Allen* (1988) the Court of Appeal held that a person who had voluntarily consumed alcohol could not claim that his drunkenness became involuntary simply because he did not realise the strength of the alcohol he was drinking. There is little authority on involuntary intoxication as a defence to a criminal charge (see *Davies* (1983)). However, one of the main factors in the judicial unwillingness to allow intoxication as a general defence to all crimes, namely the fact that the accused was responsible for his condition, is missing here. It is suggested that a plea of involuntary intoxication should be a defence to any crime if it means that the accused did not form the necessary *mens rea*. There should be no place here for the classification of crimes of basic and specific intent. Where involuntary intoxication leads an accused to commit a crime he would not have committed when sober (for example, rape) but does not deprive him of the requisite *mens rea* then it should be no defence, though it will be presumably taken into account in mitigation. Involuntary intoxication is no defence to driving whilst over the prescribed limit though it may well lead to the driver not receiving the automatic disqualification, see above, p. 95.

Where the accused is on a medically prescribed course of drugs and because of this does not form the *mens rea* required by a particular crime, he should be acquitted whether or not the crime in question is one requiring specific intent. This should also be the position where the accused's lack of *mens rea* was due to the effect of the alcohol on the course of drugs, but only where he is unaware of the effect the alcohol might have on the drugs (along the lines suggested in *Bailey*, above). A similarly understanding view was taken in *Hardie* (1985) where the accused had been given out of date valium tablets by a friend who had told him that they would calm his nerves and could not possibly do him any harm. It was held that even though the crime in question was one requiring only basic intent, he was entitled to an acquittal if, because of the effect of these drugs, he had not formed that basic intent.

III. *SELF-DEFENCE, NECESSITY AND DURESS*

These defences all have a common feature; they are all based on the concept of necessity. In other words the defendant is alleged to have committed a criminal offence but he pleads that he was forced to commit the offence. The three defences reflect the different ways in which this "force" arises. For example, suppose that D (the defendant) is a member of a mountain climbing team. As they ascend the mountain they are roped together. Ahead of D are A, B and C and behind D is E. D is alleged to have cut the rope between himself and E, sending E hurtling down the mountain side and seriously injuring him. D has been charged with causing grievous bodily harm with intent (contrary to section 18 of the Offences Against the Person Act 1861 (see below, p. 244). If his defence was self-defence, D might, for example, plead that E had a gun and was about to shoot D, and so D cut the rope to protect himself. If the defence was duress, D might plead that both he and his family had been threatened with violence if he did not seriously injure E. If the defence was necessity, he might plead that E had slipped and was gradually pulling the others with him and so D cut the rope to protect the others. We shall see that although the concept of necessity is the basis of the well recognised defences of self-defence and duress, until recently the courts have been reluctant to admit the existence of a general defence of necessity.

A. Self-Defence

The term self-defence is loosely used to cover a series of similar defences. It will arise where the accused has been charged with some form of offence against the person and seeks to justify his use of force (there is a similar defence provided under section 5 of the Criminal Damage Act 1971 for an accused charged with damaging property belonging to another; see below, p. 351). Let us suppose that X has been charged with unlawfully and maliciously inflicting grievous bodily harm on Y; he may plead one of the following fact situations by way of justification.

  (i) X may say that he was trying to prevent Y from committing a crime which may or may not have involved X.

 (ii) He may claim that Y was about to attack him and that he had to injure Y in order to protect himself.

(iii) He may claim that Y was about to attack a member of his family (or anyone else) and that X simply did all that was necessary to protect the would be victim.

(iv) He may claim that Y was in the process of burgling his house and that he simply used sufficient force to restrain him until the police arrived.

Arguably only (ii) is properly called the defence of self-defence, but the same general principles would seem to apply to all four. Number (i) is now covered by section 3 of the Criminal Law Act 1967 and since, as we shall see, Y is probably committing a crime in examples (ii) and (iv), the principles of section 3 may actually cover all four types of problem. What is common to all is the fact that unless the defence is raised by the prosecution evidence, the accused will bear the burden of introducing evidence of the defence before the prosecution will bear the legal burden of rebutting the defence beyond reasonable doubt. We can now examine each in turn. [See further Smith, *Justification and Excuse in the Criminal Law*.]

1. PREVENTION OF CRIME

This was originally covered by common law rules, but is now covered by section 3 of the Criminal Law Act 1967 which provides "(1) A person may use such force as is reasonable in the circumstances in the prevention of crime, or in effecting or assisting in the lawful arrest of offenders or suspected offenders or of persons unlawfully at large."

The crux of the provision is determining what is reasonable in the circumstances of the particular case being tried, and this is a question of fact to be determined by the jury. Thus where the accused is charged with assaulting another and seeks to rely on section 3, the question for the jury is whether they are "satisfied that no reasonable man (*a*) with knowledge of such facts as were known to the accused or [honestly] believed by him to exist (*b*) in the circumstances and time available to him for reflection (*c*) could be of the opinion that the prevention of the risk of harm to which others might be exposed if the suspect were allowed to escape, justified exposing the suspect to the risk of harm to him that might result from the kind of force that the accused contemplated using." (*Reference under section 48A of the Criminal Appeal (Northern Ireland) Act 1968 (No. 1 of 1975*); *per* Lord Diplock interpreting a provision identical in terms with section 3; in para (*a*) the word [honestly] has been substituted for "reasonably" which appeared in the original quotation. This, it is suggested, is necessary in the light of the decision of the Court of Appeal in *Gladstone Williams* (1984) and *Beckford* (1987) (above, p. 85). Thus in *Cousins* (1982) the Court of Appeal held that, in appropriate circumstances, it could be reasonable to threaten to kill another when, for example, it is believed that this would forestall a planned attack on oneself. Whether or not such a threat is reasonable is always a question of fact for the jury. Clearly a threat to kill may be reasonable in circumstances where the implementation of such a threat would not be.

What, then, if the accused was mistaken in thinking that the man he assaulted was about to commit a crime? Suppose that X was drinking in a bar when he saw Y pick up a broken glass and wave it menacingly in front of Z. It would not be unreasonable for X to suppose that Y meant to harm Z and for him to take action to prevent such injury to Z. However, it turns out that Y was just telling Z of an incident which had happened in the bar on the previous evening. It is suggested that the jury must consider the facts as they were known to X or as he honestly believed them to be. Thus, in our example, if the jury considers that X honestly thought that Y was about to attack Z, they should proceed to consider whether it was reasonable for him to have acted in the way he did. (But see *Barrett and Barrett* (1980)).

Suppose the accused reasonably believed that Y was about to strike Z but used, by any reasonable standards, too much force to prevent the crime? Let us take a rather extreme example. Suppose that X is shopping in a department store when he sees an old lady obviously about to put some jewellery in her handbag and so he grabs a heavy table lamp which happens to be on display and viciously clubs her over the head causing her really serious injury. It is possible that he honestly believes that he will be praised by the authorities for his action, but no one in their right mind would consider that the action was reasonable. Here the jury should try to balance the harm prevented by the accused's action against the harm caused by his action. The question is whether the force used was reasonable in the circumstances and no use would be served by trying to speculate in the abstract about whether or not it can ever be justifiable for a woman to kill a man who is trying to rape her, or whether it is reasonable to injure someone who is about to damage a valuable work of art. But the jury should be advised that they must bear in mind the circumstances under which the accused made his decision. He was probably not afforded the opportunity to sit down and weigh up all the pros and cons; he may have had a split second in which to make up his mind (see further on excessive use of force, p. 178).

2. SELF-DEFENCE AND DEFENCE OF OTHERS

Although in many cases where the accused pleads self-defence the situation could be covered by section 3 in that if the accused's story is correct he is merely trying to prevent the other man from committing a crime—namely attacking the accused—this is not necessarily so. If D is attacked by a child he knows to be below the age of criminal responsibility then he cannot say that the force he used on the child to stop the attack was force used in the prevention of crime. He would, however, be able to rely on the common law defence of self-defence. It is clear that the common law defence of self-defence survives section 3, but since the area of overlap is, to all intents and purposes, total, it would be absurd if the common law defence were to be governed by principles different from those controlling section 3. It is therefore submitted that where the accused, who is charged with an offence against the person, relies on the common law defence of self-defence, the court will approach the question in the same way as a defence brought under section 3. (See also *O'Grady* (1987) above, p. 166).

Self-defence is perhaps rather a narrow term to describe the defence since it applies to force use to protect members of the accused's family, his friends or even a total stranger he sees being unlawfully attacked. In each case, the question should be the same, "was the force he used reasonable in the circumstances as he knew them to be or honestly believed them to be?" The old cases on self-defence established that the accused who sought to rely on self-defence had to show that he retreated as far as was safely possible before using serious force. In *Bird* (1985), however, the Lord Chief Justice made if perfectly clear that it was not an essential part of the defence that the accused had demonstrated by her actions that she did not want to fight. The law, he said, was correctly stated in Smith and Hogan's *Criminal Law* (5th ed., 1983), p. 327, "A demonstration by D at the time that he did not want to fight is, no doubt, the best evidence that he was acting reasonably and in good faith in self-defence; but it is no more than that. A person may, in some circumstances so act without temporising, disengaging or withdrawing; and he should have a good defence." Suppose that the accused is standing at a bar when the man next to him suggests that if he does not want a beer glass rammed in his face he should go and drink elsewhere. If the accused were seriously to injure the man who made the threats, then it would be open to the jury to take the view that this was unreasonable in the circumstances since he could simply have walked away, however undignified that course of action may have seemed. The possibility of retreat should be treated in the same way as the proportionality rule in provocation (see below, p. 222).

It is sometimes said that the defence is available only against imminent violence, which implies that it cannot be used against violence which will occur sometime in the future. Again this should be regarded as a question affecting the reasonableness of the accused's action. Clearly, if A has been kidnapped by B and he knows B will kill him if a ransom is not paid in so many hours, it should be permissible for A to use force against B to prevent the future killing. On the other hand if the facts were different and A has the opportunity of putting the matter in the hands of the police before B carries out his threats, then the use of violence by A against B may be seen as unreasonable.

Normally self-defence describes a situation in which X has been attacked by Y and takes action to defend itself. There may, however, by situations in which it will be justified to take pre-emptive action. Thus in *Finch and Jardine* (1983) two police officers approached a car in which they believed was an armed man who was extremely dangerous. It was held that in such situations it may be unreasonable for the police officers to wait for the suspect to shoot first.

In *Att.-Gen.'s Reference* (*No. 2 of* 1983) (1984) the Court of Appeal held that it might be justifiable for a man to make and possess a petrol bomb (an act which would normally be an offence) where this was done to protect his family or property by way of self-defence against an imminent and apprehended attack. Though if he continued to possess the bomb after the threat had passed, his possession would no longer be justified.

3. DEFENCE OF PROPERTY

Again this is probably covered sufficiently by section 3 and the same principles will apply; was the force used by D to protect his property reasonable in the circumstances? Can it ever be reasonable to kill in order to defend your property? (See *Hussey* (1924).)

4. Excessive Force

Now that we have looked at the various forms of self-defence, we can turn to a problem that has been hinted at in the preceding sections. We have seen that if the accused mistakenly believes that there is a need for force, he will be able to rely on the defence provided that he used only so much force as was reasonably necessary in the circumstances he believed to exist. Thus, if the accused rightly believes X is about to attack him, but wrongly believes that X plans to use a knife, the amount of force which would be reasonable will be assessed on the facts the accused believed to exist. But the more difficult problem is the one in which the amount of force used was unreasonable even in the circumstances he believed to exist. Two types of problem may arise here:

(i) X believes that he is about to be attacked by Y and reasonably decides to shoot Y in the leg as he approaches. Unfortunately, his aim is bad and Y is killed. If X is charged with murder, the first thing to remember is that the prosecution must prove that X had the necessary *mens rea*. That aside, the jury should be asked to consider the reasonableness of what the accused contemplated doing. In our case, they should ask whether it was reasonable for X to try to shoot Y in the legs to prevent the attack (see the passage of Lord Diplock, above, p. 174).

(ii) X believes that poachers are taking trout from his lake during the night. He therefore lies in wait with a twelve-bore shotgun and when he sees Y taking trout from the lake he shoots at him and kills him. In other words, we have a situation in which the jury would have probably sanctioned the use of some force, but not the killing of Y. Where does X stand now? Does this finding mean that he has no defence at all? The problem is only likely to be acute in the cases where the charge is murder, since in all other cases, if it is held that excessive use of force means that the defence fails, the judge can take the facts into account when passing sentence. However, where the accused is charged with murder, if the defence fails the accused will be convicted of murder (if the prosecution establishes the necessary *mens rea*), in which case he receives life imprisonment. For a time the Australian Courts adopted a half-way house whereby on a murder charge, the jury would be entitled to return a verdict of manslaughter if it felt excessive force had been used, though some force was justifiable; *McKay* (1957).

This approach was not adopted in England; *Palmer* (1971) and has now been rejected in Australia as being too hard for juries to understand; *Zecewic* (1987). In England and Wales therefore, self-defence and defence of property and the defence of property and the defence under section 3 are either complete defences in that they lead to acquittal or they are no defence at all. This may seem rather harsh but the recent case of *Shannon* (1980) shows that this harshness is tempered with leniency. In that case the judge had left the jury with the simple question "Are you satisfied that the appellant used more force than was necessary in the circumstances?" On its own, this would give the jury the impression that they should simply take a detached look at the facts and decide what force would have been reasonable in the circumstances. However, the Court of Appeal said that they should have been reminded of Lord Morris' qualification to this test which he propounded in *Palmer*, namely, that, if they concluded that the appellant honestly thought without having to weigh things to a nicety, that what he did was necessary to defend himself, they should regard that as "most potent evidence" that it was actually reasonably necessary. "In other words, if the jury concluded that the stabbing was the act of a desperate man in extreme difficulties, with his assailant dragging him down by the hair, they should consider very carefully before concluding that the stabbing was an offensive and not a defensive act, albeit it went beyond what an onlooker would regard as reasonably necessary." What the court is saying is that the test is reasonableness taking into account the circumstances in which the decision had to be made. The 14th Report of the Criminal Law Revision Committee favoured the introduction of a partial defence so that where the accused honestly miscalculates the amount of force needed he would be convicted of manslaughter and not murder.

B. Necessity

Let us start discussion of the concept of necessity as a defence to a criminal prosecution by considering a hypothetical example. You are driving home one night when you see in the distance a child in difficulties in a river which runs alongside the road. Unfortunately before you can reach the child you have to pass through some traffic lights which have just turned to red. You drive through the lights to rescue the child only to find that you were being followed by a police car and that despite your heroic rescue you are to be prosecuted for driving through a red light. Have you any defences? Do you consider that you ought to have a defence? You clearly cannot plead that you did not intend to disobey the traffic signal, and in any case it is an offence of strict liability. You cannot plead that it was an involuntary action. Your only hope would be that the law provides that in such circumstances you have a lawful excuse and in our example this would have to be based on a concept of necessity. Of course, as we shall soon see there are dangers in such a general defence, so possibly some might argue that it would be better to leave it up to the commonsense of individual chief constables not to prosecute. But discretion is rarely a satisfactory means of solving legal problems. Either the law should recognise such a defence or it should not. The question, therefore, is should we have such a general defence and do we, in fact, have such a defence? There would be very few who would be unwilling to see a defence of necessity applied to an example such as the one given above. Once, however, the crime becomes more serious the problems with such a defence become more apparent.

In the famous case of *Dudley and Stephens* (1884) three men and a cabin boy were forced to take to a lifeboat following a storm at sea. There was very little food in the lifeboat and the four grew very weak. After 20 days, the last eight of which were without any food, D and S killed the cabin boy with a knife and for the next four days the three men lived off his flesh and blood. On that fourth day they were picked up by a passing vessel in a very low state of health. They were put on trial for murder but the jury refused to convict them. Instead, they returned a statement of the facts they found to be proved. They found that there was no food left and there was little chance of survival for much longer. The cabin boy was in the worst state and was likely to have died first. D and S killed the cabin boy who did not consent to being killed, but had they not lived off his flesh they would probably all have died before they were picked up. There was no greater reason for killing the cabin boy other than the fact that he was the weakest. This statement of facts was referred to the Queen's Bench Division who convicted D and S of murder. Their death sentences were commuted to six month's imprisonment without hard labour.

Clearly this case raises the defence of necessity in its most extreme form—can such extraneous circumstances ever justify killing? The answer of the court in *Dudley and Stephens* is that necessity cannot possibly justify such an act—and circumstances are unlikely to get more compelling than in that case. If we imagine for one moment that the court had acquitted D and S on the ground that necessity justified their action, what sort of precedent would it have set? At what stage could people in the future resort to such acts? Are there any rules for choosing the victim? Would the cabin boy have the right to kill either D or S in self-defence? Would we test D and S's act on subjective or objective grounds?

Why did the judges reject the defence of necessity in *Dudley and Stephens*? Unfortunately, the answer to this question is not clear. It is possible to read into the case the view that no real necessity existed in that case at all (Coleridge C.J.) and it was therefore unnecessary to rule on the defence of necessity in English law. Alternatively, it might have been based on the view that there was no reason as to why the cabin boy should have been selected as the victim—thus implying that had there been a democratic choice of victim the court might have taken a different view. Or possibly, as the majority of writers would seem to believe, the court was in fact saying that there was no defence of necessity in English law.

If the court was saying that no real necessity existed in that case, then when would such a necessity exist? It is hard to imagine a more extreme case than *Dudley and Stephens*. Of course, they may have been picked up within the hour, but his hardly seems relevant. On the facts know to them there was no real hope of being picked up, coupled with the very real knowledge that if no action were taken it would soon be too late to act at all. It thus seems unrealistic to hold that *Dudley and Stephens* was based on a finding that no necessity existed in that case.

Would, then, the court have taken a different view had a more democratic method been used to select the food? Clearly, the reason for the selection of the cabin boy was that he was the least likely to resist and the most likely to die first, but there is no reason to suppose that he would not have recovered given nourishment. Should they have drawn lots? This was the suggestion made in the American case, *U.S.* v. *Holmes* (1842). There, the Supreme Court held that the crew ought to have left the overcrowded life-boat first, leaving just enough crew to look after the passengers. If more needed to be thrown overboard, then these should have been passengers chosen by lot.

It seems fairly clear that this view would not have appealed to the judges in *Dudley and Stephens*, though they might have taken a different view had all four consented to the drawing of lots, for then the killing would have been by consent. Normally consent is no defence to a murder charge, but it might have just been acceptable in these circumstances. The court obviously expected the four to lie back and gracefully accept the inevitable.

If we take the third possible view, that English criminal law knows no defence of necessity, how far was the court influenced by the fact that the crime in question was murder? Can it be regarded as a holding that necessity cannot excuse murder, but might excuse less serious crimes? We shall shortly be looking at the defence of duress which closely resembles the defence of necessity, but which the courts have been prepared to allow as a general defence to practically all crimes (see below, p. 183). It seems rather illogical to recognise the defence of duress but not that of necessity. (See Report of the Law Commission on Defences of General Application: No. 83 (1977) which recommended that necessity should not be a defence). If a doctor who was not on night duty and who had consumed a large quantity of alcohol drove his car to the scene of a road accident to help the victims, should he not have a defence of necessity to a charge of being over the prescribed limit? If a diabetic, desperate for insulin, breaks into a chemist because he can find no one to help, should he not be able to plead necessity? (See also *Buckoke* v. *Greater London Council* (1971)). Is the safer answer to say that we can leave it to the police to exercise their discretion sensibly or to the trial judge to show clemency following a conviction? It may be easier to do that, but it is hardly a satisfactory answer.

Thus, at present, we must conclude that English law does not recognise a defence of necessity in its straightforward form. However, we shall see in the next section that recently the courts have been prepared to allow a limited version of the defence of necessity in what is called duress of circumstances. In classifying this as a variant of duress the court have been able to allow what, in reality, is a defence of necessity, but a defence subject to all the stringent requirements of the defence of duress (see below, p. 187).

C. DURESS

The problem here is rather similar to that in the previous section on necessity. Again extraneous factors lead the accused intentionally to perform an act which is contrary to the criminal law. The difference is that here the extraneous facts are deliberately produced by a third party with a view to persuade the victim to break the criminal law. Let us start by posing a hypothetical situation which is, unfortunately, all too familiar today. X is visited by members of a terrorist organisation. They have discovered that X is to drive a well-known politician on his forthcoming visit to the country. They tell X that unless he stops the car at a given point on the route they will kill his wife and children (or himself). They further tell X that they intend to kill the politician. X does what he is ordered to do and the politician is killed. X is then charged as a secondary party to the killing. The question raised by this problem is whether X will be able to plead that he acted under duress and that it would not therefore be possible to say that his action was truly voluntary? In other words, does English law recognise the defence of duress and if such a defence is recognised, what are its essential ingredients?

(1) Is there a defence of duress?

Over the last few years it has been generally accepted that duress is a general defence to any crime, subject to the qualification that it was not available to a person charged as a principal offender in murder and to a person charged with treason (see *D.P.P for Northern Ireland.* v. *Lynch* (1975) and *Abbott* v. *The Queen* (1977)). Thus a man charged with murder could plead duress, but the jury would be instructed that if they found him to be a principal offender in the crime they must ignore the plea. The reasoning behind this distinction between the principal and secondary offender to murder was that the law could excuse a person who had taken a subsidiary role in the killing of another human being, but that it could not excuse the actual killer. In other words no threat could be serious enough to cause you to take another person's life. The dividing line between a principal and a secondary offender may be exceedingly hard to draw, but on it could rest the difference between a conviction for murder or a complete acquittal. This was clearly an unsatisfactory state of affairs and the House of Lords took the opportunity to review the position in *Howe* (1987). In effect, the House saw the decision lying between an extension of the defence to all murderers or a complete withdrawal of the defence in murder cases. In the result the

House decided that it should not be available to anyone charged with murder whether as a principal or secondary offender. The Lord Chancellor further held that the defence of duress on a charge of attempted murder should also be reconsidered, and one of their Lordships said that duress was not available on such a charge, though his remarks are clearly *obiter dicta*. The decision clearly simplifies the law, but it will lead to some harsh decisions. For example, if the defendant is threatened with the instant death of his wife and children if he does not drive the terrorists to a spot where they will ambush and kill a political leader he must choose between the death of his family and his own conviction for murder. It is easy to see the public policy decision behind this case; where the defence of duress is available it will be easier to coerce innocent people into providing aid. Possibly when the law is codified, there will be a chance to consider a half-way house solution, namely a conviction for manslaughter in cases where the defendant has either killed or aided a killer under duress. It is, of course conceivable, that a jury faced with a hard case might simply refuse to convict the accused of murder, and return a verdict of manslaughter instead. It would appear that duress remains unavailable to a person charged with treason.

(2) What constitutes duress?

Where the accused seeks to rely on the defence of duress he bears the burden of introducing evidence on it and it is then up to the prosecution to prove beyond reasonable doubt that the accused was not acting under duress. Many of the statements on what constitute duress speak of the need for the will of the accused to have been overborne by threats of death or serious personal injury so the commission of the alleged offence was no longer the voluntary act of the accused. Whatever the earlier courts may have meant by the use of the word "voluntary" it is now clear that it is not to be used in the sense we saw it used in relation to automatism in the sense of an act he was not really in control of. What we are concerned with is a situation in which the accused was faced with a choice of two evils and under that pressure he chose what to him seemed the lesser of the two and deliberately committed a crime. The question is whether the court should take account of the pressures and if so what sort of pressure should be needed.

In *Graham* (1982) the Court of Appeal recommended the

following approach. First, was the defendant, or may he have been, impelled to act as he did because, as a result of what he reasonably believed the threatener to have said or done, he had good cause to fear that he might be killed or seriously injured? Secondly, if so, have the prosecution made sure that a person of reasonable firmness sharing the same characteristics as the accused (*cf. Camplin*, below, p. 219) would not have responded in the way that the defendant did?

In *Howe* (1987) the House of Lords was asked to consider whether the defence of duress failed if the prosecution proved that a person of reasonable firmness sharing the characteristics of the defendant would not have given way to the threats as did the defendant. Their Lordships replied that the test for duress did contain an objective element and that the test expounded in *Graham* (above) accurately recorded this.

In *Graham* the court was considering duress as a defence to a charge of murder, a situation which is no longer possible. Where, however, a lesser crime is committed under duress, are threats of consequences less than death or serious bodily harm sufficient? It could be argued that a sliding scale of threats would be fair, though it would inevitably introduce an air of uncertainty. However, in *Valderrama-Vega* (1985) where the accused had been charged with being knowingly concerned in the fraudulent evasion of the prohibition on the importation of a controlled drug, it appeared that his will may have been overcome by a combination of factors including (1) threats of death or serious injury against him and his family, (2) threats to expose his homosexual tendencies and (3) fear of financial ruin. It was held that the defence of duress was available so long as it was reasonably possible to say that the threat of death or serious bodily injury was a *sine qua non* of his decision to offend, although it need not have been the only factor. This would suggest that threats of anything less than death or serious bodily injury will not suffice whatever the offence.

It is generally accepted that the threats do not have to be against the safety of the defendant himself. Threats to kill or seriously injure the defendant's family, and possibly anyone with whom he has a special relationship, will suffice.

A further restriction is that the defence of duress should not be open to the accused if it was open to him to avoid the threatened consequences of not committing the criminal act. Thus, if there is an opportunity for him to place himself under police protection, even if he does not believe the police will be able to protect him, then failure to avail himself of the opportunity will mean that the defence of duress will fail. A rather benevolent application of this rule was seen in the case of *Hudson* (1971) where two girls were charged with committing perjury. They claimed that they had been threatened with injury if they made certain statements at the trial in question, and that during the course of the trial they had seen one of the men who had made the threats in the public gallery. Of course, they would have been able to have asked, then and there, for police help, but the Court of Appeal held that the defence of duress should have been left to the jury. The decision seems to have been based upon the notion that police protection could not guarantee to be effective and that the threats were no less immediate because they could not be carried out until the girls had left the courtroom. However, police protection will rarely, if ever, be able to guarantee permanent protection and the decision seems to be understandable. The Law Commission recommend that the defence should not be available where the accused has had an opportunity to seek official protection and this would presumably overrule *Hudson*.

Does such a rule mean that if a man's daughter is being held hostage and threatened with death if he does not join the kidnappers on a robbery that because there will be a chance to call in the police, he cannot rely on the defence of duress? It would seem at present that a defence of duress would be available in these circumstances, but the Law Commission have recommended that in this situation the defence of duress should not be available. It may seem a harsh recommendation, but it must be seen against the policy argument that to widen the scope of the defence is to provide villains with even more incentive to use threats to gain their ends. If a person subjected to threats knows that he will have no defence to a criminal prosecution, then he is less likely to yield to those threats.

In *Sharp* (*David*) (1987) the Court of Appeal held that where the accused had committed a crime after voluntarily joining an organisation with full knowledge that it was the sort of organisation which was likely to put pressure on its members to commit the type of crime with which the accused was now charged, the defence of duress should not be available. However, if he was not aware of the risks when he joined, or he was compelled to join he is entitled to use the defence. In any event if there is evidence that the accused acted under duress, the jury should decide on the exact facts (*Shepherd* (1987)).

(3) Duress of circumstances

In *Jones* (1963) the court was not prepared to allow a defence of duress in a situation where the defendant claimed to have driven dangerously because he thought he was being chased by men who wanted to attack him; his pursuers were, in fact, police officers. The court ruled that the defence was only open to someone who had been ordered to commit a crime, and no-one had ordered Jones to drive dangerously. However, more recent decisions have tended to support the possibility of a defence of duress in these circumstances. In *Conway* (1988) C was charged with and convicted of reckless driving. He claimed that he honestly believed that the two plain clothes police officers who approached his car planned to kill his passenger T. T had been involved in a shooting incident several weeks earlier, and C believed that T had been the real target for the attack at that time. After a high speed chase through a built up area C was eventually forced to stop. On his appeal against conviction C argued that the jury should have been directed on the defence of necessity. The Court of Appeal was of the opinion that it was not entirely clear whether or not there was a general defence of necessity and if so when it was available. The Court held that it was only available in cases of reckless driving where it amounted to duress of circumstances. What this means is that the Court is saying that it would accept a defence of duress (provided that all the requirements of that defence were satisfied, see above, p. 184) but that this defence was unlike the ordinary defence of duress where the defendant is told to do something "or else." In duress of circumstances the duress is applied by the surrounding circumstances. Woolf L.J. agreed with a comment of Lord Hailsham L.L. in *Howe* where he remarked that it could make no difference whether the accused does something because he is told to "or else" or whether he does it because he perceives that in view of the circumstances he has no choice.

The position after *Conway* was somewhat obscured by the discussion in that case of two earlier decisions in which the Court did not seem to appreciate the true nature of the defence that was emerging. However following the most recent decision in this area, *Martin* (1989), it seems fairly safe to assert that we now have a general defence of necessity, the scope and requirements of which are those of the defence of duress. In *Martin* the defendant was charged with driving while disqualified The trial judge refused to allow the defence of necessity and so the defendant pleaded guilty and introduced, by way of mitigation, the facts he would have used to support his defence of necessity. He said that on the morning in question his wife asked him to drive her son (his stepson) to work as he was late and in danger of being fired. His wife had previously tried to commit suicide and she now threatened to do so again if he refused. He thus felt obliged to drive, although he had been disqualified. Allowing his appeal against conviction, the Court of Appeal said that Martin had discharged his evidential burden in relation to the defence of duress of circumstances and the trial judge should therefore have left it to the jury. The jury should have been asked two questions. (1) Was the accused, or may he have been, impelled to act as he did, because as a result of what he reasonably believed to be the situation he had good cause to fear that otherwise death or serious bodily injury would result. (2) If so, would a sober person of reasonable firmness, sharing the characteristics of the accused, have responded to that situation by acting as the accused did?

In conclusion we can say that the defence of duress of circumstances is a limited form of a defence of necessity. Limited in that by classifying it as duress it means that it is not available on a charge of murder and the requirements of the defence are the partially objective requirements of the defence of duress. It seems fairly clear that the fear of death or serious bodily injury does not have to be for oneself (see *Conway* above) and it is suggested that it could cover a situation in which there is no relationship between the defendant and the person for whose safety he fears (for example the motorist who goes through a red light to save a child from a fire; above, p. 179). Later cases may need to explore the relationship between this new defence and existing defences such as self-defence and prevention of crime. (See further Smith, *Justification and Excuse in the Criminal Law*, p. 84.)

IV. *INFANCY*

Most countries recognise that special provisions have to be made to deal with children who would otherwise be liable to prosecution in the criminal courts. For our purposes we can say that special provisions apply to the way in which those who have not reached their seventeenth birthday are treated by the law.

We shall consider first the criminal liability and prosecution of children under 17 and then we shall look briefly at care proceedings.

1. CRIMINAL LIABILITY OF CHILDREN

(1) Children under 10 years of age

The criminal law provides that children who are under the age of 10 when they commit the act which, had they been adults, would have been a criminal offence, are irrebuttably to be presumed incapable of committing the crime. In other words it is a total answer to a criminal charge that the accused was under the age of 10 at the time the act was perpetrated. Since the child is completely absolved from criminal liability it means that if X persuades a child to enter a house and to steal property from within, X will be guilty of burglary as a principal offender acting through the innocent agency of the child (see above, p. 116).

(2) Children over 10 but under 14

Children over the age of 10 may be the subject of criminal proceedings though until they reach their seventeenth birthday they are likely to be tried in the juvenile court of the magistrates' court (see Smith and Bailey, *The Modern English Legal System* (1984), pp. 46 *et seq.*). You should note that the appropriate court is determined by the age on the date of trial, whereas the question of liability is determined by the age at the time the act was allegedly committed. Where criminal prosecution is brought against a child who has reached his tenth birthday, but has not yet reached his fourteenth at the time he is alleged to have committed the offence then the prosecutor must, in addition to proving the requisite *mens rea* and *actus reus* for the offence, prove that the child had what is called a mischievous discretion. In *McC.* v. *Runeckles* (1984) the Divisional Court held that in such cases the court should start with the presumption that the child does not possess this mischievous discretion (a presumption of *doli incapax*). It lay on the prosecution to prove beyond reasonable doubt that the child did possess mischievous discretion. This meant that the prosecution must prove that the child appreciated that what it was doing was *seriously wrong*. If the child knew that what it was doing was morally wrong then this was merely a species of what was seriously wrong. It would also suffice if the prosecution could prove that the child knew that what it was doing was legally wrong and that he could be punished for it. Evidence that the child took great care to conceal what it had done would be evidence of a mischievous discretion. The younger the child, the greater the proof needed to establish mischievous discretion.

Where the child is over 14 he is fully liable to prosecution for criminal offences, but until his seventeenth birthday the trial is likely to take place in the juvenile court.

Boys under the age of 14 cannot be convicted as perpetrators in any offence requiring sexual intercourse (including buggery). They may, however, be convicted as accomplices in such offences committed against others. A boy under 14 may not be convicted of the offence of buggery, either as the agent or patient though he may be convicted as an accomplice to the offence of buggery upon another person. Offences such as indecent assault which do not require sexual intercourse may be committed by boys under 14. It is not clear whether such boys can be convicted of attempting to commit offences requiring intercourse. If D, a 13 year old boy, has intercourse with a woman without her consent, he cannot be convicted of rape, but it is arguable that he can be convicted of attempted rape (see *Shivpuri*, below, p. 204).

2. CARE PROCEEDINGS

Many people believe that, except in the rarest cases, criminal prosecution is an inappropriate way of dealing with young offenders. In fact, in all cases where a child under 17 is suspected of having committed a criminal offence (other than homicide) proceedings may be taken under the Children and Young Persons Act 1969. These proceedings are known as care proceedings and may be instituted by a local authority, constable or other person authorised by the Home Secretary. Basically the person bringing ther proceedings must show that the child is in need of care and control which he is unlikely to receive unless the court makes an order in respect of him under the section, and that one or more of a number of listed conditions exists. These conditions are set out in paragraphs (*a*)–(*f*) of section 1(2) of the Act and include such facts as the child being exposed to moral danger or being ill-treated. Condition (*f*) is that the child is guilty of an offence, excluding homicide (known as the "offence condition").

Where proceedings are brought under the Children and Young Persons Act 1969 and the police are relying on the offence condition they must prove that the child would have been convicted had he been charged with a criminal offence. Thus it would be fatal that the child was under the age of 10 at the time he was alleged to have committed the offence, or, if he was between the ages of 10 and 14, that he did not possess the necessary mischievous discretion. Where the offence condition is inappropriate the police may institute care proceedings relying on one of the five other conditions such as being beyond the control of his parent or guardian. Care proceedings can be brought against a child of any age and this factor, coupled with the offence condition, means that unless the child is suspected of having killed another there is no need for the police to use criminal proceedings. It was, in fact hoped that these proceedings would gradually supplant criminal proceedings for those under 17, but it would appear that the liberal ideals of the sixties have not been realised and criminal proceedings are still favoured by the police where possible. Section 4 of the Children and Young Persons Act 1969 provided that in the case of children under the age of 14 only care proceedings should be brought, but this section has yet to be brought into effect and it seems increasingly unlikely that it ever will be. [Major changes to care proceedings will follow the implementation of the Children Bill, now before Parliament.]

V *ENTRAPMENT*

Suppose that X approaches Y and says that he has heard that Y is an expert forger. Y denies that he possesses these skills, but X persists and says that he needs a fake passport and that he is willing to pay a high price for one. Y begins to show signs of being interested and so X tells him that it is a matter of life and death and says that he will pay £5,000 at which point Y does forge such a passport. It is quite clear that Y is guilty of forgery and also that X is a party to that forgery. X will also be guilty

of inciting Y to commit forgery (see below, p. 213) and
conspiring with Y to commit forgery (see below, p. 206). But
suppose that we now disclose that X is an undercover police
agent who was merely trying to get evidence of forgery against
Y. Does this make any difference to Y's liability?

1. Y's LIABILITY

Let us suppose that Y has now been charged with forgery, can
he raise, by way of defence, that X lured him into the crime and
that without X's incitement no crime would have been
committed? In some countries, notably the United States, this
would constitute the defence of entrapment. In such countries it
is normal to draw a line between a police officer who merely
joins in an existing venture and one who positively promotes a
crime which would otherwise not have been committed; only in
the latter case would the accused have the defence of
entrapment. However, in this country the courts have positively
rejected any defence of entrapment and furthermore the
evidence received as a result of such police activity will be
admissible evidence against the accused (*Sang* (1980)). This
does not mean to say that the courts approve of such conduct,
and they may reflect their disapproval by giving the accused
a light sentence.

2. X's LIABILITY

Suppose the X, the police officer, is also prosecuted. He could
be charged with inciting Y to forge, conspiring with Y to forge
and as a party to Y's forgery. Is it any defence for him to say
that he was merely trying to collect evidence against Y, a
suspected forger?

In relation to his role as a party to the forgery it would
appear that he would not incur criminal liability. It has been
said that a police officer in such a situation will incur no
criminal liability provided that no irreparable damage is done.
After all his participation is with the intention of thwarting the
criminal, at least eventually. Thus if he assists in a burglary or
theft he can restore the proceeds. However if the crime involves

personal injury (unless possibly it is of a trivial nature and the victim has consented) or if it involved damages to property the police should not take part and participation should result in criminal liability. In general the police should try to avoid actual participation in the crime, but if it is considered really essential, then the permission of the Chief Constable should be obtained. X's liability in relation to conspiracy (see below, p. 206) would probably get the same answer, though this may involve a rather strained interpretation of the statutory definition of conspiracy.

However, in relation to incitement the courts will probably take a different view. It is one thing to join in a plot that has already been hatched, but it is quite another matter for the police to persuade people to commit crimes so that they can obtain evidence against them. In this situation X should have no defence to a charge of incitement.

VI. SUPERIOR ORDERS

If X is charged with a criminal offence can he plead by way of defence that he was simply following the orders of somebody in authority over him? There is little or no English authority on this point and this is probably because English courts are unlikely to permit such a defence. We are envisaging here a situation in which X has the requisite *mens rea* for the offence, but simply says that he thought he was obliged to follow his orders. It may well be that the effect of an order by a superior is to deprive the accused of the requisite *mens rea*. Thus if X's boss tells him to go and take some wood from Y's yard, X may well believe that the boss has the right to the wood in which case X would not be acting dishonestly (a necessary requirement for theft). Even if X knew that his boss was not entitled to the wood, his belief that he had to do what he was told might lead a jury to find that he was not acting dishonestly. Where the prosecution have to prove that the accused acted negligently, the fact that he was following orders might be evidence that he did not act negligently. Beyond these types of example, however, it is submitted that there is no general defence of acting under superior orders (whether military or civilian). The court may, however, take such a factor into account when passing sentence.

CHAPTER 7

THE INCHOATE OFFENCES

IN Chap. 5 we saw that a secondary party to a criminal offence could be held liable for acts of assistance he had performed sometime before the commission of the offence; but his liability does not arise until the offence is actually committed (or attempted). The law would be seriously deficient if liability only arose when the offence was actually committed. It would mean that if the police were aware that X intended to assault Y they would have to choose between preventing the offence and prosecuting X. Obviously we would not wish to prosecute a man simply for dreaming up criminal plans in his head, but as soon as he begins to commit overt acts which evidence his intention to put the plan into operation it is arguable that the law should be able to intervene. This, basically, is the role of the inchoate offences of incitement, conspiracy and attempt. Consider, for a moment, the following set of events; (i) X conceives in his mind a plan to burgle Barclays Bank; (ii) he approaches Y and tells him of his plans; (iii) he encourages Y to help him and to find a getaway driver; (iv) Y agrees to help and they formulate a plan in collaboration with Z who will be the getaway driver; (v) on the night in question they render the alarm on the outside of the bank inoperative and start to force open a door; and (vi) they enter the bank.

Clearly at stage (vi) they commit the completed offence of burglary the moment they enter the bank with intent to steal from it. No offence is committed at stage (i) for our law has never punished a man for his thoughts; nor at (ii) in disclosing his thoughts to Y does X commit a crime because this is still too remote from the commission of the contemplated crime. But at stage (iii) X oversteps the mark; in seeking to persuade Y to join him he commits the crime of incitement. At stage (iv) the agreement reached by X, Y‚ and Z is a crime; they have conspired to commit burglary. At stage (v) they are guilty of attempting to burgle the bank. When the prosecution gain a conviction of inciting, conspiring or attempting to commit a criminal offence the convicted person is generally speaking liable to receive the same penalty he would have incurred had he been convicted of the completed offence.

It is important to remember that these offences do not exist in the abstract; the indictment must always contain reference to the completed offence. Thus it would be wrong to say in the indictment "X is charged with conspiracy" it should be "X is charged with conspiracy to murder, steal, etc."

The law relating to conspiracy and attempts has, within the last few years, been subject to legislative reform, but incitement remains largely a creature of the common law.

1. ATTEMPTS

Liability for attempted crimes is generally covered by section 1(1) of the Criminal Attempts Act 1981 which provides "If, with intent to commit an offence to which this section applies, a person does an act which is more than merely preparatory to the commission of the offence, he is guilty of attempting to commit the offence." Under this provision a person can be convicted of attempting to commit any offence which is either indictable or triable either way (see section 1(4)). Thus whenever Parliament creates an offence which is triable on indictment, attempted liability for the offence is automatically created at the same time without any specific words in the statute creating the offence. It is not, however, possible, under this Act, to be convicted of attempting to commit an offence which is purely summary. Thus when, under the Criminal Justice Act 1988, driving while disqualified (section 37), taking a motor vehicle without the owner's consent (section 37), and common assault (section 39) became offences triable only summarily, they ceased to be offences for which there could be liability for attempting to commit them. In this situation Parliament may decide that this gap must be filled by a specific statutory attempt. The offence of driving over the prescribed limit (i.e. the breathalyser offence) is a purely summary offence, but under section 5 of the Road Traffic Act 1988, it is specifically made an offence "to drive or attempt to drive having consumed. . . . ." It may well be that Parliament will see a need to create specific offences of attempt in relation to the above offences which have become purely summary offences.

There are further restrictions on the scope of attempted liability. These can be summarised as follows:

1. It is possible to attempt to incite another to commit a substantive crime, but it is not possible to attempt to conspire. (Section 1(4)(*a*) of the Criminal Attempts Act 1981).

2. It is possible to be convicted as an accomplice to an attempted offence, but it is not possible to attempt to aid, abet, counsel, procure or suborn the commission of an offence (section 1(4)(*b*) of the Criminal Attempts Act 1981; see also *Dunnington* (1984)). The reason for this is that aiding, abetting, counselling and procuring are not, in themselves, criminal offences. There are, however, certain offences where the perpetrator is someone who aids and abets; for example, aiding and abetting suicide contrary to the Suicide Act 1961. Where this is the case it is possible to attempt to aid and abet under section 1(1) of the Criminal Attempts Act 1981 (see *Att.-Gen.* v. *Able* (1984) below, p. 235).

3. It is not possible to attempt the commission of offences under sections 4(1) and 5(1) of the Criminal Law Act 1967 (see above, p. 137, and section 1(4)(*c*) of the Criminal Attempts Act 1981).

4. There are certain offences which, by their very nature, it is impossible to attempt. For example it is generally accepted that it is not possible to attempt to commit involuntary manslaughter (for involuntary manslaughter see below, p. 226). This is because in a prosecution for an attempted offence the prosecution must prove that the defendant intended to bring about the offence. Since any intentional killing in the absence of mitigating factors (such as provocation or diminished responsibility) will be murder there is thus no scope for attempted involuntary manslaughter. It would also seem impossible to attempt to commit any offence which is defined as an omission and where the *actus reus* does not include any consequences of the omission.

By and large the mode of trial and possible sentence for a person charged with an attempt is that of the completed offence. Indeed a verdict of not guilty of the substantive offence, but guilty of the attempted offence is always an alternative verdict for the jury (provided, of course, that the prosecution have established the ingredients of the attempt) and there is no need specifically to charge the accused with the attempted offence. Thus where the accused is charged with rape the statement of the offence in the indictment will read "rape, contrary to section 1 of the Sexual Offences Act 1956" and on such indictment the jury may return a verdict of guilty of attempted rape. Where, from the outset, the prosecution intends to prosecute the accused for attempted rape the indictment will read "attempted rape, contrary to section 1(1) of the Criminal Attempts Act 1981." As we mentioned earlier certain statutory offences expressly prohibit attempted conduct (see, e.g section 5 of the Road Traffic Act 1988), but this is by virtue of the particular statute and not under the provisions of the Criminal Attempts Act. Section 3 of the Criminal Attempts Act 1981, however, provides that the principles governing these specific statutory attempts shall be those of the 1981 Act insofar as there is no express inconsistency between the statutes.

We must now look at the various ingredients of attempted offences. In simple language we are looking at situations in which the defendant has tried to do an act, which if completed would constitute a criminal offence, but has failed. In looking at the *actus reus* we must ask, how close must the defendant have got to completing the full offence before he can be convicted of an attempt? Is the *mens rea* of the attempted offence the same as that for the completed offence? In murder we can convict a defendant who merely intended to cause the victim serious bodily harm, but if the victim had not died would it make sense to charge the defendant with attempting to murder the victim? Finally we must consider cases where the defendant was trying to do something he could not possibly achieve, such as stealing from an empty pocket. Can he be convicted of attempted theft since he could never have committed the completed offence?

(1) Actus reus

Suppose that X wishes to kill Y. He buys a gun, loads it, goes to Y's house, rings the door bell, points the gun at Y and pulls the trigger. If the bullet strikes and kills Y then X will be convicted of murder. Suppose, however, that either Y does not die from the wounds, or that X is stopped before he can pull the trigger. At what stage can we say that he has attempted to kill Y? The 1981 Act says that he must do an act which is more than merely preparatory to the commission of the offence. This may seem unduly vague and not particularly helpful, but the view is held that it is for the jury and not for the judge to decide whether the accused can be said to have attempted to kill. It would be wrong for a judge to say to the jury "if you find the following acts proved, then you will find that the acts of the accused go beyond mere acts of preparation." This would be usurping the jury's function (*D.P.P.* v. *Stonehouse* (1978)). On the other hand the judge may tell the jury that certain acts are mere acts of preparation and not sufficiently proximate to the completed offence to constitute an offence. Thus in *O'Brien* v. *Anderton* (1979) Kerr L.J. said

> "The words 'more than merely preparatory' have replaced the various ways of seeking to define the concept of an attempt which one finds in many earlier authorities. In my view, whether an act is more than merely preparatory to the commission of an offence must be a question of degree in the nature of a jury question. Obviously, acts which are merely preparatory, such as a reconnaissance of the scene of the intended crime, cannot amount to attempts. They must be more than merely preparatory. If they go close to the actual commission of the offence, they may still form part of the acts necessary to carry out the complete offence, and may, in that sense, still be preparatory. But if they are properly to be regarded as more than merely preparatory, then they constitute an attempt."

In other words the jury should ask themselves "is he getting ready to commit an offence or is he in the process of attempting to commit it?" There will be many cases in which a jury, properly directed, could reasonably convict or acquit. In these cases the appellate court will not interfere.

Before the law was codified by the Criminal Attempts Act 1981 the Courts had evolved many different tests to help juries decide whether the accused had reached a stage in his activities where he could properly be said to have attempted to commit a criminal offence. One test suggested that an attempt was committed only when the defendant did the last act required of him to bring about the intended offence. Lord Diplock in *Stonehouse* (above), said that the jury should look for a point at which the defendant could be said to have "crossed the Rubicon" or "burned his boats." Both these tests are subject to the criticism that they are too restrictive. The Rubicon test suggests that an attempt is only committed when the accused can no longer turn back. In *Boyle and Boyle* (1987) the defendants, who were found trying to kick in a door, were charged with attempted burglary. Clearly there was still time for them to change their minds and run away, but equally it is possible to say that they were no longer getting ready to commit burglary, but were now attempting to commit burglary (see also *Gullefer* (1987)).

It is probably safe to say that although an accused may have committed an attempt before he does the last act required of him, if he has done the last act it will normally be possible to convict him of an attempt. Thus if the defendant is slowly poisoning his wife with arsenic over a period of weeks, we do not have to wait until he administers the last dose before we can say that he has attempted to murder his wife. On the other hand in *Stonehouse* where the defendant faked his own drowning, having previously set up an insurance policy in favour of his wife, the jury were entitled to convict him of attempting to obtain property by deception since he had done the last act required of him to get the money out of the insurance company. One qualification to the last act doctrine has to be made; whereas it will normally be a good indicator that the stage of attempt has been reached in the case of a principal offender, it might produce an incorrect result in the case of a secondary party. For example, if X hires Y, an assassin, to shoot Z, X has done the last act required of him, but he would not be guilty of attempted murder at this stage.

In most cases if the judge were simply to ask the jury whether they thought that the defendant was merely getting ready to begin the job, or whether he was actually attempting to commit the crime, the jury will be able to reach a sensible conclusion. Where the trial judge feels that there is no evidence that the defendant has gone beyond acts of preparation, he can so direct the jury to find that the prosecution have not made out the charge of attempt.

(2) Mens rea

We have seen that in the crime of murder the prosecution will succeed if it can establish that the accused brought about the *actus reus* of the crime with the necessary *mens rea* and for this purpose *mens rea* means an intention to kill or an intention to cause serious harm. Does it follow, therefore, that where he is charged with attempted murder—a lesser offence—the same *mens rea* will suffice? The answer to this question and one of the main reasons for it can best be explained by an illustration. Suppose that X, a terrorist, has been inflicting grievous bodily harm on Y in order to extract information from him and that as a result Y dies. Even though the last thing that X wanted to happen was Y's death, we would find nothing really strange in saying that X has murdered Y. If, however, Y does not die, can we charge X with attempted murder? In other words can we say that X was attempting to murder Y? The answer to this is that we cannot, in reality, say that X was attempting to murder Y. Thus at common law the courts held that on a charge of attempted murder the prosecution must establish that the defendant intended to kill the victim (*Whybrow* (1951)). This meant, of course, that the *mens rea* for the attempted offence was often more restricted than that required for the completed offence. It would have been far simpler for the courts to have said that the *mens rea* required for the attempt is that of the completed offence, but this they refused to do.

The position is now covered by section 1(1) of the Criminal Attempts Act 1981 which provides "If, with intent to commit an offence. . . . " It is generally accepted that this was intended to preserve the common law rule. Thus it seems quite clear that where the crime requires proof of conduct or of consequences the prosecution must prove that the defendant intended to act in the prohibited manner or that he intended to produce the prohibited consequences. Thus in the crime of attempted murder the prosecution will still have to prove that the accused intended to kill. In *Pearman* (1984) the Court of Appeal assumed that *intends* still bears the meaning it had at common law, which presumably means that it will be interpreted in the way it was interpreted in *Nedrick* (see above, p. 58). Thus it is clear that it is not to be equated with foresight, although foresight may be evidence of intention. The prosecution must prove that the defendant intended to commit the offence even if the full offence is one of strict liability. Hence if in *Alpacell* v. *Woodward* (above, p. 103) the defendants had been charged with attempting to cause the pollution of the river, the prosecution would have had to prove that they intended to cause the pollutant to enter the river.

It is less clear, however, whether the prosecution has to prove intention on all aspects of the *actus reus* in an attempted offence. For example, if D is charged with the attempted rape of Y, it is clear that the prosecutor will, as in the completed offence, have to prove that D intended to have sexual intercourse with Y. It is less clear whether the prosecution will have to prove that he knew she was not consenting or whether it will suffice that he could not care less whether or not she was consenting. On one view intention should only be required by the wording of the Act in relation to the central conduct of the offence, namely to have sexual intercourse. However, it could be argued that the prohibited conduct in rape is non-consensual sexual intercourse and the prosecution must establish that this was the defendant's intention. Thus the prosecution would have to establish that the defendant knew that E was not consenting. Even if this view were to be accepted, there are still other elements in the *actus reus*. For example, in *Fortheringham* (above, p. 165) the defendant mistakenly thought, so he claimed, that he was having intercourse with his wife. Part of the *actus reus* of rape is the requirement that the woman should not be the wife of the defendant. In the completed offence it was suggested that the *mens rea* on this element is *Cunningham* recklessness; are we suggesting that had Fotheringham been charged with attempted rape the prosecution would have to prove that the defendant *knew* that the girl was not his wife?

This problem was raised in the case of *Millard* v. *Vernon* (1987) where the court was considering an attempt to commit the basic offence of criminal damage (section 1(1) of the Criminal Damage Act 1971; see below, p. 344). Here the court said that there was no real difficulty. The offence consists of a single prohibited act, namely damaging or destroying property belonging to another. Thus for the attempted offence the prosecution must prove that the defendant intended to damage or destroy property belonging to another. However, the court continued *obiter*, there are offences where the substantive offence does not consist of one result and one *mens rea*, but involves not only the underlying intention to produce the result, but also another state of mind directed to some circumstance or act which the prosecution must also establish in addition to proving the result. Rape is an example of this type of offence. In the substantive offence the prohibited act is sexual intercourse with a woman, and thus in the attempted offence the prosecution must prove that the defendant intended to have sexual intercourse with a woman. However, the substantive offence is not complete without proof of an additional circumstance, namely that she did not consent and here either knowledge or recklessness suffices. The question here is whether for the attempted offence, section 1(1) of the Criminal Attempts Act 1981 requires that the prosecution prove that the accused *knew* that she was consenting or whether recklessness will suffice. An even clearer example of such an offence is the aggravated form of criminal damage under section 1(2) of the Criminal Damage Act 1971. Here the substantive offence consists in damaging or destroying property *with intent to endanger or being reckless as to endangering life*. This element of endangerment to life forms no

part of the *actus reus* of the offence; it is purely an additional
element of *mens rea* which can be satisfied by *Caldwell*
recklessness. Again the question is whether in the attempted
offence the prosecution will succeed only if it can prove that the
defendant intended to endanger life. Unfortunately the court in
Millard v. *Vernon* merely raised the issue, it did not consider it
necessary to give any response. Possibly the answer is that the
mens rea of the substantive offence should be modified only so
far as is necessary to comply with the provisions of the Criminal
Attempts Act. Thus in the crime of attempted murder the
prosecution will succeed only if they can prove that the
defendant intended to kill, but surely the charge will not fail if it
cannot prove that the defendant intended that the victim should
die within a year and a day. Under section 1(2) of the Criminal
Damage Act 1971 it should suffice that the prosecution prove
that the defendant intended to damage or destroy property;
recklessness should suffice on the endangerment of life. Rape
remains the most difficult; here it is suggested that the court
would treat the prohibited act as non-consensual intercourse and
require that the prosecution should prove intention to have non-
consensual intercourse, but that recklessness as to whether or
not the woman was his wife should suffice.

(3) Attempting the impossible

Sometimes an accused fails to commit the full offence because
he is either stopped before he can do so or because his plan
goes astray. These are perfectly proper areas to charge the
accused with attempting to commit the offence in question,
provided he has gone beyond acts of mere preparation. On the
other hand he may fail to commit an offence because what he is
trying to do is impossible. In this section we shall look at four
different situations in which the accused may be said to have
tried to do something which is impossible. In each case the
question to be asked is whether the Criminal Attempts Act 1981
renders his activity criminal.

(a) A is caught trying to open the night safe at a bank with a
can opener. It is quite clear that the bank's money is safe from
him. On the other hand, if he were to succeed he would commit
the offence of theft. This is not so much a case of attempting
the impossible, as incompetently attempting the possible.
Provided that the jury think that he is beyond merely preparing
to commit the offence, he can be convicted.

(b) B is a pickpocket operating around King's Cross railway station. He sneaks up behind V and inserts his hand into V's pocket, but it is empty, having been emptied by C another pickpocket. Once again, if B were to achieve his purpose he would commit the offence of theft, but since there is nothing in the pocket this is impossible. This type of case is sometimes referred to as attempting the factually impossible. It is fairly certain that the general public would view this conduct as attempted theft and would be highly surprised if the law provided otherwise. In *Anderton* v. *Ryan* (1985) the House of Lords held, *obiter*, that such conduct amounted to attempted theft. Had the accused been able to achieve his purpose he would have committed theft, he only fails because there is nothing in the pocket. Section 1(2) of the Act provides "A person may be guilty of attempting to commit an offence to which this section applies even though the facts are such that the commission of the offence is impossible." This section was clearly intended to cover such cases as trying to steal from empty pockets and it is suggested that it is quite adequate to do so. The pickpocket has clearly got beyond the stage of preparation and it makes perfect sense to say that he is attempting to steal from the pocket.

(c) D has intercourse with his girlfriend. Although she is, in fact, 16 she has always told him she is 15 in order to dampen his approaches. On the evening in question, however, he has broken down her resistance and they have had intercourse, but she has not informed him that she is 16 and that he will not be committing any offence. Now if the girl had been 15 he would have committed a criminal offence (unlawful sexual intercourse contrary to section 6 of the Sexual Offences Act 1956). Unlike the situation in (b) D has done everything he set out to do; it is unlikely that he will feel disappointed when he realises that she is 16. This type of case is sometimes said to be attempting the legally impossible and occurs most frequently where the accused receives non-stolen goods in the belief that they are stolen. Again it is clear that the drafters of the Act thought that such conduct should constitute a criminal attempt and that the Act, as drafted, would criminalise such conduct. However, in *Anderton* v. *Ryan* (1985), the House of Lords reached a contrary conclusion. In that case Mrs Ryan had received a Video Cassette Recorder believing it to be stolen property, whereas it was not, in fact, stolen. She could not be charged with the offence of handling stolen property contrary to section

22 of the Theft Act 1968 (see below) since that requires proof that she handled property which was, in fact, *stolen*, knowing or believing it to be stolen. She was therefore charged with attempted handling. She was convicted, but when her appeal reached the House of Lords her conviction was quashed. Their Lordships held that handling non-stolen property was no offence and that a belief that the property was stolen could not render the person liable for a criminal offence unless such liability was created by the Criminal Attempts Act. They could find nothing in the Act which was sufficiently clear to do this. In *Shivpuri* (1987) the House of Lords had another chance to examine this area of law. Here the accused was convicted of an attempt to be knowingly concerned in dealing with and harbouring a prohibited drug. Shivpuri admitted that he thought that the substance in his possession was such a drug, but on investigation it turned out to be a harmless substance rather like snuff. The House of Lords said that they considered that they had reached the wrong conclusion in *Anderton* v. *Ryan,* and although Lord Hailsham said that he could distinguish the two cases on the facts, their Lordships preferred to invoke their power to overrule previous decisions of the House of Lords. Lord Bridge said that the correct way to approach such problems was first of all to ask whether the defendant intended to commit the offence which he was alleged to have attempted; in *Shivpuri* he clearly intended to be knowingly concerned in dealing with and harbouring prohibited drugs with intent to evade their prohibition on their importation. The second question is whether he, in relation to these offences, did an act which was more than merely preparatory to the commission of the offences? Lord Bridge held that the acts relied on were more than merely preparatory to the commission of the *intended* offence and this was sufficient. Where the facts were such that the commission of the offence was impossible, it would never be possible to prove that the accused had done an act which was more than merely preparatory to the commission of the *actual* offence and this would render section 1(2) otiose.

There has been much heated debate over this issue; suffice it to say that *Shivpuri* seems to have settled this issue for the moment in favour of the prosecution. However, in *Galvin* (1987) the Court of Appeal quashed the defendant's conviction for unlawfully receiving a document contrary to section 2(2) of the Official Secrets Act 1911 because there was evidence that the Government's own wide distribution of the document may have impliedly authorised anyone who came into possession of it to use the document as he saw fit. Thus, to put it simply, Galvin believed he was receiving the document unlawfully, when, in fact, he was not. It is strange that with *Shivpuri* still ringing in our ears, it did not occur to the Court of Appeal that this was a case of attempting to receive the document unlawfully.

A similar situation arose in *D.P.P.* v. *Huskinson* (1988). In this case the defendant was charged with theft of £279 from the Housing Services Department. He had applied for housing benefit and had been sent a cheque for £497. Although he was already £800 in arrears with his rent, he gave only £200 to his landlord and spent the remainder on himself even though he believed that he was under a legal obligation to use all the money for rental purposes. The problem for the court in this case was that theft is the dishonest appropriation of property belonging to another with the intent permanently to deprive the other of the property. It was clear that, in law, the money became his on receipt and thus he had, on the face of it, appropriated his own money. Under section 5(3) of the Theft Act 1968 he can be treated as having appropriated property belonging to another if the prosecution could prove that he was under a legal obligation to use that property in a specific way (see below, p. 276). The court held that the defendant was not on the facts of this case under an obligation to use the £479 in a specific way, even though he thought he was under such an obligation. He could not therefore be convicted of theft. The court did not consider whether he should be convicted of attempted theft; but was he guilty of attempted theft? Is not this case just like *Shivpuri*? Arguably there is a significant difference. In both *Shivpuri* and *Anderton* v. *Ryan* the defendants made a mistake of fact; one believed the substance was a controlled drug, the other that a video recorder was stolen property. Huskinson's mistake, however, was one of law. He was fully aware of the facts, namely that he had been given a sum of money by the Housing Services Department; he was mistaken as to the legal effect of this transaction. The court might say that section 1(2) of the Criminal Attempts Act 1981 is not appropriate to cover this type of situation—it only relates to mistakes of fact. However, the position is not entirely straightforward (see the commentary to this case in (1988) Crim.L.R. 620). It is very tempting to suggest that the answer the court would give would depend upon whether they wish to impose a penalty for the conduct. What is clear, however, is that the Court should have at least adverted to the issue; it would appear that just as with *Galvin* the court simply did not think that this looked like a criminal attempt.

Since nearly all the examples of this type of attempting the legally impossible occur in the areas of handling or drugs, it would be more satisfactory to amend the substantive offences so that the accused commits a full offence. Thus if handling were amended so that it was an offence to receive property knowing or believing it to be stolen, Mrs Ryan would have committed the offence of handling—there would be no need to rely on attempts at all.

(d) E has intercourse with his 17 year old girlfriend believing it to be an offence to have sexual intercourse with a girl under the age of 18. Although this may be morally indistinguishable from (c) it is suggested that the answer is clear. There is no crime known to English law with which he could be charged. The indictment (the formal document containing the charges at the trial) must accuse the defendant of attempting to commit an offence which is triable on indictment. In illustration (c) the indictment would refer to the offence of unlawful sexual intercourse which is an offence under section 6 of the Sexual Offences Act 1956. In (d) there is no offence which is triable in this country on indictment. This becomes even more obvious if the defendant, believing it to be an offence to wear a red bow tie on Thursdays, deliberately sets out to break the law. Can it be seriously imagined that he has attempted to commit an offence which is indictable in English law?

(4) Acts of preparation

Section 6 of the Criminal Attempts Act 1981 makes it clear that the offence of attempt at common law and any offence at common law of procuring materials for crime are abolished (see *Gurmit Singh* (1966)). However Parliament has specifically provided that certain acts which would be described as acts of preparation to commit offences shall, in themselves, amount to crimes. Examples of such provisions are going equipped for stealing contrary to section 25 of the Theft Act 1968; and possessing anything with intent to use it to damage or destroy property contrary to section 3 of the Criminal Damage Act 1971 (below, p. 350).

2. CONSPIRACY

While a decision by one person to commit a crime, even if there is clear evidence of his intention, is not an offence, it has long been the law that an *agreement* by two or more to commit a crime is an offence. Perhaps the reason is that where two or more persons have agreed on a course of action it is much more likely that the planned course of action will be carried out. Certainly courts have taken the view that confederacies are especially dangerous. So dangerous, in fact, that criminal conspiracies were not restricted to agreements to commit crimes. In *Kamara* v. *D.P.P.* (1974) for example, it was held by the House of Lords that an agreement to commit the tort of trespass to land, if accompanied by an intention to inflict more than merely nominal damage, was indictable as a criminal conspiracy.

That it should be a crime in certain circumstances even to agree to commit a civil wrong was thought by many to be objectionable. The Law Commission considered the matter and at first the Commission essentially expressed the idea that only agreements to commit crimes should be indictable as conspiracies. This proposal was in turn criticised as being too narrow. In particular it would have restricted the operation of conspiracy to defraud because, on the common law view of this crime, there could be a conspiracy to defraud even though there was no conspiracy to commit a crime. Take *Scott* v. *Metropolitan Police Commissioner* (1975) for example. Here A, B and others made copies of films without the consent of the copyright holders with a view to making a profit for themselves by showing the films without paying the copyright holders. In such a case as this it may have been difficult to prove that A and B had committed some crime under the Theft Acts. They did not steal anything from the copyright holders nor was there any deception of the holders. But it was held that their conduct fell within the wide net of conspiracy to defraud—"an agreement by two or more by dishonesty to deprive a person of something that is his or to which he is or would be or might be entitled and an agreement by two or more by dishonesty to injure some proprietory right of his."

The Law Commission therefore proposed that criminal conspiracy should extend to: (i) agreements to commit crime, and (ii) that the common law conspiracy to defraud should be retained, at least for the time being. Had this proposal been accepted all common law conspiracies other than conspiracy to defraud would have ceased to be criminal. But the government of the day thought it best to postpone a final decision on conspiracies to corrupt public morals and conspiracies to outrage public decency pending the outcome of another review. The result, not altogether a happy one, is embodied in the Criminal Law Act 1977. The Law Commission's proposals have been implemented to create statutory offences of conspiracy but the common law conspiracy to defraud was retained and agreements to corrupt public morals and outrage public decency were excepted from the statutory scheme as well. We thus have statutory conspiracies and common law conspiracies. (See further Law Commission W.P. No. 104, Conspiracy to Defraud.)

One problem that has troubled the courts since the introduction of statutory conspiracies in 1977 is the question of overlap between statutory and common law conspiracies. Suppose that X, Y and Z agree to a plan under which they will obtain possession of a rental television set from a local company by giving false names and addresses and that once in possession of the set they will sell it and keep the money. If the plan is put into operation they will clearly commit the offence of obtaining property by deception contrary to section 15 of the Theft Act 1968. At present, however, they have only agreed to do this. Should the prosecutor therefore charge them with conspiring to obtain property by deception (a statutory conspiracy under section 1 of the Criminal Law Act 1977) or should he charge them with conspiracy to defraud (a common law conspiracy not overruled by the statute of 1977) or does he have a choice? It seems fairly clear that the drafters of the Act intended that in such a case the accused should be charged with the statutory conspiracy. Conspiracy to defraud was meant to be retained as a long stop for those cases where the commission of the agreed plan by one person would not necessarily amount to a substantive criminal law offence. The real solution envisaged was that these loopholes would eventually be filled by substantive criminal offences and the need for conspiracy to defraud would then disappear. (An example of this type of loophole can be seen in section 3 of the Theft Act 1978. If X simply left a hotel at the end of his holiday without paying he might possibly have committed no criminal offence. If, however, he agreed with Y that they should both leave without paying, this would amount to conspiracy to defraud the hotel. Under section 3 of the Theft Act 1978 a new criminal offence of making off without payment was created so that today if X dishonestly left the hotel without paying he would commit a substantive criminal offence. See below, p. 319).

It is one thing for legislators to have a certain objective in mind. It does not necessarily follow that the legislation they pass will achieve that objective. The Criminal Law Act 1977 could not be described as the clearest of statutes. Since the Act was passed there have been conflicting decisions of the Court of Appeal as to whether the prosecution could charge an accused with conspiracy to defraud when the agreement was to commit a substantive criminal law offence. After two attempts by the House of Lords to resolve the matter (*Ayres* (1984) and *Cooke* (1986)) the position was still far from clear. Happily the matter has now been resolved by statute. Section 12 of the Criminal Justice Act 1987 provides that it is perfectly permissible to charge a defendant with conspiracy to defraud even though the facts reveal a statutory conspiracy. Although this was not the intention of the drafters of the original statute it does seem the simplest solution to a potentially complex issue. The other common law conspiracies (to outrage public decency and to corrupt public morals) may not be charged when the facts reveal a statutory conspiracy. These offences, however, make only rare appearances before the courts and are not, therefore, likely to cause serious difficulties.

The whole area of conspiracy is complex and what follows is an outline of the general principles involved.

(1) Mens rea

It was established by the House of Lords in *Churchill* v. *Walton* (1967) that conspiracy at common law involves *mens rea* in the full sense—strict liability does not apply. Thus if in *Prince* (1875) (above, p. 70). Prince and another agreed to take the girl out of the possession of her parents, both believing she was over 16, neither could be convicted of conspiracy to abduct.

Section 1 of the Criminal Law Act 1977 was intended to embody the identical principle for statutory conspiracies and provides:

> "1—(1) Subject to the following provisions of the Part of this Act, if a person agrees with any other person or persons that a course of conduct shall be pursued which will necessarily amount to or involve the commission of any offence or offences by one or more of the parties to the agreement if the agreement is carried out in accordance with their intentions, he is guilty of conspiracy to commit the offence or offences in question.
>
> (2) Where liability for any offence may be incurred without knowledge on the part of the person committing it of any particular fact or circumstance necessary for the

commission of the offence, a person shall nevertheless not
be guilty of conspiracy to commit that offence by virtue of
subsection (1) above unless he and at least one other party
to the agreement intend or know that that fact or
circumstance shall or will exist at the time when the
conduct constituting the offence is to take place."

These are complex provisions but they should be interpreted to
reflect the common law position. Thus in the example just
given Prince and his friend are not guilty of a statutory
conspiracy. Section 1(2) makes it clear that even if the
completed offence can be committed without knowledge of a
"particular fact or circumstance" (in this case that the girl is
under 16) there can be no conviction for conspiracy unless that
fact or circumstance is known to those charged with conspiracy.

Section 1(1) is intended to make it clear that on a charge of
conspiracy, *e.g.* to murder or to cause criminal damage, it must
be shown that the alleged conspirators had agreed on a course
of conduct which will necessarily result in murder or criminal
damage if the agreement is carried out in accordance with their
intentions. There is no difficulty whatever if A and B agree to
kill X by poisoning or to break Y's windows. But suppose that
A and B agreed to "knee-cap" X. A and B would here be
guilty of a conspiracy to cause grievous bodily harm and if X
dies they would have the necessary *mens rea* for murder (see
above, p. 24). Are A and B thus guilty of conspiracy to
murder? The answer is No. The course of conduct they have
agreed on will not necessarily result in death; indeed it is rare
for death to occur as a result of "knee-capping." Another
example could be where, in a street fight, A and B agree to
attack X and Y by throwing stones at them, both realising that
they might miss X and Y and break windows in the street. A
and B are guilty of a conspiracy to assault X and Y but they
are not guilty of a conspiracy to commit criminal damage. In
other words conspiracy is an intentional crime in the same
sense as attempt (see above, p. 199); the same problems would
appear to be present in conspiracy. (See also *Anderson*
(1986)).

(2) Actus reus

The *actus reus* of conspiracy consists in an agreement by two
or more persons: (i) to commit a crime; (ii) to defraud; (iii) to

corrupt public morals; or (iv) to outrage public decency. The Criminal Law Act governs conspiracies falling within (i); (ii), (iii) and (iv) are common law conspiracies.

It is common ground to both statutory and common law conspiracy that there must be an agreement by two or more persons.

As to the latter of the requirements it is a truism to say that a man cannot conspire with himself. It was accordingly held in *McDonnell* (1986) that A, the managing and sole director of A Ltd., could not be convicted of conspiring with A Ltd. even though A Ltd. could have been convicted of the substantive crime committed by A (see above, p. 143). On the other hand it is perfectly possible to convict A, A Ltd. *and* B on a charge of conspiracy; or to convict A Ltd. of conspiring with B Ltd.

For reasons of policy one spouse cannot be convicted of conspiring with the other spouse if these are the *only* parties to the agreement. So husband and wife do not commit a crime in agreeing to murder X but if their son, A, becomes a party to the agreement then all three are guilty of conspiracy. This was the rule for common law conspiracies (*Mawji* v. *The Queen* (1957)) and by section 2(2)(*a*) of the Criminal Law Act 1977 the same rule is applied to statutory conspiracies. It is also provided in section 2(2) of the Act that a person cannot be convicted of conspiracy if the *only* other party is (*b*) a person under the age of criminal responsibility; or (*c*) an intended victim of the offence. There is no common law authority on agreements falling within (*b*) or (*c*); the Law Commission was of the view that at common law a conviction for conspiracy was at least theoretically possible in both cases. The Law Commission further proposed that a person should not be liable for conspiracy if the only other party was himself or herself exempt from liability for conspiracy to commit the offence in question. Had this proposal been implemented it would have reversed the decision in *Duguid* (1906) where it was held that A could be convicted of conspiring with B to abduct a child from his guardian even though B, as the mother of the child, was exempt from liability. Since it was not implemented it continues to be the law that a non-exempt party can conspire with an exempt party even though the exempt party cannot be convicted.

As to the former requirements, the agreement that is required is a compact. Negotiations, however far advanced, will not suffice without a compact to effect a criminal purpose. Nor is it enough that A gives help to B knowing of his criminal purpose. In *Bainbridge* (1960) (above, p. 118) B in knowingly supplying oxygen cutting equipment to A became a secondary party to the burglary committed by A, but on those facts alone, it could hardly be said that B had agreed with A to commit burglary.

In relation to statutory conspiracy, section 1 requires that A and B should have agreed on a course of conduct which if it is carried out as planned will necessarily amount to a crime. Suppose that A and B agree to go on a shoplifting expedition tomorrow. Between now and tomorrow many things may go wrong and thwart the plan. They may fall ill, or the shops may be closed by a strike or by a power failure. Have they, then, agreed on a course of conduct which if carried out in accordance with that intention will *necessarily* result in the commission of a crime? Of course they have and the fact that their intentions are thwarted for some reason cannot effect the matter. Nor are they any the less guilty of conspiracy to steal because they have not decided upon the particular shop or shops from which they will pilfer, nor because they have not yet specified the goods they will steal.

It would also appear that the phrase "the commission of any offence; ... by one or more of the parties to the agreement" should be read to mean that one of the parties to the conspiracy was to act as the principal offender. If A and B agree to help E rape F, then if E were not a party to the agreement, there would not be a statutory conspiracy since none of those involved in the agreement would be planning to be a principal offender in the commission of the planned offence. However, if E were a party to the agreement, then A, B and E would be guilty of a conspiracy to rape (*Hollinshead* (1985); this was the view of the Court of Appeal. The House of Lords, on appeal, did not consider it necessary to decide this issue, but held that it should be considered *de novo* in a future case). If, however, A and B agree to help C, who is not a party to the conspiracy, to commit suicide, A and B will be guilty of a statutory conspiracy. This is because the substantive offence is itself defined as aiding and abetting suicide (see below, p. 234). Although it may not be possible to conspire to be a secondary party, it is submitted that there is nothing to prevent liability as a secondary party to a conspiracy.

When A and B are the only parties to the alleged conspiracy it is necessary to show a meeting of their minds. But if there are three or more parties it is unnecessary to show that each conspirator was in contact with every other conspirator. Suppose A agreed with B to rob X leaving it to B to get someone to provide transport and B engaged C in the enterprise. A and C have now conspired to rob X though neither may have met or even know of the other's identity, provided C knew he was joining such an enterprise and that there were other members of the gang even if he did not know their names. On the other hand, there must be a nexus between A and C in relation to the conspiracy charged. If A and B plan to kill X as well as rob him but only the intention to rob X is disclosed to C, A has conspired with C to rob X but there is no agreement between them to murder X.

Criminal conspiracies are now confined to agreements: (i) to commit crime; (ii) to defraud; (iii) to corrupt public morals; and (iv) to outrage public decency. For the sake of completeness it should be added that an agreement (v) to commit murder abroad is indictable here though not agreements to commit other crimes abroad.

Little needs to be said of (i). We have seen (above, p. 207) that (ii) is wider than (i) in embracing certain dishonest activity which would not be a crime if perpetrated by one person. As to (iii) and (iv) these seem to go much further than (i) in embracing all sorts of vague conduct which would not necessarily be a crime if committed by one person. But this may not be so. There is almost certainly a substantive offence of outraging public decency (*Knuller* v. *D.P.P.* (1973)) and if this is so (iv) adds nothing to (i). It is not clear whether there is a substantive offence of corrupting public morals (see *D.P.P.* v. *Withers* (1975)) but if there is then (iii) adds nothing to (i). These are matters which still await judicial decision or, for preference, clear statutory restatement.

As with attempts, so with conspiracy, issues of impossibility arise (see above, p. 202); it is possible for persons to agree to steal from a safe which turns out to be empty, or to receive goods which are no longer stolen. By section 5 of the Criminal Attempts Act 1981 statutory, though not common law, conspiracies are brought into line with the new law on attempts; there can be a conviction for conspiracy in both of these cases.

3. INCITEMENT

We saw at the beginning of this chapter that if X were to conceive in his mind a plan to burgle Barclays Bank and even if he were to outline his plan to Y he would commit no offence. However if the prosecution can prove that he tried to persuade

Y to join him in the venture this would amount to the common law offence of inciting Y to commit, in this case, burglary. The basis, therefore, of incitement is an attempt to persuade another to commit an act which, if committed by that other, would amount to a criminal offence. As with the other inchoate offences, incitement is divisible into *actus reus* and *mens rea*.

(1) Actus reus

The prosecution must establish that the accused by word or deed encouraged another to commit a criminal offence. One who incites another to commit a criminal offence will become a party to the offence when it is committed by that other, but the reverse is not necessarily true. If X supplies Y with a gun to kill Z, X will be a party to the killing, but he is not necessarily guilty of incitement since this requires that he urged Y to kill Z. Thus if Y approached X for the gun telling him that he was thinking about killing Z, but he had not yet made up his mind, and if X then tries to remove the lingering doubts in Y's mind X will be guilty of both incitement immediately and murder when the crime is committed.

The persuasion can be by both words and deeds and it can take the forms of encouragement or threats. It can be to a particular person or to people in general. Thus even though the government has approved the use of citizen's band radios it would constitute incitement for a seller to advertise his radios by saying that the problems of police radar speed traps were almost eliminated by careful use of the equipment. In such an advertisement there would be implied encouragement for motorists to break the speed regulations.

(2) Mens rea

As with conspiracy and attempts, incitement requires that the accused has *mens rea*. Thus the prosecution will have to show that the accused intended that as a result of his persuasion another person would commit an act which would be a criminal offence, though, of course, there is no need to prove that the accused knew that the act in question was a crime (above, p. 79).

In the following examples it is accepted that X has tried to persuade Y to receive some watches and to sell them.

(i) If we assume first that the watches are, in fact, stolen at the time of the incitement then if X is unaware of this fact he cannot be guilty of inciting Y to handle stolen property since X is unaware of the fact which would make Y's receiving of the watches a crime. Similarly if X does not tell Y that the watches are stolen and has no reason to suppose that Y knows this, then this will not be incitement by X since Y will not be guilty of any criminal offence—in other words the act incited is not a crime.

(ii) If we assume that the goods are not, in fact stolen, and if X, believing them to be stolen, tells Y that the watches are stolen and encourages Y to receive them he will be inciting Y to do an act which will not, in fact, be a crime since the watches are not stolen property. Here again the problem of impossibility arises. But unlike impossibility in attempts (see above, p. 202) and statutory conspiracies (see above, p. 213) the matter is governed by the common law. On common law principles X cannot be convicted of *inciting* Y to handle stolen goods since the goods are not stolen (this is a case of so-called legal impossibility, see above, p. 203; but, odd though it may seem, Y can be convicted of *attempting* to handle stolen goods. Factual impossibility is also a defence to incitement in some circumstances; X is not guilty of incitement where he incites Y to steal from a safe that is empty. But here the critical time is the time of the incitement; if the safe contains money at the time of the incitement X may be guilty of incitement even though the safe is subsequently emptied and contains nothing when Y tries to steal from it (*Fitzmaurice* 1983)).

CHAPTER 8

UNLAWFUL HOMICIDE

In Chap. 2 we examined the constituent elements of the crime of murder. In this chapter we will look at the remaining offences against the person which involve the death of the victim.

1. VOLUNTARY MANSLAUGHTER

There are basically two types of manslaughter; voluntary and involuntary manslaughter. Voluntary manslaughter covers those killings which, but for some mitigating factor, such as provocation, would lead to convictions for murder. Involuntary manslaughter refers to those killings where the accused does not possess the requisite *mens rea* for murder. In this section we shall cover voluntary manslaughter.

Voluntary manslaughter covers those killings in which the accused is charged with murder because the prosecution believes that it can establish the necessary malice aforethought, but where the accused is eventually convicted of manslaughter because of the existence of what can be termed as a partial defence. There are three such partial defences namely provocation, diminished responsibility and suicide pacts. All three are available only on a charge of murder; they are not available if the charge is attempted murder. In the case of provocation the burden of proof is on the prosecution to prove that the defence of provocation has not been established; in the case of diminished responsibility and suicide pacts it is up to the accused to prove the defence upon a balance of probabilities.

The reason for this category's existence stems from the fact that when a person is convicted of murder the trial judge is bound by law to impose a sentence of life imprisonment. By allowing these partial defences the offence is reduced to manslaughter for which the judge has a discretion to impose any sentence up to a maximum of life imprisonment. He is thus able to take into account factors such as the provocation which led to the accused's action. This explains why these partial defences are available only on a charge of murder. In all other crimes the judge can take account of mitigating factors.

In this section we will examine only provocation. Diminished responsibility has already been explained (above, p. 157). Suicide pacts will be covered later in this chapter (below, p. 235).

Provocation

The first question to ask is what is meant by provocation. The classic definition is usually taken to be that of Devlin J. in *Duffy* (1949) where he said "Provocation is some act, or series of acts, done by the dead man to the accused, which would cause in any reasonable person, and actually causes in the accused, a sudden and temporary loss of self–control, rendering the accused so subject to passion as to make him or her for the moment not master of his mind." We shall see later that this definition has been somewhat modified by subsequent legislation and cases but it nevertheless provides us with a useful starting point. We are concerned here with, for example, a situation in which A insults B about B's deformed nose, a characteristic about which B has very strong feelings. B loses his self-control and smashes A over the head with a beer glass he happens to be holding, thereby killing A. It is worth making the point at this stage that the accused will have been charged with murder and so you must not lose sight of the need of the prosecution to establish the necessary malice aforethought of murder; the defence only becomes necessary if the jury are prepared in the first place to return a verdict of murder.

The defence of provocation is now partially covered by section 3 of the Homicide Act 1957 which provides that "where on a charge of murder there is evidence on which a jury can find that the person charged was provoked (whether by things done or by things said or by both together) to lose his self control, the question whether the provocation was enough to make a reasonable man do as he did shall be left to be determined by the jury; and in determining that question the jury shall take into account everything both done and said according to the effect which, in their opinion, it would have on a reasonable man."

The statute clearly provides that once the judge has reached the conclusion that on the evidence before him there is evidence that the accused was provoked he must leave the issue of provocation to the jury. This does not mean that the judge must be satisfied that the accused was in fact provoked or that reasonable people would have been provoked, it is sufficient that there is some evidence on which a reasonable jury would be entitled to find that the prosecution had not proved beyond reasonable doubt that he was not provoked. Thus in *Doughty* (1986) the Court of Appeal held that there was evidence that the accused had been provoked by the crying of his 17 day old child; the trial judge was therefore under an obligation to leave the defence of provocation to the jury. The case seems to illustrate that the Court of Appeal has accepted that the phrase in section 3 " whether by things done or by things said or by both together" is wide enough to cover a baby crying. It is probably not wide enough to cover a pure act of God, such as damage caused by lighting, which causes the accused to lose his self control. Before the passing of the 1957 Act the judge was entitled to withdraw the issue of provocation from the jury on the ground that even if the accused had himself been provoked no reasonable man would have reacted in the way he did to the provocation. This led to cases where the judges held that a reasonable man only lost his self-control when he found his wife in the act of adultery and not when he had been told of it; that a reasonable man who was provoked by fists did not retaliate with a knife but only with fists; that reasonable men only avail themselves of the defence when the provocation came from the person they then killed and was in fact directed not at a third party put at themselves; that reasonable men would not lose their self-control when taunted about a peculiar characteristic, *e.g.* impotence, since reasonable men did not possess that characteristic; and reasonable men would cool off after a certain period of time and regain their self-control. It is quite clear that in so far as the judges before 1957 were entitled to withdraw the issue altogether from the jury on the basis of these rules, section 3 has removed that power. The judge must leave the issue to the jury if there is evidence that the accused was provoked to lose his self-control however unreasonable his actions might appear to the judge. It is necessary also to remember that the defence of provocation might not have been specifically pleaded by the defendant who may, for example have been relying on the defence of self-defence. If, however, the judge feels that there is evidence of provocation, he is duty bound to leave the issue with the jury. (See, *e.g. Burke* (1987).)

However, once the judge has decided that there is an issue of provocation he must leave two questions with the jury. First, he must direct them to consider whether the accused himself was actually provoked. It will not avail the accused for the jury to come to the conclusion that he was not provoked, although most reasonable men undoubtedly would have been. Secondly, the jury will be directed to consider whether a reasonable man so provoked would have responded in the way that the accused did. This could have provided the judges, should they have so wished, with an opportunity to return to all the pre-1957 cases on what reasonable men do in the face of provocation. Clearly it would no longer be possible for a judge to tell a jury that reasonable men do not get provoked by things said to them alone or at least that they would not react violently to such taunts, since this is now expressly covered by the section, but he could tell the jury that reasonable men do not get worried about taunts as to their impotence, since reasonable men are not impotent. Admittedly it would be possible for a jury so directed to ignore the judge's ruling, but this is not a satisfactory way for the law to operate. The position was examined by the House of Lords in the case of *D.P.P.* v. *Camplin* (1978). In *Camplin* the accused who had been drinking went to the house of a middle-aged Pakistani, K, who he had been blackmailing over a homosexual relationship K was having with a friend of the accused. While he was there the accused was buggered by K, according to the accused, by force. After the act of buggery the accused claimed that he was overcome with remorse and shame, especially when he heard K laughing over his sexual triumph and he hit K over the head twice with a heavy chapati pan, thereby killing him. The accused was charged with murder and at his trial rested his defence solely on the issue of provocation, thus seeking to reduce the offence to manslaughter. From the point of view of the case the major factor in dispute was whether the jury should have been advised not to pay any regard to the fact that at the time of the killing the accused was only 15 years old. In the event the jury were directed to apply the criterion of whether a reasonable man of full age would in like circumstances have acted as the respondent had done. The accused was convicted of murder but this was reduced on appeal to a conviction for manslaughter. The Court of Appeal certified that there was a point of law of general public importance involved in the case namely "whether on the prosecution for murder of a boy of 15, where the issue of provocation arises, the jury should be directed to consider the question, under section 3 of the Homicide Act 1957, whether the provocation was enough to make a reasonable man do as he did by reference to a 'reasonable adult' or by reference to a 'reasonable boy'." In the eventual appeal the House of Lords confirmed the decision of the Court of Appeal. Their Lordships took the view that if the accused possesses one characteristic which is relevant to the provocation the jury must be able to take it into consideration. Lord Diplock suggested that the proper test for a jury would be as follows: "The judge should state what the question is, using the very terms of the section. He should then explain to them that the reasonable man referred to in the question is a person having the power of self-control to be expected of the person of the sex and age of the accused, but in other respects sharing such of the accused's characteristics as they think would affect the gravity of the provocation to him, and that the question is not merely whether such a person in like circumstances would be provoked to lose his self-control, but also would react to the provocation as the accused did."

In *Newell* (1980) the Court of Appeal returned to the question of what "characteristics" a jury was entitled to consider in deciding whether the accused had responded to the provocation in the way a reasonable man would have responded. The court said that the characteristic must have a sufficient degree of permanence to make it part of the individual's character or personality. Furthermore there must be some real connection between the nature of the provocation and the particular characteristic of the offender by which it is sought to modify the reasonable man test. Thus the fact that the accused was a homosexual would have a sufficient degree of permanence to render it a characteristic, but it would be relevant only if the provocation was in some way related to that trait; it would be totally irrelevant if the provocation has taken the form of insulting the accused's talents as a pianist. Alcohol will rarely ever be relevant. It has long been held that it is no defence for the accused to suggest that he reacted more violently because he was drunk. This is partly because of the general policy of the law in relation to self-imposed drunkenness, and also because there is no sufficient degree of permanence here for the condition to be regarded as a characteristic. The position might possibly be different if the accused was suffering from a more permanent form of alcoholic illness and the provocation was directed against that condition.

In *Burke* 1987 Crim.L.R. 336 the Court of Appeal held that it was not essential to use the actual words of Lord Diplock. It was enough to remind the jury of the characteristics which might have affected the conduct of the hypothetical ordinary reasonable person. It was, however, up to the jury to say which, if any, of the characteristics should be attributed to the ordinary person. This is presumably to be read in the light if *Newell* in that the judge has the right to exclude certain characteristics, such as drunkenness or characteristics which have no sufficient degree of permanence.

We can now have a look at two cases decided before the 1957 Homicide Act to see what impact that Act and the decision in *Camplin* have had on the law of provocation. *Bedder v. D.P.P.* (1954) was a case which concerned the question of whether the accused could rely on an unusual characteristic as being at the root of the provocation. In the case the accused was a young man who was aware that he was sexually impotent. On the night in question he had gone with a prostitute to see whether he could overcome his impotence. He again failed to have sexual intercourse with the woman and she taunted him and kicked him in the genitals, whereupon he responded by stabbing her to death. The House of Lords held that there was no reason for the jury to try to work out what effect such taunts would have on a man who was impotent; the test to be applied was the effect the taunts would have upon a reasonable man, who, by the very fact that he was a reasonable man, was not impotent. The effect of the 1957 Act on such cases is, as we have already noted, to compel the judge to leave the question of provocation to the jury if there is evidence that the accused was, in fact, provoked. *Camplin* makes it quite clear that the judge should allow the jury to consider such characteristics (as impotence) as they would think would affect the gravity of the provocation to him. The House of Lords in *Camplin*, said that it would technically be possible to draw a distinction between age and impotence, but that such a distinction would be unwarranted; *Bedder* should be treated as being overruled. However the House made it quite clear that the accused is not to rely on the fact that he is unduly excitable by nature, he must possess the power of self-control to be expected of an ordinary person of the sex and age of the accused.

In *Mancini* v. *D.P.P.* (1942) the accused had reacted to a fist fight by stabbing the victim. The accused had based his defence on self-defence which would, if successful, have resulted in a total acquittal. He did not raise the issue of provocation. He was convicted and appealed on the basis that the judge should have directed the jury on the issue of provocation as this issue had been clearly raised by the evidence at the trial even though he had not expressly pleaded it. The House of Lords held that although the judge would have been under a duty to direct the jury on the issue of provocation if there had been any evidence that a reasonable man would have reacted in the way that the accused did, there was no such duty on the facts of the present case since once provoked a reasonable man would retain sufficient self-control to react in proportion to the provocation. Thus he would answer fists with fists and not with a deadly weapon. This case laid the foundation for what became known as the reasonable relationship rule. The 1957 Act clearly alters the decision in that the judge would not now be entitled to withdraw the issue of provocation from the jury once there was evidence the accused himself was provoked, however unreasonably he responded to the provocation. It would clearly be permissible for a judge to draw the jury's attention to an obvious disparity between the provocation and the retaliation as a factor to be considered in deciding whether the accused acted as a reasonable person would in the circumstances. It would be improper for a judge to suggest that reasonable men always measure the retaliation in proportion to the provocation offered.

In conclusion it is probably safe to make the following propositions:

1. Once there is evidence that the accused was provoked the issue of provocation must be left to the jury.

2. The jury should be asked to consider whether the accused himself was provoked and whether the provocation was sufficient to make a reasonable man do as the accused did.

3. The jury should be invited to take into account in assessing how a reasonable man would have reacted to the provocation, any such characteristics of the accused which would affect the gravity of the provocation to him.

4. The accused should not be entitled to rely on the fact that he is, by nature, more excitable than the average man nor on the fact that alcohol had made him more unduly aggressive on this particular occasion (*McCarthy* (1954) and *Wardrope* (1960)). However there is authority to suggest that the accused could rely on intoxication to explain why he mistakenly thought he was being provoked (*Letenock* (1917)), although it seems doubtful that this decision would be followed today in the light of recent decisions on the defence of self-induced intoxication (above, p. 166).

5. Although the judge should not tell the jury that reasonable men cool off after a period of time, and that during the time their passions are inflamed they still manage to retaliate in a reasonable way, it is surely permissible for the judge to suggest that on the facts of a particular case these would be proper considerations for a jury to help them decide whether the accused acted in the way a reasonable man would have done under the given provocation.

6. **Self Induced Provocation.** Suppose that X is blackmailing Y. On one occasion X goes to collect payment from Y who finally breaks under the strain of the demands and attacks X. X, seeing that he is in danger hits and kills Y. If X is charged with murder, could he plead that he was provoked by Y? In *Edwards* v. *R.* (1973) the Privy Council said that a blackmailer should not be entitled to rely on provocation caused by his blackmailing activities unless the reaction to the blackmail goes to extreme lengths. But if there is evidence that the blackmailer was, in fact, provoked by his victim then section 3 of the Homicide Act would seem to leave the judge no discretion—he must leave the issue to the jury, though he would presumably be entitled to refer to the accused's blackmailing activities as one of the factors the jury should consider when deciding whether a reasonable man would have acted in the way that the accused did.

2. Involuntary Manslaughter and Causing Death by Reckless Driving

Leaving aside crimes such as infanticide and child destruction, manslaughter has been used as a sort of residual crime for those unlawful killings considered deserving of punishment, but where the prosecution cannot establish the *mens rea* necessary for murder. One category of offenders caused particular difficulties. These were motorists who caused death through their bad driving. Until 1956 these offenders had to be prosecuted for manslaughter (murder would rarely be appropriate). The only alternative would be to prosecute for some motoring offence such as dangerous driving (now reckless driving) and it might be felt that this did not truly reflect the seriousness of what had happened. While logically there was no good reason to single out motor vehicles as a type of weapon which required to be covered by a special form of unlawful homicide, there was a practical reason. Juries simply refused to convict motorists of manslaughter unless the facts were really appalling. Thus Parliament created the new offence of causing death by dangerous or reckless driving. (In 1977 Parliament abolished the offence of dangerous driving and consequently removed the reference to dangerous in the offence of causing death by reckless or dangerous driving. The offence thus became simply causing death by reckless driving). The structure of this offence represented a departure in principle from previous offences as can be shown by the following example. If you consider the offence of careless driving (section 3 of the Road Traffic Act 1988) you would see that the prosecution simply has to show that the accused's driving fell below the standard expected of the reasonable driver; in other words that he was negligent. The degree of carelessness and hence the severity of his penalty will be assessed by reference to how far short of the standard of the reasonable motorist he fell and not by reference to the consequences of his negligence. Thus if we say that it is careless for X to drive round a corner on the wrong side of the road, it is no more careless because someone happens to be coming round the corner in the opposite direction, though, of course, the consequences will be much more severe. Thus the punishment should not be increased because of the fortuitous approach of the other vehicle (see *Krawe* (1985)). The same principle applies in the crime of reckless driving, but because of the reluctance of juries to convict motorists of manslaughter, Parliament created the offence of causing death by reckless driving (now section 1 of the Road Traffic Act 1988). In essence this offence requires that the prosecution proves that the accused is guilty of the offence of reckless driving (section 2 of the Road Traffic Act 1988) which is an offence carrying two years imprisonment. If the prosecutor can further establish that as a result of this reckless driving the accused caused the death of another, then they will have made out the offence of causing death by reckless driving, which carries a maximum sentence of five years imprisonment. In other words Parliament has done exactly what we said the criminal law should not do, namely increase the gravity of the offence by reference to totally fortuitous consequences.

The creation of this new offence did not mean that death caused by really bad driving could not be the subject of a manslaughter charge. In *Seymour* (1983) the facts were such that manslaughter was the obvious charge. In that case, however, the House of Lords took the opportunity to review the relationship between causing death by reckless driving and manslaughter. This was followed by a further review in the case of *Kong Cheuk Kwan* (1985), this time by the Privy Council. The result of these two cases is not altogether clear. It is proposed to examine the position as it was believed to be before *Seymour* and *Kwan* and then to attempt to state the effect of the two decisions.

The position before Seymour and Kong Cheuk Kwan.

Causing death by reckless driving

In order to obtain a conviction for causing death by careless driving (contrary to section 1 Road Traffic Act 1988) the prosecutor must prove two things;

(i) First, he must prove that the defendant has committed the offence of reckless driving (contrary to section 2 Road Traffic Act 1988). This is an either way offence which carries two years imprisonment. In *Lawrence* (1982) Lord Diplock said that in order to establish reckless driving the prosecutor must prove that "the defendant was in fact driving the vehicle in such a manner as to create an obvious and serious risk of causing physical injury to some other person who might happen to be using the road or of doing substantial damage to property; and second, that in driving in that manner the defendant did so without having given any thought to the possibility of there being any such risk, or having recognised that there was some risk involved, had nonetheless gone on to take it." Clearly this is in line with the direction he gave in *Caldwell* on the offence of criminal damage.

(ii) Secondly, he must prove that by his reckless driving the defendant has caused the death of another. If he can establish this then he has made out the offence of reckless driving which is an offence triable only on indictment and which carries a maximum sentence of five years imprisonment. It is not enough that the prosecutor establishes that the defendant was driving recklessly *and* that he killed another whilst doing so. He must establish that *but for* the recklessness of the driving the death would not have happened. Thus if the evidence reveals that even had the defendant been driving with the utmost care, he would still not have been able to avoid the pedestrian who had just stepped out from behind a parked van, then the offence is not made out. (See, *e.g. Dalloway* above, p. 43). The driver, of course, is still liable for reckless driving, we have simply failed to prove that the death was caused by the reckless driving.

It has not been decided whether the offence of causing death by reckless driving is subject to the requirement of the rule that the death must occur within a year and a day of the reckless driving. However, since this offence, as we shall see, is barely distinguishable from manslaughter, it would seem to be logical for the rule to apply to this offence. (Road traffic offences, in general, are beyond the scope of this book. However the whole subject has recently been reviewed in the Road Traffic Law Review Report under the Chairmanship of Dr. P. M. North, (1988), and this well repays reading).

Involuntary manslaughter

The law relating to involuntary manslaughter has never been noted for its clarity. It was, however, generally agreed that three distinct types of involuntary manslaughter were identifiable; gross negligence manslaughter, constructive manslaughter and reckless manslaughter.

(a) *Gross negligence as to death or grievous bodily harm*

In the civil law an action lies at the suit of a person injured as a result of the negligence of another. In general we are looking for a situation in which the person responsible for the injury failed to exercise the care that a reasonable person would have exercised. To put it another way the defendant has failed to foresee what would be the consequences of his actions, consequences most reasonable persons would have foreseen. For our purposes it is better to describe negligence as failing to exercise the care a reasonable person would take in a given situation. If it is expressed this way then it is easy to see that there can be degrees of negligence. To take a simple illustration; if it is generally accepted as safe to drive at 30 m.p.h. in certain conditions then the more you exceed that speed the more negligent you can be said to be. At 40 m.p.h. we could say that there was an increase in the likelihood that you would injure someone and at 60 m.p.h. that likelihood has significantly increased. At 80 m.p.h. we could probably say that it would be a miracle if you did not injure someone. At some stage along this line the courts hold that it is no longer sufficient that the victim can be compensated in damages for his injuries, the law should be able to punish the driver for the totally irresponsible way in which he has behaved and for the injuries he has caused. At this point his negligence can be described as gross or criminal negligence (see *Bateman* (1925)).

Just as in the crime of murder we said that the prosecution had to prove that the accused intended death or serious bodily harm, so in the crime of manslaughter the prosecution will have to prove that the accused was grossly negligent. Also just as the term intention is related to some existing circumstance or result so the term negligence must be related to some consequence. The main difference is that we are not concerned with what the accused intended or even foresaw, we are concerned here with what a reasonable man placed in the same situation would have foreseen. Thus in the crime of manslaughter by gross negligence the prosecution must prove that the reasonable man would have foreseen that had he acted in the way the accused acted he would have very likely killed someone (or possibly that he would have caused serious harm). What, in effect, the jury are asked to say is that the accused's actions were such that death was a very great probability. If the jury find that death was only a possibility then the negligence is not sufficiently gross for a conviction of manslaughter. To put this into a concrete example, suppose that the accused is on the top of a cliff at the seaside and he has a large rock in his hand which he throws onto the beach below. Clearly if he intends to kill or seriously injure someone on the beach then he will be convicted of murder. If, however, it does not occur to him that he is likely to kill or seriously harm someone even though the beach is crowded then we can say that he ought to have realised that he would very likely kill someone and this would be sufficient for a conviction of manslaughter. If the beach were practically deserted and he has no reason to suspect that there would be persons below, then his actions may be described as negligent in the sense that reasonable persons would never take such risks, but since the likelihood of killing another is remote the jury should not convict him of manslaughter.

Foresight by the reasonable man of any consequence short of death (or possibly grievous bodily harm) will not suffice as the basis for gross negligence manslaughter.

All this may seem to be very unsatisfactory. The jury is being asked to decide an issue of fact and degree without really being given much guidance as to where on the scale the critical point is reached and the negligence becomes gross. It was probably for reasons such as these that in *Kwan* Lord Roskill said that it would be better in future if judges were not to direct juries in terms of gross negligence. We shall see, therefore, that it is quite possible that this category of involuntary manslaughter no longer exists (see below, p. 231).

(b) *Constructive manslaughter*

We have already mentioned that in most common law jurisdictions there existed at some time a doctrine known as felony-murder. Under this doctrine killings in the course of committing (violent) felonies were automatically murder, the only mental state the prosecution had to prove being that of the felony. Alongside this doctrine grew up a similar one for killings that occurred during the commission of lesser wrongs; this has been named constructive manslaughter, unlawful act manslaughter and misdemeanour manslaughter. In this country during the last century the accused could be convicted of manslaughter by this doctrine if he caused the death of another whilst committing any unlawful act including wrongs which were tortious but not criminal. Eventually the doctrine was modified so that it can now be confidently asserted that the unlawful act has to amount to a crime; and during this century it has been further qualified by decisions that the act must be an act likely to cause some harm. The doctrine receives its clearest statement in the judgment of Edmund Davis L.J. in *Church* (1966), where he said "the unlawful act must be such as all sober and reasonable people would inevitably recognise must subject the other person to, at least, the risk of some harm resulting therefrom, albeit not serious harm."

What therefore must the prosecution prove to make out a charge of manslaughter under this doctrine.?

(i) They must prove that the accused committed an unlawful act (it would appear that failure to act will not suffice as the basis for constructive manslaughter, *Lowe* (1973); see p. 38 for liability generally for failing to act). This act must be an act which is unlawful in itself and not one that would have been lawful but for the negligent way in which it was performed. For example, driving a car is a lawful act, but if the car is driven negligently then it becomes a criminal offence. This is not the sort of unlawful act which would suffice for the doctrine of constructive manslaughter. If the driver kills someone while driving badly the prosecution will have to charge him either with causing death by reckless driving or with manslaughter by gross negligence described above (*Andrews* v. *D.P.P.* (1937)). On the other hand an assault is an unlawful act in itself and indeed most cases of constructive manslaughter will be based on some form of assault.

In *Arobieke* (1988) A was charged with the manslaughter of K who was electrocuted while trying to cross an electrified railway line. K feared that A was looking for him in order to injure him. K had therefore gone to the railway station in an attempt to lose A. There was evidence that A had gone to the station and had been seen looking in the windows of railway carriages. The Court of Appeal held that although the jury could properly reach the conclusion that A had gone to the station with a view to injure or threaten K, there was no evidence on any actual assault upon K. A may have been preparing to assault K, but as we saw in the previous chapter (above, p. 197) this is not sufficient even for an attempt. There was thus no unlawful act upon which a charge of constructive manslaughter could be based. It might have been different if, for example, the evidence was that at the time of the accident, A had been chasing K across the lines.

(ii) The next step is to prove to the court's satisfaction that sober and reasonable people would inevitably recognise that the act would subject the other person to, at least, the risk of some harm, albeit not serious harm. It must be noted that it is not necessary to establish that the accused himself foresaw the possibility of any harm to the victim. Since the decision in *Church* there have been instances where it was thought that the Court of Appeal was saying that the accused himself must foresee that his actions would harm the victim, but the House of Lords in *D.P.P.* v. *Newbury* (1976), where youths had thrown paving slabs from a bridge on to a passing express train thereby killing the guard, re-affirmed the law as expressed by Edmund Davies L.J.

What exactly is meant by "some harm" is not altogether clear. It presumably means that the act is likely to cause some sort of bodily injury or pain. Thus if A, during the course of an argument in the street, unlawfully but gently pushes B with the result that B loses his footing and falls under a passing bus, the jury would have to decide whether the push was likely to cause B something beyond the discomfort of being touched by A. It may be that, in the circumstances, they could find that it was likely to cause A to be struck by passing traffic, but unless this was the case or unless the jury could find that the battery was sufficiently severe as to be likely to cause bruising it would be difficult to hold that the act was likely to cause any harm. In *Dawson* (1985) the Court of Appeal held that it was not sufficient that the jury find that the unlawful act was likely to cause only an emotional disturbance; there had to be a finding that the unlawful act was likely to cause at least some physical harm. In that case three men had held up the attendant at a petrol filling station in order to rob him. Shortly afterwards he died of a heart attack. The jury were directed in terms that it was sufficient that the unlawful act of the men was likely to cause emotional disturbance. On appeal it was held that they were not entitled to hold the three guilty of manslaughter unless they found that the robbery was likely to have caused some physical harm. The case may well cause difficulties for future courts in trying to distinguish between purely emotional disturbances and physical harm, though insofar as it further narrows the ambit of constructive manslaughter it is to be welcomed.

(iii) Finally the prosecution must prove that it was the unlawful act of the accused which caused the death of the victim. In *Dawson* therefore even if the jury, properly directed, had found that the unlawful act had been likely to cause some physical harm, the prosecution would still have to prove that it was the unlawful act which had caused the attendant's heart attack. (See further *Watson* (1989)).

(c) *Reckless manslaughter*

It seems to have been generally accepted that there was a category of manslaughter known as reckless manslaughter. To some the term reckless here meant the same as gross negligence and thus the offence was the same as that established in section (*a*) above. Others, however, believed that this was a separate category and covered persons who deliberately took an unjustified risk of harming another, albeit not seriously. This category would thus also include those defendants who had foreseen that what they were doing was likely to cause death or serious harm, but who were not convicted of murder because the jury was unwilling to infer from this that they intended to kill or cause serious harm (see above, p. 23). In other words, the *mens rea* for this type of manslaughter is (*Cunningham*) recklessness as to some harm.

An illustration of this type of manslaughter is provided by *Pike* (1961) where the accused persuaded his girlfriend to sniff a cleaning fluid because in the past he had found that this improved her subsequent sexual performance. He had observed in the past that some girls had been rendered unconscious by the fumes, but none had suffered any permanent damage. Unfortunately, on the occasion in question, the girl died. He was convicted of manslaughter.

The position after Seymour and Kong Cheuk Kwan.

The law relating to involuntary manslaughter has now to be read in the light of the decision of the House of Lords in *Seymour* (1983) and of the Privy Council in *Kong Cheuk Kwan* (1985).

In *Seymour* (1983) the defendant had had an argument with the woman with whom he was living. Later in the day they literally ran into each other in their respective vehicles; the defendant was driving a lorry and the woman a car. The woman got out of her car to tell the defendant what she thought of him when he suddenly rammed her car with his lorry trapping her between the two vehicles. The woman was virtually cut in half and died later as a result of her injuries. He maintained that he was simply trying to free his lorry from the car and had not seen where the woman was standing. He was charged with manslaughter. He said that he was willing to plead guilty to causing death by reckless driving, but not manslaughter. The prosecutor would not accept his plea and so he was charged with manslaughter. This case highlights the relationship between the two crimes, together with the problem faced by prosecutors over which crime to charge. Was the prosecutor acting reasonably in refusing to accept Seymour's plea? After all, we have already said that juries are notoriously reluctant to convict motorists of manslaughter. However, a distinction has to be drawn between the motorist who has killed another through bad driving and a motorist who has, in effect, used his vehicle like a dangerous weapon (or to put it in the way it would be expressed by the average juror, between a bad motorist and a real criminal). *Seymour* is a case which may well be considered to fall into the latter category and the prosecutor was undoubtedly reasonable to insist on the charge of manslaughter.

On the law as it was understood to be at the time, a jury would have almost certainly had little difficulty in convicting Seymour of gross negligence or unlawful act manslaughter. However the trial judge gave a direction to the jury which was almost identical to that approved by the House of Lords for reckless driving (see above, p. 225). The only difference between this direction and the one approved by Lord Diplock for reckless driving was that the scope of the risk was narrowed. Whereas in *Lawrence* Lord Diplock had spoken of an obvious and serious risk of causing physical injury to some other person who might happen to be using the road or of doing substantial damage to property, the trial judge in *Seymour* spoke of an obvious and serious risk of causing physical harm to another. In other words all reference to damaging property was omitted in the manslaughter direction. The defendant was convicted and appealed ultimately to the House of Lords. Lord Roskill said that where the accused was charged with the common law offence of "motor manslaughter" the qualified causing death by reckless driving direction given in this case was totally suitable since the two offences were, in essence, the same.

On the face of it this is a strange ruling since it means that the House of Lords appears to be equating the crime of manslaughter, which carries life imprisonment, with that of causing death by reckless driving which carries only five years; the only difference being that where the court is dealing with causing death by reckless driving the risk is of physical harm *or substantial damage to property*. His Lordship appeared to recognise this difficulty since he said that in deciding whether to charge the defendant with manslaughter or causing death by reckless driving, prosecutors should bear in mind that manslaughter would be the appropriate charge only where the risk of death was high.

The decision raises a number of questions. In the first place, are we to understand that there is a separate offence known as "motor manslaughter" and, if so, does it have its own set of requirements? In the second place how can we have two crimes with virtually the same ingredients but with vastly differing maximum penalties?

Lord Roskill returned to this issue again in the case of *Kong Cheuk Kwan* (1985), which involved charges of manslaughter brought as a result of a collision between two hydrofoil ferries in Hong Kong Harbour. Again Lord Roskill approved the *Seymour* direction, but this time there was never any possibility of a charge of causing death by reckless driving. It would seem to follow that this is a straightforward case of manslaughter and therefore the direction in *Seymour* is not restricted to a category of offences known as "motor manslaughter." So what type of manslaughter is it? Lord Roskill refers to it as reckless manslaughter, so he might appear to be referring to category (*c*) (above, p. 230). However he is using the wider *Caldwell* definition of recklessness in preference to *Cunningham*. Further, he would appear to see no difference between reckless manslaughter and gross negligence manslaughter. Indeed he says that gross negligence is a most confusing phrase which should not be used in future. The overall result would seem to be a merger of the old categories (*a*) and (*c*). In other words there is a new category which we can call reckless manslaughter where the prosecution must establish *Caldwell* recklessness as to causing some physical harm. This represents a fairly substantial change. Under the law before *Seymour*, a prosecutor relying on gross negligence manslaughter had to establish that the accused's acts were likely to cause death or at least serious bodily harm, and a prosecutor relying on reckless manslaughter had to prove that the accused deliberately took the risk of causing some physical harm. Now all the prosecutor has to prove is that the accused has created an obvious and serious risk of causing physical harm to another. In *Kong Cheuk Kwan* Lord Roskill explained that his reference in *Seymour* to likelihood of death was made only for the benefit of prosecutors trying to decide between the offences of manslaughter and causing death by reckless driving. He was only trying to suggest that a jury was unlikely to convict of manslaughter unless there was a high risk of death. This was not, however, part of the definition of manslaughter to be left to the jury. Once the risk of injury is established, the prosecutor merely has to show that the defendant deliberately took that risk or that he gave no thought to it.

It seems clear that category (*b*), unlawful act manslaughter still exists (see *Goodfellow* (1986) and *Arobieke* (1988)). However, it is suggested that if the above analysis of *Seymour* and *Kong Cheuk Kwan* is correct, there is little need for this head.

In summary we can probably say that the prosecution will establish involuntary manslaughter if it can prove either—

(i) that the accused perpetrated an unlawful act which was likely to cause at least some physical harm to another *or*
(ii) that the accused created an obvious and serious risk of harm to another and was reckless, in the *Caldwell* sense, towards this harm and death resulted.

An illustration. It will probably help if we conclude this section with an illustration of how these principles work. The case of *Lamb* (1967) was decided before *Seymour* and *Kong Cheuk Kwan*, but its facts provide a useful example. In that case two young men were playing with a loaded revolver. Lamb knew that there was a live round in one of the chambers, but thought that the chambers on such a weapon revolved after the gun had been fired. In fact the mechanism revolves before the gun is fired, when the trigger is pulled. He pointed the gun at his friend and pulled the trigger. This resulted in the live round being fired and his friend was killed. In the actual case the Court of Appeal ruled that Lamb was not guilty of manslaughter since there was no unlawful act; the only conceivable unlawful act was an assault and Lamb did not possess the *mens rea* for this. Experts testified that the mistake Lamb had made was quite understandable for someone unskilled in guns; he was not, therefore, guilty of gross negligence manslaughter. If the facts were to come before the courts today following *Seymour*, would the decision be the same? The decision on unlawful act manslaughter would remain unaltered unless the decision in *Kwan* has also affected the definition of assault (see above, p. 63). The question for the court would be whether or not he was guilty of reckless manslaughter. Has he created an obvious and serious risk of harm to another? Following the expert testimony it may well be that the court would hold that the risk of harm was not an obvious and serious one in which case the decision would be the same (see *Sangha* above, p. 61). If, however, the jury believed that the risk was an obvious and serious one, they would then have to decide whether he deliberately took such a risk or whether he gave no thought to there being such a risk. Clearly he did not deliberately take a risk of shooting his friend. Equally it is not clear that he gave no thought to there being such a risk. He thought about the situation and wrongly concluded that there was no risk. If this is the jury's finding, then it is quite possible that he is not reckless within the *Caldwell* definition (see above p. 69.)

3. SUICIDE

It is no longer an offence for a person to kill himself or to attempt to kill himself. However the abolition of the crime of suicide was thought to leave an unacceptable gap in the law, namely that if a person who killed or attempted to kill himself did not commit a crime, then someone who helped him to do this could not be a party to the death and there might be good reasons for wanting to bring such a helper within the scope of the criminal law. Thus section 2 of the Suicide Act 1961 provides that "A person who aids, abets, counsels or procures the suicide of another or an attempt by another to commit suicide, shall be liable on conviction on indictment to imprisonment for a term not exceeding fourteen years."

The words "aids, abets, counsels or procures" are the words which are used to describe liability generally for secondary parties to crimes (see *Att.-Gen.* v. *Able* (1984) and above p. 125). They cover a wide variety of situations from the man who urges another to kill himself for some ulterior motive to the fond relative who gets for his dying wife some poison so that she can put herself out of pain. Possibly the section must be interpreted to mean that no liability arises until the suicide is committed or at least attempted. However one who unsuccessfully urges another to commit suicide will be guilty of an attempt (see above, p. 196).

Where the accused has killed or been a party to the killing of another, it will be manslaughter and not murder if he can establish that the killing was part of a suicide pact in which he also, at the time of the killing, intended to die; Homicide Act 1957, s.4. (see above, p. 216).

The case of *R.* v. *Coroner for Inner West London, ex p. De Lucan* (1988) makes it clear that the year and a day rule (above p. 19) applies to all the offences involving suicide. It also applies to the question whether the deceased did in fact commit suicide, although suicide itself is no longer a crime. Hence the Divisional Court quashed a Coroner's verdict that the applicant's son had committed suicide.

4. INFANTICIDE

Under the provisions of the Infanticide Act 1938, where a woman has caused the death of her child which was under the age of 12 months in circumstances which would amount to murder but for the fact that at the time of her act or omission the balance of her mind was disturbed by reason of not having recovered from the effect of giving birth to the child or by reason of the effect of lactation consequent upon the birth of the child, she may be either:
  (i) prosecuted for murder at which trial she may raise the defence of infanticide or
  (ii) she may be tried directly for infanticide.

In either case a conviction for infanticide shall be treated as a conviction for manslaughter and thus the maximum sentence will be life imprisonment, though, of course, the judge will be able to take account of the mitigating factors. Unlike the defences of insanity or diminished responsibility, the defence of infanticide does not place the burden of proof on the accused woman. She must introduce evidence of the defence, but it is for the prosecution to show that the defence has not been made out.

CHAPTER 9

NON-FATAL OFFENCES AGAINST THE PERSON

In this chapter we shall examine a selection of the many offences against the person. The first section covers the more common assault type offences and the second section outlines certain sexual offences.

1. *ASSAULTS*

1. ASSAULT AND BATTERY

At common law there were two basic offences of assault and battery. Technically assault is the offence of causing another to apprehend immediate and unlawful personal violence. Thus if X puts up his fists to strike Y, if Y apprehends that he is going to be hit then we can say that X has assaulted Y. When Y is, in fact, hit on the nose, this constitutes a battery. However over the years lawyers have come to use the word "assault" to cover both situations, and indeed the offence of common assault under section 47 of the Offences Against the Person Act 1861 covers both assaults and batteries. In *Att.-Gen.'s Reference* (*No.* 6 *of* 1980) (1981) the Court of Appeal approved with a slight addition the definition of assault given by James J. in *Fagan* v. *M.P.C.* (1969); "the actual intended use of any unlawful force to another person without his consent (or any other lawful excuse)."

Both assault and battery are crimes of basic intent to which the defence of self-induced intoxication does not apply. Although the criminal law has tended to conflate the offences of assault and battery, it will be convenient here to examine their basic ingredients separately.

(1) Assault

Actus reus. The prosecution must establish that the victim was put in fear of immediate and unlawful personal violence. Thus a very clear example of an assault would be where X, during the course of an argument, raises his clenched fist as if to punch Y in the face. Y would be in fear of immediate personal violence for which there would be no lawful excuse. The requirement that the fear be of immediate personal violence has, over the years, been given a fairly generous interpretation. Recently in *Smith* v. *Chief Superintendant, Woking Police Station* (1983) it was held that magistrates were entitled to find that a woman who saw the defendant looking through the window of her bed-sitting room late at night apprehended immediate violence. The same was true in *Lewis* (1970) where the husband was threatening violence to his wife who was on the other side of a locked door, though in this case the court may have been over anxious to find an assault in order to uphold a conviction under section 20 of the Offences Against the Person Act 1861 (see below, p. 242). It is clear, however, that immediate fear of future violence does not suffice.

There is some authority for the view that words alone cannot constitute an assault, but it is suggested that in appropriate circumstances there is no reason why they should not. For example, if X, a prostitute, was walking home in the dark one evening when a man said to her "I am continuing Jack the Ripper's crusade against prostitutes," it would be absurd if this were not to be treated as being capable of constituting an assault. However, in this case it could be argued that there is something which could be classified as an act as opposed to words alone. Would there be an assault if X telephones Y and tells Y that he has planted a bomb in the telephone Y is holding and that it will go off in two seconds? (See Glanville Williams, *Textbook of Criminal Law*, p. 176).

For the purposes of common assault the personal violence is not unlawful if the accused was acting in self-defence (or if one of the allied defences applied; see above. p. 173) or if the defence of consent was available. We shall see later (below, p. 246) that in some cases a person may consent to another doing what would otherwise be an assault or battery. Suffice it here to say, however, that consent is more likely to be in issue in relation to battery. It did, however, arise in *Lamb* (above, p. 233) where the victim clearly consented to Lamb pointing the rifle at him; though in that case the absence of an assault is equally explicable on the ground that Lamb lacked *mens rea* since he did not intend to put the other in fear of immediate harm and neither did he foresee that his friend would apprehend such harm.

Mens rea. The prosecution must prove that the accused either intended to put the victim in fear of immediate personal harm or that the accused foresaw that this would be the effect of his conduct on the victim. In *Venna* (1976) the Court held that intention or recklessness sufficed. Unfortunately in *Seymour* (1983) Lord Roskill said that the word "recklessness" should receive the same definition whether it appeared in a statute or elsewhere, and, of course, he had the *Caldwell* definition of recklessness in mind. Does this mean, therefore that the prosecution would succeed if they could establish that the accused had created an obvious risk that the victim would be put in fear of immediate personal harm, and had given no thought to such a risk? It is suggested that until a specific ruling is given on this matter, we should confine the *Caldwell* definition of recklessness to instances where the word occurs in modern statutory provisions (see above p. 59).

It is the effect that the accused intentionally or recklessly (in the *Cunningham* sense) creates on the victim that is central to the offence; it does not matter that the accused had neither the intention nor the ability to carry out the threat. Thus if X holds up Y, a bank cashier, with a water pistol, if X intends that Y should be afraid for his personal safety and Y is so affected then X has committed an assault. It is no defence for X to say that there was no assault because Y was never in any danger.

(2) Battery

Actus reus. Here the prosecution must prove that the accused inflicted unlawful personal violence on the victim. There is no need to show that the amount of force was great; in fact, any touching of another without that other's consent amounts to a battery (for the defence of consent see below, p. 246), but consent is generally implied in the sort of bodily contact that happens in ordinary everyday life. Thus we generally assume that people walking about in the street accept that others will inevitably bump into them; that others may tap them on the shoulder to attract their attention; and that in the course of conversation there are people who need to touch the other to emphasise what they are saying.

The most simple example of batteries are those cases in which the accused hits his victim either with a fist or with an object he is holding. But it is also a battery to dig a hole for someone to fall into or to cause people to fall down stairs by turning out the lights (*Martin* (1881) below, p. 242). There is no need for the victim to be aware that he is about to be struck; thus it would amount to a battery where X removes the chair Y is about to sit on, or hits him on the head from behind.

Mens rea. The prosecution must establish either that the accused intended to inflict unlawful personal violence on the victim or that he foresaw that his conduct would probably have that effect. Again it is suggested that subjectivity should remain the basis for the *mens rea* of this offence and that *Caldwell* should not apply. In *Fagan* (1969) it was held that battery was a continuing offence and where the accused accidentally drove onto a policeman's foot and then refused to drive off, it sufficed that he formed the necessary *mens rea* while the car was parked on the constable's foot; it was not essential that he formed the *mens rea* before driving onto the foot (see above. p. 75).

The result of recent decisions is that where in assault or battery consent is an available defence on the facts or where the accused relies on self-defence, it is sufficient that the accused honestly believed that the victim was consenting or that he needed to act in self-defence, even though this is not the case and he has no reasonable grounds for so thinking (see above, p. 84).

2. ASSAULT OCCASIONING ACTUAL BODILY HARM

Under section 47 of the Offences Against the Person Act 1861, it is an offence for a person to assault another thereby causing that other actual bodily harm. The offence is punishable with up to five years' imprisonment. In order to gain a conviction for this offence the prosecution must prove that the accused was guilty of an assault or battery as described above and that this caused actual bodily harm. Thus the *actus reus* consists in the *actus reus* of assault or battery which led to actual bodily harm, and the *mens rea* is the *mens rea* of assault or battery. The only question that remains to be considered is what amounts to actual bodily harm. According to the House of Lords in *D.P.P.* v. *Smith* (1961) which was examining the phrase "grievous bodily harm," the words "bodily harm" needed no explanation and "grievous" meant really serious. Thus it follows that actual bodily harm is something less than really serious, and possibly any degree of bodily injury may suffice however slight, even an injury to the state of a person's mind.

3. Offences Against the Person Act 1861, Section 20

"Whosoever shall unlawfully and maliciously wound or inflict any grievous bodily harm upon another person, either with or without any weapon or instrument, shall be guilty of an offence triable either way and being convicted thereof shall be liable to imprisonment for five years."

The first thing that should strike you about this offence is that although it sounds far more serious than that under section 47 (assault occasioning actual bodily harm) it carries precisely the same maximum penalty. This is a result of the Offences Against the Person Act being a haphazard consolidation of offences, but it does make the law look a trifle illogical.

Actus reus

The prosecution must establish that the accused unlawfully inflicted grievous bodily harm or that he unlawfully wounded the victim. The word unlawfully means that the offence is not committed if the accused was acting in self-defence or possibly that the victim had consented (see below, p. 246). Wounding will rarely cause problems: here the prosecution must prove that as a result of the accused's actions the inner and outer skin of the victim were severed. Would it suffice therefore that the accused has caused internal bleeding in his victim? If, for example, the accused has caused bleeding inside the accused's mouth this will be classified as a wounding, but probably not if he has caused a rupture of the victim's stomach lining or a bruise. The difference is that the inside skin of the lips and cheeks are readily accessible from the outside; you can trace the continuity of the skin with your finger. In no way is this true of the stomach lining. The matter is not likely to cause many problems since an attack which caused internal bleeding is likely to be said to have inflicted grievous bodily harm—or at least actual bodily harm in the case of a bruise.

We have already seen that grievous bodily harm means that the victim suffers bodily harm which can be described as really serious. Here there need be no breaking of the skin, and it is a question of fact for the jury whether the harm is or is not really serious. However it will be seen that in section 20 the accused must be shown to have "inflicted" grievous bodily harm, whereas under section 18 he must be shown to have "caused" grievous bodily harm. Is any significance to be drawn from the use of these different verbs? The answer is that no such distinction may have occurred to the original drafters of the provisions, but in interpreting them the courts have more often than not held that the word "inflicts" means that the act of the accused which results in the grievous bodily harm must itself be an assault. In the majority of cases this caused no problems since the accused usually produced the grievous bodily harm by striking the victim with his fists or a weapon. In *Clarence* (1888), however, the accused who was suffering from a communicable form of veneral disease had intercourse with a woman without revealing his condition to her. It was held that he could not be convicted of "inflicting grievous bodily harm" on her since she had consented to the intercourse and hence there was no assault (see below, p. 248 for meaning of consent). Recently in *Wilson* (1984) the House of Lords has held that the word "inflicts" did not necessarily include an allegation of assault. This still leaves open the question of whether the word "inflicts" has a meaning different from "causes" and it is possible that "inflicts" might be held to require the application of some force, whether by an assault or not, and may not, therefore, cover a situation in which grievous bodily harm has been caused by the secret administration of poison.

Whatever the eventual decision in cases of poisoning and cases such as *Clarence,* the decision in *Wilson* removes doubts from other earlier cases in which convictions under section 20 had been upheld despite the absence of any obvious assault. Thus in *Martin* (1881) the accused had caused panic in a theatre as the audience was leaving after a performance by extinguishing all the lights on the stairs and placing a bar across the doors at the bottom. In the ensuing chaos several persons were injured when crushed against the doors which would not open. The court seems to have assumed that there was an assault, though it is difficult to see how they were placed in fear of immediate and unlawful violence. Possibly there was a battery of the type involved where a pit is dug for somebody to fall into. Since, however, the word "inflicts" does not require proof of an assault there will be no difficulty in holding that the accused has inflicted grievous bodily harm on the victims. Similarly many of the problems of holding that there has been an assault in cases in which the victim has caused grievous bodily harm upon himself in trying to escape from the accused will disappear. In *Halliday* (1889) the accused advanced in a threatening manner towards his wife who tried to jump out of an upstairs window. Her daughter prevented her fall by trying to hold on to her, but the accused ordered her to let go whereupon her mother fell to the ground below. It was held that the father had inflicted grievous bodily harm. In that case it would be possible to say that there was an assault since both the mother and daughter were put in fear of immediate harm; but this is more difficult in the case of *Lewis* (1970) where the husband who was threatening the wife was on the other side of a locked door. Again the court held that there was an assault although the wife was not in fear of such immediate harm because of the locked door. The decision in *Wilson* means that a conviction in such cases as these can be upheld without the need to give an unduly wide meaning to the requirement in assault that the accused should place the victim in fear of "immediate" harm.

It is generally accepted that where the prosecution has charged the accused with wounding under section 20, and possibly under section 18, it must prove that this occurred as a result of a battery, though this is unlikely to cause any problem. (*Beasley* (1981).)

Mens Rea

The prosecution must prove that the accused acted "maliciously." We have already seen that this does not mean that the accused acted from evil motives; it means that the accused must have intended or foreseen a particular result (see above, p. 50). In *Grimshaw* (1984) the Court of Appeal held that this was still the correct definition of the word "maliciously." In other words, this word was not affected by the decision of the House of Lords in *Caldwell*. If this is the case then one would have supposed that the prosecution would have to prove that the accused intended or foresaw that his actions might wound or inflict grievous bodily harm. However in *Mowatt* (1968) the Court of Appeal held that it was sufficient if the accused foresaw that some physical injury might be caused to some person albeit of a minor nature. The accused did not have to foresee that it might be a wound or grievous bodily harm. The effect of this is to reduce the *mens rea* of section 20 to the same level of culpability required for assault occasioning actual bodily harm, and this seems to be indefensible. Admittedly both offences through an accident of history carry the same sentence, but section 20 is clearly intended to be the more serious and sense can only be made of the two offences if a higher degree of culpability (namely foresight of grievous bodily harm or wounding) is required under section 20. However, at present this is not the requirement, and this aspect of *Mowatt* was confirmed by the Court of Appeal in *Grimshaw* (1984).

Thus in conclusion if X punches Y and foresees that Y will suffer slight harm, X will be guilty of an offence under section 20 if Y is wounded or if he suffers really serious bodily injury as a result of the punch. He also commits an offence under section 47.

In *Sullivan* (1981) the Court of Appeal held that an intention to frighten the victim, without more, would not suffice as the *mens rea* for section 20. Where, for example, A drives his car perilously close to B intending to scare him, A may well realise that he might cause some injury to B. Unless, however, he does realise that there is a risk of injury there is no offence under section 20, though there may be an offence under section 47.

4. OFFENCES AGAINST THE PERSON ACT 1861, SECTION 18

"Whosoever shall unlawfully and maliciously by any means whatsoever wound or cause any grievous bodily harm to any person with intent to do some grievous bodily harm to any person, or with intent to resist or prevent the lawful apprehension or detaining of any person, shall be guilty of an offence, and being convicted thereof shall be liable to imprisonment for life."

The maximum possible sentence of life imprisonment clearly shows that this offence is reserved for the most culpable of non–fatal offenders against the person.

Actus reus

The *actus reus* of this offence is to a large extent identical to that of the offence under section 20. It should be noted however that this section speaks of the accused "causing" rather than "inflicting" grievous bodily harm, and thus there is no question of the need to show an assault here.

Mens rea

The prosecution must prove (i) that the accused intended to do grievous bodily harm or intended to resist arrest, and (ii) that he acted maliciously.

(i) The prosecution must prove that the accused caused the *actus reus* with the intention either of doing grievous bodily harm to some person or with the intention of resisting or preventing the lawful apprehension or detaining of any person. *Belfon* (1976) makes it clear that nothing short of intention will suffice on this part of the *mens rea*. Where, therefore, an explanation of "intention" is required, the trial judge may well turn to the guidelines suggested by Lord Lane C.J. in *Nedrick* (1986); see above, p. 58). We need say nothing more about an intention to do grievous bodily harm. In relation to intention to resist, etc., we can safely say that if the accused believes that the arrest is unlawful and it is, in fact, unlawful, he will have a defence. The position is less clear if he believes the arrest is unlawful, but it is in fact lawful. On principle he should have a defence as long as his belief is genuine. This would seem to follow from *Morgan* (above, p. 82) but there is old authority to the contrary (*Bentley* (1850)).

(ii) In addition to the intent described in (i) above the prosecution must establish that the accused was acting "maliciously." In *Mowatt* (1968) the Court of Appeal said, *obiter,* that this word is superfluous in section 18, presumably thinking of a case in which the accused is charged with maliciously causing grievous bodily harm with intent to do grievous bodily harm. Similarly it would not add much to wounding where this was charged coupled with an intent to do grievous bodily harm. Where, however, the accused is charged with wounding or causing grievous bodily harm with intent to resist arrest it has a full part to play. Consider a situation in which X, in trying to resist lawful arrest, pushes the arresting officer who falls and is seriously injured. If the word malicious is given no role to play it means that the only *mens rea* required of X would be his intent to resist arrest and this would be satisfied even if he used only the slightest force to break away. This would surely be wrong. Thus the word maliciously should be employed so as to require that in addition to the ulterior intent the prosecution should also have to prove that the accused at least foresaw grievous bodily harm or a wound whichever was specified in the indictment. Thus in our illustration X would only be liable on an indictment charging him with causing grievous bodily harm with intent to resist arrest if he did intend to resist arrest and if he also foresaw that his act might cause grievous bodily harm. The extended meaning given to maliciously by the Court in *Mowatt* for section 20—*i.e.* foresight of any degree of injury— should not be applied to section 18, however inconsistent this may appear.

5. CONSENT AS A DEFENCE TO OFFENCES AGAINST THE PERSON

The questions we must ask in this section are whether consent can ever be relied upon as a defence to offences against the person and, if so, what does the criminal law mean by the term "consent?"

(1) Is consent any defence to a charge involving an offence against the person?

It has been said that the least touching of another without his consent amounts to a battery. Put another way we can say that an element of battery is lack of consent. Clearly everyday life requires that you consent to others touching you; if this were not so you would not be able to visit the hairdresser without being the victim of a battery. When you walk down the crowded high street you impliedly consent to other pedestrians bumping into you. But can you consent to more violent contact? Again a moment's thought will show you that you can. For instance most of pay painful visits to the dentist from time to time and thousands of people engage in sporting activities where bodily contact can be quite violent. If we were not allowed to consent to such activities we should not have sports such as rugby or boxing. In such sports the participants consent to the amount of violence that is legally permissible under the rules of the game and also to fouls that occur in normal games. However, it would be no defence where a member of one team violently punched a member of the other team in a game of rugby to say that it was all in the game.

Equally we know that in some sports very serious harm or even death can result. Does this mean that you can consent to the possible infliction of really serious harm? The general policy has been recently reviewed by the Court of Appeal in *Att.-Gen.'s Reference (No. 6 of 1980) (1981)*. There it was held that, contrary to one line of argument put forward, it mattered not whether the act occurred in public or in private; "it is an assault if actual bodily harm is intended and/or caused." The Court of Appeal however, added that their decision was not intended to cast doubt upon the accepted legality of properly conducted games or sports, lawful chastisement or correction, reasonable surgical interference, dangerous exhibitions, etc. Of these lawful chastisement is the exercise of a legal right and the remainder can be justified on the ground of being for the public good.

Thus the position would appear to be that where actual bodily harm is not intended or is not actually caused, lack of consent is an essential ingredient of the crimes of assault and battery. Where, however, actual bodily harm is intended and/or caused, consent is irrelevant unless the act falls within one of the exceptions such as a properly conducted sport. Here the victim's implied consent to the risks of the sport will be a defence to any allegation of an assault. In *Jones* (1987) the Court of Appeal held that consent to rough and undisciplined play where there was no intent to injure was a defence. This would seem to allow exemption from the Attorney-General's reference even where the activity is seen to involve risk of serious injury and is based on the notion that boys will indulge in this sort of horse-play. The Court also endorsed the principle that a belief that the other was consenting to such activity was a defence even though the belief was not reasonably entertained, as along as it was a genuine belief.

Within these recognised exceptions such as properly conducted sports and reasonable surgical interference how wide is the scope of the defence of consent. Let us consider sport first. Society has accepted that sport is something to be encouraged even if this means some degree of bodily injury. Take boxing as an example. In that sport the contestants intentionally inflict some bodily injury on each other and clearly when they enter the ring they consent to such injuries and the law allows such consent. Equally clearly it would not be acceptable if the object of the game was for the participants intentionally to inflict really serious injury on each other. Thus bare-fist boxing (prize-fighting) was banned many years ago. But we all know that even boxing with gloves can lead to very serious injuries, even to death. Does this mean that the law allows participants to consent to the risk of receiving really serious injury? The participants in professional boxing know that they could cause really serious injuries to each other, so this means that the law allows them to consent to such risks. What the law does here is to balance the risks of serious harm against the social good of the sport. Since the risks of really serious injury are slight and the public benefit is seen to be large, boxers are allowed to consent to such injuries.

Similarly in medical treatment. If the patient does not consent to the treatment the doctor is guilty of an assault. But surely you can always consent to medically prescribed treatment. The position is not quite so straightforward. Under no circumstances may you consent to the intentional infliction of death on you, whatever your condition. However some operations carry with them the risk of death and there, as with boxing, a balancing of the risks must be taken. If it appears that the risk is worth taking as the only way in which the patient will be brought back to normal life (as with a heart transplant operation) then the patient will be entitled to consent to the treatment and the doctor will incur no liability for a death which he foresaw as possible; this is a balancing of the risk with the possible benefit. You may not consent to treatment which has no social benefit. For example you would not be entitled to have your leg surgically removed so that you could take part in the disabled persons' Olympic Games. But what of cosmetic surgery such as reducing the size of the patient's nose? At first it was said that such operations served no therapeutic value. Now it appears that the psychological benefit they confer on the patient is recognised and thus one may consent to such surgery. Sex change operations and sterilisations which were once regarded as being against the public interest are now generally recognised as valuable operations.

In the field of sexual offences consent plays an important role. For example it is obvious that persons over the age of 16 can consent to sexual intercourse and their consent is a complete defence to a charge of rape. Girls who are under 16 can clearly give consent to intercourse, provided they understand the nature of the act, (below, p. 249) and this will be a defence to a charge of rape, but not to a defence of unlawful sexual intercourse which is an offence to which consent is irrelevant. (See below, p. 252.)

(2) What is consent?

It is often said that to constitute a defence the consent must be real. This means that if the person submits to some act because of duress, there is no real consent. Equally the law takes the view that some children are too young to give any meaningful consent. A 15 year old girl's consent to intercourse may save the man from a charge of rape if not unlawful sexual intercourse, but if the girl was much younger then the court is likely to discount the fact that she agreed to what was being done. There is no rule of thumb about the age at which a person can give meaningful consent, it depends on the facts of the case and the actual child.

More problematical are the cases where consent is procured by fraud. In *Bolduc and Bird* (1967) a doctor permitted a friend who was a jazz musician to attend a vaginal examination. He introduced his friend to the woman as a medical student and asked if she minded his presence. She said she did not mind and so the examination took place. When she learned the truth she was, not surprisingly, furious, and the doctor and his friend were prosecuted for an assault. Now obviously if the woman consented to being examined there was no assault; but can you say that she really consented when it is perfectly clear she would not have consented had she known of the true facts. The criminal courts take a rather simplistic approach to such problems. If the act which follows the consent is the act which the person was consenting to, then it is irrelevant that the person would not have consented had he or she known of all the surrounding circumstances. Thus in *Bolduc and Bird*, the woman consented to the doctor performing a vaginal examination and that is what he did. It was irrelevant that the woman would not have consented had she known his friend was a voyeur and not a student. Similarly, in *Clarence* which we discussed earlier (above, p. 242), the woman consented to intercourse and that is what took place albeit in circumstances that would have led her to withdraw her consent. In *Williams* (1923) a singing master was charged with the rape of a girl of 16. The prosecution's case was that he had told her her voice needed improving and that he would help her. She then let him have intercourse with her. If the prosecution could establish that she was totally unaware of sexual matters and that she thought this was some form of operation to improve her voice, then there would be no consent. If, on the other hand she knew that he was proposing sexual intercourse but wrongly believed him when he said that this would improve her voice then there would be effective consent.

II. SEXUAL OFFENCES

Although non-consensual sexual offences might be subsumed under the general category of non-fatal offences against the person, many sexual offences have the unusual feature that they may be committed even where the conduct was consensual. It is therefore customary to treat sexual offences as a separate category and a further justification may lie in the fact that sexual *offenders* constitute a special category of offenders.

The law relating to sexual offences was reviewed by the Criminal Law Revision Committee which reported in 1984 (15th Report, Sexual Offences, Cmnd. 9213). In its draft Criminal Code the Law Commission has incorporated, with certain exceptions, the Criminal Law Revision Committee's recommendations into the section on sexual offences (Law Com. No. 177, (1989)).

Among the plethora of sexual offences the following need to be noted.

1. RAPE

Under section 1 of the Sexual Offences Act 1956 it is an offence for a man to rape a woman. The definition of rape is to be found in section 1 of the Sexual Offences (Amendment) Act 1976 which was passed as a result of controversy following the decision of the House of Lords in *D.P.P.* v. *Morgan* (1976); the Act supported the decision of the House of Lords. (See above, p. 82.)

Actus reus

In a prosecution for rape the prosecutor must prove—
First, that the man had sexual intercourse with the woman and for this purpose the slightest penetration of the vagina by the penis suffices (Sexual Offences Act 1956, s.44).

Secondly, that the woman did not, in fact, consent to have sexual intercourse. It does not have to be proved that intercourse was achieved by force or threats of bodily harm. Thus in *Olugboja* (1981) it was held that where a girl submitted to intercourse through fear of what might happen if she did not, even though no specific threats had been made, the intercourse was non-consensual. There is no requirement that the woman should put up at least some resistance. The prosecution would also succeed if it could prove that intercourse was achieved by fraud, provided that the fraud resulted in the woman being mistaken either as to the identity of the man or as to the nature of the act performed (see *Williams* (1923)). Where the woman is too young, too drunk or too mentally deficient to be able to give a meaningful consent, intercourse would be held to have taken place without her consent.

Thirdly, that the man is not the husband of the woman. At the present time, the common law rule that a husband cannot rape his wife prevails. He can, of course, be charged with assaulting his wife if he forces her to have intercourse with him and the force satisfies the normal requirements of one of the assault offences (see above, p. 237). He may also be charged with indecent assault (*Kowalski* (1988)). The rule does not apply if the spouses are living apart or if a decree nisi of divorce or annulment has been granted. Furthermore the rule does not apply to persons who are cohabiting but who are not a husband and wife.

Fourthly, that the man is over the age of 14. There is an irrebuttable presumption that males under the age of 14 are incapable of having sexual intercourse. It follows, therefore, that they cannot be the principal offender in any offence which requires sexual intercourse, including buggery. They can, however, be charged as secondary parties to such offences or with the offence of indecent assault.

Mens rea

The prosecution must prove that, at the time of the intercourse, the man *either* (i) knew that the woman was not consenting *or* (ii) was reckless as to whether or not she was consenting. The main problem here is the meaning to be given to the word "reckless." Since it is being used in a modern statute it would be natural to suppose it would be interpreted in accordance with the principles laid down by Lord Diplock in *Caldwell* (above, p. 59). This would mean that the prosecutor would succeed if he could prove that the defendant gave no thought to a serious and obvious risk that at the time of the intercourse the woman was not consenting. This initially was the approach taken by the Court of Appeal in *Pigg* (1983). However in *Satnam and Kewal* (1984) the Court of Appeal adopted a different approach. First the jury should be told that if they were sure that the defendant *knew* that the woman was not consenting, they should find him guilty. If, however, they were not sure about that, they should consider whether he genuinely believed that she was consenting, even if he was mistaken. If they found that he did have such a belief, they must acquit. If they found that he had no such belief then he should be convicted. If they came to the conclusion that, at the time of the intercourse, he could not care less whether or not she was consenting, but pressed on regardless, then he was "reckless" within the meaning of the Act. A test under which the jury have to assess whether the defendant "could not care less" is clearly a subjective one since it is not possible to say of a person that he could not care less unless he has first given some thought to the matter.

Although for the purposes of rape, intercourse is complete as soon as there is the slightest penetration of the vagina by the penis, rape is a continuing act. It has been held by the Privy Council in relation to the New Zealand law of rape, and almost certainly would be so held in relation to English law, that if a man realises only after the intercourse has commenced that the woman is not consenting he will be guilty of rape if he continues after that time. (*Kaitamaki* v. *The Queen* (1985).)

2. Unlawful Sexual Intercourse

In seeking to protect young girls from what are seen as the adverse social and psychological effects of having sexual intercourse at an early age the law provides that it is an offence, punishable with two years imprisonment, for a man to have sexual intercourse with a girl who is under the age of 16 (Sexual Offences Act 1956, s.6). Where the girl is under the age of 13 the man is guilty of a more serious offence which carries life imprisonment (Sexual Offences Act 1956, s.5). Since the purpose of the law is to protect young girls against these adverse effects it is irrelevant that she consented to the intercourse; though, of course if she did not consent the man would also have committed the offence of rape.

It is no defence for a man to plead that he thought that the girl was older than she in fact was, since liability on the age element of the *actus reus* is strict. However in relation to the less serious offence under section 6 there are two statutory defences. Under section 6(2) it is a defence for the accused to show that he had gone through a form of marriage with the girl and that he honestly and reasonably believed that she was his wife. Under section 6(3) it is a defence for the accused to show that at the time of the intercourse he was under the age of 24, that he honestly and reasonably believed that the girl was over age of 15 and that he had never been previously charged with such an offence. In keeping with the principle which underlies the defence under section 6(3) it is probably safe to say that where the offence is committed by a young man who himself is not much over the age of 16 it is more likely that he will be cautioned by the police rather than prosecuted. As the age gap widens between the parties, prosecution becomes more probable.

3. INDECENT ASSAULT AND OTHER OFFENCES OF INDECENCY

The offence of indecent assault can be committed by both men and women against both men and women (Sexual Offences Act, 1956, ss.14 and 15). Until recently the penalty was higher for an indecent assault upon a male than for an indecent assault upon a female. The penalty in both cases is a maximum sentence of ten years imprisonment.

Until recently the law relating to indecent assault appeared to be reasonably settled if not well defined. It was generally accepted that the prosecution had to prove that the defendant had assaulted (assault here including a battery) the victim in circumstances of indecency. Very little attention was paid to the *mens rea* of this offence, apart from recognising that it required the *mens rea* of a common assault or battery. In *Court* (1988), however, the issue was the subject of an appeal before the House of Lords. The problem facing the House was whether the prosecution had to establish any *mens rea* over and above the *mens rea* needed to prove an assault. Was it sufficient that the defendant had assaulted the victim in circumstances which a jury or bench of magistrates held to be indecent?

Consider a case in which a traveller on a crowded underground train while alighting from the train removes a woman's blouse with his umbrella. It may be that in his fear of not getting out of the train before the doors closed, he has used more force than he is entitled to use. He may thus be guilty of an assault, but would we call it an indecent assault because the lady was embarrassed? On the other hand the explanation may be that he saw an excellent opportunity for stripping the unfortunate woman. Should he be convicted of an indecent assault because of the sexual motive which is not communicated to the woman?

On the other hand there may be cases which outwardly appear to be indecent assaults, but which conceal a motive which was not indecent. Suppose that a medical student forces a fellow student at gunpoint to strip, so that he can measure his genitals, should this be an indecent assault if the sole purpose of the assault was to obtain scientific data? In *Pratt* (1984) two boys were fishing at night when they were approached by the defendant who, at gun point, forced each to strip off their clothes while the other held a torch so that the defendant, who stood a few feet away and touched neither boy, could see their naked bodies. This would appear to be a clear example of an indecent assault, but the defendant claimed that he had reason to believe that the boys had stolen a quantity of cannabis from him and he was merely searching them for it. The Crown Court judge directed the jury that they could not convict him of an indecent assault unless they found an indecent intention.

These and other issues were considered by the House of Lords in *Court* where the defendant had forced a 12 year old girl to lie face down over his lap while he struck her about twelve times on the buttocks. He later confessed to the police that he had a "buttock fettish." Lord Ackner delivering the main speech for the majority said that on a charge for indecent assault the prosecution must prove three things, namely:—

(i) *The defendant must have intentionally assaulted the victim.* Hence there must be an assault or battery in the normal sense of the word. Lord Ackner approved a definition of assault given by Lord Lane C.J. in *Faulkener* v. *Talbot* where he said this amounted to 'any intentional touching of another without the consent of that person and without lawful excuse. It need not necessarily be hostile or rude or aggressive, as some cases seem to indicate." Lord Ackner continued "But the 'assault' relied on need not involve any physical contact but may consist merely of conduct which causes the victim to apprehend immediate and unlawful violence." Hence in *Fairclough* v. *Whipp* (1951) the accused exposed his penis to a nine year old girl and invited her to touch it. At no stage did he give any intention that he would touch her. However indecent the incident, the defendant could not be convicted of indecent assault since there was no assault. In *Faulkener* v. *Talbot* the Court of Appeal held that a woman who lay perfectly still and allowed a 15 year old boy to have sexual intercourse with her would not commit the offence of indecent assault. If, however, she touched him in order to stimulate him, this would amount to an assault since the consent of a 15 year old would be irrelevant.

It is interesting to note that Lord Ackner said that the assault must be intentional. Does this mean that recklessness, which normally suffices for an assault, will not suffice here? It seems likely that Lord Ackner took the view that it is highly unlikely that an indecent assault could take place recklessly. If, however, the defendant deliberately took the risk that the victim was not consenting, the offence would be made out.

(ii) *That the assault, or the assault and circumstances accompanying it, are capable of being considered by right-minded persons as indecent.* Basically this means that the jury or magistrates must decide whether what occurred was so offensive to contemporary standards of modesty and privacy as to be indecent. It may be that the assault itself is indecent, as where the defendant touches the private parts of the victim, or it may be that the indecency lies in the surrounding circumstances. Hence in *Beal* v. *Kelly* (1951) the defendant exposed himself to a 14 year old boy and invited the boy to handle him. When the boy refused, the defendant grabbed his arm and pulled the boy towards him. Clearly the pulling of the boy constituted an assault and this, in itself, was not indecent. The surrounding circumstances, however, were clearly indecent. On the other hand, in *George* (1956) although there was an assault constituted by the defendant attempting to remove a girls shoe, the court held that there was no evidence of any circumstances of indecency since the indecency was all in the mind of the accused.

(iii) *That the defendant intended to commit such an assault as referred to in (ii) above.* It would seem that Lord Ackner saw the cases as falling in to one of three categories.

(a) Cases in which the incident, viewed objectively, could not be said to involve any element of indecency. In this type of situation there is no indecent assault, however indecent the motives of the defendant. Here the trial judge should not admit evidence of the accused's indecent motives since this would be highly prejudicial but irrelevant (*e.g. George*, above).

(b) Cases in which the incident is unambiguously indecent. Again the motives of the defendant are irrelevant. Thus Lord

Ackner said that if a man strips the coating off a woman then it can matter not whether he does this for a sexual purpose or simply to get his own back on her. It is sufficient that he is aware of the circumstances which would lead right-minded persons to consider the assault to be indecent. It would seem to follow in such a case that evidence of any indecent motive should be excluded as irrelevant. The only *mens rea* required, apart from that of the assault, is that he was aware of the circumstances which are considered to be indecent. Lord Ackner appears to recognise that it would be open to the defendant to show that he had a lawful excuse for his conduct.

(c) Cases where the assault is not unambigously indecent, but where it is capable of being so considered. In this type of case his indecent motive will be decisive. Lord Ackner clearly considered *Court* to fall into this category and thus he held that the evidence of the defendant's "buttock fettish" to have been rightly admitted.

Lord Ackner concluded by saying that counsel for the Crown had agreed that the requirements he had set out should give rise to no difficulty or complications; this may turn out to be an over optimistic prediction.

It would seem, therefore, that at future trials for indecent assault the trial judge will have to decide whether the case before him falls into category (a), (b) or (c). Only if it falls into category (c) should he admit evidence of the defendant's indecent motives. If a doctor is charged with indecently assaulting a 15 year old girl by submitting her to a vaginal examination it would appear that the judge should first determine whether consent was properly obtained. If consent has been obtained and the examination is medically necessary, the doctor cannot be guilty of an indecent assault even though he gains sexual enjoyment from the examination. If, however, the examination is not necessary it will fall into category (b) and will be considered an indecent assault whether the doctor's motive is sexual enjoyment or scientific research. Similarly the example quoted above of the medical student who forcibly measures the genital organs of a fellow student; this would clearly amount to an indecent assault despite the fact that the defendant had no indecent motive. It is sufficient that he is aware of the circumstances which right-minded people would regard as indecent. It is difficult to reconcile with these examples the approval Lord Ackner gave to *Pratt* (above). That was surely a case which came within category (b). If the doctor is not allowed to plead that he had no sexual motive in conducting his examination and the medical student is similarly prevented, why should *Pratt* be allowed to escape liability because he was looking for cannabis? He was fully aware that what he was doing would be regarded as highly embarrassing by the boys and this is all the *mens rea* Lord Ackner said was required in category (b) cases.

Before leaving the offence of indecent assault we should note two points. First, if a man is charged with having unlawful sexual intercourse with a 15 year old girl (Sexual Offences Act 1956, s.6), we have seen that he will have a defence if he can prove he was under the age of 24, believed her to be over 15 and had never been charged with such an offence before; but this defence is not available on a charge of indecent assault. Thus if the police charge him with indecently assaulting the girl (by having intercourse with her) he will not be able to raise such a defence. The defence under section 6(2) (above, p. 252) is, however, available on a charge of indecent assault.

Secondly, the law has provided for the *Fairclough* v. *Whipp* type of case, where the accused is acquitted because there is no actual assault. The Indecency with Children Act 1960 makes it an offence for any person to commit an act of gross indecency with or towards a child under the age of 14 or to incite a child under that age to do such an act with him or with another. Thus mere incitement may constitute an offence. The accused in *Fairclough* v. *Whipp* would now commit an offence under this Act. This would also have been the appropriate charge to have been brought against the accused in *Sutton* (1977). Sutton had taken photographs of naked and partially clad boys in poses designed to draw attention to their genital organs. He had only touched them on their arms, legs and torsos so as to indicate a pose. The Court of Appeal held that the touching was not of itself indecent and so there was no indecent assault. The use of the word "gross" to qualify "indecency" suggests that the act must be more indecent than that required for an indecent assault and is probably confined to activity concerning the genital region.

Thirdly, under the Criminal Justice Act 1988 a new offence of possession of an indecent photograph of a child (under 16) has been created (section 160). There is no definition of "indecent" in the Act, but it is assumed that it will be interpreted in line with the principles laid down in cases like *Court* (above). It would be a defence for the defendant to prove (i) that he had a legitimate reason for having the photograph in his possession, or (ii) that he had not himself seen the photograph and neither knew, nor had any reason to suspect, it to be indecent, or (iii) the photograph had been sent to him without his prior request and he had not subsequently kept it for an unreasonable time. The punishment for this offence is a fine not exceeding £2,000.

4. INDECENT EXPOSURE

It is an offence under section 4 of the Vagrancy Act 1824 for a man wilfully and indecently to expose his penis, in public or in private, with intent to insult any female. If the man indecently exposes any other part of his body in a public place he may be guilty of a common law offence.

CHAPTER 10

OFFENCES AGAINST THE THEFT ACTS 1968 AND 1978

THE Theft Acts of 1968 and 1978 provide us with a fairly comprehensive list of offences which broadly speaking involve the dishonest dealing with other people's property. They do not, however, provide a complete code on what might be termed as property offences. Forgery for example is covered by the Forgery and Counterfeiting Act 1981 and offences involving damage or destruction of property are contained in the Criminal Damage Act 1971 which will be examined in Chapter 11. Included in the Theft Acts are such offences as theft, obtaining by deception, burglary, robbery, blackmail and handling.

The Theft Act 1968 represents an overhaul of the existing assortment of offences which had become rather complex and unwieldy. The 1978 Act created three new offences to replace a subsection of the 1968 Act which had been found to be unworkable. Between them the Acts have produced a simplification of the law in this area and we can say from the outset that the great majority of cases brought under them present very few difficult legal problems. They may present difficult problems of proof for the court of trial—but this is a totally different issue. For example many cases involving thefts from supermarkets may hinge upon the ability of the prosecution to prove that the defendant deliberately tried to avoid paying for a given item and that it was not simply a case of absentmindedness. We all know how easy it is to arrive at the other side of the checkout counter without having paid for an item, hence the difficulty in individual cases of proving that the defendant was dishonest. But to repeat what was said earlier, this is not a difficulty arising from the interpretation of the Act itself; it is one of proving that the essential elements of the offence exist. That is not to say that the Theft Acts have got rid of all the legal difficulties; this is probably an impossible task given the complex nature of the rights the law is seeking to protect. Take theft itself, for example; this consists in the interference with the property rights of another. These property rights are controlled at the outset by the civil law, and so in theft cases it is sometimes necessary to take account of difficult civil law rules before criminal liability can be sorted out. Occasionally judges have said that complex rules relating to property rights have no place in the criminal law, but it would be impossible to divorce the law of theft from the property rights it is seeking to protect. One of the major problems in this area has been the failure of prosecutors to make full use of the wide range of offences created by these Acts. In many cases which have led to questionable appellate decisions, the problem would not have arisen had the prosecutor selected a more appropriate offence. The judiciary, for their part, should avoid strained interpretations of the law in their attempts to uphold convictions where the prosecutor has selected the wrong offence. As it is there is a grave danger that the Theft Acts will become as complex as the law they were designed to replace. The golden rule in every case is that the prosecutor must be able to establish each of the required elements of the *actus reus* and *mens rea*. In nearly every case where the court has got itself into difficulty there was a more appropriate charge which could have been successfully brought against the defendant.

Since we shall occasionally have to get involved in some of these property rights it will be useful at the outset to mention certain concepts which will be in use throughout the chapter. Let us stay with the crime of stealing. When we say X has taken Y's book what do we mean by Y's book? Normally we would mean that Y is the owner of the book. Ownership is the ultimate right over property; it usually means that Y will have the right to determine what happens to the book. It does not, however mean that Y has possession of the book or even that he has the right to possess it. He may have lent the book to Z. Under normal circumstances Y would be able to demand the return of the book, but this is not always so. Consider a common everyday situation. Y has rented a television set from B company. He is paying £10 a month for the loan of the set. Y is therefore in possession, but B company is still the owner of the set. Although B company is still the owner of the set, they will not be in possession of it and nor will they have the right to immediate possession unless Y defaults on his payments or breaks some other clause in the rental agreement. It is common for judges to say that the property or title in the television set is in B. This is another way of saying that B owns the television set. If B now sells the set we can say that the property or title in the set passes to whoever buys it.

It will also be useful to say a few words about money as a form of property. If Y lends B his book, the ownership remains with Y; B merely gets possession. B cannot make X the owner of the book by purporting to sell it to him because B has no "property" in the book to pass on to X, this is still with Y. On the other hand if Y lends B a five pound note, B's only obligation is to restore an equivalent amount of money. If B passes on the five pounds to X, X receives ownership of the money. This goes even further. If B steals the note from Y, ownership in the five pounds remains with Y, but if B passes on the note to X for valuable consideration and X is acting in good faith X will receive a good title to the money which he can pass on to others. What is the difference between the book and the five pound note? The answer is that money is negotiable whereas a book and most other forms of property are not. If B had stolen Y's book he could not pass on a good title to the book to X even if X was acting in good faith and paid a fair price. The need for such a rule in relation to money is obvious; it will usually be very hard to identify your particular pound coin and one could only imagine the havoc that would be caused if one's right to spend money could be made dependent upon showing that you received it from someone who was in a position to pass ownership in it to you.

The word "possession" can also be hard to pin down. Normally it means control over property. Thus in the example of the rented television set we can clearly say that Y is in possession. When however an employee is cleaning his employer's silverware it would be odd to say that he was in possession of the silverware. It is probably more accurate to say that he is in control of it as long as he is engaged on its cleaning.

In this chapter we shall concentrate mainly upon the offences of theft and deception and the chapter will conclude with a summary of the other well known offences.

I. THEFT

The offence is defined by section 1 of the Theft Act 1968 as follows:

"(1) A person is guilty of theft if he dishonestly appropriates property belonging to another with the intention of permanently depriving the other of it; and 'thief' and 'steal' shall be construed accordingly."

Sections 1 to 6 of the Act amplify the meaning of words and phrases used in this definition and section 7 provides that the offence of theft shall be punishable with a maximum of 10 years imprisonment. It should be borne in mind that the offence of theft covers all cases of stealing whether it be of a great or a small sum; we have no division into petty theft and grand theft; though theft is an offence which is triable either way (see above, p. 7). There is no separate offence of shoplifting; this is a colloquialism which is used to describe a particular form of theft, which has the unfortunate tendency of suggesting that there is a separate, less serious offence.

From the definition in section 1 we can see that the *actus reus* comprises (a) an appropriation (b) of property (c) which property belongs to another. The *mens rea* requires (a) dishonesty and (b) an intention permanently to deprive the other of the property.

As is usual in the criminal law there is no difficulty in applying the definition of the offence to the typical, or everyday, case. But cases do arise which lie at the edge of the definition where complexities can occur. In this context it might be noted that there is a close relationship—indeed there is an overlap—between the offence of theft under section 1 and the offence of obtaining property by deception under section 15. In this grey area great care needs to be taken to determine whether the facts will best support the elements of the offence of theft or the offence of deception. Facts which might easily establish the one offence may only doubtfully, or not at all, support the other. The classic instance of this is *Lawrence* (1972), discussion of which will be taken up (below, p. 309) after the elements of both theft and deception have been considered. The moral is plain: faced with a particular set of facts (whether in an examination paper or a solicitor's office) it pays to give careful consideration as to whether those facts will prima facie support *all* the elements of the offence which is to be charged.

1. THE ACTUS REUS OF THEFT

(1) Appropriates

This requirement is defined in section 3(1) of the Act as

follows: "any assumption by a person of the rights of an owner amounts to an appropriation." In *Morris* (1984) Lord Roskill said "the concept of appropriation in section 3(1) involves an element of adverse interference with or usurpation of some right of the owner." Thus, although section 3(1) seems clearly to state that the defendant must have assumed *the rights* of the owner, or in other words to have treated himself as the owner of the property, it appears that the assumption of just one of the owner's rights by the defendant will suffice (see further, p. 266, below and the label switching cases).

To illustrate the meaning of appropriation we can consider the most commonly occurring form of appropriation, the case of appropriation by taking. A enters B's bookshop and takes a book belonging to B; C enters D's room and takes D's watch; E puts his hand in F's pocket and removes F's wallet. In these cases it is as clear as can be that A has appropriated the book, C the watch and E the wallet. A, C and E are treating themselves as owners of property which belongs to B, D and F.

But two things need to be noticed. The first is that although taking is by far the most common mode of appropriation that laymen still think of theft as a taking, it is not the *only* mode of appropriation. The definition says that *"any"* assumption of the rights of an owner amounts to an appropriation. Strictly, therefore, it amounts to an appropriation to destroy another's property. Thus if A pushes B's car over a cliff and thereby destroys it, it can properly be said that he has appropriated the car. Most laymen would not recognise this as a case of theft (and no doubt A would be charged under the Criminal Damage Act 1971, below, p. 344) but a charge of theft could be supported on such facts. This is clearly an appropriation (what could be a clearer assumption of B's rights than destroying his car?) and section 1(1) makes it clear that the prosecution does not have to establish on a charge of theft that A intended to make any gain from his action.

The second point to note is that while the layman might think that, in the examples first given, A, C and E appropriate the property when they take it *away, i.e.* when they remove the goods from the control of B, D and F into their own control, in law the appropriation has occurred at an earlier stage. When, for example, E put his hand on the wallet inside F's pocket, and *before* he removes it, he may be said to have appropriated it because, at that instance, he is assuming the rights of the owner, F. One of F's rights is to enjoy the undisturbed possession of his wallet; in asserting a right to possess it himself,

E is assuming F's right. This point may be further illustrated by reference to *Corcoran* v. *Anderton* (1980). A and B attacked a woman intending to take her bag. A got his hands on the bag and there was a struggle for its possession during which the bag fell to the ground. A and B then ran off empty handed. This to the layman might look like a case of *attempted* robbery because the youths failed to get what they were after but they were convicted of the full offence. Robbery is theft accomplished with force (below, p. 291) and the theft was complete when the handbag was appropriated, *i.e.* when A grabbed it and tried to take it from her—that conduct was an assumption by A of the owner's rights.

An appropriation, therefore, is something done in relation to the property that only the owner can properly do. It follows that if the owner authorises the accused to deal with the goods in a certain way, the accused cannot appropriate the goods by dealing with them in the *authorised* way. Thus, for example, a cashier in a supermarket is authorised to sell goods on behalf of his employer. The sale of the goods by the cashier at the correct price cannot, therefore, constitute an appropriation. In doing what he is employed to do by his employer, he cannot be assuming any of the employer's rights as owner. On the other hand, if the cashier sells the goods below the authorised price he will have assumed the rights of the employer and this will constitute an appropriation (see *Att.-Gen. for Hong Kong* v. *Nai Keung* (1988)). Now suppose a somewhat different case. Imagine that B lends A his car to drive from London to Brighton. When B, in London, hands over the car keys, A secretly makes up his mind to sell the car in Brighton and decamp with the proceeds. Obviously when A sells the car (or even attempts to do so) he is assuming rights which he is in no sense authorised to assume and would at that stage appropriate the car. But does A appropriate the car when he takes possession of it with intent to sell it on arrival in Brighton? One thing is clear: B would not have parted with possession of the car had he known that he might never see it again. But though B would not authorise A to drive the car to Brighton had he known of A's dishonest intent, he does nevertheless authorise A to drive the car to Brighton. Until A deviates from his authorisation there is no conduct of his which can be described as an appropriation; an appropriation involves more than a mental resolution to steal. The point is made by *Skipp* (1975), where the accused, posing as a genuine haulage contractor, was instructed to pick up three loads of oranges from different places in London and to deliver them to Leicester. All the time he was collecting the oranges he intended to abscond with them, thereby depriving the owner permanently of his property. The Court of Appeal, however, held that he did not appropriate the property until he did an act inconsistent with the owner's instructions. Thus while he was on the designated route he had not appropriated the property. Therefore, if he intended to drive down the road almost to Leicester, there would presumably be no appropriation until he left the Leicester road. (You might wonder how such a point arose for discussion. Skipp was charged in an indictment containing one count of theft. It is a rule of procedure that a count must only contain one offence and Skipp argued that there were three separate offences of theft. The court held that since the appropriation took place only after the three loads were on board, there was only one theft).

In line with *Skipp* is *Eddy* v. *Niman* (1981). A and B went into a supermarket with the intention of stealing goods and in pursuance of this plan they took goods from the shelves which they placed in the receptacle provided by the store. B then had a change of heart and left the store. It was held that he could not be convicted of theft because there was nothing that could be described as an appropriation; in doing what he was authorised to do, albeit with a dishonest intention, he had not yet assumed the rights of the owner. It would have been different, however, if A had put the goods, not in the receptacle provided, but in his pockets with a view to passing through the checkout without accounting for them; such an act would have provided evidence of "an element of adverse interference with or ursurpation of some right of the owner," (*McPherson* (1973)). It might be noted in passing that an appropriation may occur before a customer leaves the store. For practical reasons (such as to negative a possible defence of forgetfulness or mistake or accident) store detectives do not usually challenge the customer until he has left the store. The appropriation, however, occurs not when he leaves the store but when he assumes the rights of the owner.

A more difficult case to explain on this basis is *Monaghan* (1979) where a checkout cashier was seen to place money, given to her by a customer for the purchase of goods, into the till, without ringing up the price. When questioned she admitted that she was acting dishonestly and that it was her intention to take from the till an equivalent sum at a *later* stage. It was held that she had appropriated the money when she failed to record the correct price and she was therefore convicted of theft. It has been argued that this is difficult to reconcile with *Skipp*. In relation to the money she had done exactly as she was bidden by placing it in the till; her misdeed related solely to the matter of keeping a correct financial account. However the court seems to have regarded the use of the till as one complete transaction; she was entitled to put money into the till only if she recorded the correct amount. Her action was therefore not authorised by the store owner and constituted an appropriation of the money. It is interesting to note that whereas this approach solved a procedural problem in *Skipp* because it meant that there was only one theft, it must lead to the opposite result in *Monaghan*; *i.e.* that there would be a separate theft each time the cash was put into the till. This point was not taken in *Monaghan*, nor was the point that Monaghan did not "steal" the money she put into the till; she intended to "steal" an equivalent amount at the end of the day. In other words she was getting ready to steal at the end of the day's trading. The prosecution would have been better advised to charge her with false accounting (section 17 of the Theft Act 1968) which is a better description of what, at this stage, she was really up to.

The *Skipp* line of cases, however, received approval by the House of Lords in *Morris* and therefore it does not amount to an appropriation of property to do something to that property which is authorised by the person to whom it belongs. Since *Skipp* must have committed the offence of obtaining each load of goods by deception at the three pick-up points it also follows that obtaining goods by deception does not, of itself, necessarily constitute an appropriation for the purposes of theft. (See below, pp. 305 and 309. The decision of the house of Lords in *Lawrence* is also difficult to reconcile with the decision in *Skipp*, but it is submitted that ways can be found to do so; see below, p. 310).

We can now take the issue a stage further by considering the response of the courts to what is generally known as label-switching. In these cases the accused removes a price label from an item on display in a shop and replaces it with a label showing a lower price. He then presents this item at the checkout, thereby offering to buy it at the reduced price. Unless the checkout operator notices the incorrect price, the offer will be accepted and under the law of contract the customer will become owner of the item under a voidable contract and will remain so until the shopkeeper avoids the contract. Thus when he leaves the shop he is taking his own property. He has committed the offence of obtaining the property by deception and that should be the charge which is brought against him. Unfortunately prosecutors seem intent to prosecute this as theft and the courts have leapt to their aid. Now it is quite clear that we cannot say he appropriated the property when he left the shop, since this would amount to appropriation of his own property. The appropriation must occur before he becomes the owner of the goods. Thus in *Anderton* v. *Wish* (1980) the Divisional Court held that the appropriation occurred when the labels were switched. Clearly at this point he did assume one of the owner's rights namely the right to price the goods in the shop. It cannot be said, however, that he appropriated all the owner's rights; he did not treat himself as the owner of the goods because it was his intention to present the goods at the checkout and offer to buy them—one would not do this with property one regarded as one's own. The Divisional Court appeared to recognise the strength of these arguments in the later case of *Oxford* v. *Peers* (1980) but felt itself bound to follow *Anderton* v. *Wish*. Finally in *Morris* (1984) the Court of Appeal took a dramatic approach by holding that the appropriation in these cases took place when the accused removed the items from the shelf; the later switching of the labels was merely evidence of the accused's dishonesty. Such a decision was totally irreconcilable with the principle of cases such as *Skipp*. In the House of Lords, Lord Roskill said that his reading of the various statutory provisions led him to the conclusion that it was not necessary for the prosecutor to prove that the accused had assumed all the rights of the owner; it sufficed that he had assumed any of the owner's rights. Further he held that mere removal of the goods from the shelf did not in itself constitute an appropriation since this is an act which the shopkeeper authorises his customers to do. In these cases it is the removal of the goods from the shelf coupled with the switching of the labels which "*evidences adverse interference with or usurpation of the rights of the owner.*" Thus the appropriation occurs at this time. His Lordship added that it would normally be better to charge such persons with obtaining the goods by deception (contrary to section 15 of the Theft Act 1968), but this might not be possible if the shopper had not reached the checkout point at the time he was arrested, in which case he could be charged with theft. The decision in *Anderton* v. *Wish*, is thus followed, and the principle of the *Skipp* line of cases is preserved.

We can now take a look at one or two further situations in the light of *Morris*.

(i) A takes a bottle of whisky from the shelf in a supermarket and places it in his raincoat pocket, intending not to pay for it. These were the facts of *McPherson* (1973) where the court held that the accused had appropriated the bottle of whisky at the time he put it in his pocket. This decision was approved in *Morris*. The evidence clearly indicates adverse interference with the rights of the owner. The facts do not provide such clear evidence of dishonesty as do those in the label switching case, but provided the court is satisfied that the accused was acting dishonestly, theft has been committed at this stage.

(ii) B substitutes lower price labels on a whole range of goods in a supermarket. He has no intention of obtaining any of the property for himself; it is merely his idea of a mischievous trick. Lord Roskill in *Morris* thought that this would not normally "without more" amount to an appropriation of the property. In truth it is difficult to see how Lord Roskill reaches such a conclusion. It may well be that B has not committed theft because he lacks any intention permanently to deprive the store of the property, but his activity surely falls within Roskill's definition of appropriation. He has usurped one of the owner's rights, and should therefore be held to have appropriated the property. The distinction between this example and *Morris* lies not in the *actus reus*, but in the *mens rea*.

(iii) C discovers that the store has wrongly underpriced certain goods. She therefore takes them to the checkout counter and hands them to the cashier without drawing the cashier's attention to the mistake. In her own mind she believes that she is acting dishonestly. These are basically the facts of *Kaur* v. *Chief Constable of Hampshire* (1981) where the magistrates held that this constitutes theft since, because of the cashier's mistake, no contract came into existence by which Kaur could become owner of the goods. Thus when she left the shop she appropriated property belonging to another. The Divisional Court held that the mistake on the part of the cashier merely rendered the contract voidable and so Kaur became owner of the goods before she did any act which could amount to an appropriation. It therefore followed that she did not commit theft. Lord Roskill thought that this case had probably been wrongly decided and so the precise answer to this example cannot be given with any degree of confidence. However it is a useful illustration of how complex civil law concepts can influence the outcome of a criminal case. For the present we might content ourselves by asking whether such conduct should amount to theft or obtaining property by deception. Should customers be under any duty to point out such mistakes by stores? It will be a rare prosecutor who would press charges in such circumstances and an even rarer jury who would find dishonesty. Should it make any difference that C, in our example, has deliberately taken advantage of the prank played by B in illustration (ii)?

Thus far it has been suggested that an appropriation requires some *conduct* on the accused's part. Certainly it is difficult to see how a pure omission could amount to an assumption of the user's rights. If, for example, A has mislaid his umbrella, B could hardly be said to have appropriated it because he knows where it is and fails to tell A—even if B hopes that A will fail to find it so that he, B, can make off with it later on. On the other hand section 3 goes on to say that there is an appropriation where X has come by the property (innocently or not) but without stealing it and has assumed a right to it "... by keeping it or dealing with it as owner." This is meant to deal with the sort of case where A "comes by" (A may have borrowed it, or found it or had it delivered to him by mistake, etc.) B's property and decides to keep it. A's mental resolution to keep it is probably not enough; the section says that A must keep it "as owner." Suppose then that A borrows B's lawn mower or bicycle or book for a week. At the end of the week A fails to return the goods and his intention is never to do so. Probably this will not make A a thief; but A will become a thief if, with the necessary intent, he removes the lawn mower to his new premises, or he continues to drive the bicycle, or he writes his name in the book.

Where however A receives the property in good faith from B for consideration, if it later turns out that B had no right to sell the property, no assumption of the rights of an owner by A over that property can amount to an appropriation for the purposes of a charge of theft (see section 3(2)). Thus if A buys a car from B in circumstances where A believes that B is the lawful owner of the car, then if he is later told that C is the rightful owner of the car and that B had stolen it, A's refusal to restore the car to C would not amount to theft. However, if A later sells the car to D, he may be guilty of obtaining property by deception contrary to section 15 (see below, p. 305) since he will have impliedly represented that he had title to sell, when he clearly did not.

(2) Property

(a) The general position

The definition of what can amount to property for the purposes of being stolen is to be found in section 4. The general position is covered by section 4(1) which provides that "property" includes money and all other property, real or personal, including things in action and other intangible property. The reference to real property means that land is included in the definition of property, but subsection 2 specifically provides that with one or two exceptions land cannot be stolen (it can, however, be obtained by deception; see p. 306). Before we look at the special problem with land we ought to mention one or two points in relation to the general definition. The effect of subsection 1 is that virtually all tangible property with the exception of land is capable of being stolen. One or two difficulties may, however, arise:

(i) Gas, water and electricity

Gas and water are clearly within the definition of property in section 4(1) and are thus capable of being stolen. Electricity, on the other hand, does not constitute property and cannot therefore be stolen. There is a separate offence to deal with the unlawful abstraction of electricity (see below, p. 341).

(ii) Intangible property

Section 4(1) makes it clear that choses in action and other intangible property are capable of being stolen. Choses in action are rights which can only be enforced by taking legal action. Thus if X owes Y £50, X can sue Y for the £50 and this right to sue is known as a chose in action. Other examples of choses in action are copyrights, trademarks; patents are not choses in action but they are clearly a form of intangible property. In *Att.-Gen. for Hong Kong* v. *Nai Keung* (1988) the Privy Council held that *export quotas* fell within the meaning of *other intangible property*. They are transferable for value and can be bought and sold. Since the defendant had sold export quotas belonging to another at a gross undervalue he was rightly convicted of stealing them.

(iii) Intellectual property

In *Oxford* v. *Moss* (1978) a student borrowed an examination paper and photographed the questions. He could not be charged with stealing the question paper since he intended to return it and the court held that he could not be charged with theft of the confidential information since this did not amount to property under section 4(1). It would seem to follow that trade secrets are not property which is capable of being stolen.

(iv) *Human remains*

Under the previous legislation it appears to have been accepted that it was not possible to steal a corpse since corpses are incapable of being the subject of ownership by anyone. There seems no logical reason why a corpse should not be capable of being stolen. Where a person has expended time or money in preserving a corpse or parts of a corpse (such as kidneys for use in transplants) it would seem sensible to hold that these should be capable of being stolen. Presumably where a corpse has been cremated and the ashes retained by a relative, the ashes should be capable of being stolen. While it is quite reasonable to hold that a living body cannot be stolen, there seems no logic in the rule that this position continues after death.

(b) *Land*

Although land is contained in the definition of property in subsection 1, subsection 2 provides that "A person cannot steal land, or things forming part of land and severed from it by him or by his directions" except in certain cases. Before we look at the exceptions we should note that in law, land includes not only the earth, but also things attached to it so as to become part of the land. Whether or not something is sufficiently attached to the land so as to be counted as part of the land depends upon the degree of annexation and the degree of permanency. Clearly trees and other growing things can be treated for this purpose as land; equally houses which are not only well and truly fixed to the soil but are usually designed with a degree of permanency in mind. On the other hand a workman's portakabin which is just erected on the land while the workmen are there would not be regarded as part of the land; it can therefore be stolen as ordinary property. In between the distinction sometimes becomes rather blurred.

When can land be stolen? There are three exceptions to the general rule that land cannot be stolen, these are:

(i) s.4(2)(*a*). Land or things forming part of it can be stolen by a person who falls into a certain category of individual for example a trustee or personal representative who deals with the property in breach of the confidence reposed in him.

(ii) s.4(2)(*b*). A person who is not in possession of the land and appropriates anything forming part of the land by severing it or causing it to be severed, or after it has been severed. Thus this section does not apply to an owner who is living on the land or someone living on the land by virtue of a tenancy.

(iii) s.4(2)(*c*). A person in possession of the land under a tenancy who appropriates the whole or any part of a fixture or structure let to be used with the land.

We can see how these provisions work in practice by considering the following situations:

(i) X has moved a boundary fence so that two acres of Y's land now appear to belong to X. Since this involves the land itself and no act of severance is involved, only if X falls within section 4(2)(*a*) can this amount to theft. In fact persons falling within section 4(2)(*a*) would be guilty of theft in all the following situations and so no further mention will be made of them.

(ii) X removes a layer of turf from Y's land which he then sells. If X is not in possession of the land he will be guilty of theft by virtue of section 4(2)(*b*). If he is in possession of the land by virtue of a tenancy he will not be guilty of theft since turf cannot be regarded as a fixture or structure under section 4(2)(*c*).

(iii) X cuts down a tree on land belonging to Y and removes it for firewood. Again, unless he is in possession as a tenant, he will be guilty by virtue of section 4(2)(*b*)—he has severed the tree and removed it from Y's land. A tenant in possession would not be guilty of theft since this is presumably not what is meant by a fixture or structure let for use by the tenant. (See section 4(3) below for further rules relating to wild trees and plants).

(iv) X dismantles Y's brick garage and gives it to Z. X will be guilty by virtue of section 4(2)(*b*) if he is not in possession of the land and section 4(2)(*c*) if he is a tenant in possession of the land. You should note that a person in possession of the land under a tenancy will be guilty of theft if he merely sells it to Z with a promise to dismantle it later; section 4(2)(*c*) does not require severance.

(v) X dismantles Y's greenhouse and gives it to Z. The answer is the same as in (d) except that if the greenhouse is of a temporary nature and not fixed to the land it may be regarded as an ordinary item of property and stealable by virtue of section 4(1).

(c) *Wild plants, etc.*

If the section stopped at subsection 2 then a trespasser who picked wild flowers would be guilty of stealing them. Section 4(3) therefore provides "A person who picks mushrooms growing wild on any land, or who picks flowers, fruit or foliage from a plant growing wild on any land does not (although not in possession of the land) steal what he picks, unless he does it for reward or for sale or for other commercial purpose." (Mushrooms includes any fungus, and plant includes any shrub or tree).

A few illustrations will show how this section works.

(i) X goes on to Y's land and picks some mushrooms and some strawberries. If these are wild and if X intends them for his own domestic use he commits no offence. If however they are cultivated or he intends to sell them he commits an offence.

(ii) X goes on to Y's land and digs up a holly tree and saws the top off a fir tree. He has committed theft in both instances since the exemption in the subsection refers only to picking from plants, and neither digging up the whole tree nor sawing a portion off a tree can be regarded as picking.

(d) *Wild creatures*

These are covered by section 4(4) which provides "Wild creatures, tamed or untamed, shall be regarded as property; but a person cannot steal a wild creature not tame nor ordinarily kept in captivity, or the carcase of any such creature, unless either it has been reduced into possession by or on behalf of another person and possession of it has not since been lost or abandoned, or another person is in course of reducing it into possession."

Thus it is theft to steal a wild animal which has been tamed or which is in captivity. Therefore if X takes a rattlesnake from London Zoo he is guilty of theft.

Where the creature has not been tamed or placed in captivity it is not capable of being stolen unless it has been reduced into possession or it is in the process of being reduced into possession. Thus if X shoots rabbits on Y's land he will not be guilty of theft. If, however, Y has already shot and stored the rabbits or if they are in traps set by Y or even another trespasser and X takes them he will be guilty of theft (poaching is covered by other legislation).

(3) Belonging to another

The prosecution must establish that at the time of the appropriation the property belonged to another. This seems an obvious requirement as theft is generally understood to be the taking of someone else's property. What then do we mean by the phrase "belonging to another?" Clearly it must include the case where the property is owned by the victim at the time when the accused takes it. But that alone would be too restricting. Suppose that X dishonestly appropriates a television set which A rents from B. Does X steal the set from A or from B? If we said that belonging to another meant only "owned by another" then the indictment would have to charge X with stealing the television from B. This might present few problems in our illustration, but there will be cases where the true owner would be hard to identify. In any case a law of theft which in our example would allow X to defeat a charge of stealing from A on the ground that A was not the real owner would be open to ridicule. Suppose that it was B, the owner of the television set, who secretly took it back from A, intending both to resell the set and claim the cost of a new set from A. Should we not in such a case be able to charge B with stealing the set from A? It is for reasons such as these that the phrase "belonging to another" receives a much wider definition in section 5 of the Act.

Section 5(1) provides "Property shall be regarded as belonging to any person having possession or control of it, or having in it any proprietary right or interest (not being an equitable interest arising only from an agreement to transfer or grant an interest)."

Thus property can be stolen from a person who owns, possesses or has control over it. In the example of the television set it can therefore be stolen from either A, who has possession of it under a rental agreement or from B who owns it. If A takes the set to C for repairs it could also be stolen from C while it was in his premises awaiting repairs. But then the question arises, can one of the persons with a recognised interest in the property steal it from one of the others? If A, the person renting the set, sold it and told B that it had been stolen, could A be charged with stealing it from B? If B, the owner, took it from A and claimed that A had lost it and was therefore under a contractual obligation to pay for it, could B be charged with stealing it from A even though B is the owner? The answer to both of these questions is clearly yes. In *Turner* (1971) the accused had left his car for repair with a garage. Later he returned after it had been repaired and took it from outside the garage intending not to pay the bill. Despite the fact that the car belonged to Turner it was held that the garage had sufficient control of it to come within the phrase "belonging to another," and so Turner's conviction for theft was upheld (*cf. Meredith* (1973)).

In *Philippov* (1989) it was held that the two defendants, who were the only persons involved in a limited company, could steal from that company. Does the victim need to be aware of the property? In *Woodman* (1974) the X company were running down one of their factories and sold off a quantity of scrap metal to Y company. This gave Y company the right to enter the factory and remove the metal. Y company did, in fact, remove most of the scrap metal but left some there as not being worth the cost of salvaging it. X company remained owners of the site and put up a barbed wire fence and notices to discourage trespassers. It became clear that X company was not aware that any metal remained at the site. Some two years after X company's business had ceased at the factory, Woodman entered the site and took some of the scrap metal. He was charged with stealing the metal from X company. The trial judge took the view that there was no case to go to the jury on the basis that X company owned or possessed the property, but that there was a case of theft which could be left to the jury on the basis that X company controlled the property. The accused was convicted and appealed on the basis that X company could not be said to control the scrap metal since they were under the impression that it had all been removed by Y company. The Court of Appeal held that in the ordinary case if "it is once established that a particular person is in control of a site such as this, then prima facie he is in control of items on the site even though they were unaware of the existence of specific items." It might be that if the scrap metal had been placed there by a third party after the barbed wire had been erected then a different result could follow, but that was not the case here. In one sense the property was abandoned, but at least in relation to *Woodman* the X company could be said to be in control of it. (See *Small* (1988), below, p. 286).

Similarly where householders throw rubbish into a dustbin for collection by the corporation, they have in a sense abandoned the property; but not for the purposes of theft. This does not give the public the right to rummage through the bin to see if there is anything worth taking. Thus even in a situation where the householder is expected to place his dustbin in the street outside his house for collection, if X, a passerby or even the dustman, takes anything from the bin there is a prima facie case of theft from the householder (see also *Hibbert* v. *McKiernan* (1948)).

Equitable interests in property are also protected. If T is the trustee of property under a trust and B is the beneficiary, the property can be stolen from either T who has the legal interest or from B who has the equitable or beneficial interest. However it does not cover a person who has an equitable interest which arises solely from an agreement to transfer property (see also section 5(2)).

Section 5(3) and 5(4)

Subsections 3 and 4 of section 5 provide for two situations in which the phrase "belonging to another" is given an extended meaning in order to widen the scope of the offence in section 1. It should be remembered that in both cases the provisions of section 5 enable the accused to be prosecuted for the offence of theft under section 1; they do not create separate offences of theft, the tendency to speak of charging the accused under section 5(4) is therefore inaccurate.

Section 5(3)

Section 5(3) provides "Where a person receives property from or on account of another, and is under an obligation to the other to retain and deal with that property or its proceeds in a particular way, the property or proceeds shall be regarded (as against him) as belonging to the other."

This is intended to cover the situation in which the accused has been given property, money or otherwise, and is supposed to act in a particular way with that property and where he has acted against his instructions. Why is this a problem? Let us assume a case in which X's fellow employees have given him five pounds to go and buy some fish and chips for lunch. Clearly they are not making a present of the five pounds to X, but, under the civil law, ownership in the five pounds passes to X upon delivery of the money to him. He is under an obligation either to buy the fish and chips or to restore the money, but in the latter case any five pound note will do. The same is true when you deposit money in a bank; the bank's only obligation is to restore an equivalent amount. The ownership in the money you leave with the bank passes to the bank. If then X, on the way to buy the fish and chips, suddenly decides to put it all on a horse at the local betting shop, he is using money of which he is now the owner and he will pass a good title in the five pounds to the bookmaker. He is therefore appropriating money which belongs to himself—the fellow employees have neither owner-ship nor possession nor control of the money. Thus under the definition of belonging to another in section 5(1) he cannot steal the money. However under section 5(3) the money will be, for the purposes of theft, regarded as belonging to the employees if X was under an obligation to use that particular five pounds in a particular way. This means that the property, though it may be owned only by D, must be, as it were, earmarked in D's pocket for certain specific purposes of P. Fine; then he can be convicted of theft? Well this is not quite so simple. Was he expected to use that particular money, or any money so long as he came back with the chips and change? In *Hall* (1973) the accused had set up as a travel agent and had taken various sums of money from customers for the purpose of booking them on flights to America. He paid all the monies into the general trading account. Later, business went wrong and he told the customers that he had no money and that no flights had been booked. He was charged under section 1 with theft, the prosecution relying on section 5(3) to prove that the money belonged to the customers. On the face of it it looks like a classic example of section 5(3), but a moment's reflection will show that it is not quite so simple. Was Hall supposed to use the actual monies paid in, or was his sole duty to use the firm's money to make the bookings? Clearly in the world of business it would be unreasonable for him to put each sum of money into an envelope and book each customer's flight with their particular money. Nor would you expect the travel agent to put the money in a specific fund for that particular flight. His sole duty is to make sure the booking is made and if this is impossible to return the equivalent amount of money to the customer. But section 5(3) says the property or its proceeds; does not this cover *Hall*? No; this is intended to cover a situation in which the rogue has converted the original property into something equally identifiable. For example if a shopkeeper gives his assistant a twenty pound note to "pop next door to the bank and get it changed" the change he receives from the bank will be the proceeds of the twenty pound note and if he absconds at this stage he will be caught by section 5(3). Thus Hall's conviction was quashed. Our example of the five pounds for the fish and chips is probably nearer the line and it could be argued that it might be possible for a jury to find that he was expected to use *that* five pounds. Where, for any reason, the ownership is not transferred to the accused, section 5(3) is not needed.

In *Lewis* v. *Lethbridge* (1987) the Divisional Court held that where the defendant had collected money on behalf of the London Marathon Charity, he merely owed a debt to the Charity. He could not become a thief merely by not paying the debt. The Court added that the words "property or its proceeds" made it clear that the defendant need not be under an obligation to retain particular monies to come within section 5(3). It is sufficient that he is obliged to keep in existence a fund equivalent to that which he has received. Thus in *Davidge* v. *Bunnett* (1984) the Divisional Court held that it was sufficient the defendant was under an obligation to keep a fund of money which would cover the gas bill.

Whether or not an obligation arises is a matter of law for the judge since the obligation referred to is a *legal* obligation (see, e.g. *D.P.P.* v. *Huskinson* (1988) above, p. 205). While it is for the jury to find the facts, it is for the judge to rule on which facts give rise to an obligation. In *Mainwaring* (1982) the Court said:

> "Whether or not an obligation arises is a matter of law, because an obligation must be a legal obligation. But a legal obligation arises only in certain circumstances, and in many cases the circumstances cannot be known until the facts are established. It is for the jury, not the judge to establish the facts.
>
> What, in our judgment, a judge ought to do is this: if the facts relied upon by the prosecution are in dispute he should direct the jury to make their findings on the facts, and then say to them: 'If you find the facts to be such-and-

such, then I direct you as a matter of law that a legal obligation arose to which s.5(3) applies'."

Section 5(4)

This is possibly one of the most complex provisions of the entire Act yet arguably one of the least needed. It is supposed to cover the situation in which, due to a mistake by the victim, ownership in the property passes to the rogue before any act of appropriation, so that when the appropriation occurs he is appropriating his own property. The section provides:

> "Where a person gets property by another's mistake, and is under an obligation to make restoration (in whole or in part) of the property or its proceeds or of the value thereof, then to the extent of that obligation the property or proceeds shall be regarded (as against him) as belonging to the person entitled to restoration, and an intention not to make restoration shall be regarded accordingly as an intention to deprive that person of the property or proceeds."

It might be easiest to understand the workings of the section if we first consider the case of *Moynes* v. *Coopper* (1956) which it was designed to overrule. In that case the accused was given an advance on his wages during the course of the week. At the end of the week the wages clerk paid him a full salary, totally unaware that he ought to have made a deduction for the amount already advanced. When Moynes later discovered the error he decided to keep all the money.

At this point it is necessary to consider the *civil* law. No one can doubt but that Moynes was acting in a thoroughly dishonest way but, as we have just seen, dishonesty is not enough. So far as the civil law is concerned the fact that the person delivering property makes a mistake does not necessarily prevent ownership from passing and, of course, if ownership passes the recipient cannot steal the property because it is his own property. Generally, a mistake will prevent ownership from passing only where the deliveror is mistaken as to the identity of the recipient or the identity of the property. The clerk in *Moynes* v. *Coopper* was mistaken in neither of these senses: he intended to pay the Moynes the exact amount he in fact paid.

Prima facie, therefore, Moynes was merely a dishonest debtor—he owed his employers the seven pounds approximately which had been overpaid—but the law stops short of making thieves out of dishonest debtors. Moynes, however, was not quite like other dishonest debtors. He did not merely owe seven pounds to his employers: he was under a quasi-contractual obligation to restore either the actual seven pounds or its proceeds or its value. Section 5(4) is there to deal with this sort of case. It is not there to deal with the case where A is under an obligation to pay money to B (because that would make thieves of all dishonest debtors) but only where A is under an obligation to restore B the *very* property which he received from B or the proceeds or value of *that* property. Where A is under such an obligation can be a very complicated question but the complications arise in the civil law not the criminal law. For our purposes it is enough to note that section 5(4) comes into play only in the unusual sort of case because:

(1) If the ownership does not pass to the accused but remains with the person handing over the property, then the property still belongs to another without the need for section 5(4). Thus if X asks Y if he can give him a ten penny piece in exchange for ten pennies and Y mistakenly hands over a 50 pence piece it is arguable that Y retains ownership in the 50 pence and thus it is property belonging to Y. (See *Gilks* (1972)). It is conceivable also that the effect of the decision in *Chase Manhattan Bank N.A.* v. *Israel-British Bank* (*London*) (1981) is that whenever money is paid under a mistake, the payer retains an equitable proprietary interest in the property, thus rendering reliance on section 5(4) unnecessary. (See, *e.g.* commentary on *Davis* at [1988] Crim.L.R. 765.)

(2) In many cases where ownership in the property does pass despite the mistake, it has been caused to pass by fraud on the part of the recipient, in which case the prosecution would be better advised to prosecute the rogue for obtaining property by deception.

(3) In a large number of cases in which X receives ownership of property from Y on the basis of a mistake by Y there will be no obligation on X's part to make any restoration. For instance, if the mistake induces a voidable contract, ownership in the property will pass under that voidable contract and there will be no obligation in the recipient to make restoration until the other party has realised the mistake and has avoided the contract, even if the mistake was induced by fraud. Suppose that X goes into a supermarket and finds a jar of coffee with no price tag on. When he tenders this at the checkout he tells the girl that other such jars were priced at 50 pence; they were in fact one

pound. If the girl accepts his statement the property will pass to X under a voidable contract and there is no obligation to make restoration in whole or in part until the supermarket avoids the contract. This means that when he appropriates the property (by taking it out of the shop) he is appropriating his own property— section 5(4) is of no avail. (See further *Att.-Gen.'s Reference No. 1 of 1983* (1984).)

2. THE MENS REA OF THEFT

The Act provides that the prosecution must prove that the appropriation of property belonging to another was dishonest and that at the time of the appropriation the accused had the intention of permanently depriving the other of the property. The effect of the dishonesty requirement is, in part, that the prosecution must be able to establish intention or *Cunningham* recklessness (above, p. 59) in relation to each element of the *actus reus*. There is no requirement that the accused did it for personal gain; it would be theft if the defendant takes property belonging to another and simply throws it on the fire (s.1(2)).

(1) Dishonesty

Dishonesty is peculiarly difficult to define. Dishonest conduct is conduct which is regarded by people generally as dishonest. In most cases, of course, there is general agreement as to what is viewed as honest or dishonest. No one doubts but that it is dishonest to take goods from a store without paying for them, or to surreptitiously remove books from a library, or to get goods from a machine by using a washer instead of coinage, and so on. But cases can arise, and arise not infrequently, where views may differ as to whether particular conduct is dishonest.

The Theft Act does not attempt a comprehensive definition of dishonesty. Section 2 provides only a partial definition and details three cases where a person's conduct is not to be regarded as dishonest. Before these are examined, it will be noted that in addition it is provided by section 2(2) that a person's appropriation of property *may* be dishonest notwithstanding an intention to pay for it, and by section 1(1) that it is immaterial that the appropriation is not made with a view to gain. Suppose A wants to purchase a painting from B which B refuses to sell; A may be convicted of theft if he takes the picture though he leaves in its place money which more than represents its value. Alternatively A may wish merely to deprive B of the painting without intending to enjoy it himself or to sell it for his own profit; A may be convicted of theft because he intends the painting to be lost to B though he has no view to gain for himself.

Section 2(1) states that an appropriation is not to be regarded as dishonest in three cases: (i) where he believes that he has in law the right to deprive the other of it on behalf of himself or another; (ii) where he appropriates the property in the belief that he would have the owner's consent; and (iii) where he appropriates the property in the belief that the owner cannot be traced by taking reasonable steps.

(a) *Belief in legal right*

The only belief that is relevant here is a belief in a *legal* right. That A feels that he has a moral claim to the property, or that he is in some vague way justified in taking it, is not relevant under this head though it may be otherwise relevant to the issue of dishonesty. If A believes he has a *legal* right, his conduct cannot be accounted dishonest though his claim is entirely unreasonable or even though the claim is one which the law does not recognise. An honest belief in legal right, however arrived at, is inconsistent with dishonesty (see *Robinson* (1977) below, p. 291).

(b) *Belief in consent*

If A honestly believes that B, the owner, would have consented to his appropriation, his conduct cannot be regarded as dishonest. That A's belief is unreasonably arrived at is irrelevant except to the extent that it may cast doubt on the honesty of his belief.

It is useful to remember here that the law also requires that the accused must intend permanently to deprive the owner of the property so that unlawful borrowing of another's property even where you know the other would most certainly have refused to lend the property does not amount to theft. Unlawful borrowing may be a social nuisance but it has long been held that this is not an appropriate subject for criminal sanctions (but see section 6 below, p. 286; unlawful borrowing of a motor vehicle may amount to a separate offence under section 12. See below, p. 341). It should also be remembered that where the property "borrowed" is consumable such as money or cups of sugar, the borrower will intend permanently to deprive the other of *that* money or sugar, he will have an intention merely to replace an equivalent amount.

Suppose that X enters a shop intending to purchase a bottle of milk. He finds that there is no one serving in the shop and so he simply takes the bottle of milk and leaves. His criminal liability will depend upon the circumstances. For example:

(i) If he honestly believed that the shopkeeper would not object to his taking the milk and paying up later then he will have a defence under section 2(1)(*b*).

(ii) If, however, he does not know the shopkeeper and has no reason to believe that the shopkeeper would consent to his simply taking the milk, he might suppose that it would be all right if he either left a note of his name and address and a message that he would call in to pay later, or more likely that the owner would not object if he left the money on the counter. The only difficulty here is that section 2(2) says that the appropriation *may* be dishonest notwithstanding that he is willing to pay for the property. Thus if A owns a valuable Ming vase which B has always wanted, if B were to go to A's house and take the vase, leaving a cheque for the market value of the vase, a jury would be entitled to find that B dishonestly appropriated A's vase despite his willingness to pay. But in the example of the bottle of milk, a jury would be equally entitled to find that the leaving of the money or I.O.U. was evidence that X honestly believed that the owner would have consented or simply that X was not dishonest (see below, p. 284).

(c) *Belief that the owner cannot be traced*

This provision essentially deals with property which is found by A; he is not to be treated as a thief if he appropriates that property in the belief that the owner cannot be traced by taking reasonable steps. If, for example, A finds a £1 note in the street it could only be exceptionally that he would believe that the owner can be traced so that in appropriating it he would not be guilty of theft. If, however, A finds in the same street Goya's portrait of the Duke of Wellington, he is unlikely to believe that the owner cannot be traced by taking reasonable steps.

Nevertheless, if A is a philistine who regards the painting as worthless so that it does not occur to him to take steps to trace the owner, he cannot be convicted of theft. If it does occur to A that the owner might be traced, he may be convicted of theft if he fails to take *reasonable* steps. He is not required to take every conceivable step; no doubt the most usual reasonable step would be to hand the property to the police on the assumption that the owner, if he cares about his loss, will have reported it to them.

(d) *Dishonesty in other cases*

The partial definition does not of course provide for all cases and the question arises as to how dishonesty is to be defined in circumstances not falling within the partial definition. The courts have considered the matter in a number of cases, *Feely* (1973), *Boggeln* v. *Williams* (1978); *Landy* (1981); *McIvor* (1982)) and in *Ghosh* (1982) the Court of Appeal, recognising that the law was in a complicated state, attempted a restatement.

Whether conduct is to be regarded as dishonest is a matter for the jury to determine. The judge should, however, direct the jury that A acts dishonestly if (a) his conduct would be regarded as dishonest by the ordinary standards of reasonable people; and (b) A realises that his conduct is so regarded. If (a) and (b) are satisfied then (c) A's conduct is dishonest however he might regard his conduct; A cannot set up a personal standard which he knows to be at variance with the general standard.

As to (a) the issue is one for the jury who have only their own knowledge and experience to guide them. No doubt on any given set of facts most juries would reach the same decision, but on certain facts juries may reach different conclusions. Take cases where A, C and D "borrow" money from B without permission. A may take 75p from the till of his employer B, to pay a taxi driver because he has no small change; C may take £5 from B's till to lay a wager on a horse (*Feely* (1973)); D may take £200 from B's safe to pay a deposit on his holiday (*McIvor* (1982)). All intend to pay the money at a later stage, but, of course, the money which they take is not "*borrowed*" but is appropriated since B is deprived permanently of the notes and coins taken. (See also *Velomyl* (1989)).

Would any or all of these takings be regarded as dishonest by the generality of reasonable people? No doubt the jury would wish to consider such factors as whether B had expressly forbidden "borrowing," the extent to which A, C and D had an ability to repay, whether the borrowing was done openly or secretly and so on. It seems difficult to lay down a general principle for such cases (but see Elliott at [1982] Crim.L.R. 395) so it may be that different juries would reach different conclusions.

As to (b) it is not simply a question of whether the defendant regards his conduct as dishonest according to his own standards. It is a question of whether he knew that ordinary people would regard his conduct as dishonest. It is generally regarded as dishonest to travel on buses with intent to avoid paying the fare but, as the court pointed out in *Ghosh*, a person who came from a country were public transport was free, would not act dishonestly if he boarded a bus believing that public transport here was similarly free; he would not be aware that ordinary people in this country would regard the conduct as dishonest.

If, then, a modern Robin Hood thought it was right for him to rob the rich in order to feed the poor, he would be acting dishonestly if he realised, as is the fact, that people generally regard such a taking as dishonest. But if he is out of touch with community standards and genuinely thinks that people generally do not regard such conduct as dishonest, then his conduct cannot, it seems, be accounted dishonest. Cases where the defendant is mistaken about the prevailing standards of dishonesty will be expectional, but they may occasionally happen.

In *Roberts* (1987) the Court of Appeal held that it would not, in every case, be necessary for the trial judge to give a full *Ghosh* direction. If the defendant did not raise an issue with regard to the second part of the test, the judge need not leave it to the jury. Thus there is a burden on the defendant to introduce evidence that he did not think that ordinary people would regard his conduct as dishonest.

(2) With intention permanently to deprive

During the period of debate before the Theft Act 1968 was enacted, it was suggested that the prosecution should no longer have to prove the accused intended permanently to deprive the other of his property. This would have had the effect of making dishonest borrowing theft. It was finally decided that the requirement should be retained and that cases of unlawful borrowing were better dealt with by the civil law. (But see below, p. 341 for special provisions for some instances of unlawful borrowing, especially of motor vehicles.

Thus the prosecution must prove that at the time of the appropriation the accused intended permanently to deprive the owner of the property. This ordinarily presents no problems because when A takes money from B's pocket or when C takes a book from D's shop the prosecution is usually not hard pressed to prove that A and C intended permanently to deprive. Equally, where the accused believed that the property had been abandoned, he cannot be said to have intended permanently to deprive another of it (*Small* (1988)). But *evidential* difficulties can occur. Where C takes the book from the university library, his claim that he intended to return the book at the end of term may be plausible and the prosecution may in such a case have difficulty in proving the intent. It has been known even for law students to take books from the law library without signing for them and then to leave them at the end of term outside the library door. This is a deplorable practice but it is not theft for it is obvious that the miscreant does not intend the university to lose the books permanently. What, then, if the miscreant left the books in the students' union or on the London underground? Given that the books were stamped as the property of the university of X, the probability is that they would be returned to the university in the first case, though this is much less likely in the second. But in either case the test of C's liability is the same: did he *intend* permanently to deprive the university of its books? If C believes that by leaving the books where he does they will be returned to the university he cannot be said to intend permanent deprivation even if he leaves them in a place which makes it highly unlikely that they will ever be returned.

In the normal run of case, then, the intent permanently to deprive raises only evidential problems. But in exceptional cases it can raise legal problems. Such cases tend to be those where A takes property of B's which, in a sense, he returns to B but only after A has treated himself as owner of that property. It is for these exceptional cases that section 6 is there to provide:

"A person appropriating property belonging to another without meaning the other permanently to lose the thing itself is nevertheless to be regarded as having the intention of permanently depriving the other of it if his intention is to treat the thing as his own to dispose of regardless of the other's rights; and a borrowing or lending of it may amount to so treating it if, but only if, the borrowing or lending is for a period and in circumstances making it equivalent to an outright taking or disposal."

Consider the following examples:

(1) A is a shopkeeper who stores empty beer bottles, on which he has paid the refund, in his yard. B enters the yards, takes some bottles and then enters B's shop where he gets a refund on the bottles. Such a case as this is perhaps best treated as obtaining by deception, but B may alternatively be convicted of stealing the bottles. In a sense he intends that A should get his bottles back but only after A has paid for them, B is clearly treating the bottles as his own to dispose of regardless of A's rights; A can get his own bottles back only by paying for them. This is just the situation the first part of section 6(1) was designed to cover; *per* Lord Lane C.J. in *Lloyd* (1985).

(2) D, a first year medical student, takes a copy of Gray's *Anatomy* from the library intending to return it on completion of his course in five years' time. Five years is a long time, so can it be said that D's "borrowing... was for a period and in circumstances which made it equivalent to an outright taking or disposal?" The difficulty with this view is that it could leave the courts with an impossible task in determining what period of borrowing would be so equivalent. The section says it must be *equivalent* to an outright taking. Borrowing for a fixed term falls short of being so equivalent, and the courts have held it to be a misdirection for a judge to direct a jury that X may be convicted of stealing Y's goods where X intends to keep those goods indefinitely (*Warner* (1970)). A taking or borrowing is equivalent to an outright taking probably only where all the value of the property is consumed. So if X takes Y's season ticket to a football ground, intending to use it for *all* the games for which it is valued and then return the ticket to Y, X has stolen the ticket, for the borrowing is now equivalent to an outright taking. In *Lloyd* (1985) a cinema projectionist handed over to an associate films which were currently being shown at the cinema. The associate produced a master video tape of the films which were then returned to the cinema in time for its next showing. It was clear that there was no intention permanently to deprive the owner of the films since they were returned none the worse for wear; they had lost none, let alone all, of their virtue.

In *Coffey* (1987) the prosecution alleged that the defendant had obtained a machine from the victim by deception (a worthless cheque). Although this was a charge under section 15 of the Act, namely obtaining property by deception, it also required that the prosecution prove that the defendant intended permanently to deprive the other of the machine. It appeared that the defendant was in dispute with the owner of the machine and had obtained the machine so as to give himself a bargaining counter in the negotiations. It was not altogether clear what would have happened to the machine if the negotiations were not settled to the defendant's satisfaction. It was held that this was a situation in which the trial judge should give the jury a full direction on section 6(1). The prosecution would have to satisfy the jury that the defendant intended not to return the machine until he got what he wanted, or, at least, that he intended to keep it so long as to be regarded as an outright taking of it; in other words, till all the virtue had gone out of the thing.

(3) E, knowing that F is out of town for the day and is in no position to interfere, takes G to F's home. There, representing himself as the owner of the house and contents, he sells F's furniture to G. E is obviously guilty of theft if he anticipates that G will remove the furniture, but what if E knows that F will return in time to prevent removal? The simple answer would be to charge E with obtaining by deception but it is arguable that he would still be guilty of stealing. E may not "mean" F to lose the thing (the furniture) itself but by purporting to sell it to G he has treated the furniture as his own to dispose of (*Pitham* v. *Hehl* (1976)). This conclusion is supported by the decision of the Privy Council in *Chan Man-sin* v. *Att.-Gen. for Hong Kong* (1988). In that case the defendant had, by means of forged cheques, caused money to be transferred from M and H's accounts with S.C. Bank into his own personal account with O.T. Bank. The defence argued that once it was discovered that the cheques were forgeries, M and H would be able to insist on having the transactions reversed, and would thus lose nothing. Since the defendant, who was an accountant, would know this to be the position, it could not be said that he intended permanently to deprive them of their property. (The property in this case were the debts owed by the Bank to M and M—*i.e.* choses in action; see above, p. 270). The Privy Council held that this was covered by a provision in the Hong Kong statute which was identical to section 6 of our Theft Act 1968. The defendant's intention was to treat the thing as his own to dispose of regardless of the rights of M and H.

(4) H hires a car from J for a week. K takes the car, uses it for a week and then returns it to J. No doubt K would be charged under section 12 (taking a conveyance, see p. 341) but he may also be guilty of theft. He has not stolen the car from J

but so far as H is concerned he has deprived H of the whole of his interest.

(5) A takes B's silver goblets and pawns them. He keeps the money he receives from the pawnshop intending to redeem it later. This is covered by section 6(2) which gives a further extended meaning to the phrase "with the intention permanently to deprive."

> "If any person in possession of another's property (whether lawfully or not) parts with that property under a condition he may not be able to perform he may be regarded as treating the property to dispose of regardless of the other's rights."

(3) Conditional intention

A problem which has caused much controversy in recent years has been that of so-called conditional intent. In a sense all intention may be said to be conditional. A may set out with the firm intention of stealing B's painting but his intention will be subject to certain conditions such as that he will be able to effect an entry to the place where the painting is kept or that B will not be guarding the painting. But it would be quite unrealistic to say that if A leaves empty handed because he cannot effect an entry or because B was on guard that he therefore did not intend to steal the painting.

But what if the painting is not in the building at all because B has moved it to another place? Until recently this sort of case caused a problem because of a House of Lords ruling (in *Haughton* v. *Smith* (1975)) that a person could not be convicted of an attempt to commit a crime which was a physical impossibility. This position has been reversed by the Criminal Attempts Act 1981 (above, p. 203) and now a person may be convicted of an attempt even though, in the circumstances, he could not have effected the complete crime. So if A is found in the room where the painting used to hang he may be convicted of attempting to steal it; moreover in entering the building with intent to steal it he commits the crime of burglary.

A somewhat similar problem arose where A has not yet made up his mind whether and what to steal. Take the case of the rogue, A, whose practice it is to search other people's cars to see whether there is anything that takes his fancy. In B's car he finds nothing at all; in C's car he notices that there is a copy of the bible but he is not interested in that; in D's car he finds a handbag but having ascertained that the contents (lipstick, handkerchief, nail file) are of no value to him he returns the handbag to its place. In none of these cases can A be convicted of theft since he has stolen nothing. Now that the rule in *Haughton* v. *Smith* has been changed by statute, A may be convicted even though it was impossible for him to commit the completed crime (theft) owing to the fact that there was nothing he was remotely interested in stealing. But there is another matter to consider. A cannot be charged with stealing nothing, nor with attempting to steal nothing. He must be charged with attempting to steal some property belonging to another. Nor can he be properly charged with attempting to steal property which he just does not intend to steal. A cannot be charged with attempting to steal C's bible or the lipstick from D's handbag because his conduct proves that he had no intent to steal these.

But when A saw the handbag in D's car he no doubt hoped that it would contain money and, had it done so, it is certain that he would have taken it. If so, A can be charged with and convicted of attempting to steal money from D. In the other two cases it may be that A had no expectation of finding money, nor did he find anything else that took his fancy. But if A had found something that had taken his fancy he would certainly have taken it, and in such a case it is proper to charge him with attempting to steal "property belong to" B or C without specifying any particular property (*Bayley* v. *Easterbrook* (1980)).

It really boils down to this. If, in the indictment, you charge A with stealing or attempting to steal a specific item of property, you must prove that he actually intended to steal that item. In a case where you are alleging that A has committed the completed offence of theft, you will obviously need to specify the property, alleged to have been stolen, in the indictment. In cases of attempted theft, however, where you are faced with the sort of problem illustrated above in which A has been looking through the boots of cars, the court will allow an indictment which simply alleges that A has attempted to steal property from B. A similar problem occurs in burglary where the accused is charged under section 9(1)(*a*) of the Theft Act 1968 (see below, p. 323). In this type of burglary the prosecution may have to prove that at the time the accused entered the building he intended to steal property from within. Again it has been held that there is no need to specify particular items of property in the building, nor would it be fatal to the prosecution that the building turned out to be empty. (See *Att.-Gen.'s References Nos. 1 and 2 of* 1979 (1980).)

II. *ROBBERY*

Section 8 of the Theft Act 1968 provides:

"(1) A person is guilty of robbery if he steals, and immediately before or at the time of doing so, and in order to do so, he uses force on any person or puts or seeks to put any person in fear of being then and there subjected to force.

(2) A person guilty of robbery, or of an assault with intent to rob, shall on conviction on indictment be liable to imprisonment for life."

In order to succeed on a charge of robbery the prosecution must establish (a) that the property was stolen; and (b) that the theft of it was accomplished by force. Thus all the defences open to one charged with theft are open on a charge of robbery. If the jury believe that the accused honestly thought that he had the right to take the property they must acquit him of theft, and therefore of robbery. In *Robinson* (1977) the accused was owed £7 by I's wife. The prosecution alleged that R and two others approached I in the street and that R was brandishing a knife. In the course of a fight which followed, I dropped a £5 note. R picked it up and asked for the remaining £2 he was owed. The judge directed the jury that for a defence under section 2(1) of the Theft Act the accused should honestly believe he had the right to take the money in the way he did. His appeal against conviction for robbery was allowed by the Court of Appeal. The prosecution had to establish the basic offence of theft and it would be a defence to that charge that the accused honestly believed he had a right in law to deprive I of the money, even if he knew he was not entitled to use a knife to get it. If the prosecution failed to prove theft, then an indictment for robbery must also fail.

What then turns an act of theft into one of robbery? In the first place the prosecution must prove that in order to steal the accused used force on any person or sought to put any person in fear of such force being then and there used on him. It is important to note that the section does not say that the force or threat has to be used on the person from whom the property is stolen. It can be used on any person provided that it is used "in order to steal." Thus if the accused sees Mr. and Mrs. A walking along the street, it would be robbery if he knocked Mr. A unconscious and snatched Mrs. A's handbag. The prosecution must, however, establish that the force was used against a person (and not just against the property) though very slight force will suffice. It is enough to constitute robbery that there is a struggle for possession of the goods and that A pulls them from B's hands (*Corcoran* v. *Anderton* (1980)). In *Clouden* (1987) the defendant followed a woman and then, coming up behind her, grabbed the shopping bag which she was carrying in her left hand. He wrenched it from her grasp. Before the Theft Act 1968 the prosecution would have had to prove not merely that the force was used to gain possession of the goods, but that it was used to overpower the victim and prevent resistance. It is clear that the drafters of the Act intended to preserve this distinction. However, the Court of Appeal said that the trial judge should not concern himself with these distinctions of the old law, but should direct the jury's attention to the wording of section 8. Whether or not the defendant used force on any person in order to steal was an issue for the jury. It is possible, on facts such as those in *Clouden*, to say that the defendant used force on the woman in order to steal. But surely the man in the street would say that these facts look more akin to a case of pickpocketing than to robbery.

The Act, however, says that the force or threat of force must be used immediately before or at the time of stealing, and this raises difficult problems of fact and degree. What does the Act mean by immediately before? If a gang intend to break into a factory and one of the gang knocks out the night-watchman before the main part of the gang break in to steal, this would be robbery. If, on the other hand, they were to threaten the night-watchman with a beating up if he did not draw them a plan of the factory so that they could steal from it a week later, this would not be robbery since force or threat of force was not used immediately before the stealing.

At the other end of the time span, the Act says that the force must be used (immediately before or) at the time of the stealing. Here it is important to remember the other qualification that the force or threat must be used in order to steal. A strict interpretation would mean that once the theft is complete, in the sense that the accused could be charged with the substantive offence of theft, the use of force will not turn the crime into an offence of robbery. For example, if X is a pickpocket and has got his hands round Y's wallet and is in the process of removing it from Y, we have said that since he has now assumed rights of an owner over (*i.e.* appropriated) the wallet, the offence of theft is complete even though he has not yet removed it totally from Y. If Y now realises what is being done, resists and is hit in the stomach by X, does this mean that it is not robbery because the force is used after X has stolen the wallet? Could X argue that since the theft was complete the force was not used "in order to steal?" Clearly, the words must be given a wider meaning than "up to the time when there is a completed act of appropriation." Similar problems arise in handling (below, see p. 338), where the phrase "otherwise than in the course of stealing" appears) and presumably a uniform answer should be given. It must be robbery when the accused uses force on the victim to enable him to get the wallet out of his control, or to get the goods off the premises in a bank raid (see *Hale* (1979)). Even though there is already a completed act of theft when the accused appropriated the property, it would probably still be robbery if X hit Y to stop him immediately recovering the wallet. On the other hand, if X has got hold of Y's wallet and is running down the street when he is stopped by P.C. Z, force now used on P.C. Z would be after the commission of the theft and would not turn the offence into robbery. "At the time of" committing the theft must be viewed in a commonsense way; the test is whether X can sensibly be said to be stealing the goods when the force is used on Y.

III. *OFFENCES INVOLVING DECEPTION*

So far we have been considering the offence of theft which is concerned largely with those situations in which the accused has taken property belonging to another. In this section we shall be concerned with those situations where the accused has, by fraud, induced the victim to act in a way he would not, but for the fraud, have acted. In some cases the accused will have tricked the victim into handing over property that falls within the definition of section 4 and in these cases it would undoubtedly be possible to draft an offence which would embrace both theft and obtaining property by deception. However, other acts of deception do not result in the handing over of property but, for example, cause the victim to perform a service for the accused and in these cases it would not be appropriate to say that he stole the service. For this and other reasons it is seen as preferable to separate the offence of theft from those involving deception. It should be remembered, however, that when property falling within section 5(4) of the Act is involved it may sometimes be difficult to decide whether it is correct to charge the accused with theft or obtaining property by deception. In these cases it may be safer to charge him with both offences in the alternative (see below, p. 307).

Under the Theft Act 1968 there are two basic offences of deception. Under section 15 it is an offence to obtain property by deception and under section 16 it is an offence to obtain a pecuniary advantage by deception. Common to both offences is the need to establish that the property or the pecuniary advantage was obtained as a result of the deception practised by the accused. The need for two sections arises from the fact that Parliament thought it necessary to distinguish between those situations in which the accused obtained property and those in which he obtained a financial advantage but nothing tangible. For example, if you go into a car rental agency and by showing a false driving licence and insurance you induce him to rent you a car for the day, you will have obtained possession of the car by deception and this is clearly the obtaining of property. If, however, when it comes to paying for the car which the garage has already let you take away, you trick the owner into giving you time to pay then you have not obtained any property by deception, you have gained a financial advantage—namely more time to pay. Under the Theft Act 1968 "pecuniary advantage" was defined to mean three things under section 16(2)(a) (b) and (c). Unfortunately section 16(2)(a) gave rise to so many difficulties that it was thought better to repeal it and replace it with three new offences to be found in the Theft Act 1978. Under the new Theft Act it is an offence to obtain services by deception, to evade liability by deception and to make off without paying. The resulting position is that there are now four basic offences of deception and these are the dishonest obtaining by deception of:

    (i)   property (Theft Act 1968, s.15);

   (ii)   pecuniary advantage (the unrepealed parts of section 16 of the Theft Act 1968—*viz.* s.16(2)(b) and (c) which deal with defined cases and which have as yet given rise to few problems);

  (iii) services (Theft Act 1978, s.1);

  (iv) evasion of liability (Theft Act 1978, s.2).

Finally there is the offence of dishonestly making off without paying (Theft Act 1978, s.3—but this offence does not require any deception). In this section we shall first consider the elements common to the deception offences and then examine the four things which have to be obtained. We shall then consider the offence of making off.

1. ELEMENTS COMMON TO DECEPTION OFFENCES

There are three basic elements which the prosecution must prove in all four crimes, namely (i) deception; (ii) that the deception was instrumental in the obtaining of, *e.g.* the property; and (iii) dishonesty.

(1) What can constitute deception for the purposes of the Theft Acts?

In the majority of cases it will be quite clear that the accused has deceived the victim into handing over some property or into performing some task and there will be no problem over the definition of the word "deception": the accused will have made a statement of fact which he well knows to be false. Thus if A, a well-known art dealer, tells B, a customer, that the picture he is interested in is a genuine Constable, when he knows full well that it is a reprint, then this will be a deception within the meaning of the Acts. If this is so, then what about the television commercial which says that X soap powder washes whiter than any other brand? Are we saying that if A buys this brand because of the advert and discovers that it washes no whiter than any other brand, that the advertisers obtained his money by deception? If not, what is the difference between this case and the art dealer? There are two points to be made here. In the first place, we should note that section 15(4) says that "deception" means any description (whether deliberate or reckless) by word or conduct as to fact or law...." This means that in relation to commercials the deception must involve a false statement as to an issue of fact. It could be argued that television commercials are statements of opinion and not of fact. If A therefore falsely tells B that he believes one car to be better than another this is a statement of opinion and not of fact and is not within the definition of deception. However, many statements of opinion are simply statements of fact expressed as opinion. For example, in the case where A tells B that he thinks that one car is a better buy than another he may have no factual basis for saying this. On the other hand, he may be aware of facts which make one car better than the other; for example, he may be aware that the second car's engine will need replacing in about a thousand miles. If, knowing this, he deliberately tells B that he thinks that the car with the faulty engine is a better car and B buys on the strength of that opinion, then he should be held to have made a false statement of fact. To the purchaser of a car from a salesman, the statement "This car is a better buy than the other one" implies to the buyer that the seller is saying he is not aware of any facts which would prove otherwise.

The second point to note concerning commercials is that in today's world there is the general assumption that most television watchers are immune to sales pressures through adverts and there is the general view that no one actually believes the inflated claims of the advertisers. However, this does not mean to say that in appropriate circumstances commercials could not be the basis of a deception charge. Much greater care can rightly be expected where the adverts are directed at children. Equally, if it can be shown that the advert makes a false statement of fact, such as "X Co. ball point pens last longer than Y Co. ball point pens," then if it can be shown that viewers were induced to buy the product for this reason, there is no reason why a deception charge should not be made. (See *Bryan* (1857)).

(a) *Misrepresentation of law*

It is quite clear from the definition of deception in section 15(4) that a deliberate or reckless misrepresentation of law can amount to a deception for the purposes of these offences. Thus if a solicitor deliberately misrepresented the effect a certain clause in a will would have, so that he became a beneficiary under the will, he would, on receipt of the legacy, have obtained property by deception.

(b) *Statement of intention*

X offers to paint Y's house for £100 cash in advance. He intends all along to abscond with the money without painting the house. This is a statement of intention of what he will do in the future if Y gives him £100, and not a statement of fact. Under the pre-1968 law this could not amount to a deception, but section 15(4) concludes that deception includes a "deception as to the present intentions of the person using the deception or any other person." Thus in our example X's present intentions are to take the money and leave and thus the statement is capable of amounting to a deception within the Act.

In *Silverman* (1987) the defendant gave an excessively high quotation for work to be done on property owned by two elderly sisters. The defendant had worked for the family in the past and it was clear that the negotiations had taken place in an atmosphere of mutual trust. The question for the court was whether his excessively high quotation could amount to deception for purposes of section 15. Obviously the court was mindful of the implication of holding that high quotations could constitute deception. However, it held that, in the special circumstances of this case where there was a relationship of trust, a representation of a fair charge which the defendant, but not the sisters, know to be dishonestly excessive could amount to a deception. In one respect the statement was a statement of opinion, but it amounted to a representation of the present state of his mind. In these circumstances his silence was as eloquent as if he had said that he was going to make no more than a modest profit.

(c) *Does there need to be words; will conduct suffice?*

We have already seen above in the definition of deception under section 15(4) that conduct can amount to a deception. This will be conduct which the accused knows or believes will cause another to draw certain conclusions. Thus in *D.P.P.* v. *Ray* (1974) the House of Lords held in a case where Ray left a restaurant without paying for a meal he had just eaten, that there was evidence which could support a finding that by staying in his seat after forming the intention not to pay, Ray had caused the waitress to leave the room, enabling Ray to walk out. Similarly, if you were to drive into a self-service station intending not to pay when you had filled up your tank, then you would be inducing in the attendants, by your conduct, a belief that you would be paying when you had got your petrol. When you sit down in the hairdressers's chair you are impliedly telling him that it is your present intention to pay for the haircut.

What of the accused who tenders a cheque or cheque card in payment? Let us consider the straightforward unaccompanied cheque first. Following the decision in *M.P.C. v. Charles* (1977) it would appear that, in the absence of any statement to the contrary, a person who tenders a cheque is impliedly stating that to the best of his knowledge, the cheque will be met when it is presented to the bank. This is not without its difficulties, since you are really saying that your bank manager will authorise payment of the cheque when he sees it. As we have already said, the deception must be as to a question of fact or present intentions and this is a statement concerning how you believe someone else will act in the future. Nevertheless, it does represent a statement of the presenter's present beliefs. He is saying that at that precise moment he has no reason to think that the cheque will not be met. Thus, for example, if he knows that he no longer has an account at that bank or that the manager has specifically told him that all future cheques presented will be dishonoured, it is suggested that this will amount to a deception within the meaning of the Act. In *Gilmartin* (1983) the Court of Appeal held that where the accused had written a post-dated cheque he was making the same sort of representation—that he had no reason to believe that the cheque would not be honoured when presented.

We shall see later that cheque cards and credit cards present special difficulties owing to the way in which they operate. It is suggested, however, that the presenter of such a card is stating that he has the authority to use it (see below, p. 301).

(d) *Can there be a case of deception by silence?*

In many cases of sales the seller is aware that the buyer is slaving under a misapprehension as to the qualities of the goods he is about to purchase. Is the seller therefore guilty of obtaining property by deception if he fails to correct the buyer's misapprehension? There exists at civil law, the motto *caveat emptor*, which translated means, "let the buyer beware"; in other words, he must take the risks. It would be odd if the criminal law were to punish the seller for simply following a civil law maxim. However, the seller must do nothing actively to promote the mistake. If the customer were to say "I am going to use this paint for outside work" and the shopkeeper knew it was extremely unsuitable for that purpose, his silence could be taken as an implied statement that the paint was suitable for outside work. It is suggested that this should amount to a deception within the Act. Similarly, if X warrants that the car he is selling Y is roadworthy but discovers before Y pays him the money that there is a serious defect in the car which makes it extremely unsafe, X would be guilty of obtaining the money by deception if he failed to draw this to the attention of Y before he received the money.

(e) *Can you deceive a machine?*

The simple answer to this question is, not for the purposes of these four offences. The deception must cause a human being to act in a way he would not have done but for the deception. Thus, if you insert a valueless metal disc into a cigarette machine for the purpose of getting cigarettes out for nothing, then you have stolen the cigarettes just as much as if you had forced the machine open with a crowbar; but you have not obtained them by deception. The Law Commission in their Working Paper on Computer Misuse (1988) suggest that this constitutes a gap in the law which should be amended to permit the conviction of a defendant who deceives a machine and thereby obtains property, a pecuniary advantage, services or the evasion of liability. (See Law Commission Working Paper No. 110, Computer Misuse, p. 67.) However, if the machine is used to deceive a human being, there may be a deception. For example, if X takes the afternoon off work and alters the machine which prints his time of leaving so that his record card shows that he left at the proper time, when he gets paid his full amount at the end of the week it will be because he had used the machine to deceive his employers. Thus he will be guilty of obtaining property from his employers by deception. (He would also commit the offence of false accounting section 17 of the Theft Act 1968).

(2) The causal link

It is not sufficient for the prosecution to prove that the accused practised a deception on the victim and that he then obtained an item of property from the victim. They must prove that the deception was the reason why the accused obtained the property. In other words there must be a causal link between the deception and the obtaining of the property. A few illustrations will help to make this clearer.

(a) A offers to sell B his copy of *Smith and Hogan*. He tells B that it is the current edition when he knows full well that there has just been a new edition and that B will need the new edition for his classes. The jury should only convict A of obtaining the property (*i.e.* the sale price) by deception if they are satisfied beyond reasonable doubt that B would not have bought the book but for the deception. If, on the other hand, they feel that B knew that the book was out of date but that he had some reason for still wanting to buy it, then despite A's belief that he has duped B, his attempt to deceive B did not cause B to buy the book and so the purchase price was not obtained by A's lies. (Can A be charged with attempting to obtain property by deception? See above, p. 203.)

(b) C drives into a petrol station. He intends to fill up with petrol and then drive off without paying. If the jury are satisfied that his representations caused the petrol station attendants to believe that C intended to pay and thus allowed him to fill his car then clearly C has obtained the petrol by deception.

(c) D writes a begging letter to E saying that she is the impoverished widow of a sailor who was drowned at sea. E knows whom the letter is from and that it is an attempt to trick him. Nevertheless E sends D the money in an attempt to trap D. Care is needed here. D has told E lies and E has sent D some money, *but* it was not D's deception which caused the money to be sent because E was aware it was a trick (*Hensler* (1870)). That was a relatively easy case in which to see absence of a causal link between the deception and the obtaining, but it is not always so simple. Let us consider a case in which A and B who are travelling on a train from London to Leeds, go to the buffet car for a snack. In the buffet car a bystander tells them that he suspects that the attendant is selling his own sandwiches and keeping the money. A says that he will only buy a sandwich if it is a British Rail sandwich, for which the money will have to go in the till. B, on the other hand, says that he could not care less who made the sandwich as long as it is fresh. They ask the attendant whose sandwiches are on sale and he falsely tells him that they are British Rail sandwiches. Both are deceived by the attendant, but the deception is material only to A since B would have bought the sandwiches even if the attendant had told them that he had made the sandwiches himself. The attendant obtains property only from A by deception.

An interesting illustration of this point was provided by the case of *King and Stockwell* (1987). In that case the defendants were charged with attempting to obtain property by deception from a 68 year old woman to whom they had falsely represented themselves as employees of a reputable firm of tree surgeons. They told her that certain trees on her property needed felling as they could cause damage to the foundation of her house and to her gas supply. They argued that they had committed no offence since any money paid over would have been in return for the felling of trees; the lies they had told merely gave them the opportunity to do the work and had, in effect, ceased to be operative. The Court of Appeal held that this reasoning was fallacious. The question in every case is: was the deception an operative cause of the obtaining of the property? There was plenty of evidence in the present case that had the attempt succeeded, the money would have been paid over by the victim as a result of the lies told to her by the defendants. In the present case it would seem that the work recommended was unnecessary and so it is easy to say that the deception was an operative cause of the obtaining of the payment. However, it would be less clear cut if the work was essential and if the defendants had performed it well and at a reasonable price. The deception need not be the only reason for the handing over of property, but the jury must be satisfied that but for the deception the property would not have been obtained by the defendant.

A similar situation may arise where credit or cheque cards are used. You will know that one common feature of these cards is that a shopkeeper who sells goods to a person using one of these cards is guaranteed payment provided that he has fulfilled the regulations relating to them. In the case of credit cards these regulations require that the shopkeeper checks the signatures, checks that the card number is not on a stop-list, and telephones the company if the money involved is over a certain amount. In the case of cheque guarantee cards the seller must ensure that the signatures are in order. In both cases he need not actually be aware that the customer is no longer authorised to use the card. Where a person uses such a card he is impliedly representing that he is authorised to use the card. Thus if the shopkeeper is induced by a false representation that the card-holder is authorised to use the card to sell the goods, the holder has obtained the goods by deception. Before the introduction of such cards many shopkeepers were reluctant to accept cheques or grant credit. One purpose of the cards is to remove his fears that he will not be paid for the goods. As long as he is not actually aware that the authority to use the card has been withdrawn by the bank or credit card company, he will be paid. It is no longer necessary for him to ask embarrassing questions to ensure the customer's bona fides. He is, in theory, allowed to be like B on the train; he need not care whether the customer is authorised to use the card, so long as he does not actually know that the authority has been withdrawn. So when he accepts a cheque from X backed by a cheque guarantee card, does he do so because of X's implied assertion that he is authorised to use the card, or because he knows that he will be paid whether or not X is in fact authorised to use the card? If the prosecution cannot prove that he was influenced by the implied assertion of authority to use the card, there is no casual link between X's deception and the obtaining of the property.

The House of Lords has twice considered this issue.

In *M.P.C.* v *Charles* (1977), Charles, who was overdrawn, was told by his bank manager that he could cash only one cheque a day for 30 pounds and then only at a bank. What Charles did was to go to a gambling casino where in the course of the evening using his bank card he cashed 25 cheques for 30 pounds each in return for gambling chips. Unfortunately his luck was out and his bank had to meet all of these cheques. On a charge of obtaining a pecuniary advantage by deception it was argued on Charles' behalf that his deception (for there was a deception in his implicit representation that he was authorised to use the card as he had) was not an *effective* cause of the obtaining. The manager of the casino, it was agreed, handed over the chips not because he believed that Charles had authority but because *he did not know that Charles lacked authority*. This might be thought to be a play on words but it is not really that. We have noticed that cheque cards were introduced because of the reluctance of shopkeepers to accept cheques from customers they do not know. How much more reluctant must be the managers of gambling casinos to accept cheques from customers of whose creditworthiness they are unsure! The reason why such a manager parts with gambling chips is because he can be sure—so long as he does not know that a customer lacks authority—that the bank will pay. In short, it pays the manager not to know.

As it turned out, though, the House of Lords upheld Charles' conviction for obtaining by deception. The manager said that he would not have accepted the cheques had he known of Charles' lack of authority. The House of Lords seized on this as showing that Charles had made a deception which *caused* the manager to act on it. But was this really so? No gambling casino manager in his right mind would accept cheques from a customer of whose creditworthiness he was unaware unless there was a guarantor. The idea behind cheque cards, after all, is to assure shopkeepers and others that they can safely part with the property even though they do not know that, or are uncertain whether, the customer is creditworthy. The actual decision in *Charles* can be defended if the casino manager can be regarded as like our scrupulous A in that he considered whether Charles had authority and decided that he would not accept Charles' cheques but for Charles' implicit assurance that he had authority. This was the view taken by the House of Lords but, with respect, it seems an odd view having regard to the actual facts. The casino made no actual inquiry of Charles regarding his authority and it would be an odd casino manager who did. To make such an inquiry (a) runs the risk of offending the customer and thereby losing his custom; and (b) cannot leave him any better off because if he meets the cheque being unaware of, or uncertain as to, the customer's creditworthiness he knows that this is just the sort of situation for which cheque cards were introduced.

In *Lambie* (1982) the accused was charged with obtaining a pecuniary advantage by deception. She was the holder of a Barclaycard (which is a credit card as well as a cheque guarantee card) and had a debit balance of over £900. She knew that Barclays were trying to contact her and so she deliberately changed address without informing them. On December 15 she bought goods in Mothercare for £10.35 and tendered her Barclaycard as a credit card. The assistant checked the current "stop-list" and finding the accused's name was not on it, completed the voucher. She was convicted at her trial and appealed. The Court of Appeal held that there was adequate evidence that the accused had made a false representation to the shop, namely that she was authorised to use the card. However, it was the question of the inducement that gave rise to difficulty. The shop assistant made it perfectly clear that she regarded the state of the customer's credit as nothing to do with her. It was therefore very difficult to say that she was induced by the false representation to act in a way she would not otherwise have done.

The Court of Appeal found a distinction between cheque cards and credit cards based on the differences in the way they each secure payment for the shopkeeper. They held that this enabled them to distinguish *Charles* and hold *Lambie* not guilty because there was no evidence that the shopkeeper had been influenced by the implied representation that the accused was

authorised to use the card. Suffice it to say that the House of
Lords, in *Lambie*, held that there was no relevant distinction to
be drawn between cheque and credit cards. The question then
remained of whether Lambie had obtained a pecuniary
advantage by holding herself out as an authorised credit card
user. The House took the view that had the shop assistant been
asked whether, if she had known that Lambie was acting
dishonestly and had no authority to use the card, she would
have completed the transaction, she would obviously have
answered "no." The House, therefore, held that it followed that
the shop assistant was induced to perform the contract by
Lambie's implied assertion that she was an authorised user.
With respect, it is not at all clear from the report that this was
a logical deduction. However, the effect of this decision appears
to be that the Courts will fictitiously imply that all those who
permit their customers to use credit and cheque cards do so
motivated by the belief that their customers are authorised to
use the cards.

(d) X buys a book from Y and hands Y a cheque in payment.
The following day X discovers that the cheque will not be met
by the bank, but he does not inform Y. There is no obtaining of
a book by deception since this has already occurred when X
handed Y the cheque. If however X did not take possession of
the book until after he has discovered that the cheque will be
met then his silence would amount to a deception in that he
would be impliedly representing that there is no reason to think
that Y will not get his money, and this would cause Y to hand
over the book.

(e) X sells Y a car and makes several representations about
its qualities. All of the representations are true except for the
one in which X tells Y that the car has never been involved in a
serious accident. Could X defend himself against a charge of
obtaining property by deception on the basis that Y bought the
car acting on representations most of which were true? This is a
question of fact for the jury. If they are satisfied that Y would
not have bought the car had he known about the serious
accident then the charge is made out.

(f) X drives into a petrol station intending to pay. When he
has filled the tank he discovers that he has left all his money at
home. He therefore simply drives off without paying. Even if
you could find any form of deception here it would be at a time
when the ownership in the petrol had already passed to X (it

passes to him when he puts it in the tank) and so it would be impossible to say that he obtained the property by deception. Nor is it theft because the property in the petrol has already passed to him before he dishonestly appropriates it. (See now the Theft Act 1978, s.3, below, p. 319.)

(3) Dishonesty

All deception offences require dishonesty. The partial definition of dishonesty which is provided in section 2(1) for the purposes of theft is not made applicable to the deception offences. Obviously this partial definition is for the most part inapt for deception offences but otherwise the concept of dishonesty is the same for the deception offences as it is for theft. So a person would not commit a deception offence if he used a deception with a view to obtaining something to which he believed he was legally entitled. But just as a person's conduct may be accounted dishonest for the purposes of theft notwithstanding any intention to pay for the property, so too a person may dishonestly obtain by deception though he gives full value for what he obtains. If, for example, A sells Christmas cards by pretending that the profits will go to charity, he may be convicted of obtaining by deception though his cards are fair value for the price charged (see *Potger* (1970)).

2. WHAT MUST BE OBTAINED BY THE DECEPTION?

The prosecution must prove that as a result of the deception the accused obtained:
(1) property (Theft Act 1968, s.15); or
(2) a pecuniary advantage (Theft Act 1968, s.16); or
(3) services from another (Theft Act 1978, s.1); or
(4) the evasion of liability (Theft Act 1978, s.2).

(1) Obtaining property

The best known of the deception offences is that of by deception dishonestly obtaining property belonging to another with intent permanently to deprive that other of it contrary to section 15 of the Theft Act 1968.

(a) *What constitutes property for the purposes of section 15?*

Section 4(1) of the Theft Act 1968 applies for the definition of property throughout the Acts, but the complex provisions contained in section 4(2)–(4) relate only to the offence of theft. Thus the section 15 offence can be committed in relation to virtually any type of property including land, though probably not intellectual property (see *Oxford* v. *Moss,* above, p. 270). The property must belong to another at the time it is obtained by the accused in the sense that the other must own, possess or have control of the property.

(b) *When does D obtain the property?*

Section 15 provides that D obtains the property when he gets ownership, possession or control of the property. Thus if X goes into a do-it-yourself store and by means of a cheque he knows will not be met induces the shopowner to (a) sell him a chain saw or (b) loan it to him for three days, if X intends to abscond with the saw before the cheque is dishonoured he will have committed the offence under section 15. Equally if he persuades the shopkeeper to allow him to take the saw outside for closer examination to see if it is the sort he wants, intending to run off, he will have obtained control of the saw by deception and would be equally guilty under section 15.

(c) *Must he obtain the property for himself?*

No. The Act provides that D is to be regarded as obtaining the property if he acquires it for another or enables another to obtain or retain the property.

(d) *Mens rea*

Apart from (i) dishonesty which has been discussed above, it must also be proved that (ii) the deception was deliberate or reckless; and (iii) that there was an intention permanently to deprive.

As to (ii) there must be a representation which is in fact untrue which the maker knows to be untrue or which he makes not caring whether it be true or false. This requirement is really an essential adjunct of the requirement for dishonesty. It follows that D does not commit an offence where he is merely negligent for no amount of negligence can make an honest man a dishonest man. It would appear clearly to follow that the objective test of recklessness endorsed in *Caldwell* (above, p. 59) can have no place in this context.

(e) *Is there an overlap between the offences of theft and obtaining property by deception?*

It should be noted at the outset that there is no reason why there should not be an overlap between these offences. After all the Criminal Law Revision Committee did at one stage consider whether to define theft in such a way as to include cases of obtaining by deception. In the end they decided against this course but at least some members of the Committee thought it possible to subsume the deception offence within a more broadly drawn definition of theft. But having decided on two separate offences, the Committee never had it in mind so to define them that there could be no conceivable possibility of overlap. The fact that in particular circumstances the defendant might be convicted of either theft or deception is of no great consequence.

Suppose, then, that A obtains a television set from B on a hire-purchase term, that A has no intention of paying the instalments and makes off with the set. This looks like, and is, a case of obtaining by deception contrary to section 15. It is also a case of theft. Under a hire-purchase transaction the purchaser gets possession but does not get ownership of the goods hired. The ownership here remains in B so when A make off with (*i.e.* appropriates) the set he is then appropriating property belonging to B. So there are at least some cases in which the defendant may be convicted of theft or deception. What we need to explore is the extent of this overlap.

The first question that arises is whether *all* cases of theft can be charged as deception. The answer must be an obvious "No." If A puts his hand in B's pocket and extracts B's wallet this is theft, but by no stretch of the imagination can it be said to be an obtaining of the wallet by deception. Thus by far the most common form of theft (*i.e.* theft by taking) cannot fall within deception—because there is no deception.

The second question is whether *all* cases of deception can be charged as theft. It would certainly be surprising if this turned out to be the case, if only because the Criminal Law Revision

Committee, though it anticipated some overlap, can hardly have thought that the offence of deception was entirely superfluous. Sometimes, though, statutory provisions do not always have the effect they were intended by their framers to have and there is Court of Appeal authority, though the statement was obiter, that it might be the law that all cases of deception can be charged as theft. This opinion by the Court of Appeal is obviously wrong in at least one respect. The range of property which is capable of being obtained by deception is wider than the range of property which can be stolen. Land, for example, can be obtained by deception but it cannot be stolen (see above, p. 271). If, then, A obtains Blackacre from B by deception he may commit the offence under section 15 but not the offence of theft under section 1. The court's opinion, therefore, can only be applied to cases where the property involved can be both obtained by deception and stolen. Even in such cases the view is still a surprising one and needs a word or two of explanation.

Before this question is examined further it will be useful to remember that where the prosecution has charged the defendant with theft it must establish that the defendant has *appropriated* property *belonging to another*. Where the defendant has obtained property by deception from his victim, then it may well be that the defendant may have obtained ownership of the property as well as possession. In such a case, if the prosecutor charges the defendant with theft it should follow that he should establish that the defendant appropriated the property before he became owner of it, otherwise he would be appropriating his own property and not property belonging to another. We can now consider two situations.

(1) A, by deception, obtains possession of goods belonging to X. He then makes off with the goods intending never to return them. In such a case A may be charged with both theft and obtaining property by deception, but if the case of *Skipp* is correct (see above, p. 271) the two offences do not occur at the same moment. You will remember that in *Skipp* the defendant had picked up three loads of oranges from different places in London for delivery to Leicester. His intention all along was to keep the oranges. It was held that he did not steal the oranges until he deviated from his proper course some time after picking up the third load. It was only at this stage that he appropriated the property. However, it is clear that he obtained each load of goods by deception as he picked them up in London, by impliedly representing that it was his present intention to take

them to Leicester as directed. Thus it is possible to say that the act which constitutes the offence of obtaining property by deception does not necessarily constitute theft; in other words obtaining goods by deception from another does not, in itself, amount to an appropriation.

(2) B, by deception, obtains ownership of property which belonged to Y. He then takes the goods intending to keep them. This clearly constitutes the offence of obtaining property by deception, but equally clearly should not be charged as theft. This is because when B does not act which, according to *Morris*, can amount to an appropriation, namely the taking away of the property, he is appropriating his own property. Whether, and at what time ownership passes to the rogue is a question of civil law (see *e.g. Lewis* v. *Averay* (1973)).

Since in both cases a case of obtaining property by deception can be made out, that is the charge which should be brought. The major difficulty lies in the case of *Lawrence* which seems difficult to reconcile with *Skipp* and passages from which might seem to suggest that a charge of theft could be brought even in illustration (2). In *Lawrence* (1972), Occhi an Italian student arrived at Victoria station with little knowledge of English and even less of the breathtaking rapacity of certain of our taxi drivers. He asked Lawrence, the driver of the taxi, to take him to a certain address in Ladbroke Grove which was written on a piece of paper. Lawrence told him that that was a long way and would be expensive. Occhi opened his wallet and took out a pound note which he gave to Lawrence who then took a further £6 out of the wallet which was still open. Lawrence then drove Occhi to his address in Ladbroke Grove for which the correct fare would have been about 50 pence. He was charged with and convicted of theft of the £6.

It is quite clear that had Lawrence been charged under section 15 the case could hardly have given rise to difficulty, for he had falsely represented that the address was a long way off and that £7 was the correct fare. For some reason, however, Lawrence was charged with theft and of course the prosecution had to substantiate that charge. Under the law preceding the Theft Act 1968, in order to prove larceny, the forerunner of theft, the prosecution would have to prove that the taking and carrying away of another's property was done without that other's consent. The Court of Appeal, in *Lawrence*, held that since the words "without the consent of the owner" did not appear in the Theft Act, Lawrence could be convicted of theft.

The Court went on to say, rightly enough, that Lawrence might have been convicted on a charge under section 15, but then concluded, as something of a non sequitur, that it might be that as a result of their decision that any facts which would support a charge under section 15 would also support a charge under section 1.

The decision of the House of Lords does little to clarify the matter. It was there said again, rightly enough, that *some* cases of deception might be charged as theft but the House of Lords did not commit itself to the view that all cases of deception could be charged as theft, but neither did it say that such a view was wrong. Their Lordships contented themselves with the view that Lawrence had appropriated property which, at the time he took it from the wallet, belonged to Occhi. The charge of theft was therefore made out. The questions we should ask is did ownership of the £7 pass to Lawrance and if so did it do so before he appropriated it. If the answer to both questions is yes, then on the views expressed here, Lawrence could not be guilty of stealing the money. The House of Lords did not decide this point but held that even if ownership had passed Lawrence could still be convicted of theft. The House of Lords did this by taking what might be thought an ingenious point. It will be recalled that though Occhi *gave* Lawrence the first £1, Lawrence himself *took* the other £6 from his wallet. While the money was in the wallet it was still Occhi's and *at the very instant Lawrence put his hand on it he was appropriating property which was still Occhi's*.

But this view creates problems in another respect. In what sense did Lawrence *appropriate* the £6. As we have seen an appropriation has to be an *unauthorised* act (above, p. 264) and it looks as though Occhi authorised the taking by allowing Lawrence to take the notes without protest. An answer to that, which is hinted at in the House of Lords decision, is that Occhi was so confused he did not know what Lawrence was taking, so the case might be likened to that where by slight of hand A gets property from B which B does not realise he is getting and such a case would amount to theft.

If the decision in *Lawrence* is treated in this way it is reconcilable with the principals stated at the beginning of this section and with the decisions in *Morris* and *Skipp*. Thus in conclusion we can say that some cases of deception will amount to theft, but that where D has, by any deception, induced P to transfer ownership to him before he does any act which could constitute an appropriation, this should not amount to theft.

Prosecutors would be well advised that where D has by any deception obtained ownership, possession or control of property from P, D should be charged under section 15 and not section 1 of the Theft Act 1968.

(2) Obtaining a pecuniary advantage

If X goes into a hairdresser's and allows the hairdresser to cut his hair intending not to pay when the haircut is over, you could say that he has obtained the haircut by deception. But is a haircut property? Clearly not within the definition of section 4 of the Theft Act 1968. Of course, if shampoo or conditioner have been used you could say that he obtained those items by deception. It would, however, be absurd to say that liability should depend upon whether the haircut involves the use of shampoo. Similarly if A gives false information on an application form for a job and as a result of that false information he obtains the employment, what has he obtained by deception? So far he has obtained the right to work for the firm. At the end of the month when he is paid, this will be for the work he has done during the month and not because of the deception. So does he commit no offence?

These examples should show that whereas theft can be limited to items of property (albeit a widened definition to cover such property as things in action) the definition of property is just not suitable to cover the examples given above. It was therefore felt necessary to include a separate offence to cover situations where the accused by his deception obtains some form of financial advantage. Thus section 16 provided a criminal offence of obtaining a pecuniary advantage by deception. The phrase pecuniary advantage was defined in three ways by section 16(2)(a)–(c). Paragraphs (b) and (c) provided for a fairly restricted range of situations and these will be discussed below. Paragraph (a) was a wide ranging definition of pecuniary advantage which was intended to cover, for example, the cases like the hairdresser described above. Unfortunately this section caused the courts so many problems, being described at one stage as a "judicial nightmare," that Parliament repealed this one small part of the Theft Act and replaced it with three new offences under the Theft Act 1978. The end result is that the offence of obtaining a pecuniary advantage survives in section 16, but the definition of pecuniary advantage is now limited to paragraphs 16(2)(b) and 16(2)(c).

What therefore is a pecuniary advantage for the purposes of section 16?

(i) *Section* 16(2)(*b*):

> "He is allowed to borrow by way of overdraft, or to take out any policy of insurance or annuity contract, or obtains an improvement of the terms on which he is allowed to do so";

Thus if X falsely tells his bank manager that he is expecting a cheque from his father in five weeks time and as a result is allowed to create an overdraft, then even before he has begun to take advantage of the overdraft facilities he has committed the offence under section 16 of obtaining a pecuniary advantage by deception. It is the obtaining of the facility that is the crux of the offence.

If Y gives false information about his state of health and thereby obtains a life insurance policy, he has committed an offence at the time he is granted the policy.

(ii) *Section* 16(2)(*c*):

> "He is given the opportunity to earn remuneration or greater remuneration in an office or employment, or to win money by betting."

Our earlier example of the applicant for a job who gives false information on the application form which induces the employer to give him the job will be caught by this definition of pecuniary advantage. Similarly a university lecturer who gains promotion by supplying the university with a false list of publications would also commit the offence under section 16. Recent concern has centred around persons who have been obtaining licences to drive taxis or private hire vehicles without disclosing serious criminal convictions as required by the application forms. This may clearly constitute obtaining a pecuniary advantage by deception; the offence is complete at the moment when the defendant obtains employment and not at the later time when he obtains his first wage packet.

In one case, X went into a bookmaker's shop and said he wanted to place a bet on a certain horse. It was just before the race began. The bet was placed and X then took a wad of notes from his pocket and began to count the appropriate sum out very slowly. In the meantime the race had begun and as soon as it became apparent that X's horse would not win he scooped up the money and walked out. Now had the horse won, X would have paid over the stake and collected his winnings. He would, however, not have obtained those winnings by any deception about being willing to pay for his bet, but because his horse had won. As it was his trick enabled him to get the chance to win money on a bet and it is the obtaining of this opportunity which is the offence under section 16 (*Aston and Hadley* (1970)). Although section 16 describes only one offence, the indictment should reveal what type of pecuniary advantage is involved. In *Aston and Hadley* the accused's conviction was quashed because although the facts may well have supported an indictment based on section 16(2)(*c*), the prosecution had alleged a section 16(2)(*a*) type of pecuniary advantage which was not supportable on the facts.

(3) Obtaining services by deception

Section 1 of the Theft Act 1978 provides:
(1) A person whom by any deception dishonestly obtains services from another shall be guilty of an offence.
(2) It is an obtaining of services where the other is induced to confer a benefit by doing some act, or causing or permitting some act to be done, on the understanding that the benefit has been or will be paid for.

This offence is designed to deal with the defendant who, by deception, induces another to perform a service either for the defendant or for a third party. It suffices that the deception causes the person deceived to perform the service, or to instruct a third party to perform the service or that because of the deception the defendant is permitted to do something, *e.g.* to enter a cinema without paying. An essential element of the offence is that the service is performed on the understanding that it will be paid for. (An excellent introduction to the three offences under the Theft Act 1978 can be found in J.R. Spencer "The Theft Act 1978" [1979] Crim. L.R. 24.)

A few illustrations should serve to illustrate the scope of the offence:

(i) X deliberately allows a hairdresser to cut his hair, fully intending to leave without paying. Clearly the barber is "induced to do some act" by the deception and there is obviously an understanding that the service will be paid for when it is completed and before the customer leaves the shop. (If he decides to leave without paying only after the haircut is completed then he will commit an offence under section 3, see below, p. 319.)

(ii) The following example is based on a newspaper report. E was a student at school Y where he was studying for his A level examinations. He was dissatisfied with the instruction he was receiving in history and so, putting on the school tie of Z school, he attended the history lessons at that school. The history master at Z school did not realise that there was an interloper in the class and gave the lesson. Did E commit an offence under section 1?

(a) Is he dishonest? This is a question for the jury (see above, p. 284). His wearing of Z school tie tends to suggest that he knows he has no right to be there. But is that enough?

(b) Is there a deception? Clearly he wears the tie to deceive the authorities at Z school into allowing him onto the premises.

(c) Does he obtain a service by the deception? Presumably F was going to deliver his class that day for his own pupils, in which case it would be rather straining the section to say that E's deception deceived F into conferring a benefit upon E. If F had spotted E before the class he would no doubt have expelled E, but that does not seem to be the same as saying that E caused F to perform the act. There is a further difficulty. The Act says that the act must be done on the understanding that it has been or will be paid for. Now F will be paid for by the local authority (if it is a state school) for his work as a teacher. He therefore gives each class on the understanding that he will be paid. It is submitted, however, that this is not what the Act means. It surely means that an understanding exists between the deceiver and the deceived that there will be payment though not necessarily payment made by the deceiver. If X were to go to a car repairers and falsely tell them that he worked for a firm which had an account with that garage, when the mechanics repaired the car it would be because the deception had created in their minds the understanding that they would be paid, not by the rogue, but by his firm. In our school example no such understanding exists and it is submitted that no offence under section 1 is committed.

(iii) H sneaks into a cinema without being observed by the ticket seller. It is probable that this does not amount to an offence under this section. The section requires that somebody provides a service because they have been deceived; but since no-one has seen him enter, how can it be said that anyone has been deceived?

(iv) J by deception persuades his neighbour to drive him to the station. This would only be an offence under this section if there was an understanding between them that J would pay for the service and this is unlikely. If J gets into a taxi intending not to pay at the other end he will obtain the service by deception, but if, by deception at the beginning of the ride, he persuades the taxi driver to carry him free then no offence under section 1 will be committed. (But see Theft Act 1978, s. 2(1)(c), below, p. 318).

(v) K and his secretary book into a local hotel as husband and wife. They know that the hotel is run by people with strict moral principals who would never allow them to stay there if they knew what was afoot. After their night of passion they pay the bill and leave. If the prosecution can establish that K and his secretary were dishonest and that the services were provided because the hoteliers thought that K and his secretary were man and wife, it would appear an offence under section 1 has been committed. Normally, of course, the deception will concern payment for the services, but the statute does not limit it to this. It suffices that the deception causes the service to be performed and that it is a service which is performed on the understanding that it will be paid for and in fact is paid for.

(vi) A visits B, a prostitute, for the purpose of having sexual intercourse and intends to walk off without paying. It is submitted that an offence under section 1 is committed; the section makes no reference to the payment needing to be one which is legally enforceable. (But see also Theft Act 1978, section 3, below, p. 322).

In conclusion we should note that there is a good deal of potential overlap between this section and section 15 of the Theft Act 1968. Thus if D books into a hotel for bed and breakfast intending never to pay, he obtains both goods and services by deception. Again there is no harm in such an overlap provided that common sense is used. In all cases where the accused has obtained property by deception he could be said to have obtained a service, but this is clearly not what is intended. In most cases, however, the correct charge should be obvious. (See also *Harkindel Atwal* (1989)).

(4) Evasion of liability by deception

Section 2 provides an offence to cover the situation where the accused dishonestly and by deception evades a financial obligation. Although the section contains only one offence it may be committed in one of three ways and the prosecution would be expected to make clear in the indictment in which of the three ways it was alleged the accused committed the offence.

Section 2(1)(a)

Section 2(1)(a) covers the situation where D, by any deception, "dishonestly secures the remission of the whole or any part of any existing liability to make payment, whether his own liability or another's."

D's girl friend, E, is £45 in arrears in the rental payments on her flat. D goes to her landlord and falsely tells him that E's mother is slowly dying and that E is having to spend nearly all her money in travelling to care for her mother and this is the reason for her rental arrears. Out of kindness the landlord tells D that he will accept £20 in full settlement of the arrears.

D has committed an offence within the meaning of section 2(1)(a). There is no requirement that the liability which has allegedly been evaded is that of the defendant; this applies to all three subsections. The £45 rental arrears is an existing liability which D had dishonestly tricked the landlord into reducing. Most commentators seem to suggest that the use of the word "remit" in section 2(1)(a) indicates that there must be an agreement by the person deceived either to wipe the slate clean as far as the existing liability is concerned or to make a reduction in the amount of money that will have to be paid. It would not be sufficient that the landlord is tricked into believing that he has already been paid, although this might amount to inducing the landlord to forego payment under s.2(1)(b). He must be aware that there is an existing liability and decide to extinguish or reduce that liability. If the landlord also says that he will accept half rent until the situation alters, this would be an offence under section 2(1)(c) (below, p. 318).

Section 2(1)(b)

Section 2(1)(b) covers the situation where by any deception

the accused "with intent to make permanent default in whole or in part on any existing liability to make payment, or with intent to let another do so, dishonestly induces the creditor or any person claiming payment on behalf of the creditor to wait for payment (whether or not the due date for payment is deferred) or to forego payment."

(i) A has rented a television from B Ltd. for the last four years, paying monthly instalments. He is now five months in arrears of payments and the shop manager has called round to tell him that if he does not give the money owed they will take immediate possession of the set. A is about to emigrate to Australia in three days' time, but is very eager to see the Cup Final on his set the day before he leaves the country. He therefore hands the manager a cheque for the full amount, knowing full well that he has closed that account and that the cheque will be dishonoured. He believes, however, that by the time the cheque is returned to the television company, he will have seen the Cup Final and have left the country for good.

Has he dishonestly and by deception induced the manager to wait for payment on an existing liability? Has he not, in fact, paid the manager by the cheque? Section 2(3) expressly provides for a case in which the creditor is given a cheque in payment; he is to be treated not as one who has been paid but one who has been induced to wait for payment. The answer to the initial question is, therefore, yes. There is, however, one more requirement; the accused must have the intention to make permanent default in whole or in part on any existing liability. In our example, this condition is clearly met. He is simply buying himself time so that he can get out of the country and avoid payment altogether. If, on the other hand, A was short of money and not about to emigrate and so sent his son to the door to tell the manager that his father was away for a few days, intending to pay the bill when he received his monthly salary, then this would not amount to an offence since he had no intention to make permanent default. This is a difficult area. The father who sends his son to the door to tell the rent collector that "dad is out" is clearly dishonest, but should he be treated as a criminal? Parliament decided that he should not be so treated unless the deception was practised with the intention that the debt would never be paid.

(ii) Let us imagine another type of debt situation but one in which the liability A evades is to a prostitute C, for services rendered.

Unfortunately for C, A commits no offence under section 2 because liability is defined in section 2(2) as "legally enforceable liability" and as you will know, the prostitute could not sue A for the recovery of the money owed for her sexual services. And this applies to all three types of evasion of liability under section 2.

(iii) X while driving his car, runs into the back of Y's car, causing about £50 worth of damage. X denies that he was to blame, but he tells Y that to save any bother he will give him a cheque for £30, knowing that the cheque will not be met. Section 2(2) provides that throughout section 2, liability does not include a liability which is not accepted or established (presumably by a court) to pay compensation for a wrongful act or omission. Since X has not accepted that he was to blame for the accident, there is no offence committed under section 2.

(iv) A, who owes B's bookshop £20, dishonestly and falsely tells them that he has paid them already. The manager accepts that his sales staff have made a mistake and enters "paid" in the accounts. This would be an example of dishonestly and by deception inducing another to forego payments (*cf.* section 2(1)(*a*) above, p. 316).

Section 2(1)(*c*)

Section 2(1)(*c*) covers the situation where the accused by any deception "dishonestly obtains any exemption from or abatement of liability to make a payment."

Unlike the other two types of evasion in paragraphs (*b*) and (*c*) this provision makes no reference to an existing liability. It is therefore suitable to cover a situation in which the deception is practised before any liability is incurred with the result that either the liability which is eventually incurred is less than it should have been or that no liability at all is incurred.

(i) A and his friend B are desperate to catch a train. The local station is next to the hospital and so B pretends to be taken ill while A flags down a passing taxi driver. The driver agrees to take them to the hospital free of charge. This would clearly amount to an offence under this provision. But for the deception A and B would have incurred a financial liability for the ride.

(ii) A local authority passes a bye-law under which senior citizens who satisfy certain financial requirements can obtain a pass which will enable them to travel free on local buses. C, a senior citizen, misrepresents the true state of his finances and as a result he is issued with a pass. He commits an offence under this section. He would be liable to pay his fares on any bus journey but for the deception which he has practised on the local authority.

(iii) D gets on board a local bus by flashing a fake season ticket at the driver as he enters. Arguably this case differs from the two previous cases in that here the driver would regard the "season ticket" as evidence that this passenger was under no liability to pay since he would assume that payment had already been made. There is thus no conscious decision on the part of the driver to grant any exemption from or abatement of D's liability to make a payment since he believes that there is no such liability. It would seem more appropriate to charge D with an offence under section 2(1)(b) (by deception inducing the driver to forego payment) or with making off without payment (section 3 of the Theft Act 1978 below) when he leaves the bus at the end of the journey. However the Court of Appeal has held that this would amount to an offence under section 2(1)(c) (see *Sibartie* (1983)).

IV. *MAKING OFF WITHOUT PAYMENT*

Before the Theft Act 1978 came into effect there was a common, and quickly growing, fraud for which the 1968 Act made inadequate provision. The fraud was simplicity itself and consisted merely in making off without paying for goods or services provided. Typical examples are provided by the motorist who, having filled up his tank with petrol, drives away without paying; or by the customer who, having consumed a meal in a restaurant, runs off without settling his bill. If the goods or services are obtained by deception there will usually be an offence under section 15 of the 1968 Act or under section 1 of the 1978 Act (formerly there may have been an offence under section 16(2)(a) of the 1968 Act) but if no deception is made before the goods are obtained or the service provided then these provisions are inapplicable.

On the other hand the law does not in general make it an offence for a debtor dishonestly to resolve not to pay his debts. It is not an offence dishonestly to resolve not to pay the quarterly gas or electricity bill. But since the gas and electricity boards know with whom they are dealing, they can be left to pursue their *civil* remedies and there is no need to make a crime of such conduct. Moreover, if such conduct was made criminal there is a real danger that people who cannot pay, as opposed to those who will not pay, would find themselves in the criminal courts.

Section 3 is accordingly not aimed at dishonest debtors in general but at the kind of debtor who, if he cannot be brought to book on the spot may never be traced and made to pay. Hence the offence of making off is made an arrestable one because without a power of arrest it would, as a practical matter, be impossible to give effect to the section. However, unlike the power of arrest conferred in the case of arrestable offences, section 3(4) does not permit the arrest of a person who has already completed the offence under section 3: *Drameh* (1983).

Section 3(1) provides "a person who, knowing that payment on the spot for any goods supplied or service done is required or expected from him, dishonestly makes off without having paid as required or expected and with intent to avoid payment of the amount due shall be guilty of an offence."

You will note from section 3(1) that there is no requirement of a deception in this offence; it suffices that he dishonestly makes off without payment. Again we can examine the working of the offence by reference to some hypothetical examples.

(i) A eats a meal in a restaurant fully intending to pay. At the end of the meal he discovers that he has come out without any means of paying and so he simply runs out intending to avoid payment. Before the Theft Act 1978 the prosecution would have had to discover some deception on A's part which enabled him to make his escape. Under section 3 no such mental gymnastics are required. The prosecution must prove that the accused knew that payment on the spot was required. It is clear that people eating in a restaurant will expect to pay before they leave. Even if they expect to arrange for credit or to use a credit card, this will clearly be covered by the section as long as the customer knows that he must make some deal with the restaurant owner before he leaves. Secondly, the prosecutor must prove that the accused made off from that spot. (For where payment is expected or required: see *McDavitt* (1981); *Brooks and Brooks* (1983). What will constitute making off will depend upon the facts of the individual case; but there will be no difficulty in holding that a person who runs out of a restaurant without paying has "made off." Thirdly, the prosecutor must establish that the accused was dishonest and fourthly that in making off he did so *with intent to avoid payment.* This last phrase is somewhat ambiguous. It could be interpreted to mean that it was sufficient that the accused intended not to pay when expected or it could mean that the prosecutor must establish that the accused intended never to pay. In *Allen* (1985) the House of Lords held that this ambiguity should be resolved in favour of the defendant; no offence shall be committed unless the prosecutor proves that the accused intended never to pay.

From a practical point of view it may be easier to use this offence even where you suspect that the accused intended to avoid payment even before he ate the meal. Technically, he should be charged with obtaining property by deception which carries a much higher penalty. On the other hand where it is obvious that no use will be made of this greater sentencing power, it may well prove attractive to the prosecution to avoid the need to prove that the deception occurred from the outset. Similarly where the accused drives off from a petrol station without having paid, he may well have committed offences of theft, deception and making off, but the prosecution may well settle for the making off charge.

(ii) G pays for a repair to his car with a cheque which he knows will be dishonoured when presented. The garage owner, however, is quite happy and hands G the keys to the car and G leaves intending never to pay. The issue raised by this example is whether the concept of "making off" is satisfied when the accused leaves with the consent of a person who has been tricked into thinking that he has been paid or does "making off" cover only those cases where the accused leaves without the consent of the victim? This point has not yet been settled by the courts.

(iii) X travels each evening between Leeds and Menston on a local pay train (on such trains the guard issues tickets in the same way that tickets are issued on buses, there being no station staff to collect such tickets at the local stops such as Menston). One evening the train is particularly full and the guard has not reached X by the time the train reaches Menston. X gets out of the train and walks off without paying.

This may seem an obvious example of an offence under section 3, but is it? He clearly makes off without paying (would hiding in the toilet constitute a making off?); a service has been provided for him and payment on the spot was expected. However the section requires that the accused should have acted dishonestly and with intent to avoid payment. You will recall that the word "dishonestly" is a question of fact for the jury (above, p. 284); they will have to consider whether people in general would regard such conduct as dishonest and, if so, whether the defendant knew that this conduct would be so regarded by people in general. It is therefore quite on the cards that a jury would not find the accused to have acted dishonestly. Further it is rather hard to say that he made off with the intention of avoiding payment. Experience may have taught him that it is not advisable to stay on the train to look for the guard since the train will probably move on as soon as other passengers have dismounted. Clearly if he gets off at an earlier station because he sees that the guard will reach him before the train gets to Menston then it will be possible to say that he has dishonestly made off with intent to avoid payment. This may also be the position if, when he alights from the train at Menston he sees the guard standing on the platform ready to receive fares from those who have not yet paid and then deliberately avoids taking the opportunity to pay. This problem clearly raises issues as to the duties owed by persons travelling on buses or such pay trains; is there a duty to seek out the fare-collector? Considerations such as these will affect how the jury tackles the requirements of dishonesty.

(iv) X has just had intercourse with a prostitute who now requires payment. X simply walks off saying "Take me to court and try to get your money." There is no difference in principle between this example and that in number (i). However section 3(3) provides that if the supply of goods or the doing of the service is contrary to law, or if the service done is such that payment is not legally enforceable, then the offence is not committed. Here the prostitute would not be able to sue X to recover damages for breach of contract and so X commits no offence when he walks off. However, if from the outset he intended not to pay, X would probably commit the offence of obtaining services by deception contrary to section 1 of the Act, since no such qualification is expressed to section 1 (above p. 315). Thus in *Troughton* (1987) where the defendant had allegedly made off without paying a taxi fare, it was fatal to the prosecutor's case that the taxi-driver had broken his contract by not taking the accused to his desired destination. In those circumstances he was in no position to demand payment on the spot.

V. BURGLARY AND AGGRAVATED BURGLARY

1. BURGLARY

Burglary is traditionally thought of as breaking and entering a dwelling-house in the night with intent to steal. It was once so defined and separate provision was made for less serious entries where the building was entered by day or where buildings other than dwelling were entered. All these distinctions have been swept away.

Burglary can now be committed in buildings generally, and nothing turns upon whether the entry (for there is no longer any requirement for a breaking) was during the day or night (except that the more alarm the burglars cause the heavier the eventual sentence they may receive). Section 9(1) of the Theft Act 1968 provides for two distinct ways in which burglary may be committed namely by a person who

> "(a) enters a building or part of a building as a trespasser and with intent to commit any such offence as is mentioned in sub-section (2) below. (These are stealing from the building or part of the building, inflicting grievous bodily harm on any person therein, raping any woman therein, or unlawfully damaging the building or anything therein), or
> (b) having entered any building or part of a building as a trespasser he steals or attempts to steal anything in the building or that part of it or inflicts or attempts to inflict on any person therein any grievous bodily harm."

Burglary is, in effect, a form of aggravated trespass. In both types of burglary the prosecution have to prove that the accused has entered a building (or part of the building) either knowing, or being reckless as to the fact that, he is a trespasser. If the charge is brought under section 9(1)(a) the prosecution must, in addition, prove that at the time he entered the building the accused intended (and here recklessness will not suffice) to commit one of the offences specified in section 9(2) which are listed above. If the charge is brought under section 9(1)(b) the accused must be shown to have actually committed one of the offences specified in paragraph (b) and at the time of committing the offence he either knew that he entered as a trespasser or was reckless as to that fact.

We shall now consider the elements which are common to both forms of burglary, namely (1) entry; (2) trespassing; (3) a building; (4) part of a building.

(1) Enters

In both forms of burglary the prosecution must prove that the accused entered the building as a trespasser. Under section

9(1)(a) they must prove that the accused entered and that at the time he either knew that he was a trespasser or was reckless as to that fact. Under section 9(1)(b) the prosecution must prove that at the time of committing the specified offence he knew that he had entered as a trespasser or was at least reckless as to that fact.

The prosecution must prove that the accused actually entered the building in question. As with many elements of criminal offences this will pose no great problems in the general run of cases since the accused will be apprehended in the building or some days later when he has actually removed property from the building. However on occasion it may be difficult to say whether or not there has actually been an entry into the building within the meaning of section 9.

There are various possible views as to what constitutes an entry. One view is that entry requires that the accused, A, should be entirely within the building. On this view, if he still had so much as a foot on the window ledge outside the building he would not be guilty of the complete offence though he would be guilty of an attempt. Another view is that A has entered if any part of his body is within the building; on this view A would be guilty should his hand, or even his fingertips, penetrate beyond the door or window. The one case on this point (*Collins* (1973)) holds that there must be "an effective and substantial" entry which seems to suggest a half-way house between these two views. As a practical test it seems to be less satisfactory than either of the two first suggested tests because it is not clear cut. Whether A's body is entirely within the building or whether any part of his body has penetrated the building, admit of definite answers; but whether enough of his body is within the building so as to constitute an effective and substantial entry must be something on which views may differ. The subsequent decision of the Court of Appeal in *Brown* (1985), in which it was said that "substantial" did not materially assist in the matter, but that a jury should be directed that in order to convict they must be satisfied that the entry was "effective," would appear to add little in the way of clarification to the matter.

A further complication is introduced where A employs an innocent agent. A might, for example, employ a boy below the age of criminal responsibility to enter the building and bring out property to him. In such a case it must be tempting to use the innocent agency principle (above p. 116) and conclude that this is to be treated as an entry by A himself. Suppose, then, that

A, while remaining outside the building, uses some instrument to withdraw property from the building. Is it to be said that, by parity of reasoning, the implement is to be regarded like the boy so that its insertion into the building is to be regarded as an entry by A himself? Since burglary may now be committed when there is an entry with intent to do serious bodily harm, is A guilty of burglary when the bullet from his gun, fired from the highway, enters the victim's house?

If regard is paid to the wording of section 9, it would appear that these last two illustrations cannot constitute burglary. A person is guilty of burglary if "he enters" with certain intents, or "having entered... he" commits certain offences. To hold that "he" enters or has entered when an instrument is inserted by him would seem to be at odds with what the section expressly requires.

It is further suggested that the natural meaning of the words employed in the section require a complete entry by A. "Enters" or "having entered" means just that; it can hardly be supposed to mean "being in the process of entering" or "having half-entered." If A is in the process of entering he may always be convicted of an attempt.

Where an innocent agent (the boy under the age of criminal responsibility) is employed the same argument should hold good. The "he" referred to in section 9 is the person who is charged with burglary and "he" has not entered the building.

(2) As a trespasser

The word trespass is largely a civil law concept. It basically means entry on to property which is in the possession of another without the consent of that other. At civil law it would not be a defence to show that you had entered by mistake. So does this mean that for purposes of burglary the prosecution need show only that the accused was, by civil law definitions a trespasser? Fortunately the Theft Act seems to be one area in which the courts have adopted a subjective approach and in prosecutions under section 9 the prosecution will have to prove that the accused was at least (*Cunningham*) reckless as to the fact of being a trespasser; in other words he was aware of facts which might mean he was trespassing. If the prosecution is brought under section 9(1)(*a*) of the Theft Act the prosecution must prove that he was reckless as to being a trespasser at the time he entered the building. In the case of a prosecution under section 9(1)(b) the prosecution would have to prove that at the time he committed the offence inside the building he was reckless as to his entry being as a trespasser. If the accused mistakenly thinks that he has the consent of the owner to entering, even if his mistake is unreasonable, he should not be convicted; equally if he believes that he is entering his own house, since then he would not even consider the issue of consent. More problematical is the situation where the accused is invited into the house by a person who has no right to give that consent. Again the answer should be that if the accused honestly believes that he has entered with consent he should not be convicted. In *Jones and Smith* (1976) the accused and an accomplice were charged with and convicted of burglary, the offence consisting of stealing TV sets from the house of Smith's father. At the trial it was accepted that Smith's father had given his son a sort of blanket permission to enter his house. So how could you say he entered as a trespasser? James L.J. said that the jury were entitled to hold that the son and his friend were trespassing if they found they had entered the premises of another knowing that they were entering in excess of the permission that had been given to them, or being reckless whether they were so entering. Here it is clear that his father's permission to enter did not extend to entry for the purpose of stealing and the son and friend well knew this.

Where X is charged under section 9(1)(b) it would seem that *mens rea* to entry as a trespasser is not needed until the moment the crime is committed. So that if X enters a building thinking he has the consent to enter it would suffice that he realised that he did not have consent by the time he committed the theft inside.

Yet more difficulties arise where X manages to gain entry by deceiving the owner. Suppose that X enters Y's house by pretending to be the gas meter reader. In a way he enters not by force but with the consent of the owner, but on the other hand he is fully aware that the owner would not have let him in had he known the truth. It is suggested that there should be no difficulty in saying that X entered knowing that he was a trespasser. Does this mean that if X enters a supermarket intending to steal from within, he commits burglary as he enters? X knows that if the shopkeeper knew of his intentions he would not allow him into the shop and his case is thus not really different from the example of the gas meter reader. The major difficulty here is that the jury will have to be sure that he had that intention when he entered the store, and once the rogue has actually hidden a bottle of Scotch in his coat, the offence of theft is usually sufficient to deal with him.

Now that we have considered some of the rules surrounding the offence of burglary it might be helpful to examine a decision in which many of the above points arose in a somewhat bizarre factual setting. *Collins* (1973) was a young man who had been out drinking heavily into the early hours of the morning. On his way home he passed the house where he knew lived a girl he rather fancied. He found a ladder in the garden of the house and placed it against a window he thought might be the girl's bedroom. He climbed the ladder and seeing her lying naked on the bed he climbed down again, removed all his clothes, except for his socks, and climbed back up. The girl awoke to see the frame of a naked man with an erect penis silhouetted against the window. She took it to be her boyfriend who was in the habit of paying her ardent nocturnal visits. She therefore bade him enter. He climbed into the room and had intercourse with the girl. It was only after the act of intercourse that the girl realised that it was not her boyfriend. Collins was charged with burglary. It seems that there was evidence upon which the jury were entitled to find that he intended to have intercourse with her whether or not she consented, but the Court of Appeal held that the jury had not been properly directed on the question of entry as a trespasser. It was clear that Collins was kneeling on the window sill when the invitation was made, but it was not clear whether at that moment he was on the part of the sill which was inside the bedroom. To a layman this is just the sort of distinction which causes the law to seem absurd. However the fact remains that if he had crossed the centre line of the sill before the invitation was made, he had entered the building as a trespasser and then the jury would have had to consider whether or not he did intend to have sexual intercourse with the girl whether or not she consented. The Court of Appeal ruled that since the jury had not been asked to consider the question of whether he entered as a trespasser, the conviction had to be quashed. Clearly the girl made the invitation under a mistake and possibly Collins should have realised this, but so long as he honestly believed he had consent to enter before he made "an effective and substantial entry" he did not commit the offence of burglary. This can be contrasted with *Jones and Smith* above, p. 326; in that case they knew they had no permission to enter and to steal; here, Collins must have assumed that any girl who would invite a naked male with an erect penis into her bedroom was giving consent to his entry for the purpose of intercourse (but see Williams, *Textbook of Criminal Law, (2nd. Ed.)* pp. 845 *et seq.*). It was up to the prosecution to prove that he did enter before he was invited. As one commentator put it, this case lends a new meaning to the old maxim that the law varies with the length of the Chancellor's foot.

(3) A building

Under the law before 1968 burglary could only be committed from a dwelling-house. The new Act is not so restricted, and burglary can be committed in a building or part of a building.

Little would be gained here in trying to give an exhaustive definition of what constitutes a building. It is a word generally used to convey some idea of permanence, and probably there is a requirement of a roof, but beyond this no firm guidelines can be given. Clearly burglary can now be committed from such places as offices, barns, garages. A tent, on the other hand, although it may constitute a dwelling is probably not sufficiently permanent to be regarded as a building. (See *B. and S.* v. *Leathley* (1979)).

The Act specifically extends the definition of buildings to cover inhabited vessels or vehicles, including the times when the person who inhabits them is not there. The word "inhabited" does, however seem to require that the vehicle at the time of the entry is used as a dwelling, and it would not therefore cover an ordinary car or a dormobile which is being used as a form of transport at the time. But if a family use their dormobile as an ordinary form of transport for 50 weeks in the year but as a holiday home for the other two, it would be an inhabited vehicle for those two weeks. In *Norfolk Constabulary* v. *Seekings and Gould* (1986) the definition of "building" did not extend to two articulated lorry trailers which for a year were used by a supermarket as temporary storerooms. Although they remained static, with steps attached and with an electricity supply, the court held they were still vehicles and as such they only constituted "buildings" if they were inhabited.

(4) Or part of a building

The Act provides that the accused must have entered a building or part of a building as a trespasser. This second part is designed to cover situations where the accused is lawfully entitled to be in one part of the building but not in another. For example if X is a student in a hall of residence he will be entitled to enter his own room and those parts of the hall designed for common use and connecting corridors, but he will not be entitled a fellow student's room without permission. Thus if he goes into student Y's room to steal money from his desk, he would enter Y's room as a trespasser. He has therefore entered a part of the building as a trespasser and thus he would commit burglary as well as theft. One problem arising out of the use of the concept of parts of a building is that where the prosecution are alleging that the accused has entered part of a building as a trespasser with intent to steal contrary to section 9(1)(a), they must prove that he intended to steal from that part. Suppose that X enters a department store intending only to purchase some gardening equipment. While in the store, where he is legally entitled to be, he conceives a plan to steal money from the manager's office. To reach this office he must first pass through the staff common room which like the manager's office is out of bounds. If X is apprehended in the staff room and confesses that he was on his way to the manager's office can we say that he has entered a part of the building intending to steal in that part, or is the manager's office another part? Possibly the most sensible answer in cases such as these is to treat the building as having two parts—one part where customers are entitled to be, and the other part which is for staff only. If this interpretation is adopted, then as soon as X enters the staff room he has entered a part of the building he is not entitled to enter, and this part includes the manager's office. In *Walkington* (1979) the accused was charged with burglary from a till in a department store. The till was standing on a three-sided counter and the questions for the jury were (1) did the management regard the floor area within the three sides of the counter as being restricted to staff; (2) if the answer to (1) was yes, then did the accused realise that this area was so restricted and (3) if he did, did he enter it with intent to steal from it?

(5) Mens rea

Apart from a trespassory entry which has already been considered the offence of burglary requires an intention to commit one of the specified offences. Burglary is no longer confined to cases where the intention is to commit theft and it will be noted that this range of specified offences is wider under section 9(1)(*a*) than under section 9(1)(*b*). (For discussion of conditional intent, see above p. 289).

2. *AGGRAVATED BURGLARY*

Section 10 of the Theft Act 1968 provides for the offence of aggravated burglary which carries a possible maximum sentence of life imprisonment. A person is guilty of aggravated burglary if he commits any burglary and at the time has with him any firearm, any weapon of offence, or any explosive (see *Francis* (1982)). Whereas burglary under section 9 is in some senses a form of aggravated trespass, section 10 is designed both to deter would-be burglars from taking offensive weapons with them when they burgle a house and to enable the court to reflect in the sentence the full fact that burglary where offensive weapons are carried is a far more serious offence than when they are not.

VI. *MAKING UNWARRANTED DEMANDS WITH MENACES: BLACKMAIL*

Section 21 of the Theft Act 1968 provides:

> (1) A person is guilty of blackmail if, with a view to gain for himself or another or with intent to cause loss to another, he makes any unwarranted demand with menaces; and for this purpose a demand with menaces is unwarranted unless the person making it does so in the belief—
> (a) that he has reasonable grounds for making the demand; and
> (b) that the use of the menaces is a proper means of reinforcing the demand.

The word "blackmail" is a word commonly used in everday language to describe a situation in which X is threatening Y with unpleasant consequences unless Y does what X wants. This is, in fact, the gist of blackmail under section 21, but as we shall see the scope of the offence is somewhat more restricted than the everyday use of the term.

Suppose that one evening as he was driving home X is involved in an accident with Y. X demands that Y admit liability for the accident but Y refuses, whereupon X says he will call the police. Y asks him not to do this as he has been drinking that evening and he cannot risk a breath test since he is a driving instructor. X repeats his demand that unless Y signs a written statement admitting liability, X will now certainly call the police. Y agrees. Has X committed an offence under the section? We can examine each element that the prosecution must prove in turn:

(1) There must be a demand

This will generally present no problems and the word will be given its ordinary meaning. What is required is that the accused acts in such a way as to demonstrate that he wants the victim to do something. It does not matter whether the request is made in the form of an order or a humble plea. The offence is demanding with menaces and so it does not matter whether the request is complied with or even that it was heard, provided that it was made. It is immaterial whether it was made orally or in writing. Where it is made in writing and sent through the post the demand is made as soon as the letter is posted and it continues to be made until it is received. Thus if A posts, in England, a demand to B in America, the demand is made and therefore the offence is committed in England; if the facts are reversed the offence is committed in England at the latest when the letter reaches England (*see Treacy* (1971)). Thus in our case X has clearly made a demand.

(2) The demand must be accompanied by menaces

This does not mean that there must be a threat of violence; it is sufficient that something detrimental or unpleasant is threatened. (*Thorne* v. *Motor Traders Association* (1937). The use of the word "menaces" however rather than "threats" suggests that there might be certain threats which would be too trivial to be classed as menaces. In *Garwood* (1987) the Court of Appeal considered threats made by the defendant to a youth the jury considered to be unduly timid. The Court held that in the majority of cases the judge would not need to spend time in defining "menaces." However, there were two cases where guidance would be needed. The first was where the threats, although likely to affect the mind of a normal person, did not affect the defendant's; this would clearly amount to "menaces." The second is where the threats are unlikely to have affected the mind of a person of normal stability, but have affected the particular victim because he was unduly susceptible. In this type of case it all depends upon the knowledge of the defendant. If he knows the likely effect of his actions on the victim, then what he has done constitutes menaces. Thus a threat to expose A's sexual perversions would probably influence most stable citizens, but a threat to poison A's pet budgie may be an example of a threat which would only be a menace if the accused knew that A, an old lady, was very timid and devoted to the budgie.

In our example X had clearly reinforced the demands with menaces which he knows will influence Y to comply with the demands.

(3) The demand must be made with a view to gain for the maker or another, or with intent to cause loss to another

The words gain and loss are defined by section 34(2) of the Act as being restricted to gains and losses in money or other property; the gain or loss may be temporary or permanent. Gain includes a gain by keeping what one has, as well as a gain by getting what one has not; and loss includes a loss by not getting what one might get as well as a loss by parting with what one has. Thus if A threatens to expose B's cheating in an examination if she does not have sexual intercourse with him, this will not be a gain under section 21, but if his demand is for the £50 which she owes him then it may be an offence under section 21 even though the money is legally owed to him. It would appear that so long as the defendant is demanding money or other property, his ulterior motive will be irrelevant. Thus, in *Bevans (Ronald)* (1988) B went to a doctor's surgery and, at gun point, demanded to be injected with a pain-killing drug. The Court of Appeal upheld the trial judge's direction to the jury that "with a view to gain" related to money or other property and that the drug could clearly constitute property. It was irrelevant that his ulterior motive had been the relief of pain and not economic gain. He had clearly made his demand with a view to gain and he certainly intended to cause the doctor loss.

Difficulties may arise when the thing demanded is not money or other property. Here it may be necessary to examine the defendant's motives. For example if he is demanding that the woman marry him, his demand could properly be said to be made with a view to gain if she was an heiress and the demand was made with a view to getting his hands on her money. However it may be that the monetary gain can become to remote, as where A threatens Professor B that he will expose him as a homosexual if he does not give him a place as a student in the university law school. Presumably A will be hoping to earn good money with the law degree he will obtain in a few years time—but it is likely that the court would hold that this monetary gain is too remote.

Thus again in our original example it would appear that the demand is made by X with a view to monetary gain.

(4) The demand must be unwarranted

If the accused raises the issue that the demand was not unwarranted then the prosecution must prove either that the accused did not believe that he had reasonable grounds for making the claim or, if he did, that he did not believe that it was proper to use menaces as a means of reinforcing the demand. In the majority of cases it is likely that the accused will believe that he had reasonable grounds for making the claim, Even a prostitute or bookmaker, who knows that the courts would not enforce the demand, may genuinely believe that they have the right to demand payment for a "debt of honour." It is far more likely that the accused will know that he should not have used menaces as a means of reinforcing the demand. In *Harvey and Others* (1981) the Court of Appeal held that no act which the accused believed to be a crime could be considered by him to be a proper means of enforcing the demand. However, even here, it is for the jury to decide what the accused actually believed. Thus, in practice, the more serious the threat, the less likely the jury are to believe that the accused considered his conduct to be "proper."

In our example X probably believes he has the right to demand a statement admitting liability—if he believes that Y was the cause of the accident. More likely the crucial question will be whether he honestly believed that the use of menaces was a proper means of backing up the demand. In our example it is quite possible that X believed his threats were proper. The test is for the jury to ask themselves did the accused actually believe that he was acting in a socially acceptable way. Thus the lower the accused's standards, the less likely he is to be convicted. If X had said he would have Y beaten up if he did not sign a statement, it is less likely that the jury would believe that he honestly thought this was a proper way of reinforcing his demands.

VII. *HANDLING*

When thieves have got away with their stolen property, the next step is to dispose of it. Clearly, if the stolen property is money there will be no difficulty, but where the property is readily identifiable there is every danger that the thief will get caught trying to sell it or use it. It is for this reason that specialist criminals exist whose function is to dispose of the goods for the original thieves. These are the persons regularly known as "fences." In some respects these people are a greater social menace than the original thieves since without them the thieves would have to dispose of the stolen property personally and might find the whole enterprise less attractive and rewarding. Most fences probably commit theft in relation to the property they deal with, but this is not always the case and this fact, coupled with the generally accepted need to be able to punish big time fences more severely than the thieves for whom they act, has led to the creation of a separate offence. Until 1968 this was known as "receiving" but under the Theft Act 1968 its scope has been increased and it is now termed handling. The basic offence is defined by section 22 of the Act which provides:

"(1) A person handles stolen goods if (otherwise than in the course of the stealing) knowing or believing them to be stolen he dishonestly receives the goods, or dishonestly undertakes or assists in their retention, removal, disposal or realisation by or for the benefit of another person, or if he arranges to do so."

A person who is convicted under this section is liable to up to 14 years' imprisonment. It should be noted that while there are about 18 methods of handling stolen goods outlined in this section, there is only one offence.

1. THE ACTUS REUS OF HANDLING

(1) Stolen goods

"Goods" for the purpose of section 22 are defined to include "money and every other description of property except land,

and includes things severed from the land by stealing" (section 34(2)(*b*)). Subject to minor exceptions goods which may be handled extends to the same property that may be the subject of theft.

Such goods must be "stolen" and for this purpose goods are not only stolen when obtained in circumstances amounting to theft but also when they are obtained by blackmail or by deception contrary to section 15(1) (section 24(4)). Provision is also made for goods stolen abroad which are brought to this country.

Not only must the prosecution establish that the goods were at some time "stolen" as defined in section 24, they must prove that they were "stolen" at the time of the handling. Problems can arise when the act which is alleged to constitute the handling occurs either before the goods have been stolen or at a time when the law deems that the property has ceased to have the characteristics of stolen property. Thus in *Park* (1988) the defendant was charged with handling certain property in that he had arranged to deal with the property in a way prohibited under section 22. His conviction was quashed because at the time he made the arrangement the money could not yet be described as stolen property.

In relation to handling property after it has ceased to be stolen section 24 provides that goods which may have been "stolen" within the meaning of section 24(4) may cease to be stolen in one of three ways, namely where

(i) they have been restored to the person from whom they were stolen; or

(ii) they have been restored to other lawful possession or custody; or

(iii) the person from whom they were stolen (or anyone claiming through him) ceases to have any right to restitution of the goods.

Other lawful possession or custody in (ii) covers the situation in which the police recover the stolen property. Here and in (i) the major difficulty is to decide when the property has actually been restored either to its owner or to other lawful possession. The problem was considered in *Att.-Gen.'s Reference (No. 1 of 1974)* (1974). A police officer suspecting, correctly as it turned out, that the goods in the back of a car were stolen, immobilised the car and kept watch for the driver. When the driver arrived the officer questioned him and, because the driver's replies were unsatisfactory, he arrested him. It was held that in such a case the jury should be invited to consider whether the officer had taken custody of the goods before the driver returned or whether he had postponed the decision to take custody until he had the chance of confirming or disaffirming his suspicions by questioning the suspect. Merely to prevent the suspect from having access to the goods until questions are asked is not necessarily to take possession of the goods.

Sometimes the owner, or the police, become aware that A has stolen the goods but, with a view to catching the handler as well, follow the goods to their destination. Such conduct by the owner or police does not constitute a resumption of possession and the receiver may be convicted of handling.

An illustration of property ceasing to be stolen under (iii) would be where X has obtained property from Y under a contract which is voidable because of X's deception. If, when he realises what has happened, Y ratified the contract, he would cease to have any rights in the property and at that stage the property would cease to be stolen.

Section 24(3) contains some rather complex rules concerning the proceeds of stolen goods. Two examples will serve to illustrate the general idea of the section. If X steals a car and then sells that car, the money he receives in exchange will be stolen goods and so will the car. Equally, if the handler of stolen property exchanges it for other property, the newly acquired property will be classified as stolen goods. Where, however, stolen property comes into the hands of someone who is not a thief or handler (for example because he is totally unaware that the property is stolen) then although the property is still stolen property, anything he acquires in exchange for it does not become stolen property:

(2) Handling

The prosecution must prove that the accused handled the stolen property. While goods may be handled in a wide variety of ways, these ways fall into two groups:

(a) *Received or arranged to receive*

This is the clearest example of handling. If the prosecution allege that the accused received the goods they will have to show that he took them into his possession whether personally or by his agents. It is a question of fact and degree for the jury to decide whether the alleged receiver had possession or control of the goods. If the accused has not actually received the goods and has not yet done enough to be charged with an attempt he may nevertheless have arranged to receive. Thus a typical case of arranging to receive would be where the thief has got in touch with a fence and has arranged to deliver the property to the fence who will then dispose of it. But you should remember that the goods must be stolen at the time of the arrangement.

(b) *Undertakes or assists in their retention, removal, disposal or realisation by or for the benefit of another person, or arranges to do so*

This form of handling casts the net very wide. Assist would seem to suggest a situation in which the accused joins forces with the thief or other handlers and works with them; undertakes on the other hand would seem more suitable to cover the situation where the accused has acted on his own. A few illustrations will serve to show how this part of the section works.

X negotiates with Y that Y will buy stolen property from the thief Z. X has undertaken the disposal of stolen goods for the benefit of Z.

X helps Y, the thief, store stolen property in a barn where it will stay until the police search dies down. X will have assisted Y in the retention of the stolen goods.

X lends Y, the thief, a van to take the stolen goods abroad. X has assisted Y in the removal of the stolen goods.

The section, however, goes further, if, X arranges to do any of the above acts he will also be guilty of handling. Thus, in the first example, if X agreed with Z that he would try to find him a buyer, X has arranged to undertake the disposal of the goods for Z.

Where the prosecution is relying on forms of handling other than receiving or arranging to receive, he must prove that the acts were done by or for the benefit of another person. If these words were not present it would mean that thieves who tried to dispose of their goods would automatically become handlers. Thus, if X had stolen a painting and he approached

Y to see if Y would buy the painting, he would have undertaken the disposal of the painting. However, the addition of the words by or for the benefit of another mean that X is not a handler since he has only undertaken the disposal of the painting for his own benefit. In each of the examples discussed above the acts were done by or for the benefit of another (see *Bloxham* (1983)).

(c) *Otherwise than in the course of the stealing*

All forms of handling are subject to the requirement that the act which constitutes the handling must not be in the course of the stealing. If these words were not present, it would mean that if X and Y were to burgle Barclays Bank and X handed Y the money from the safe, Y would be guilty of handling. This phrase is similar to that used in the definiton of robbery and it is suggested that it should be given the same interpretation (see above, p. 293). Thus, in our example of X and Y burgling Barclays Bank, the stealing would presumably be deemed to continue until at least they have left the premises and possibly whilst they are making their getaway. (In *Cash* (1985) the Court of Appeal held that the prosecution do not always have to prove this element in every case. Only where the jury have to decide whether the accused is a thief or a handler, is it likely to be relevant. This has recently been followed by the Privy Council in *Att.-Gen. for Hong Kong* v. *Yip Kai-Foon* (1988)).

2. THE MENS REA OF HANDLING

A person is guilty of handling if he dishonestly receives, etc., the *stolen* goods knowing or believing them to be stolen. Notice that the goods must be proved to be stolen goods at the time of the handling. A person may believe goods to be stolen even where they are not; such a person cannot be convicted of the completed offence of handling. Can he be convicted of attempted handling (see above, p. 203)?

(1) Knowing or believing that the goods were stolen

The expression *knowing or believing* has caused many

problems for the courts and the Court of Appeal has shown a great reluctance to give clear guidance to trial judges in the correct way to direct juries on this issue. However in *Hall* (1987) the Court said that a person might be said to *know* that goods were stolen when he was told by someone with first hand knowledge. Belief is something short of this, but not much short. It might be the state of mind of a man who said to himself, "I cannot say I know for certain that those goods are stolen, but there can be no other reasonable conclusion in the light of all the circumstances of all that I have heard and seen." It would even be enough that the defendant had said to himself, "despite all that I have seen and heard, I refuse to believe what my brain tells me is obvious." What will certainly not suffice is a finding that the accused *suspected* that the goods were stolen. Possibly the trial judge will not go far wrong if he follows the statement of Glanville Williams: "The preferable view is that [the section] extends the notion of knowledge to the case where the defendant, while lacking explicit information, is virtually certain in his own mind that the fact exists" (*Textbook of Criminal Law* (2nd ed., 1983), p. 875). In *Toor* (1987) the Court of Appeal said that it will often be unnecessary for the trial judge to give a full direction along the lines of *Hall*. However, where in the trial much reference has been made to "suspicion," the trial judge should ensure that the jury fully appreciate the meaning of the word "believing."

(2) Dishonesty

This is a question of fact for the jury though it will normally add nothing to the requirement that the prosecution must prove that the accused knew or believed that the goods were stolen. However, if X received goods knowing that they were stolen, but intending to return them to their true owner, the jury would no doubt find that X was not dishonest. (See also *Roberts* (1987)).

(3) Proof of mens rea

"Stolen goods frequently pass quickly from hand to hand. Many of those who deal in them knowing or believing them to be stolen tell lies when they are asked to explain how the goods came into their possession. Others prefer to give no explanation. This has been the experience of the courts for generations. So when a defendant is found to have been in possession of goods recently stolen and either gives no explanation of how he came to acquire them innocently or gives an explanation which is patently untrue, it is the practice of judges to tell juries that they may, if they think it right, infer that he acquired them knowing or believing that they were stolen." (*per* McCullough J. in *Ball* (1983)).

This is the so-called doctrine of recent possession. It is really misnamed since it has nothing to do with goods recently *possesed*, but with goods recently *stolen*. It is not even a doctrine, but simply an application of general principles relating to circumstantial evidence. In other words it is an invitation to the jury to draw certain common sense conclusions, if they see fit to do so.

In addition to this common law doctrine of recent possession, section 27(3) of the Theft Act 1968 provides for the reception of evidence, which would otherwise be inadmissible, to assist the jury in their search for the *mens rea* of handling. This section provides:

"Where a person is being proceeded against for handling stolen goods (but not for any offence other than handling stolen goods), then at any stage of the proceedings, if evidence has been given of his having or arranging to have in his possession the goods the subject of the charge, or of his undertaking or assisting in, or arranging to undertake or assist in, their retention, removal disposal or realisation, the following evidence shall be admissible for the purpose of proving that he knew or believed the goods to be stolen goods:

(*a*) evidence that he has had in his possession, or has undertaken or assisted in the retention, removal, disposal or realisation of, stolen goods from any theft taking place not earlier than twelve months before the offence charged; and

(*b*) (provided that seven days' notice in writing has been given to him of the intention to prove the conviction) evidence that he has within the five years preceding the date of the offence charged been convicted of theft or of handling stolen goods."

VIII. *OTHER OFFENCES UNDER THE THEFT ACT 1968*

In this chapter on the offences under the Theft Acts we have concentrated on the basic offences. It is important to remember that there are other offences under the Theft Act 1968 which have not been covered. In outline these offences are:

(1) Offences of temporary deprivation

You will recall that a charge of theft requires that the prosecution prove that the accused intended permanently to deprive the other of the property. There were those who argued that this element should be dropped from the definition of theft in the 1968 Act, but it was finally decided that it should form part of the new definition of theft. However it was decided that specific offences should be provided for two examples of temporary deprivation. Under section 11 it is an offence to remove articles from places open to the public. This is clearly designed to cover such cases as where a rogue removes a famous painting from an art gallery and offers to return it only upon payment of a ransom. Under section 12 it is an offence to take a motor vehicle or other conveyance without the consent of the owner. Before this provision there was very little the police could do about the rogue who "borrowed" another's car for a joyride and then left it where it was eventually found and returned to the owner. With a car it was very difficult to show that such a rogue intended permanently to deprive the other of the car. Of course it was possible to charge him with stealing the amount of petrol used, but this was hardly satisfactory. Under section 12 he now commits a substantive offence. It is also an offence for a person who knows that a motor vehicle has been taken without the owner's consent, to drive it or to allow himself to be driven in it.

(2) Abstracting electricity

Under section 13 it is an offence dishonestly to use electricity without authority, or dishonestly to cause the electricity to be diverted or wasted. Such a section was needed because electricity is not property within the definition of property under section 4 of the Act; it cannot therefore be stolen. Gas and water, on the other hand, are items of property within section 4

and are capable of being stolen. Thus it would be an offence
under this section for a tramp who has broken into premises for
a night's shelter to turn on the electric fire (if it was a gas fire he
could be charged with stealing the gas); or for students involved
in a sit-in to operate without authority any electrical equipment.

(3) Business frauds

Sections 17 to 20 provide for a number of offences relating to
commercial fraud such as false accounting (s.17) liability of
company officers (sections 18 and 19) and suppression of
documents (section 20).

(4) Advertising rewards

Under section 23 of the Act it is an offence to advertise
publicly a reward for the return of stolen property or lost
property, where the words used have the effect of promising
immunity from apprehension or inquiry, or that any money paid
for the purchase of the goods or advanced by way of loan on
the goods will be repaid. The offence is committed by anyone
who advertises the reward and anyone who publishes or prints
it.

(5) Going equipped for stealing

Under section 25 of the Act it is an offence for a person not
at his place of abode to have with him any article for use in the
course of or in connection with any burglary, theft or cheat.
This offence clearly allows the police to stop a suspected burglar
well before he has begun to force open the window of a
dwelling house, though the maximum sentence of three years is
far less than that available if they apprehend him having entered
a building as a trespasser. (See *Doukas* (1978) for an illustration
of the width of the offence and also *Minor* v. *D.P.P.* (1988)).

(6) Restitution and compensation

Under section 28 of the Theft Act 1968 the court may order
that the stolen property should be returned to its rightful owner
or if this is not possible that the victim should be compensated
by money from the convicted offender; also that where the

court orders that restitution be made, that the convicted person should compensate the person who gave good value for the goods which are now being taken from him to be returned to the rightful owner.

CHAPTER 11

CRIMINAL DAMAGE TO PROPERTY

IN this chapter we shall look briefly at some of the provisions of the Criminal Damage Act 1971 which covers, amongst other matters, the damaging or destroying of property. As we saw in the previous chapter it is possible to steal property belonging to another by destroying it so that he is permanently deprived of the property. However, where the property is not destroyed, theft would not be committed and in any case it is asking too much of the law of theft to cover all instances of vandalism and damage to property. Until 1971 offences of damage to property were known as offences of malicious damage; these were to a large extent repealed by the Criminal Law Act 1971 and the offence is now called criminal damage. We shall now look at the basic offences and defences in this Act. (For an excellent survey of these offences see "Criminal Damage" by Professor Elliott, [1988] Crim.L.R. 404).

1. THE BASIC OFFENCE

Section 1(1) provides that "A person who without lawful excuse destroys or damages any property belonging to another intending to destroy or damage any such property or being reckless as to whether any such property would be destroyed or damaged shall be guilty of an offence." This offence is punishable under section 4 by imprisonment for 10 years (see also above, p. 8).

(1) Actus reus

The prosecution must establish (i) damage or destruction of (ii) property belonging to another (iii) absence of lawful excuse.

(a) *Damage or destruction*

The word destroy would tend to suggest some irreparable damage which renders the property in question useless. Thus if D sets fire to P's car so that it is completely burned out, it can properly be said that D has destroyed the car, even though there may still be a metal shell. Damage, on the other hand, suggests any physical harm which produces impairment of the property's use or value. If D scratched his name on P's car, this can clearly be described as damaging the car in that its value has been clearly reduced. In *Cox* v. *Riley* (1986) it was held that erasing the memory from a plastic circuit card which controlled a computerised saw constituted damage. Difficulties may arise when the harm inflicted is trivial and may, for example, be easily rectified. Several cases concerning graffiti have appeared before the courts and the results are not easy to reconcile. In *Roe* v. *Kingerlee* (1986) the court held that "What constitutes criminal damage is a matter of fact and degree, and it is for the justices, applying their common sense to decide whether what has happened was damage or not." It is not necessarily fatal to the prosecution's case that the harm is rectifiable. However, where the harm can be easily remedied, as in *A. (Juvenile)* v. *The Queen* (1978) where the defendant spat on a policeman's raincoat, it might be a reason for holding that there has been no damage.

(b) *Property belonging to another*

Section 10 says that property of a tangible nature, whether real or personal, and including money, may be the subject of a charge of criminal damage. Wild animals, which are covered by section 4(4) of the Theft Act 1968, are covered but not wild flowers as under section 4(3) of the Theft Act (see above, p. 273). It was noted earlier that there is no clear answer to the question of whether or not a corpse is capable of being stolen (above, p. 271). If, as was suggested, there is no reason why a corpse should not be capable of being stolen, then it should be equally capable of being criminally damaged. (It was reported in *The Times* for December 27, 1984 that a Welsh presbyterian Minister had been charged, *inter alia*, with criminally damaging a corpse.)

In general terms you cannot be guilty of destroying your own property under this provision. Thus if you own a valuable building you may knock it down to build a car park without committing an offence under this provision. (You may, however, have committed an offence against other regulations designed to preserve particular buildings or property.) However section 10(2) goes on to provide that in certain cases you may be guilty of an offence of damaging your own property if the property is in the custody or control of another or if another has a proprietary right or interest in it or if another has a charge over it. Thus a landlord who has leased his house to Y may be guilty of criminal damage to that property if he deliberately damages it.

(c) *Without lawful excuse*

It is part of the prosecution's case that they prove that the accused had no lawful excuse either by virtue of common law or under section 5 of the Criminal Damage Act 1971. This will be discussed after we have considered the other offences (below p. 351).

(2) Mens rea

The prosecution must prove that the accused intended to destroy or damage the property or that he was reckless as to whether the property would be destroyed or damaged. The word *intention* needs no further explanation here (see above, p. 53). It is necessary, however, to make one or two comments about the meaning of "recklessness" in criminal damage. Until the decision of the House of Lords in *Caldwell* (1982) a subjective interpretation had prevailed (see *e.g. David Smith* (1974)). In *Caldwell*, however, it will be recalled that Lord Diplock said that this interpretation of the word recklessness in modern statutes was too narrow. He said that a person was "reckless as to whether or not any property would be destroyed or damaged if (1) he does an act which in fact creates an obvious risk that property will be destroyed or damaged and (2) when he does the act he either has not given any thought to the possibility of there being any such risk or has recognised that there was some risk involved and has none the less gone on to do it." To all intents and purposes the effect of this decision is to render criminal damage an offence which can be committed by gross negligence on the part of the accused (see above, p. 68 for the fuller treatment of this development). It is also clear that this is the meaning the word is to receive throughout the statute.

The prosecution must also establish that the accused knew or was reckless as to the fact that the property belonged to another.

Since *Caldwell* recklessness suffices for every element of the *actus reus* of this offence, voluntary intoxication is irrelevant, since it is of no concern to the court why the defendant gave no thought to the serious and obvious risk of damage or destruction he has created. (The offence is generally said to be an offence of basic intent, but for reasons given above this nomenclature is not strictly necessary in offences requiring only *Caldwell* recklessness; p. 162; but see also *Jaggard* v. *Dickinson*, below, p. 352.)

2. AGGRAVATED DAMAGE

Section 1(2) provides that "A person, who without lawful excuse destroys or damages any property, whether belonging to himself or another—

    (*a*) intending to destroy or damage any property or being reckless as to whether any property would be destroyed or damaged; and

    (*b*) intending by the destruction or damage to endanger the life of another or being reckless as to whether the life of another would thereby be endangered;

shall be guilty of an offence.

Under section 4 this offence is punishable with life imprisonment.

(1) Actus reus

The *actus reus* of this offence is basically the same as that for the offence under section 1(1) with the exception that under this section the offence can be committed in respect of one's own property. Thus if X knows that Y is asleep inside X's house but nonetheless sets fire to it in an attempt to swindle the insurance company, if he is reckless as to Y's life being endangered he is guilty of an offence under section 1(2).

In *Steer* (1987) the defendant had fired a rifle at the bedroom window and door of the bungalow belonging to his former business partner who was in the bedroom at the time. It is clear that the defendant committed the basic criminal damage offence under section 1(1) of the Act. He was charged, however, with being reckless as to whether the life of another was endangered contrary to section 1(2). The House of Lords held that the danger to life has to stem from the damage caused by the accused's conduct and not from the conduct itself. In this case the threat to the victim's life arose from the bullets fired by the defendant and not from the damage he had caused to the property. It may have been different had he been firing into a room full of explosives or if the prosecution had been alleging that the danger to the victim's life stemmed from the flying glass. Similarly in an arson case, it is not the match or inflammable material which causes the danger to life; it is the ensuing conflagration which occurs as the property which has been set on fire is damaged or destroyed. In *Steer* the prosecution should have charged the defendant with an offence against the person arising from the use of the gun.

(2) Mens rea

The prosecution must establish:
  (i) that the accused intended to destroy or damage property or that he was reckless as to whether the property would be damaged or destroyed and
 (ii) that the accused intended by the destruction or damage to endanger the life of another or that he was reckless as to whether the life of another would be thereby endangered.

In *Sangha* (1988) the Court of Appeal held that when considering whether the test to be applied under section 1(2) was whether it had been proved that an ordinary prudent bystander would have perceived an obvious risk that property would be damaged and that life would thereby be endangered. It was irrelevant that, as in the present case, experts would have appreciated that the building which had been set on fire was constructed in such a way that the risk of the fire spreading so as to endanger life was minimal. Ordinary people would have been of the opinion that the defendant's action created an obvious and serious risk of danger to life.

Whether or not the defendant intended to endanger life or was reckless in this respect must be determined at the time he does the act which causes the damage to or destruction of the property, and not by reference back from the damage or destruction actually caused. Thus in *Dudley* (1989) the accused threw a fire bomb at the complainant's house. This clearly created the risk of serious damage to the property likely to endanger life. However the complainants managed to extinguish the fire before it had caused more than trivial damage to the house. The defendant argued that there was no evidence that the damage which was actually caused was either intended to or likely to endanger life. The Court of Appeal held that the words "destruction or damage" in section 1(2)(b) referred back to the damage or destruction intended or as to which there was recklessness, in section 1(2)(a). In this case it was clear that the defendant's conduct created a serious and obvious risk that the property would be damaged in a way likely to endanger life and he, therefore, committed the aggravated offence under section 1(2) even though the actual damage caused was not likely to have this effect. The reverse is equally true. If D is reckless as to causing damage which is not at all likely to endanger life, the fact that a chance happening causes a serious life endangering destruction of the property will not render him liable to the more serious charge.

It must, however, be remembered that the offence under section 1(2) requires some actual damage to the property. If the complainant's in *Dudley* had managed to extinguish the bomb before any damage had been caused to their property, the offence under section 1(2) would not have been committed even though his conduct was likely to endanger life.

Until the decision of the House of Lords in *Caldwell* this offence was regarded as a crime of specific intent to which the defence of voluntary intoxication could apply. This was certainly in keeping with an observable pattern, namely that in many cases voluntary intoxication would provide a defence to a very serious charge, but still leave the accused liable to conviction for a lesser charge (see above, p. 165). However, the decision in *Caldwell* means that voluntary intoxication will only be a defence where the accused is charged with intentionally seeking to endanger life and common sense would suggest that it will be only in the rarest of cases that the prosecution would so restrict the charge. It is much more likely that the defendant will be charged with either *recklessly* endangering life, or with *intentionally or recklessly* endangering life, in which case the intoxication will be relevant only so far as the allegation of *intentionally* endangering life. *Cunningham* ((1957), above, p. 50) would today be charged with an offence under section 1(2) of the Criminal Damage Act 1971. It is fairly clear that he intentionally damaged the gas meter and that this created a serious and obvious risk that life would be thereby endangered. It is unlikely that he could have any defence to an allegation that he gave no thought to such a risk.

From a procedural point of view it is likely that where the prosecution is relying on "intention or recklessness as to endangerment of life" the indictment will contain two counts, one containing a charge that the accused intended to endanger life and the alternative count that he was reckless as to endangering life. In this way the jury will be forced to indicate which of the two states of mind they found to be proved since this will be of relevance in the sentencing, (see *Hoof* (1980) a decision on arson under section 1(3) which seems equally applicable to section 1(2)).

3. ARSON

Arson was a common law offence of damaging property by fire. It is abolished by the Criminal Damage Act 1971 but the term arson is retained to describe the situation where offences under section 1 are committed by means of fire. Where the damage has been perpetrated by fire the offence shall be charged as arson and whether or not the basic action contravenes section 1(1) or section 1(2) the penalty available is life imprisonment. This reflects the law's great disapproval of the use of fire which of course is a completely uncontrollable means of destroying property (see *Hoof* (1980) above).

4. THREATENING TO DESTROY OR DAMAGE PROPERTY (SECTION 2)

If a person threatens without lawful excuse to commit an offence under section 1 intending that the other shall fear that the threat will be carried out, he commits a separate offence of threatening damage which is punishable by 10 years. You should note that he must intend that the other should be put in fear that he will carry out the threat; recklessness that the other will be put in fear is not enough.

5. POSSESSION OF ANYTHING WITH INTENT TO DAMAGE OR DESTROY PROPERTY (SECTION 3)

It is an offence for a person to have anything in his custody or under his control intending without lawful excuse to use it or to cause or permit another to use it to commit an offence under section 1 of the Act. This offence is punishable by 10 years' imprisonment. Thus if X buys matches from a shop intending to burn down the local public house, he has already committed an offence contrary to section 3 of this Act, though there may be difficulty in proving that he had the requisite intent.

6. THE DEFENCE OF LAWFUL EXCUSE

In all the offences we have considered the prosecution have to establish that the accused acted without lawful excuse. For all offences except those under s. 1(2) and s. 1(3) and those under section 2 where the threat was to cause destruction or damage in a way likely to endanger life and section 3 where the possession was with intent to destroy or damage in a way likely to endanger life, the defence receives a partial definition under section 5 of the Act. In addition to the defence under section 5 the phrase lawful excuse means that the general common law defences are available to offences under the Act (this is expressly provided under section 5(5)).

(1) Lawful excuse under section 5

Under section 5(2)(a) the accused shall be treated as having a lawful excuse if at the time of the acts alleged to constitute the offence he honestly (s.5(3) makes it clear it need not be a reasonably held belief) believed that the person whom he believed to be entitled to give consent to the destruction of the property had or would have given consent. Thus if, following a storm, X sees that his neighbour's garage is in a dangerous condition and likely to fall causing injury to passers-by, if X pulls down the garage to prevent such possible injuries in the belief that Y would have consented, he will have a lawful excuse. In *Denton* (1981) it was held that, where any employee damaged property belonging to his employer at the request of his employer who wished to make a fraudulent claim in relation to the property, the employee was entitled to rely on his honest belief that the person entitled to give consent to the damage to the proprty had, in fact, done so.

In *Jaggard* v. *Dickinson* (1981) the accused had gained entry to what she thought was a friend's house by breaking a window and damaging a net curtain. Later it transpired that the house belonged to someone else altogether. She had her friend's permission to treat his house as her own and her mistake as to which house it was clearly stemmed from intoxication. She was charged under section 1(1) of the Act and the justices held that she was not entitled to rely on section 5(2), since the belief relied on was induced by intoxication. The Divisional Court held that the conviction should be quashed. Section 5(3) directed the court to focus on the existence of the belief and not its intellectual soundness. A belief could be just as much honestly held if it was induced by intoxication as if it stemmed from stupidity, forgetfulness or inattention. This case highlights the absurdity of the rules relating to intoxication. If this woman had stumbled against the window in a blind intoxicated stupor she would have had no defence (see *Majewski,* above, p. 163). But since her defence was based on a more specific claim of right which is interpreted as requiring no more than an honestly held belief, she is acquitted despite the fact that she is charged with a crime of basic intent. Whether or not this case would be decided in the same way after the decision in *Caldwell* is open to debate. It is suggested that until it is expressly held to be wrong, it should be regarded as representing the present law.

Under section 5(2)(*b*) if the defendant believes that he is protecting property belonging to himself or another and that the property was in immediate need of protection and that the means he adopted or professed to adopt were reasonable in all the circumstances then he has acted with lawful excuse. Again it is sufficient that this belief is honest even though unreasonable. Let us suppose that the defendant has been charged with criminal damage to property because he has shot a dog belonging to his neighbour. The evidence at his trial reveals that the dog had got into a field in which there were young sheep belonging to the defendant. The defendant gives evidence that the dog appeared to be attacking the sheep and he took what he considered reasonable steps to protect his sheep. On these facts the magistrates will have little difficulty in accepting as genuine his belief that the steps he took were reasonable. Suppose, however, that he admits that he shot the dog because he wanted to get his own back on his neighbour, or that the evidence is that the dog was not in the field with the sheep but in the next field and that the defendant still says that he honestly believed that his sheep were in need of immediate protection. A strict reading of section 5(2)(*b*) would suggest that as along as his belief is genuine, he is entitled to an acquittal, and it is probably this that has led the Court of Appeal to say that the test of whether an act is done "in order to protect property" is an objective one (*Hunt* (1977) and *Ashford and Smith* (1988)). However, a purely objective approach would provide a defence to the defendant in a situation where he had no genuine belief that the destruction of another's property was necessary to protect his own, but where objectively viewed it would appear that he would be entitled to hold such a belief.

In *Hill* (1989) the Court of Appeal appears to have provided some answer to these problems. In that case the defendant was charged with possessing a hacksaw blade with intent to damage property (section 3). The plan had been, along with others, to cut through the perimeter fencing around a U.S. naval base. The defendant claimed that the presence of the naval base placed their homes around the base in imminent danger of a nuclear attack and that by rendering the base insecure they might avert the danger by persuading the authorities to move the base elsewhere. In dismissing her application for leave to appeal against conviction the Court of Appeal held that the correct approach was for the judge (or magistrates) first to determine what was in the defendant's mind (a subjective test) and then secondly to decide, as a matter of law, on the facts believed by the defendant, whether cutting the strand of wire could amount to something done to protect her home or the homes of adjacent friends (an objective test). In the present case there was no evidence that the defendant believed that there was a need for protection from immediate danger.

What this seems to mean in the case of the defendant who shot his neighbour's dog is that he can have no defence unless he actually believes that his sheep were in immediate need of protection and that what he did was reasonable to achieve this protection. However the magistrates are not bound to accept, for example, his assessment that the need for protection was immediate. If on the facts believed by him to exist the magistrates are not prepared to hold that the need for protection was immediate or that the steps he took were reasonable, he will have no defence.

In both situations it would appear that the accused must raise the issue, but the prosecution must prove beyond reasonable doubt that the accused was acting without lawful excuse.

(2) Lawful excuse outside of section 5

As we said earlier, section 5(5) makes it quite clear that the partial definition of lawful excuse provided by section 5(2) must not be taken as casting doubt on any defence recognised as a general defence to criminal charges. Where the offence is one involving intention or recklessness as to endangering life the accused must rely on the general defences since section 5(2) does not apply. Thus the defences of self-defence, defence of property, prevention of crimes, duress, etc., all apply to offences under the Act. If X were being pursued by Y and he picked up Z's garden gnome and flung it at Y, he would be able to plead self-defence. It would seem in keeping with the Act and the way it has been interpreted that if, in such a case, X were mistaken about Y's intentions, it should suffice that he honestly believed he was about to be attacked.

BIBLIOGRAPHY

THIS book is intended to be an introduction to the principles of criminal liability. It is hoped that the reader might have been tempted to undertake a more thorough study of the subject and to that end I have listed some suggestions for further reading. This list is not intended to be exhaustive, but merely a guide. Where a book has been cited in the text by its author's name alone, a fuller reference will be found below.

1. STANDARD WORKS ON THE CRIMINAL LAW

The standard recommended textbooks for Criminal Law are Smith and Hogan, *Criminal Law* (6th ed., Butterworths, 1988) and Glanville Williams, *Textbook of Criminal Law* (2nd ed., Sweet and Maxwell, 1983). Cross and Jones, *Introduction to Criminal Law* (11th ed., by Richard Card, Butterworths, 1988) provides a somewhat shorter account. There are works on particular aspects of the criminal law, but it is sufficient to mention here Professor Smith's Hamlyn Lecture on *Justification and Excuse in the Criminal Law* (Sweet and Maxwell, 1989) and two books on the law of theft; these are Griew, *The Theft Acts 1968 and 1978* (5th ed., Sweet and Maxwell, 1986) and Smith, *The Law of Theft* (5th ed., Butterworths, 1984). Attention must be drawn to the great work of reference on the general principles of the criminal law; this is Glanville Williams, *Criminal Law—The General Part* (2nd ed., Sweet and Maxwell, 1961)—time spent reading any part of this is time well spent. Fletcher, *Rethinking the Criminal Law* (Little Brown, U.S.A.) provides an excellent and different approach to the subject. Collections of cases and materials, particularly useful to those with no access to law libraries, are available to complement both Smith and Hogan, and Cross and Jones. Elliot and Wood's *Casebook on Criminal Law* (5th ed., Sweet and Maxwell, 1989) and Clarkson and Keating, *Criminal Law: Text and Materials*

(Sweet and Maxwell, 1984) are further examples of this type of book.

2. GENERAL SOURCES

Any student of criminal law should make frequent use of the monthly *Criminal Law Review* which provides, *inter alia*, an excellent survey of recent cases with commentaries. In addition to this, much useful material is to be found in the Working Papers and Reports of the Law Commission and Criminal Law Revision Committee who are at present engaged in a thorough overhaul of the criminal law. Particularly useful reading at the present time is Law Commissions Draft Criminal Code and Commentary (Law Comm. No. 177; April 1989).

3. BACKGROUND

Probably the most authoritative work on the history of the criminal law is Stephen's *History of the Criminal Law* in three volumes. If this seems rather daunting, then a good place to start is Christopher Hibbert, *Roots of Evil* (Minerva Press, 1968). An outline of criminal procedure can be obtained in Barnard, *The Criminal Court in Action* (3rd ed., Butterworths, 1988) or Emmins, *A Practical Approach to Criminal Procedure* (4th ed., Blackstone Press, 1988); reference should be made to the Report of the Royal Commission on Criminal Procedure in England and Wales (1981 Cmnd. 8092). Other useful books on criminal procedure are Street, *Freedom, the Individual and the Law* (5th ed., 1982, Penguin); D. G. T. Williams, *Keeping the Peace: The Police and Public Order* (1967); Whittaker, *The Police*; Devlin, *The Criminal Prosecution in England* (1960). Guides to the recent far-reaching changes made by the Police and Criminal Evidence Act 1984 (to the law relating to police powers, evidence in criminal proceedings and police complaints procedure) can be found in Zander, *The Police and Criminal Evidence Act* 1984 (2nd ed. Sweet and Maxwell, 1989) and Bevan and Lidstone, *A Guide to the Police and Criminal Evidence Act* 1984 (Butterworths, 1985).

On the trial itself, good pictures of the trial process are provided by Blom Cooper, *The A6 Murder*; and Kennedy, *The*

Trial of Stephen Ward (1964). The *Notable British Trials Series* provides an opportunity to read full accounts of individual trials. A more formalistic description of the trial process can be found in Glanville Williams, *The Proof of Guilt* (3rd ed., 1963); Devlin, *Trial by Jury* (1966); and Cornish, *The Jury* (1968).

4. SENTENCING PROCESS

Excellent works on the sentencing process are Walker, *Crime and Punishment in Great Britain* (1968); Thomas, *Principles of Sentencing* (2nd ed., 1979); Ashworth, *Sentencing and Penal Policy* (1983); and Emmins, *A Practical Approach to Sentencing* (1985).

INDEX